Advance Praise for
Post Traumatic Success

"Post traumatic growth is one of the fascinating and inspiring themes within positive psychology. Bannink describes eloquently how positive psychology and solution-focused strategies can assist clients in coping successfully with traumatic events. A practical guide I highly recommend."
—**Prof.dr. Ernst Bohlmeijer**
Department of Psychology, University of Twente, the Netherlands

"For far too long, we were ignorant about the sometimes strong aftereffects of trauma on clients' lives. Then, with the naming and articulating of the diagnosis post-traumatic stress, we became more sensitive to these signs and signals. But like everything, it can be taken too far.

In recognizing and treating trauma aftereffects, our field overlooks that the vast majority of people are resilient and often bounce back from even the most horrific and intrusive traumas. And, in focusing on the negative aftereffects, we often inadvertently help people see themselves as damaged and unchangeable. Bannink's *Post Traumatic Success* finds a nice balance between problem and solution, challenges and change, damage and growth. Her application of the latest research and methods for strength- and solution-building can be used for therapists of any persuasion to enhance their effectiveness with people who have lived through extraordinary experiences and help them come out the other side 'strong at the broken places'."
—**Bill O'Hanlon**,
Author of *Out of the Blue: Six Non-Medication Ways to Relieve Depression*

"Bannink's *Post Traumatic Success* is a landmark work, and in my mind the most important book on treating trauma and post traumatic stress disorder in the last 20 years. The book
From thinking about treatment as ameliorat

focusing on the trauma—which isn't always successful and can be a slow, painful process—to focusing on exceptions, strengths and resiliencies so that clients may thrive. Integrating current research in positive psychology and solution-focused brief therapy, the book offers concrete and specific interventions that can be used immediately in clinical practice. I highly recommend this book for new and seasoned therapists alike." **—Terry S. Trepper, PhD**
Professor of Psychology,
Purdue University Calumet

"As always with Bannink, she has read widely around her topic. The overlap described between Positive Psychology, Solution Focus and other forms of psychotherapy, such as CBT, will be of particular interest to many practitioners. The text highlights the new future-focus being brought into Positive Psychology and includes many tried and tested exercises to increase the client's resources. The many anecdotes and stories demonstrate the concepts well and add to the readability of the volume. There is something in this book to interest all psychologists and post-modern therapists."
—Alasdair J. Macdonald, MB, ChB, FRCPsych, DPM, DCH, Consultant psychiatrist, UK.

POST TRAUMATIC
SUCCESS

Post Traumatic Success

Positive Psychology and
Solution-Focused Strategies to
Help Clients Survive and Thrive

FREDRIKE BANNINK

W. W. NORTON & COMPANY
New York • London

All cases are composites.

TEN LESSONS FROM THE BAMBOO: Used with permission from Garr Reynolds.

APA 10 WAYS TO BUILD RESILIENCE: This content has been excerpted from American Psychological Association (2002). The Road to Resilience. Retrieved from http://www.apa.org/helpcenter/road-resilience.aspx. Copyright 2002 by the American Psychological Association. Reproduced with permission. No further reproduction or distribution is permitted without written permission from the American Psychological Association.

SESSION RATING SCALE: Used with permission from Scott Miller

For information about permission to reproduce selections from this book, write to Permissions, W. W. Norton & Company, Inc., 500 Fifth Avenue, New York, NY 10110

For information about special discounts for bulk purchases, please contact W. W. Norton Special Sales at specialsales@wwnorton.com or 800-233-4830

Manufacturing by R. R. Donnelley, Harrisonburg
Book design by Gilda Hannah
Production manager: Leeann Graham

Library of Congress Cataloging-in-Publication Data

Bannink, Fredrike.
    Post traumatic success : positive psychology & solution-focused strategies to help clients survive & thrive / Fredrike Bannink. — First Edition.
        pages cm. — (A Norton professional book)
    Includes bibliographical references and index.
    ISBN 978-0-393-70922-3 (pbk.)
1. Post-traumatic stress disorder. 2. Positive psychology. I. Title.
    RC552.P67B336 2014
    616.85'21--dc23
                            2014016414

ISBN: 978-0-393-70922-3 (pbk.)

W. W. Norton & Company, Inc., 500 Fifth Avenue, New York, N.Y. 10110
                            www.wwnorton.com
W. W. Norton & Company Ltd., Castle House, 75/76 Wells Street, London W1T 3QT

1 2 3 4 5 6 7 8 9 0

Carl Jung, a Swiss psychiatrist (1875–1961), stated,

"I am not what happened to me.
I am what I choose to become."
(1965, p. 38)

Jung's quote is the theme of this book.

Contents

• • • • • • • • • • • • •

Preface

Although many individuals experiencing a wide array of challenging life circumstances recover and even experience post traumatic growth, there are also a significant number of people who experience little or no growth in their struggle with trauma. This is a book written ultimately to help individuals who need assistance in the form of therapy that will enable them to transform what happened to them in the past to make them better instead of bitter. When therapists help clients to let their experiences make them better, there can be a range of outcomes. For some clients, post traumatic success implies a full, or even only a partial, recovery from the symptoms of post traumatic stress (disorder), and that is as far as these clients can go. For other clients, post traumatic success entails not only a full or partial recovery from symptoms but also simultaneous post traumatic growth. It is possible for post traumatic growth and (symptoms of) post traumatic stress disorder (PTSD) to coexist. For still other clients, post traumatic success implies finding a resiliency that allows them to go on with their lives, often on their own, and thus therapists will usually not see this group of trauma survivors in their office.

This book aims to offer you, as a professional working with trauma survivors, practical direction for helping individuals who are struggling with events in their past. By introducing new skills and viewpoints, this book invites you to change your focus from what *is* wrong with your clients to what is right with them, and from what is not working in their lives to what is working for them. Throughout this book, 117 exercises, 33 cases, and 40 stories are provided to give you the opportunity to integrate this new approach through action learning.

Traditional treatments have been strongly influenced by the medical model. The structure of problem-solving—first determining the nature of the problem and then intervening to minimize suffering—influences the content of the interaction between therapists and clients: They focus on pathology and on what is wrong with the client. Many therapists tend to be preoccupied with client problems, limitations, and deficiencies. Client assessments by interdisciplinary teams are often negative and mention few or no client strengths and abilities.

However, it is not this negative way of thinking but clients' strengths, abilities, and resources that are most important in bringing about change. The mission of the helping professions is to empower clients to live more productive and satisfying lives and to flourish. Empowering clients means assisting individuals, groups, families, and communities in discovering and expanding the resources and tools within and around them and providing them with the processes to do so. In the medical model, the term *patient* is used; in this model, to emphasize the theme of empowerment, we use the term *client*.

Seligman (2011), cofounder of the positive psychology movement, stated that if we want to flourish and if we want to have well-being, we must minimize our misery; and we must have positive emotion, meaning, accomplishment, and positive relationships. Therefore, it's about time to turn the tide on trauma and shift the focus from (only) reducing distress and merely *surviving* to building success and positively *thriving*.

Mental health is more than the absence of mental illness. In the past thirty years there has been a development of competency-based, more collaborative approaches to working with clients. Positive psychology (PP) and solution-focused brief therapy (SFBT) are among these approaches, which are predominantly directed toward clients' strengths and preferred futures instead of their deficits and past problems. The focus in PP and SFBT is on increasing the well-being of clients, exploring what makes life worth living, and building the conditions that enable such a life. The good news is that within each of us can be found the solutions to most of the problems in which we find ourselves.

Outcomes in psychotherapy, particularly longer-term outcomes, leave a substantial margin for improvement. What would it take to help more trauma survivors benefit more substantively from therapy? What more can therapists do to support their clients in developing longer-term resilience? How can therapists use the least demanding interventions with their clients? How can therapists increase clients' self-efficacy and self-esteem? What would it take to make psychotherapy better, faster, and therefore more cost effective? And last but not least: How can therapy be more kind to the therapists who employ it?

In this book I will explore how traditional approaches to post traumatic stress become positive approaches to *post traumatic success* (PTS). PP and SFBT are aimed at stimulating recovery, resilience, and post traumatic growth. The focus is no longer on pathology, on what is wrong with clients and on repairing what is worst, but first and foremost on strengths, on what is right with clients and on creating what is best. Therapists often consider amelioration of client distress the most important therapy outcome, and they generally assume that their clients share this view. However, the most important outcomes for clients are (a) attaining positive mental health qualities, such as optimism and self-confidence; (b) a return to one's usual, normal self; (c) a return to one's usual level of functioning; and (d) relief from symptoms (Kuyken, Padesky, & Dudley, 2009).

The features of this positive focus not only ensure that psychotherapy is shorter in time but also ensure autonomy for clients (Gingerich & Peterson, 2013; Stams, Dekovic, Buist, & Vries, 2006). According to many therapists who use this positive focus, conversations with clients become more lighthearted, which in turn may result in less stress, depression, and burnout for clients as well as less secondary traumatization among therapists.

This is a big book, but it has to be, because it is the first book on trauma in which the theory and practice of PP and SFBT are combined with traditional approaches. The book is written for all professionals and students working with trauma survivors (both adults and children) and their families and friends who would like to adopt a (more) positive approach or would simply like to increase the range of techniques available to them. Therapists trained in (positive) cognitive behavioral therapy (CBT), PP, or SFBT may also find useful elements to add to their approach.

Although this book is primarily aimed at therapists, I also hope that people suffering from trauma who do not see a therapist may find useful information and helpful exercises contained within its pages.

I hope you find this book useful and invite you to share your comments via email at solutions@fredrikebannink.

FREDRIKE BANNINK
www.fredrikebannink.com

Ten Lessons from
the Bamboo

∎∎∎∎∎∎∎∎∎∎∎∎∎

The famous aikido master Ueshiba stressed the importance of studying the teachings of the pine tree, the bamboo, and the plum blossom. Pine, bamboo, and plum are regarded as linked by the season of winter because they flourish together at that time. For this reason, they are commonly known as the "Three Friends of Winter." The pine and plum blossom add their fragrance to the cold air and are therefore valued as providers of a sensory boost in adverse conditions. This uplifting is further emphasized by the evergreen qualities of pine and bamboo, which, together with the early flowering of the plum while snow is still on the ground, make all three symbols of perseverance, integrity, and modesty.

Let's take a closer look at the bamboo plant, depicted on the cover of this book as a symbol of recovery, growth, and resilience. In Japan, the symbolism of the bamboo runs deep and offers many practical lessons for life. These ten lessons (see www.youtube.com/watch?v=9g8T8MsFIp0) are summarized below:

1. Remember: What looks weak is strong. Bamboo endures cold winters and hot summers, and these trees are sometimes the only ones left standing in the aftermath of a typhoon. Like the bamboo, stand tall, believe in your strengths, and know that you are as strong as you need to be. Remember that there is strength in kindness, compassion, and cooperation.

2. Bend but don't break. Bamboo is harder than steel or oak and yet sways gently in the breeze. The trees' foundation is solid even though they sway with the wind, never fighting against it. In time, even the strongest wind tires itself out, but the bamboo remains, standing tall and still. A bend-but-don't-break or go-with-the-flow attitude is one of the secrets for success in dealing with difficult aspects of life.

3. Be strongly rooted yet flexible. Bamboo is remarkable for its flexibility, made possible in part by its complex root structure, which makes the ground around a bamboo forest very stable. The challenge for many of us is to remain the mobile and flexible people that we are while making the effort and taking the time to be rooted in the community right outside our door.

4. Slow down your busy mind. We have more information available than ever before, and most of us live at a fast pace. Life can seem quite hectic, at times chaotic. It is important for us to take the time to slow down and calm our busy minds so that we can see things more clearly. A Taoist proverb says, "We cannot see our reflection in running water. It is only in still water that we can see."

5. Be always ready. Unlike other types of wood, which take a good deal of processing and finishing, bamboo needs little of that. Aikido master Kensho Furuya stated that the warrior, like bamboo, is ever ready for action (1996). Through study and practice, we can do our best to be ready for any situation.

6. Find wisdom in emptiness. One cannot fill a cup that is already full. The hollow bamboo reminds us that we are often too full of our own conclusions and ourselves; we have no space for anything else. To receive knowledge and wisdom, we have to be open to what is new and different. When you empty your mind of prejudices, pride, and fear, you become open to the possibilities.

7. Smile, laugh, and play. Bamboo has an association with laughter because of the sound its leaves make on a windy day. Bamboo also has a connection with playfulness, as it has been used in traditional Japanese kite and doll making. These elements play an important role in one's mental and physical health.

8. Commit yourself to growth and renewal. Bamboo is one of the fastest-growing plants in the world. How fast or slow you grow is not your concern, only that you're moving forward. With sustained effort you are always growing. Do not be discouraged by

what you perceive as a lack of growth or improvement. If you have not given up, then you are growing; you just may not see it until much later.

9. Express usefulness through simplicity. Bamboo in its simplicity expresses its usefulness. Often we complicate the simple to impress and fail to simplify the complex for fear that others may know what we know. We could be more creative and find simpler solutions to even complex problems that ultimately provide the greatest usefulness for us.

10. Unleash your power to spring back. The essence of bamboo is "Fall seven times, get up eight." Bamboo has the ability to bounce back after experiencing adversity. In winter, the heavy snow bends the bamboo back until the snow becomes too heavy and begins to fall off, and the bamboo snaps back up tall again as if to say, "I will not be defeated." *Be like the bamboo.*

Used with permission from Garr Reynolds

Acknowledgments

An author never writes a book alone. It is always a product of many people who work together and ultimately ensure that the name of the author appears on the cover.

I thank my colleagues, students, and above all my clients, including hundreds of trauma survivors at home and abroad, who have helped me discover, apply, and improve my work over the years.

In my work as a trainer for the Mental Health Team of Doctors Without Borders (MSF), I visited many countries in Asia and Africa. I am deeply impressed by the suffering, but also by the recovery, growth, and resilience shown by people living in these conflict areas. I often wonder whether I would even survive in such terrible conditions as living for years on end in refugee camps, being raped by people who are supposed to protect you, or being abused as a child soldier. My deepest respect goes to those who survive and even thrive.

I thank my publisher Deborah Malmud, my friend and translator Suzanne Aldis Routh, and everyone else who has contributed to the realization of this book. I thank my husband Hidde for giving me the opportunity and encouragement to write my books.

Grazie also to my three Italian cats, rescued as kittens, for keeping me company during the many pleasant hours of writing this book.

PART ONE

......

THEORY

CHAPTER 1

••••••••••••

Post Traumatic Stress

Experiencing trauma is an essential part of being human; history is written in blood. Throughout evolution, humans have been exposed to terrible events: serious accidents; medical complications or serious illnesses such as cancer; childhood physical or sexual assaults or witnessing of such events; adult experiences of physical or sexual assault; warfare, policing, and other occupations involving exposure to violence and disaster; and violent, life-threatening natural disasters. Yet most people who are exposed to dreadful experiences survive without developing psychiatric disorders. To be distressed is a normal reaction to the horror, helplessness, and fear that are the critical elements of a traumatic experience. In this chapter, the concept of post traumatic stress (disorder) is described and several myths about stress and trauma are debunked.

One of the myths about stress and trauma is that there are only negative effects, including negative *affect*. But research has shown that there is a concurrence of positive and negative affect during chronic stress, with positive affect having adaptive functions. According to the "broaden-and-build" theory of positive emotions, balancing negative and positive emotions combines relieving suffering and building well-being, and negative affect sometimes better helps to achieve certain types of goals. Balancing negative and positive emotions, however, is not an easy task. Chesterton (1908), an English writer, stated, "It's easy to be heavy, hard to be light."

POST TRAUMATIC STRESS DISORDER

Most people who experience a traumatizing event will not develop post traumatic stress disorder (PTSD). They may suffer acute symptoms like numbing, detachment, derealization, depersonalization or dissociation, dreams and nightmares, or thoughts and flashbacks of the event, and they may avoid any stimulation that reminds them of what happened. These symptoms last for a couple of days and may resolve themselves with time, usually within four weeks of the event, or they may develop into a more severe disorder such as PTSD. Even though the symptoms of PTSD have been recognized throughout history, it wasn't until 1980 that the diagnosis as we know it today came to be. Before that time, symptoms of PTSD were primarily referred to as *shell shock, combat fatigue,* or *war neurosis*.

Since 1980, there has been an extensive amount of research on the symptoms and consequences of PTSD. As of 2012, Pentagon statistics showed that more soldiers had died from suicide than from combat. Tens of thousands of soldiers returning from the wars in Iraq and Afghanistan are suffering from psychological trauma, and many of them show symptoms of PTSD. Also, hundreds of thousands of children, men, and women all over the world are experiencing psychological trauma from emotional, physical, or sexual abuse or from natural or manmade disasters. The financial consequences are at least $42 billion a year in the United States alone (Williams, 2012).

The essential feature of PTSD is the development of characteristic symptoms following exposure to an extreme traumatic stressor entailing direct personal experience of an event involving actual or threatened death or serious injury or another threat to one's physical integrity (like sexual violation); witnessing an event involving death, injury, or a threat to the physical integrity of another person; learning about the unexpected or violent death, serious harm, or threat of death or injury experienced by a family member or other close associate; or experiencing repeated exposure to distressing details of an event, such as a police officer (or therapist) repeatedly hearing details about child sexual abuse. In the DSM-IV (American Psychiatric Association, 1994), PTSD was listed under the category "Anxiety Disorders"; in the DSM-5 (American Psychiatric Association, 2013), a new category called "Trauma- and Stressor-Related Disorders" hosts PTSD.

Complex PTSD (C-PTSD) is not a formal diagnosis, although many therapists use this concept in their work with trauma survivors. This type of PTSD is referred to as the dissociative subtype in DSM-5, because complex trauma is often identified in conjunction with dissociative symptoms and/or a personality disorder. These dissociative symptoms can be either experiences of feeling detached from one's own mind or body, or experiences in which the world seems unreal, dreamlike, or distorted. Clients suffering from C-PTSD often have problems trusting other people, even their therapists; they may have a tendency to harm themselves (e.g., through cutting or other self-injury, suicide attempts, or high-risk acting out, such as extreme drug or alcohol intoxication leading to hospitalization); and they often have a number of other psychological disorders, such as borderline personality disorder, an eating disorder, substance abuse or dependence, panic disorder, or schizoid or schizotypal personality disorder.

STORY 1. Give Up 13.6 Years of Your Life

The following research gives an impression of how clients may suffer from PTSD. Doctor, Zoellner, and Feeny (2011) interviewed 184 persons seeking treatment for PTSD at two treatment sites in different regions of the United States. They found that distressing recollections of a traumatic event and avoidance of certain activities and thoughts, both commonly conceived of as dysfunctional behaviors, had little correlation to an individual's reported sense of well-being. However, symptoms tied to heightened arousal, such as trouble sleeping, irritability, and vigilance, were associated with lower quality of life. Anxiety and depression were also associated with lower quality of life. The effect of avoidance on quality of life may be limited because it is a coping strategy and may, in the short term, improve well-being.

The researchers found that, on average, a person with PTSD was willing to give up 13.6 years of his or her life to live unburdened by the symptoms of the disorder! On average, the participants were willing to accept a treatment with up to a 13-percent chance of immediate death to achieve total relief of PTSD symptoms.

DEBUNKING MYTHS ABOUT STRESS AND TRAUMA

Seligman (2005, p. 4) tells us:

> The message of the Positive Psychology (PP) movement is to remind our field that it has been deformed. Psychology is not

just the study of disease, weakness, and damage; it also is the study of strength and virtue. Treatment is not just fixing what is wrong; it also is building what is right.

Because of this deformation, many psychologists and psychiatrists became *pathologizers* and *victimologists* with a focus on assessing and curing individual suffering (how to make miserable people less miserable). Therapists went about treating mental illness within the disease-patient framework of repairing damage. This focus on pathology ("What's wrong with you?") generated several myths about mental illness and about trauma. Therapists forgot to ask the question "What's right with you?" Below are several myths about stress and trauma:

- Everyone who experiences a traumatic event will develop post traumatic stress.
- People must have psychotherapy to get over post traumatic stress.
- The only effective treatment for post traumatic stress is long-term psychotherapy in which one reexperiences or remembers everything that happened during the traumatic incident.
- There are only negative effects from trauma.

In the military, the police force, and other occupations exposed to violence and disaster, other myths and worries exist, such as:

- Seeking help will kill my career because I will be perceived in a negative light.
- If I see a therapist, everyone will know about it, and that will not be good.
- Treatment does not work.

An example of the premise that only negative effects come from trauma is found in the study of the life expectancy of Polish Holocaust survivors. Previous studies had shown that a traumatic experience may shorten life expectancy and even found genetic proof that trauma may lead to a shortening of the chromosome ends in the human DNA responsible for the lifespan of human body cells. These facts led researchers at the University of Haifa (Israel) and Leiden University (the Netherlands) to examine whether Holocaust survivors really did have a shorter lifespan. However, it turned out that male Holocaust survivors had a *longer* life expectancy compared to those who hadn't experienced the Holocaust (Sagi-Schwartz, Bakermans-Kranenburg, Linn, & van IJzendoorn, 2013). This was the first study to examine data on the entire Jewish Polish population that emigrated from Poland to Israel before and after World War II. Holocaust survivors not only suffered grave psychosocial trauma but also famine, malnutrition, and lack of hygienic and medical facilities. This led to the assumption that these conditions damaged their later health and reduced life expectancy. Surprisingly, findings showed that the life expectancy in the survivors' population was 6.5 months longer than that of the immigrant population that did not experience the Holocaust. There was no significant difference in life expectancy between female survivors and women who hadn't experienced the Holocaust. The differences in the male populations, however, were significant, with male Holocaust survivors living on average fourteen months longer. One possible explanation for these findings, according to the researchers, might be the *post traumatic growth phenomenon*, according to which the traumatic, life-threatening experiences Holocaust survivors had to face, which engendered high levels of psychological distress, could have also served as stimuli for developing personal and interpersonal skills and gaining new insights and a deeper meaning to life. All of these could have eventually contributed to the survivors' longevity.

POSITIVE AFFECT

One of the myths about stress and trauma is that they produce only negative effects, including negative *affect*. But research shows that positive affect co-occurs with negative affect during chronic stress, with positive affect having adaptive functions (Folkman & Moskowitz, 2000).

Although research on *coping* over the past several decades has produced convergent evidence about the functions of coping and the factors that influence it, the focus until recently has been almost exclusively on negative outcomes. However, positive affect has not been entirely neglected in models of stress. It has been discussed in relation to stressful situations that have been appraised as *challenges*, a label that signals the possibility of mastery or gain and implies emotions such as eagerness, excitement, and confidence. It is also discussed in relation to the appraisal of the resolution of stressful encounters as favorable or successful, leading to emotions such as happiness and pride. And it is discussed as a response to the cessation of aversive conditions, when people are likely to experience an offsetting positive emotion such as relief.

In general, however, most models of stress do not emphasize positive affect or, in particular, its adaptational significance, nor do they describe the kinds of coping processes that people use to generate or sustain positive affect in the midst of personally significant, enduring stress. Folkman and Moskowitz (2000) argue that:

- Positive affect can occur alongside distress during a given period.
- Positive affect in the context of stress has important adaptational significance of its own.
- Coping processes that generate and sustain positive affect in the context of chronic stress involve meaning.

The Broaden-and-Build Theory of Positive Emotions

In the *broaden-and-build theory of positive emotions* (Fredrickson, 2000, 2009), the function of positive emotions is explained. In contrast to negative emotions, which lead to narrowing of attention and specific action tendencies, positive emotions (interest, contentment, enjoyment, serenity, happiness, joy, pride, relief, affection, love) broaden the individual's attentional focus and behavioral repertoire and, as a consequence, build social, intellectual, and physical resources—resources that can become depleted under chronically stressful conditions. People who are feeling positive show patterns of thought that are more flexible, unusual, creative, and inclusive. Their thinking tends to be more efficient and more open to information and options. It is suggested that positive emotions enlarge the cognitive context, an effect recently linked to increases in brain dopamine levels. The broaden-and-build theory is an exploration of the evolved function of positive emotions and has substantial support. Longitudinal studies show that positive emotions play a role in the development of long-term resources such as psychological resilience and flourishing. Individuals who express or report higher levels of positive emotions show more constructive and flexible coping, more abstract and long-term thinking, and greater emotional distance following stressful negative events.

Furthermore, Fredrickson (2000) found that positive emotions serve as particularly effective *antidotes* for the lingering effects of negative emotions, which narrow individuals' thought-action repertoires. In other words, positive emotions have an *undoing effect* on negative emotions, since positive emotions are incompatible with negative ones. Positive emotions have a unique ability to reduce the lingering cardiovascular aftereffects of negative emotions. Beyond speeding physiological recovery, the *undoing effect* implies that positive emotions counteract any aspect of negative emotions that stems from a narrowed thought-action repertoire. For instance, negative emotions can sidetrack people toward narrowed lines of thinking consistent with the specific action tendencies they trigger. When angry, individuals may dwell on getting revenge or getting even; when anxious or afraid, they may dwell on escaping or avoiding harm; when sad or depressed, they may dwell on the repercussions of what has been lost.

Fredrickson (2009) found that the connection between the *positivity ratio* and flourishing (see Chapter 7) is evident at three very different levels of human experience. Whether you are one person, two partners, or a team, this positivity ratio is worth attention. The positivity ratio is the amount of heartfelt positivity relative to the amount of heart-wrenching negativity. Stated formally, the positivity ratio is the frequency of positivity over any given time span, divided by the frequency of negativity over that same time span. Below a certain ratio, people get pulled into a downward spiral fueled by negativity, yet above this same ratio, people are drawn along an upward spiral energized by positivity. Fredrickson (2009, p. 16) stated, "Downward spiral or upward spiral. As I see it, that's your choice."

Subjective well-being is a function of three different factors: high positive affect, low negative affect, and high life satisfaction, whereby positive and negative affect are on different continua. A key to emotional flourishing is having a high positive-to-negative emotion ratio. We can improve our state, either by increasing positive emotions or by decreasing negative emotions (or both). Research has shown that when individuals flourish, with a positivity ratio of 3:1 or more, health, productivity, and peace follow. Although recently there has been criticism regarding the empirical evidence of the positivity ratio, the fact that positivity is important remains untouched.

And the good news is that happiness, in the long run, turns out to be more contagious than depression (Fowler & Christakis, 2008), so an upward spiral of positivity will occur.

STORY 2. *The Power of Positive Emotions*

Scientists examined the ways physicians make medical diagnoses by having them think aloud while they solved the case of a patient with liver disease. Astonishingly, this research team found that when they gave physicians a small gift—simply a bag of candy—those physicians were better at integrating case information and less likely to become fixated on their initial ideas and come to premature closure in their diagnosis

—Isen, Rosenzweig, & Young, 1991

Exercise 1. TURN ON POSITIVITY

We all have the power to turn positivity on and off for ourselves. Experiment with this and turn positivity on right now. Take a moment to notice your physical surroundings. Whether you are in your living room or in your bathroom, on the bus or on the train, ask yourself: "What is right about my current circumstances? What makes me lucky to be here? What aspect of my current situation might I view as a gift to be treasured? How does it benefit me or others?" Taking time to think in this manner can ignite the inner glow of gratitude. Take a few moments to savor and enjoy the good feeling you have created for yourself.

Now turn positivity off. Positivity-spoiling questions include: "What is wrong here? What is bothering me? What should be different and better? Who is to blame?" Try asking yourself these kind of questions, follow the chain of thoughts they produce, and see how quickly your positivity plummets (Fredickson, 2009).

STORY 3. I Can Choose

The comedian Groucho Marx (2002) stated that each morning when he opened his eyes, he said to himself, "I, not events, have the power to make me happy or unhappy today. I can choose which it shall be. Yesterday is dead; tomorrow hasn't arrived yet. I have just one day, today, and I am going to be happy in it."

Increasing Positive Affect

Research by Isen and colleagues (1991) showed that positive affect promotes creativity and flexibility. Positive affect also facilitates the processing of important (e.g., self-relevant) information, even if that information is negative and may potentially damage self-esteem (Reed & Aspinwall, 1998).

Another route through which positive affect may offset the deleterious physiological effects of stress is through the neuroendocrine system. In Epel, McEwen, and Ickovics's study (1998), people who reported finding positive meaning in response to a traumatic event had more adaptive hormonal responses, making them more resilient in the face of stressful events. This finding is further reinforced by research showing that positive affect and negative affect are associated with different neural structures (Cacioppo & Gardner, 1999).

Positive affect in the context of chronic stress may also help prevent clinical depression. Intense, prolonged negative affect, such as that experienced in chronically stressful conditions, without compensatory experiences of positive affect may overwhelm the regulatory function of emotion and result in clinical depression (Gross & Munoz, 1995). Experiences of positive affect in the midst of stressful circumstances may interrupt and thereby short-circuit this rumination spiral and prevent the decline into clinical depression. Ways to increase positive affect include:

- *Positive reappraisal.* This refers to cognitive strategies for reframing a situation in a more positive light (seeing the glass half full as opposed to half empty). The focus is on the value of people's efforts and appraising them positively.
- *Coping.* This refers to efforts directed at solving or managing the problem that is causing distress. It includes strategies for gathering information, making decisions, planning, and resolving conflicts. It also includes efforts to acquire resources to help deal with the problem as well as instrumental, task-oriented actions.
- *Infusion of ordinary events with positive meaning.* This refers to the finding that people may be more likely to bring about, note, or remember ordinary positive events during chronically stressful conditions, possibly as a way of offsetting the negative affective consequences of a negative event. Therefore, making a game of finding something positive in every situation is useful. A high percentage of our emotions are determined by how we interpret events.

STORY 4. *Value Positivity*

A few years ago I came across a greeting card that read: "Life gives us negativity on its own. It's our job to create positivity." I like this phrasing because it reminds us that positivity is a choice—a choice we all need to make again and again, day after day. I'd like to remind you that your emotions are as far from random as they are from being fixed by your genes. They stem to a large degree from your daily activities and your entrenched mental habits. Perhaps more than you ever thought possible, you get to choose them. Sure enough, negativity that's necessary will always know where to find you. But you can choose to minimize the gratuitous kind. And the more you value positivity, the more often its upward spiral will lift you to new heights.

—Fredrickson, 2009, p. 230

BALANCING POSITIVE AND NEGATIVE AFFECT

Negative affect is not always wrong. Beck (2011) stated that the aim of cognitive behavioral therapy (CBT) is not to get rid of all distress; negative emotions are as much a part of the richness of life as positive emotions and serve as important a function as does physical pain, often alerting us to potential problems that may need to be addressed. However, therapists should seek to increase clients' positive emotions through discussion of their interests, positive events that occurred during the week, and positive memories. Therapists should often suggest homework assignments aimed at increasing the number of activities in which clients are likely to experience mastery and pleasure. More information on positive emotions and the positivity ratio can be found in Chapter 7.

Seligman (2011) stated that when he had started out as a therapist almost forty years before, it was common for his clients to tell him that they just wanted to be happy. Seligman translated this into the clients' wish to get rid of their depression. Back then he did not have the tools of building well-being at hand and was blinded by Freud and Schopenhauer (who taught that the best humans can ever achieve is to minimize their misery); the difference had not even occurred to him. He had only the tools for relieving depression. But he found that every individual just wants to be happy, and realizing this legitimate goal combines relieving suffering and building well-being. Cure, to his way of thinking, uses the entire arsenal for minimizing misery—drugs and therapy—and adds positive psychology.

We all want to feel pleasure and avoid pain, and although people generally prefer happiness, they sometimes prefer being angry or anxious, as they see these emotions as providing long-term benefits. Tamir, Mitchell, and Gross (2008) stated that people typically prefer to feel emotions that are pleasant (e.g., excitement) and avoid those that are unpleasant (e.g., anger). They tested whether people prefer to experience emotions that are potentially useful, even when they are unpleasant to experience. They tested whether individuals are motivated to increase their level of anger when they expect to complete a task where anger might enhance performance. Participants were told that they would play either a violent or a nonviolent computer game. They were then asked to rate the extent to which they would like to engage in different activities before playing the game. They found that participants preferred activities that were likely to make them angry (e.g., listening to anger-inducing music, recalling past events in which they had been angry) when they expected to play a violent game. In contrast, participants preferred more pleasant activities when they expected to play a nonviolent game.

To examine whether preferences to increase anger resulted in improved performance, participants were assigned at random to either an angry, neutral, or excited emotion induction and then played a violent and a nonviolent computer game. As expected, angry participants performed better than others in the violent game by successfully killing more enemies. However, angry participants did not perform better than others in the nonviolent game, which involved serving customers. Such findings demonstrate that what people prefer to feel at any given moment may depend in part on what they might get out of it. A factor that ought to be considered where anger is concerned is that it can be very arousing, and thus can actually feel good in a certain way.

Interestingly, people sometimes opt for less arousing and less pleasant feelings such as fear. This is particularly true when people are pursuing avoidant, rather than approach, goals (see Chapter 6). Approach goals involve pursuit of a positive outcome, as in "I want to go to bed early tonight because I want to feel fit tomorrow morning." Avoidance goals are based on avoidance of a negative outcome, as in "I don't want to go to bed late tonight because I don't want to be sleepy at work tomorrow morning." Tamir and colleagues (2008) found that people prefer fear when they are pursuing avoidance goals. Despite the unpleasantness of fear, people appear to recognize that it will help them better achieve certain types of goals.

THE DECLINE OF VIOLENCE

This chapter started with the observation that human history "is written in blood." Yet the good news is that violence has gone down over the course of history. Despite the constant stream of news about war, crime, and terrorism, violence of all kinds has been decreasing. Barbaric practices such as human sacrifice, torture-executions, and slavery have been abolished; rates of death from war and homicide are dramatically down; and brutality toward minorities, women, children, and animals is in steady decline. This decline has not been smooth; it has not brought violence down to zero; and it is not guaranteed to continue. But it is an unmistakable development, visible on scales spanning millennia or just a few years and evident in phenomena ranging from the waging of war to the spanking of children. Although the very idea invites skepticism, incredulity, and sometimes anger, today we may be living in the most peaceable era in the existence of our species. With the knowledge that something has driven violence down, we can look not just at what we have been doing wrong but also at what we have been doing right. Instead of asking, "Why is there war?" we might ask, "Why is there peace?" (Pinker, 2012). In the next chapter we will look at trauma with a similarly positive focus.

SUMMARY

- The concept of post traumatic stress disorder is described.
- Several myths about stress and trauma are debunked; one myth is that stress and trauma have only negative effects, including negative affect.
- Research has shown co-occurrence of positive and negative affect during chronic stress, with positive affect having adaptive functions.
- Balancing negative and positive affect helps in relieving suffering and building well-being.
- Negative affect helps to better achieve certain types of goals.
- The good news is that violence has gone down over the course of history.

CHAPTER 2

∎∎∎∎∎∎∎∎∎∎∎∎

Post Traumatic Success

The Greek philosopher Epictetus (55–135 AD) said, "It is not what happens to you, but how you react to it that matters." Results of several studies suggest that traumas need not be debilitating and that most people are resilient; they recover and may even grow in the wake of a trauma. Bonanno, Rennicke, and Dekel (2005) have stated that resilience, a stable trajectory of healthy functioning, is the most common outcome following a traumatic event. Understanding and highlighting the sources of recovery, resilience, and post traumatic growth, with a focus on hope and optimism as supporting elements, helps therapists foster this positive development in their clients, unlike focusing on what is wrong with them, which may have a discouraging effect. As mentioned in Chapter 1, many therapists became pathologizers and victimologists. A focus on pathology has generated several myths about mental illness and about trauma. However, if an individual is asked, "Did your difficult childhood make you stronger or weaker?" he or she is likely to reply that it actually made him or her stronger. The following quote by Nietzsche has become famous: "What does not kill me makes me stronger."

In this chapter, the concept of what I refer to as post traumatic success (PTS) is addressed (Bannink, 2008a), including the theory and research of its 3R's (components)—Recovery, Resilience, and enRichment (post traumatic growth)—which are each described. A description of findings about grief and resilience and brain and body resilience follows.

Recovery means that an individual eventually returns to pretrauma functioning levels *after having experienced significant symptoms or PTSD.*

Resilience means that an individual maintains a stable equilibrium in the face of adverse events. The individual quickly returns to baseline functioning following a highly stressful or traumatic experience (O'Leary & Ickovics, 1995).

EnRichment, or *post traumatic growth,* means that an individual eventually arrives at a higher level of psychological functioning than he or she had before the negative event happened. This is a positive change that the individual experiences as a result of his or her struggle with the traumatic event (Calhoun & Tedeschi, 2000). In other words, the experience is transformative and represents a *value-added* or *better-off-afterward* state. Other descriptions of this general construct include *thriving* (O'Leary & Ickovics, 1995), *stress-related growth* (Park, Cohen, & Murch, 1996), *perceived benefits* (McMillen, Smith, & Fisher, 1997), and *adversarial growth* (Linley & Joseph, 2004; Bohlmeijer & Bannink, 2013).

POST TRAUMATIC SUCCESS

Most people exposed to trauma do not develop PTSD. Because early studies on trauma focused solely on individuals seeking treatment, researchers have underestimated the potential for human resilience. Until recently, resilience was considered to be the exception, or worse, a pathological state in which the individual was not "working through" his or her problem. According to Seligman (2011), there is a bell-shaped distribution of the human response to high adversity. At the extremely vulnerable end, the result is pathology: depression, anxiety, substance abuse, suicide, and PTSD. But the human species has evolved through millennia of trauma, and the usual response to high adversity is *resilience*—a relatively brief episode of depression, plus anxiety, followed by a return to the previous level of functioning.

However, a substantial number of people also show intense depression and anxiety after high adversity, often to the level of PTSD, but then they *recover* and *grow*. In the long run, they arrive at a higher level of psychological functioning than before. This is called *post traumatic growth* (PTG). For example, Terry Waite, an envoy for the Church of England, traveled to Lebanon to try to arrange the release of four hostages. He was himself held captive in solitary confinement from 1989 to 1991. According to Waite, suffering is universal. However, he attempted to subvert it so that it did not have a destructive, negative effect. He was able to turn it around so that it became a creative, positive force.

Thus, only a minority of people will go on to develop PTSD, and with the passage of time the symptoms will resolve in approximately two-thirds of these (McFarlane & Yehuda, 1996). Epidemiological studies of the prevalence of PTSD in trauma-exposed populations have shown that *recovery* and *resilience* are the norm, not the exception. A study using data from the National Comorbidity Survey (NCS) showed that although 50 to 60 percent of the US population are exposed to trauma at some point, only about 8 percent of the population meet full criteria for PTSD (Kessler, Sonnega, Bromet, Higher, & Nelson, 1995).

The relationship among recovery, resilience, and PTG is complex. Bonanno (2004) states that recovery is distinct from resilience and that resilience is even more common than recovery (see below). Some researchers speculate that PTG is a kind of resilience, while others suggest that resilience plays an important role in the development of PTG (Lepore & Revenson, 2006). Calhoun and Tedeschi (2006) conceptualize a complicated relationship between PTG and resilience. Studies have shown an inverse relationship between PTG and resilience, where highly resilient people experience less PTG than less resilient people do (Tedeschi & McNally, 2011). That is, as PTG increases, one's resilience decreases, and as PTG decreases, one's resilience increases. Highly resilient individuals may have stronger coping skills and are less likely to struggle with the psychological consequences of trauma, but they are also less likely to experience as many opportunities for change proceeding from the emotional struggle with trauma.

Resilience has demonstrated an inverse relationship with "Relating to Others" (one of the subscales of the PTGI; see below). What this means is that those who are more resilient are less likely to have an increased sense of closeness to others, especially significant others, or to develop greater compassion and empathy toward others. Thus, while resilience has distinct positives, it may not make an individual more empathic or compassionate toward others going through a similar experience or have greater feelings of closeness to those he or she is intimately connected to in times of difficulty.

My definition of post traumatic success (thanks to my colleague Bill O'Hanlon for introducing this term) includes recovery from significant symptoms (which may include PTSD) as well as resilience and post traumatic growth, since I regard these three constructs all as forms of post traumatic success.

| –10 | 0 | +10 |

Figure 1. Scale of psychological well-being.

To clarify the difference among *recovery*, *growth*, and *resilience*, I use a scale of psychological well-being from –10 to +10 (see Figure 1). The point –10 indicates the worst possible psychological situation while +10 indicates perfect personal thriving. For an individual who started off at 0 before a traumatizing event, *recovery* means that the traumatic event causes him or her to drop well below 0 but then move up the scale from, for instance, –8 to –2, or even back to 0. *Post traumatic growth* means that an individual moves from, for instance, –8 to +2 or further up, functioning at a higher psychological level than he or she did before the trauma. *Resilience* means that an individual may temporarily move to, for instance, –1 or –2, but will come back quickly to 0 or maybe +1.

Therapists will usually see clients with (symptoms of) PTSD, who are rather low on the scale, and not individuals who are resilient. The use of scaling in therapy is explained in detail in Chapter 6.

RECOVERY

Recovery means a return or restoration from pathology to a normal, former condition.

The term *recovery* connotes a trajectory in which normal functioning temporarily gives way to (sub)threshold psychopathology (e.g., symptoms of depression or PTSD), usually for a period of at least several months, and then gradually returns. Full recovery may be relatively rapid or may take as long as one or several years. The term is derived from the medical model of treatment, where the relief of—or better still, the absence of—symptoms is the goal of treatment.

Many authors have distinguished levels of functioning. Aldwin (1994) suggested that coping may lead to either a homeostatic function, that is, recovery, or it may be transformational, a process that produces positive change (growth) or negative change (no recovery or partial recovery). Carver (1998) developed a model delineating four different levels of functioning following a negative event: (a) submitting, (b) surviving with deteriorated ability to function (partial recovery), (c) recovering to a former level of functioning, or (d) recovering to a higher level of functioning (growth).

When individuals experience a positive change following a negative event or gain a higher level of functioning, the concept of *thriving* comes to the fore. O'Leary and Ickovics (1995) described thriving as the ability to reach beyond the original psychosocial level of functioning, to grow and to become both mentally and physically vigorous, even to *bloom*. They implied that an individual may react to a negative event in one of three ways: (a) by surviving, (b) by recovering to the previous level, or (c) by climbing to a higher level than that reached before the trauma (thriving).

An individual's experience of stress is highly subjective. Several mechanisms may influence an individual's reaction to a negative event, such as his or her profile of positive versus negative affect, intellectual ability, willingness to take personal risks, flexibility, and social support variables.

Most traditional—that is, problem-focused—treatments are aimed at recovery, not at growth: They aim to relieve symptoms or PTSD by helping clients deal with the trauma they have experienced. Among these treatments are CBT, eye movement desensitization and reprocessing (EMDR), and mindfulness-based therapy (Bannink, 2012a). Rather than avoiding the trauma and any reminder of it, these treatments encourage clients to activate resources so that they can be strong enough to then recall and process the emotions and sensations they felt during the negative event. In addition to offering an outlet for negative emotions clients have been bottling up, treatment helps restore their sense of control and reduce the powerful hold the memory of the trauma has on their life. In these treatments, clients explore their thoughts and feelings about the trauma; work through feelings of guilt, self-blame, and mistrust; and learn how to cope with and control intrusive memories and address problems in their lives and relationships.

Benish, Imel, and Wampold (2008) performed a meta-analysis to investigate the relative efficacy of psychotherapies, and their results "suggest that despite strong evidence of psychotherapy efficaciousness vis-à-vis no treatment or common factor controls, bona fide psychotherapies produce equivalent benefits for clients with PTSD." However, as will become clear in this book, there are other approaches that are (more) solution-focused than problem-focused. These treatments actively avoid bringing back the negative feelings associated with the trauma and focus on the clients' preferred future and positive feelings instead.

RESILIENCE

Resilience refers to how people negotiate adversity to maintain their well-being. The term describes the psychological processes through which people draw on their strengths to adapt to challenges. Resilience (*resilio* is Latin for "I bounce back") is defined as the ability to survive and persevere in the face of various obstacles and threats. Bonanno (2004) defined resilience as the ability of people in otherwise normal circumstances who are exposed to a potentially highly disruptive event, such as the death of a close relation or a violent or life-threatening situation, to maintain relatively stable, healthy levels of psychological and physical functioning. They are also able to maintain the capacity for generative experiences and positive emotions. This definition contrasts resilience with a more traditional recovery pathway characterized by readily observable elevations in psychological symptoms that endure for at least several months before gradually returning to baseline, pre-trauma levels (see above).

A key point is that although resilient individuals may experience some short-term dysregulation and variability in their emotional and physical well-being, their reactions to a potentially traumatic event tend to be relatively brief and usually do not impede their ability to function to a significant degree. Thus, resilient individuals among an exposed population report little or no psychological symptoms and have the ability to continue fulfilling personal and social responsibilities and to embrace new tasks and experiences.

Galea and colleagues (2003) investigated trends in probable PTSD prevalence in the general population of New York City in the first six months after the September 11 terrorist attacks. They found that the prevalence of probable PTSD declined from 7.5 percent one month after the attacks to 0.6 percent six months after the attacks. These data suggest a *rapid resolution of most of the probable PTSD symptoms* in the general population of NYC in the first six months after the attacks.

CASE 1. *My Kids Keep Me Going*

A colleague explained to me how he worked with soldiers in psychotherapy. When he asked the soldiers what had helped them survive, the most common response was: "My kids. They keep me going."

Then he typically proceeded to inquire how the kids were important, and encouraged the soldiers to explain, as concretely as they could, how thinking about the children enhanced their will to survive and contributed to their resilience.

There are two important distinctions: one between *resilience* and *resources* and one between *resilience* and *recovery*. Research done by Masten (2001) shows a distinction between personal resources and resilience. *Resources* refers to attributes of a person, such as good coping abilities, or protective circumstances, such as a supportive partner. *Resilience* refers to the processes whereby these resources enable adaptation *during times of challenge*. Thus, once therapists help clients identify resources, those resources can be incorporated into conceptualizations of client resilience.

As stated above, resilience is also distinct from recovery. Bonanno (2004) states that the term recovery connotes a trajectory in which normal functioning temporarily gives way to subthreshold or threshold psychopathology, usually for a period of months or even years, and then gradually returns to pre-event levels. By contrast, resilience reflects the ability to maintain a stable equilibrium. A further distinction is that resilience is more than the simple absence of psychopathology. Recovering individuals often experience (sub)threshold symptom levels. Resilient individuals may experience transient perturbations in normal functioning (e.g., several weeks of sporadic preoccupation or restless sleep) but generally exhibit a stable trajectory of healthy functioning across time as well as the capacity for generative experiences and positive emotions.

The grandfather of resilience theory is Garmezy, who by the 1970s had begun asking why some children of schizophrenic parents fared better than others (Garmezy & Streitman, 1974). Masten joined Gar-

---

Exercise 2. RECOGNIZING RESILIENCE

Ask your clients these two questions:

1. How will you notice that you are acting in a resilient way during/after this negative event?
2. How will others notice that you are acting in a resilient way during/after this negative event?

mezy, and they started a project spanning more than two decades. Masten's (1989) study showed that children with a schizophrenic parent may not obtain comforting caregiving compared to children with healthy parents, and that such a situation has an impact on children's development. However, some children of ill parents thrived and were academically competent, leading researchers to make efforts to understand such responses to adversity. While children of average or above-average intelligence were more likely to exhibit resilience, the researchers noted that good relationships with adults could exert a mitigating effect that was just as powerful as, if not more powerful than, the effects of adversity.

The early research on resilience was devoted to discovering the protective factors that explain people's adaptation to adverse conditions such as maltreatment, catastrophic life events, and urban poverty. The focus of empirical work then shifted to understanding the underlying protective processes and uncovering how some factors may contribute to positive outcomes.

The American Psychological Association (APA) has described "10 ways to build resilience." These strategies will be further elaborated throughout this book.

1. *Make connections.* Good relationships with close family members, friends, or others are important [see Chapter 11]. Accepting help and support from those who care about you and will listen to you strengthens resilience. Some people find that being active in civic groups, faith-based organizations, or other local groups provides social support and can help with reclaiming hope. Assisting others in their time of need also can benefit the helper.
2. *Avoid seeing crises as insurmountable problems.* You can't change the fact that highly stressful events happen, but you can change how you interpret and respond to these events [see Chapters 5 and 7]. Try looking beyond the present to how future circumstances may be a little better. Note any subtle ways in which you might already feel somewhat better as you deal with difficult situations.
3. *Accept that change is a part of living.* Certain goals may no longer be attainable as a result of adverse situations. Accepting circumstances that cannot be changed can help you focus on circumstances that you can alter. [See Chapter 6.]
4. *Move toward your goals.* Develop some realistic goals [see Chapter 5]. Do something regularly—even if it seems like a small ac-

complishment—that enables you to move toward your goals. Instead of focusing on tasks that seem unachievable, ask yourself, "What's one thing I know I can accomplish today that helps me move in the direction I want to go?"

5. *Take decisive actions.* Act on adverse situations as much as you can. Take decisive actions, rather than detaching completely from problems and stresses and wishing they would just go away. [See Chapter 7.]

6. *Look for opportunities for self-discovery.* People often learn something about themselves and may find that they have grown in some respect as a result of their struggle with loss [see below]. Many people who have experienced tragedies and hardship have reported better relationships, greater sense of strength even while feeling vulnerable, increased sense of self-worth, a more developed spirituality and heightened appreciation for life.

7. *Nurture a positive view of yourself.* Developing confidence in your ability to solve problems and trusting your instincts helps build resilience. [See Chapter 6.]

8. *Keep things in perspective.* Even when facing painful events, try to consider the stressful situation in a broader context and keep a long-term perspective. Avoid blowing the event out of proportion. [See Chapter 7.]

9. *Maintain a hopeful outlook.* An optimistic outlook enables you to expect that good things will happen in your life. Try visualizing what you want, rather than worrying about what you fear. [See Chapter 4.]

10. *Take care of yourself.* Pay attention to your own needs and feelings. Engage in activities that you enjoy and find relaxing. Exercise regularly. Taking care of yourself helps to keep your mind and body primed to deal with situations that require resilience. [See Chapters 6 and 7.]

Additional ways of strengthening resilience may be helpful. For example, some people write about their deepest thoughts and feelings related to the trauma they have experienced or other stressful events in their life. Meditation and spiritual practices help some people build connections and restore hope. The key is to identify ways that are likely to work well for your clients as part of their own personal strategy for fostering resilience.

From a solution-focused point of view, a good way to explore a client's resilience is to look for fluctuations within the experience of the problem: Ask clients in detail about the times they did not experience the problem even though they expected they would (or experienced it to a lesser extent than they thought they would); find out what happens as the problem ends or starts to fade; and ask why the problem is not worse (see Chapters 3 and 6). It is also helpful to look for success stories in the past. How was the client able to survive or find protection? Achieving a sense of distance from one's negative past actions and a sense of connection to one's positive past actions promotes a favorable view of the present self (Ross & Wilson, 2002).

ENRICHMENT OR POST TRAUMATIC GROWTH

In recent years, psychologists have become increasingly interested in the positive life changes that accompany highly stressful life events, such as being diagnosed with a chronic or terminal illness, losing a loved one, witnessing others being hurt or dying, or sexual assault. This phenomenon has been referred to as *benefit finding, stress-related growth, post traumatic growth* (Park & Helgeson, 2006) or *enRichment* (Bannink, 2014).

The literature has documented PTG for many diverse areas of trauma and stress, including illness, bereavement, natural disasters, sexual assault, military combat, and terrorist attacks. PTG is a direct contrast to PTSD, where individuals find no benefit from their trauma, only pain and anxiety (Haidt, 2006). However, some symptoms or some form of PTSD might come first and then PTG may occur; there is no PTG without traumatization.

Increasingly, longitudinal studies are becoming available and beginning to paint a clearer picture of which factors lead to positive change. In a study of 206 long-term cancer survivors (Schroevers, Helgeson, Sanderman, & Ranchor, 2010), the more the emotional support received at three months after diagnosis, the greater the experience of positive consequences of the illness at eight years after diagnosis, even after controlling for concurrent levels of emotional support at that follow-up.

Linley, Joseph, and Goodfellow (2008) found that people who report positive change are less likely to experience problems of post traumatic stress six months after the trauma. Frazier, Steward, and Mortensen (2004) asked 171 rape survivors to complete a specially designed questionnaire to measure positive changes at two weeks following the assault and then again at two, six, and twelve months later. This study allowed the investigators to see how positive changes related to well-being over time. Four groups were created: (a) those who reported low levels of positive change at two weeks and high levels at twelve months (gained positive change group), (b) those who reported high levels of positive change at two weeks and low levels at twelve months (lost positive change group), (c) those who reported low levels at both time points (never had positive change group), and (d) those who reported high levels at both time points (always had positive change group). Results indicated that those in the "always had positive change group" did the best, showing the lowest levels of depression and post traumatic stress.

Affleck, Tennen, Croog, and Levine (1987) reported that heart attack patients who found benefits immediately after their first attack had reduced recurrence and morbidity statistics eight years later. Dunigan, Carr, and Steel (2007) reported that among patients with hepatoma (liver cancer), those scoring high on positive change survived 186 days longer than their lower-scoring peers due to higher peripheral blood leukocytes. Furthermore, Bower, Kemeny, Taylor, and Fahey (1998) reported that lower AIDS-related mortality was associated with self-reported benefit-finding among bereaved HIV-positive men. Milam, Ritt-Olson, and Unger (2004) also reported greater immune system functioning among HIV patients with higher levels of positive change.

Carver (1998) indicated the socioeconomic necessity of pursuing research that explains why some individuals emerge reinforced from trauma and are able to thrive. The identification and understanding of factors underlying this thriving ability may offer several advantages in the health care arena.

Areas of Growth
At some point, trauma survivors may be able to engage in a sort of metacognition or reflection on their own processing of their life events, seeing themselves as having spent time making a major alteration of their understanding of themselves and of their lives. This then becomes part of their life narrative and includes an appreciation for new, more sophisticated ways of grappling with life events. One helpful question therapists might ask their clients is: "What evidence of your ability to grow and evolve might you notice during tough situations that life sometimes brings about?"

There are five particular areas of growth that often spring from adversity: (a) a renewed appreciation for life, (b) enhanced personal strength, (c) the ability to identify and act on new possibilities for one's life, (d) improved interpersonal relationships, and (e) spiritual deepening. Data are available to support this. In just one example, 61.1 percent of airmen who had been imprisoned and tortured for years by the North Vietnamese said that they had benefited psychologically from their ordeal. What's more, the more severe their treatment, the greater the PTG. "This is not to suggest that we celebrate trauma itself; rather, we should make the most of the fact that trauma often sets the stage for growth, and we must teach others about the conditions under which such growth is most likely to happen" (Seligman, 2011, p. 161).

Hefferon, Grealy, and Mutrie (2009) reviewed the qualitative literature (fifty-seven published journal articles) on PTG and life-threatening physical illness. Four key themes were (a) reappraisal of life and priorities, (b) trauma equals development of self, (c) existential reevaluation, and (d) new awareness of the body. The findings suggest that there are unique elements to illness-based PTG and also suggest a need for additional research into the processes and outcomes of physical trauma (Bohlmeijer and Bannink, 2013).

Post traumatic growth is different from *religious practice*. Religious involvement (e.g., turning to religion, praying) as a coping mechanism predicted "Spiritual Change" on the PTGI (see below) but not any of the other four dimensions, suggesting that post traumatic growth involves an existential domain that is not limited to or coextensive with religion (Butler et al., 2005).

Tedeschi and Calhoun (2006) developed the Post Traumatic Growth Inventory. The PTGI is an instrument for assessing positive outcomes reported by people who have experienced traumatic events. This twenty-one-item scale includes factors on five subscales: (a) New Possibilities, (b) Relating to Others, (c) Personal Strength, (d) Spiritual Change, and (e) Appreciation of Life (see Appendix E). Women report more benefits than men, and people who have experienced traumatic events report more positive change than people who have not experienced extraordinary events. The PTGI is modestly related to optimism and extroversion. The scale appears to have utility in determining how successfully individuals coping with the aftermath of trauma have reconstructed or strengthened their perceptions of self, others, and the meaning of events. There is also a PTGI for children.

CASE 2. *Quotes From Survivors on Their Post Traumatic Growth*

Following are a few quotes taken from a qualitative study of adult survivors of sexual, emotional, and physical abuse (Woodward & Joseph, 2003, pp. 278–279).

I have learned to appreciate what I have, a loving husband and three children with whom I have a warm and affectionate relationship.

***

There are times when I wish I could return to a time of less self-awareness, a kind of blissful ignorance, but the gain perhaps of increased self-awareness is an increase in the depth of feeling good/bad, happy/sad, etc., which I wouldn't now be without.

***

I enjoy every day to the full, I don't worry about silly things anymore, and if something is important to me, I make an effort to do something about it. I realize now that however unjust or unfair R's death was that this is part of life.

CASE 3. *An Example of Post Traumatic Success*

"What matters most of all is the attitude we take toward suffering, the attitude in which we take our suffering upon ourselves" (Frankl, 1963, p. 178). Frankl is often cited as an example of post traumatic success. He said of his stay in a German concentration camp that a prisoner who no longer believed in the future—his future—was doomed. Frankl described an incident where he was staggering along in a row of prisoners on his way to the work area, in the cold and without food. He forced himself to think about something else. Suddenly he saw himself standing on the stage of an auditorium where he was giving a lecture about the psychology of the camp system. In this way he succeeded in lifting himself above the suffering of the moment and was able to view the torment as if it were already in the past. His focus on the future saved him for that moment. And this vision of the future even became reality, as after the war he conducted many successful lecture tours. In his logotherapy, Frankl explained that the meaning in suffering is resilience itself: The trick is to handle as well as possible the challenges that we face in life.

STORY 5. *Comprehensive Growth Ability*

Being a thriver involves either PTG (post traumatic growth) or PEG (post-ecstatic growth). PEG is defined as growth through positive life events. Mangelsdorf (2013) proposed the concept of comprehensive growth ability (CGA), a new framework that unifies the concepts of post traumatic growth and post-ecstatic growth. According to this model, people who are more likely to experience post traumatic growth are also more likely to experience post-ecstatic growth.

CGA is a traitlike capacity to flourish after either traumatic or positive life events. A counterfactual mindset—which performs the role of meaning-making in growth processes—partially mediates the effect of the event on growth. The direct effect of the event is moderated by the presence of supportive positive relationships and the prevalence of positive emotions. By unifying post traumatic and post-ecstatic growth, CGA proposes a new understanding of positive human development. It suggests that fostering a counterfactual mindset, enhancing positive emotions, and helping people to strengthen supportive relationships increases their likelihood of thriving, whatever their life path will be.

Caveats

The relationship between trauma symptoms and growth is not yet clear. A recent study of HIV-positive women who were sexually abused as children found that the more severe the past trauma, the greater the improvement experienced in an intervention program designed to ease psychological suffering (Chin et al., 2013). Those whose sexual abuse was most severe showed the greatest overall reduction in their symptoms of depression, post traumatic stress, and anxiety. This is somewhat surprising at first glance, as one might assume that with more trauma comes more difficulty in improving one's symptoms. One explanation may be that the more severe the trauma, the more severe the symptoms and the greater the amount of change possible in returning to a normal level of functioning.

However, there is also research indicating that a moderate level of traumatization has the strongest connection to PTG (Butler et al., 2005). In some cases, a curvilinear relationship between trauma symptoms and growth has been noted wherein higher growth is reported by those with intermediate levels of exposure or symptoms, suggesting that there may be a range of traumatic experience most conducive to growth. This may involve life events that disturb psychological equanimity enough to prompt cognitive reorganization but not enough to undermine or overwhelm one's capacity to adapt.

Another issue that needs to be clarified is the distinction between *PTG as a process and PTG as an outcome*. The literature does not distinguish between PTG as a process and PTG as an outcome, which may have important implications for the way PTG research is conducted (e.g., if PTG is an outcome, is it accurate to link PTG to other outcomes of trauma, such as well-being?). It may be that constructs that occur in light of trauma (such as growth and depression) are not polar opposites. Rather, they may be seen as independent dimensions of well-being. Further research is required.

Tedeschi and Calhoun (2004) offered some important caveats on PTG. They stated that PTG occurs in the context of suffering and psychological struggle. A focus on growth should not come at the expense of empathy for the pain and suffering. As a matter of fact, PTG and symptoms of PTSD may coexist. Posttraumatic growth emerges from the struggle with coping, not from the trauma itself, which is not good in any way and undesirable. Also trauma is not necessary for growth or universal or inevitable. There are also a significant number of people who experience little or no growth at all in their struggle with trauma and this should be quite acceptable.

In sum, the idea of PTG has become one of the most exciting topics in modern psychology because it changes how we think about psychological trauma. Psychologists and psychiatrists are beginning to realize that post traumatic stress following trauma is not always a sign of disorder. Instead, post traumatic stress can signal that the person is going through a normal and natural emotional struggle to rebuild his or her life and make sense of what has happened. For example, in contrast to pathological denial marked by little or no insight, *healthy denial* (Druss & Douglas, 1988) early in the adaptation process may aid in the ultimate assimilation of the event. Sadly, it often takes a tragic event in our lives before we make changes. Survivors and thrivers have much to teach those of us who haven't experienced such traumas about how to live.

STORY 6. *The Shattered Vase*

The metaphor of the shattered vase is often used in therapy with trauma survivors. Post traumatic growth involves the rebuilding of

the shattered assumptive world. Imagine that one day you acciden-
tally knock a treasured vase off its perch. It smashes into tiny pieces.
What do you do? Do you try to put the vase back together as it
was? Do you collect the pieces and drop them in the trash, regarding the vase as a total loss? Or do you pick up the beautiful pieces
and use them to make something new—such as a colorful mosaic?
When adversity strikes, people often feel that at least some part of
them—their view of the world, their sense of themselves, their relationships—has been smashed. Those who try to put their lives back
together exactly as they were remain fractured and vulnerable. But
those who accept the breakage and build themselves anew become
more resilient and open to new ways of living.

These changes do not necessarily mean that the person will be entirely free of memories of what has happened, grief, or other forms
of distress. But they may mean that he or she will live life more
meaningfully in light of what happened.

GRIEF AND RESILIENCE

When does a broken heart become a mental disorder? Grief is a natural
response to loss. It is the emotional suffering you feel when something
or someone you love is taken away. Grief associated with death is familiar to most people, but people may grieve in connection with a variety
of losses throughout their lives, such as unemployment, ill health, or
the end of a relationship.

However, besides the negative outcomes of the loss, there are often
positive ones. People commonly say that one of the positive outcomes
of loss they have suffered is that it signaled a *wake-up call*. Priorities in
their lives underwent a change. No longer is it all about pursuing success in work, but about cherishing and improving their relationships
with people dear to them. People also mention that they live more in the
present and are not so preoccupied with the past or future. Enjoying a
sunny day, admiring the beauty of nature, and enjoying good company
with nice people become more important. Theories about coping state
that taking stock of your resilience after a setback, or reconsidering the
meaning of life or the importance of relationships with significant others, prevents feelings of loss or helplessness. This, in turn, can lead to
experiencing existence as significant, which is connected to feelings of
well-being and self-respect. A traumatic incident or the loss of a loved
one can also ensure further development in life, perhaps because one

has to adopt a new role, such as that of widow or head of the family.

Nolen-Hoeksema (2000) interviewed people in bereavement at intervals of six, thirteen, and eighteen months after their loss. She found that people who after six months could report something positive experienced less fear and depression than people who did not experience a positive dimension. Her research shows that it is not a question of how many positive things someone can discover but of whether the person can find anything positive at all.

Nolen-Hoeksema's research into coping mechanisms of the bereaved has found that those who find something positive use different coping styles than those who do not. The former try hard to find something positive, seek out more support, express their emotions more, and actively look for diversion.

Although the loss of a significant loved one can be a highly distressing experience, research done by Nolen-Hoeksema and Davis (2005) showed that the majority of bereaved people report finding something positive in their loss experiences. Common positive themes include a sense of personal growth and personality change, realization of personal strengths, reprioritization of life goals, greater appreciation for relationships, and a diminished sense of fear about death. Nolen-Hoeksa and Davis also discovered a strong link between optimism and finding significance in life after a loss. People who have positive expectations—optimists—are actively committed to seeking ways of transforming bad times into good times. They actively search for positive ways to look at the situation. And the more they preoccupy themselves with that, the greater the chance that they will find something positive. In turn, people who find something positive in their losses show better psychological adjustment to the loss, both shortly after the loss and long afterward.

Research also shows that people who can experience something positive amid feelings of grief for their loved ones recover much faster (Ong, Bergeman, Bisconti, and Wallace, 2006). Some people, reflecting on the qualities of their loved ones and the years they spent together, find contentment in recalling the wonderful times they shared. Others find consolation in the comfort and support they receive from family and friends. Another group find significance in their lives through altruistic acts, like starting a self-help group or doing volunteer work. Whatever it is, there will be space to develop plans and set goals for the future, whereby a further widening can take place and creativity can increase. Fredrickson (2009) states that it could well be this positivity that is the deepest resource in times of crisis, because this is what is required to stop the downward spiral of negative emotions and bounce back.

A focus on recovery from a loss to a previous level of functioning misses the true process of change that many people experience following a loss. During times of loss and trauma, therapists should, while acknowledging the pain of that loss, more clearly focus on positive emotions and discovering a new significance in life. Therapists' focus should not be merely on a *return to normal*, but, together with their clients, they should look at how positive emotions can contribute to personal growth and new levels of functioning.

It is important for therapists to keep in mind that no therapy can change the events of a life; it can only influence the effects of those events. Thus, in relation to a loss, it is not the loss itself that we work with, but merely the change in our client's sense of self and the reformulation of his or her life following the loss. A useful questions is: "Imagine that you are living a life that does you justice and does justice to your relationship with [the deceased person]. How will you know that you're doing that?" Imagining that picture and making moves to turn it into reality are what open up possibilities.

STORY 7. A Buddhist Tale

This is an old Buddhist tale. A long time ago in India, there lived a woman named Kisa. She met a man whom she fell in love with and who also loved her. They married and had a son. They were very happy as they watched their son grow. However, at the age of two, he fell ill and died. Kisa's world collapsed. She was overcome by grief so strong that she denied his death altogether. She wandered around, carrying her dead son and asking people desperately for a medicine that would cure him. Eventually, she found her way to the Buddha and asked him to cure her son. The Buddha said with deep compassion, "Yes, I will help you, but I'll need a fistful of mustard seeds for that." When Kisa told him that she was willing to do anything to get the mustard seeds, the Buddha added, "The seeds must be from a house where no one has lost his or her child, spouse, or parents. All the seeds have to be from a house that hasn't been visited by death."

Kisa went from house to house, but everywhere the reply was the same: "We do have mustard seeds, but there are fewer of us alive than dead." Everyone had lost a father or a mother, a wife or a husband, a son or a daughter. Kisa visited many houses and heard many stories of loss. After she had visited all the houses in the village, her eyes were opened and she realized that no one is safe from loss and grief and that she wasn't alone. Her grief turned into compassion for the other grieving people. She was then able to grieve the death of her son and bury his body.

—Furman (1988)

BRAIN AND BODY RESILIENCE

The brain can be changed by experiences for better or for worse. We develop good or bad habits, actually changing the structure of the brain and altering the reward system of the brain. Studies of early trauma and neglect have revealed that the neural structure and function within the brain can be severely affected, leading to long-lasting and extensive effects on the brain's capacity to adapt to stress. If a certain pattern has been stimulated in the past, the probability of activating a similar profile in the future is enhanced. If the pattern is fired repeatedly, the probability of future activation is further increased. This increased probability is created by changes in the synaptic connections within the

Exercise 3. FINDING NEW MEANING

This is an exercise aimed at finding new meaning in life and positive aspects after the loss of a loved one. Nestled in the saying "It is better to have loved and lost than never to have loved at all" is a kernel of positivity. This morning one of my clients canceled his appointment: His eighty-year old mother had just died. He told me that he was very sad but relieved that she had been spared a long period of suffering, dependency, and loss of dignity. He also found consolation in the fact that she had hardly suffered.

However sad clients are, and however difficult they may find it in the beginning, invite them to discover something positive in their situation. Perhaps there is something for which they can be grateful. Could something have been worse? What is it about their situation that prevents it from being even worse? Research has shown that it doesn't matter how small the positive aspect is, so long as people can eventually find something positive. This small aspect can be the seed they sow to harvest more positivity in the future.

network of neurons. This is called *Hebb's axiom*: Neurons that fire together, wire together. However, neuroscientists have discovered that the human brain does not remain stable for the rest of its life but changes throughout one's lifetime. New connections are made and some areas of the brain can even generate new cells, a process called *neurogenesis*. Recent research suggests that physical exercise and cognitive stimulation enhance such *brain plasticity* and increase the brain's information-processing capacity.

Fredrickson (2009) found that positivity alters the brain and changes the way people interact with the world. One of the consequences of positivity is enhanced creativity, as demonstrated by Rowe, Hirsh, and Anderson (2007), who "injected" volunteers with positivity, negativity, or neutrality by using music to induce emotions and then tested them on two different tasks. One task measured the scope of visual attention by tracking the influence of peripherally presented information. The other task measured verbal creativity by asking volunteers to come up with a single word that related to three given words (e.g., mower, atomic, and foreign > power) using the Remote Associates Test. When people felt positive, their performance on the two tasks changed in tandem: The broader the scope of their visual attention, the greater their creativity on the verbal task. This is an important linkage because it documents that positivity broadens minds in multiple, interrelated ways.

The Optimism Bias

The belief that the future will be better than the past and present is known as the *optimism bias*. A growing body of scientific evidence points to the conclusion that optimism may be hardwired by evolution into the human brain. The science of optimism opens a new window into the workings of human consciousness. Our brains aren't just stamped by the past; they are constantly being shaped by the future as well. To think positively about our prospects, we must be able to imagine ourselves in the future. Optimism starts with what may be the most extraordinary of human talents: mental time travel, the ability to move back and forth through time and space in one's mind, which is critical to our survival.

To make progress, we need to be able to imagine alternative realities—better ones—and we need to believe that we can achieve them. Such faith helps motivate us to pursue our goals. Optimists work longer hours and tend to earn more. Economists have found that optimists even save more. And although they are not less likely to divorce, they are more likely to remarry.

Even if that better future is often an illusion, optimism has clear benefits in the present. Hope keeps our minds at ease, lowers stress, and improves physical health. Researchers studying heart disease patients found that optimists were more likely than nonoptimistic patients to take vitamins, eat low-fat diets, and exercise, thereby reducing their overall coronary risk (Affleck et al., 1987). A study of cancer patients revealed that pessimistic patients under the age of sixty were more likely to die within eight months than nonpessimistic patients of the same initial health, status, and age (Dunigan et al., 2007).

Should something unpleasant happen to us, we soon see the cloud's silver lining and rapidly return to our former level of happiness. This capacity to envision the future relies partly on the hippocampus, a part of our brain crucial to memory. Patients with damage to their hippocampus are unable to recollect the past, but they are also unable to construct detailed images of future scenarios. They appear to be stuck in time. Research shows that most of us spend less time mulling over negative outcomes than we do positive ones. Positive expectations enhance the odds of survival (Sharot, 2011).

The optimism bias is distinct from the *negativity bias*, which indicates that negative stimuli get more attention and processing, that we generally learn more from pain than from pleasure, and that people work harder to avoid a loss than they do to attain an equal gain.

Amygdala Whisperers

We as therapists are *amygdala whisperers*. We want our clients to be conscious of their amygdala activation and be able to say to themselves, "Don't worry; everything will be fine." Amygdala activation takes place if constitutional features, traumatic experiences, or negative attachments have produced maladaptive emotion regulation, restricting people in their ability to achieve emotional resilience and behavioral flexibility. Addressing the neocortex can override these responses and bring the deeper structures of the amygdala into a more tolerable level of arousal. This can be done by a number of *self-talk* strategies in which imagery or internal dialogue is activated. Over time and with continued practice, the frequency and intensity of these responses can be significantly decreased and the speed of recovery can be enhanced. Siegel (1999) described a client who was afraid of dogs after having been mauled by one, losing part of his left ear and sustaining deep wounds to his arms and chest. Teaching him about the nature of the fear response and the neural circuits underlying it was relieving for him, and relaxation techniques and guided imagery with exposure to self-generated images of dogs were provided. Nevertheless, he still had an initial startle response to dogs, so a *cognitive override* strategy was then tried. The client learned to acknowledge the relevance of his amygdala's response to the present dog and the past trauma (the initial arousal mechanism). He then would say to himself, "I know that you [the amygdala] are trying to protect me, and that you think this is a dangerous thing. [This was the specific appraisal stage.] I do not need to see this sense of panic as something to fear or get agitated about." He would then imagine his amygdala sighing with relief, having discharged its duty to warn, and the sense of doom would dissipate. After several weeks of performing these internal override discussions, he felt ready to proceed with the purchase of a (small) dog for his children. Six months later, he and his family were doing well with the new addition to their household.

A Positive Outcome

Rock (2009) stated that unless you take care to label your emotions when they are at a high level (see Chapter 7) and then not dwell on them, thinking of problems will increase limbic arousal, making it harder to solve them. Solving difficult problems involves getting through an impasse. It requires a quiet and generally positive and open mind. Getting lost in large amounts of history and detail does not make the brain quiet at all. The more negative connections you make, the less dopamine you have, the fewer resources you have for solving the next problem, and the more negative connections you make. In this low-energy state, everything looks hard. Increasingly risk adverse, you don't have the motivation to take action. The decision to focus on a positive outcome instead of a problem impacts brain functioning in several ways:

• When you focus on a positive outcome, you prime the brain to perceive information relevant to that outcome rather than to notice information about the problem. You can't be looking for solutions and problems at the same time.
• When you look for solutions, you scan your environment widely for cues, which activates more of the right hemisphere of the brain, rather than drilling down into information that activates the left hemisphere. Activating the right hemisphere is helpful

in having insights, which is how complex problems are often solved.

• When you focus on problems, you are more likely to activate the emotions connected with those problems, which will create greater noise in the brain. This inhibits insight, whereas focusing on solutions generates a toward state because you desire something. You are seeking, not avoiding. This increases dopamine levels, which is useful for insight. And if you are expecting that you might find a solution, these positive expectations help release even more dopamine.

In all these ways, focusing on solutions can significantly increase the likelihood of having insights and even make you feel happier.

Another way to boost your dopamine level is to hold a pencil or pen between your teeth (across from cheek to cheek) for two minutes. This simple action forces your mouth and face to smile, and bizarre as it sounds, this has shown to have a real positive effect on your happiness level.

STORY 8. *The Drip System*

In changing the brain, repetition is key. Rock (2009) used the metaphor of the brain as a garden. In this garden it is sunny almost all the time, although it rains naturally once in a while. If you want to grow some nice tomatoes, you first plant seedlings, which need careful daily watering. Once the plants are a bit hardy, you need to water them regularly to keep them growing. How often is the right amount? If you water once a year, it will probably wash everything away. Once a quarter won't do much. Once a month will help, maybe. Once a week does make a difference for some plants, but watering twice a week seems to make a sustainable and noticeable difference. It seems that the best technique for growing plants is what they do on hydroponic farms, which is to water them several times each day using a drip system. Rock proposes that creating healthy new circuits in the brain is similar: You need to pay regular attention.

The Body

Fredrickson (2009) cites an impressive amount of research conducted in recent years wherein there appears to be a positive association between positive emotions and health benefits such as a better immune system, less stress, lower blood pressure, less pain, fewer colds, better sleep patterns, lower risk of medical conditions like diabetes and stroke, faster production of new cells in the body and in the brain, and even longer life. More information on neuroscience (e.g., the roles of dopamine, oxytocin, endorphins, cortisol, and gamma-aminobutyric acid) can be found in *Practicing Positive CBT* (Bannink, 2012a, 2013).

The standard fairy tale ending phrase is "and they lived happily ever after." Positive psychology and solution-focused brief therapy may give this ending phrase a whole new meaning. In the next chapter, PP and SFBT, with their positive focus, will be described in greater detail.

SUMMARY

- Most people are resilient and may even grow in the wake of a trauma.
- Resilience, a stable trajectory of healthy functioning, is the most common outcome following a traumatic event.
- Post traumatic success (PTS) includes recovery from (symptoms of) PTSD, resilience, and post traumatic growth.
- Grief is a natural response to loss and is associated with resilience.
- Research shows that the brain can be changed by experience and that one's outlook has a significant effect on one's health.

CHAPTER 3

•••••••••••••

The Positive Focus

Suppose you are hungry and decide to eat in a restaurant. After having waited for some time, you are invited to take a seat and the manager introduces himself. He asks you questions regarding your hunger: "How hungry are you? For how long have you been preoccupied with this feeling? Were you hungry in the past? What role did hunger play at home with your family or with other relatives? What disadvantages and possibly advantages does hunger have for you?" After this, having become even hungrier, you ask if you can now eat. But in addition the manager wants you to complete some questionnaires about hunger (and perhaps about other issues that the manager finds important). Once everything is finished, a meal is served to you that you did not order, but that the manager claims is good for you and has helped other hungry people. What are the chances of you leaving the restaurant feeling satisfied?

—Bannink, 2010a, p. xii

In traditional psychotherapies, the medical model is used: The focus is predominantly on problems and how to reduce them. Client assessments often mention few or no client strengths, resources, and abilities. It is, however, the clients' abilities, strengths, and resources that are most important in helping to bring about change. Kuyken and colleagues (2009) state that in CBT there has been a much greater emphasis on identifying precipitating, predisposing, and perpetuating factors for problems. They advocate the inclusion of strengths whenever possible. It should be emphasized, however, that a positive focus and positive interventions should not be used at the expense of attention to the suffering of clients, and they are appropriate only after individuals' acute physical and psychological needs have been met.

In this chapter, a paradigm shift from problem-solving to solution-building is described, and both positive psychology and solution-focused brief therapy are explained in detail. A short comparison of the two approaches is also given. Differences between the traditional approach to trauma and the strengths-and-solutions-focused approach are outlined, showing how this paradigm shift is applied in helping clients change.

A PARADIGM SHIFT

According to the traditional cause-effect model (also called the *medical model* or the *problem-focused model*), one must find out exactly what is the matter and declare a correct diagnosis before a remedy can be provided. This is the *problem-solving paradigm*. In our Western thinking, the cause-effect model is the preeminent model for making the world understandable. The model is useful if one is dealing with straightforward problems that can actually be reduced to simple and unambiguous causes, as is the case with many medical or mechanical problems. When you have a toothache, the first question you ask is: "What's wrong with my teeth?" When your vacuum cleaner breaks down, the first question you ask is: "What's wrong with my vacuum cleaner?" The medical model can be stated thus: Diagnosis + prescribed treatment = symptom reduction. As far as psychotherapy is concerned, however, this model has a major disadvantage: It is heavily problem-focused. If the problem and its possible causes are studied in depth, a vicious circle may develop, with ever-growing problems. The atmosphere becomes laden with problems, which poses the risk that solutions will recede ever further from view and that the hope of improvement will dwindle. In this manner, psychology becomes a victimology and psychologists and psychiatrists become pathologizers. Exploring or analyzing the factors that cause or perpetuate a problem does not automatically result in improvement of the problem. Einstein (1954) stated that we cannot solve problems by using the same kind of thinking we used when we created them. Duncan (2010) stated that psychotherapy is not a medical endeavor; it is first and foremost a relational one. Yet the medical model is still the predominant description of what therapists do.

The British Psychological Society, in its response to the proposed DSM-5 (2011), stated its concern that clients and the general public are negatively affected by the continued and continuous medicalization of their natural and normal responses to their experiences—responses that undoubtedly have distressing consequences that demand helping responses, but that do not reflect illnesses so much as normal individual variation.

Furthermore, research shows that among professionals using the problem-solving model, there are high percentages of stress, depression, suicide, burnout, and secondary traumatization. These findings warrant closer examination.

Shortcomings of the Problem-Solving Paradigm

The problem-solving paradigm has become popular in business, in government, and in coaching, psychotherapy, and conflict management. In traditional forms of psychotherapy, the focus is on pathology. The diagnosis of the problem is the first step. The next step is finding the causes of the problem, using the cause-effect model (the *medical model* or *mechanical model*) as previously mentioned.

This is a very common perspective: Something has gone wrong and we have to put it right. In medicine and psychotherapy, problems are called a deviation from the normal. Health is normal; sickness is a deviation and has to be removed.

The problem-solving model is very straightforward: Identify the cause and remove it. And indeed, "Analyze the problem, find the cause, put it right" is a simple and attractive idiom. It makes sense, and it is action-oriented. But unfortunately, it is often inadequate for a number of reasons:

- In a complex interactive situation, we may never be able to isolate one cause.
- There is a danger in fastening onto a particular cause because it is easy to identify while ignoring the rest of the situation.
- We may identify the cause but be unable to remove it.
- The notion that once the cause is removed, the problem will be solved and things will be back to normal, is usually erroneous.
- In defining the goal and deciding how to get there, our perceived destination may be inaccurate or imprecise.

There is growing dissatisfaction among clients and professionals with problem-focused models of therapy. Studying problems in depth often leads to the premature discontinuation of sessions, because nothing changes and the client loses hope of improvement. The good news about psychotherapy is that the average treated client is better off than 80 percent of the untreated sample. Psychotherapy facilitates the remission of symptoms and improves functioning. It also often provides additional coping strategies and methods for dealing with future problems (Lambert & Ogles, 2004).

The bad news, however, is that there has been no improvement in psychotherapy outcomes in more than thirty years, that the dropout rates are often very high (47 to 50 percent), and that there is a lack of consumer confidence in therapy outcomes. For example, Monson and colleagues (2006) described a wait-list controlled trial of cognitive processing therapy (CPT: a CBT approach) with sixty veterans (fifty-four men and six women) with chronic military-related PTSD. They found that the dropout rate was over 16 percent (20 percent from CPT, 13 percent from the waiting list). Forty percent of the CPT sample did not meet criteria for a PTSD diagnosis, and 50 percent had a reliable change in their PTSD symptoms at post-treatment assessment. Monson and colleagues stated that this trial provided some of the most encouraging results of PTSD treatment for veterans with chronic PTSD. However, half of the treated subjects showed no reliable improvement!

In spite of these disappointing outcomes, there is a continued emphasis on the medical model, and there are continued claims of superiority among models despite the absence of evidence. As Wampold (2001, p. 204) stated, "Research designs that are able to isolate and establish the relationship between specific ingredients and outcomes have failed to find a scintilla of evidence that any specific ingredient is necessary for therapeutic change."

STORY 9. *Shot by a Poisoned Arrow*

If a man is shot by a poisoned arrow and says, "Don't take this arrow away before you find out exactly by whom and from where and how it was shot," this man's death is inevitable.

—Buddha

The Solution-Building Paradigm

A *strengths-and-solutions-based approach*, which has its roots in PP and SFBT, is a meta-view—an overarching philosophical perspective in which people are seen as capable and as having abilities and resources within themselves and their social systems. When activated and integrated with new experiences, understandings, and skills, strengths offer pathways to reduce pain and suffering, resolve concerns and conflicts, and more effectively cope with life stressors. The outcome is an improved sense of well-being and quality of life and a higher degree of interpersonal and social functioning. Strengths-based positive psychologists and solution-focused professionals promote this "change from wrong to strong" through respectful educational, therapeutic, and operational processes that encourage and empower their clients.

Exercise 4. FIND MORE HELPFUL QUESTIONS

Consider a typical problematic situation. Write down the typical questions you ask yourself or your clients about it. Examine these questions closely. Does asking them help you feel better or worse? Does asking them help move you forward to where you want to be or merely give you an explanation of why you are stuck or can't change? If your questions are not helping you, find some more helpful questions.

Saleebey (2007) called this view the *strengths perspective* and saw it as encompassing the following assumptions:

- Despite life's struggles, all persons possess strengths (i.e., resources) that can be marshaled to improve the qualities of their lives. Therapists should respect these strengths and the directions in which clients wish to apply them.
- Client motivation is increased by a consistent emphasis on strengths as the client defines them.
- Discovering strengths requires a process of cooperative exploration between clients and therapists; expert therapists do not have the last word on what clients need to improve in their lives.
- Focusing on strengths turns therapists away from the temptation to judge or blame clients for their difficulties and toward discovering how clients have managed to survive, even in the most difficult of circumstances.
- All environments—even the most bleak—contain resources.

POSITIVE PSYCHOLOGY

Positive psychology is an umbrella term encompassing the basic academic discipline principally concerned with understanding positive human thought, feeling, and behavior; the empirical, systematic investigation of psychological phenomena; and finally an applied discipline in which certain interventions are created and employed. The "positive psychology family" consists of optimism, hope, self-efficacy, self-esteem, positive emotions, flow, happiness, gratitude, and so forth. Over the last decade, much research has taken place and many books have been published on PP (Bannink, 2009a, 2011; Fredrickson, 2009; Seligman, 2011; Snyder & Lopez, 2005).

PP is the study of what makes life worth living and what enables individuals and communities to thrive. It is also the study of the conditions and processes that lead to optimal functioning in individuals, in relations, and in work. The label PP represents the efforts of professionals to help people optimize human functioning by acknowledging strengths as well as deficiencies, and by noting environmental resources in addition to stressors. The study of mental health is distinct from and complementary to the long-standing interest in mental illness, its prevalence, and its remedies (Keyes & Lopez, 2005).

According to PP, getting rid of unhappiness is not the same thing as achieving happiness. Getting rid of fear, anger, and depression will not automatically fill you with peace, love, and joy. Getting rid of weaknesses will not automatically maximize your strengths. In traditional psychotherapy book titles, you find the same way of thinking: *Overcoming Depression*, *Coping With Obsessive-Compulsive Disorder*, *Your Route Out of Perfectionism*. PP finds that happiness and unhappiness are not on the same continuum. Strategies to minimize fear, anger, and depression are not identical to strategies to maximize peace, joy, strength, and meaning. In this respect, PP differs from SFBT. SFBT uses the same continuum by asking, "What would you like to have instead of the problem?" SFBT assumes that this strategy is helpful in inviting clients to move from a minus point on the scale (given a scale of –10 to +10) to a plus point.

We see the same paradigm change in Appreciative Inquiry (AI), which is used in management and leadership (Cooperrider & Whitney, 2005). It is profoundly strengths-based in its assumptions and founded on the premise that people and organizations excel only by amplifying strengths, never by fixing weaknesses. Small shifts can make seismic differences: Strengths-based change obeys a tipping point. Instead of focusing 80 percent on what is not working and 20 percent on strengths, AI reverses this 80/20 rule. This "80/20 deficit-bias" (Cooperrider & Godwin, 2011) still pervades the media, the helping professions, our culture at large, and almost every systemic and global change effort. Cooperrider and Godwin state that the deficit-based industry—focused primarily on problem analysis, error reduction, and repair—represents a $350 billion market. By reversing the 80/20 rule, challenges or crisis are not ignored (there is still a 20-percent focus on those challenges), but the main focus (80 percent) is on progress markers, successes, strengths, and solutions. Drucker (2002), an influential management consultant, has even stated that the great task of leadership is to create an alignment of strengths in ways that make a system's weaknesses irrelevant.

Exercise 5. RAISE THE PERCENTAGE OF STRENGTHS AND SOLUTIONS TALK

What percentage of time in your intake process and treatment do you as a therapist spend asking clients about their strengths, their successes, and what works in their life and in reaching their preferred future? Is it 10 percent? Is it 20 percent? Is it 50 percent, or maybe zero? Suppose you were a client. How would you like your therapist to spend his or her time during your therapy? Would you like to be invited to talk about your strengths and resources? You probably would! So why not raise the percentage of time you normally spend by just 10 percent (e.g., if you use 10 percent, make it 20 percent) and notice what a difference this makes for both your clients and yourself. Or do as AI does (see above): Raise the percentage to 80/20.

STORY 10. *The Comprehensive Soldier Fitness (CSF) Program*

Seligman developed the Comprehensive Soldier Fitness program to promote the idea that it is possible for the 1.1 million soldiers in the US army to be just as psychologically fit as physically fit. Seligman proposed that the US army could move the entire emphasis of the reaction to adversity in the direction of resilience and growth. This would not only help prevent PTSD but also increase the number of soldiers who bounce back readily from adversity. Most important, it would increase the number of soldiers who grow psychologically from the crucible of combat.

The CSF program, begun in 2009, is the largest well-being intervention, military or civilian, ever undertaken. Preliminary findings from the testing of over 800,000 soldiers indicate that as psychological fitness increases, PTSD symptoms decrease and healthcare costs decline (Seligman, 2011).

The program consists of four fitness modules: the emotional fitness module, the family fitness module, the social fitness module, and the spiritual fitness module. It is described in more detail in Seligman's book *Flourish* (2011).

Exercise 6. THREE BLESSINGS (HUNT THE GOOD STUFF)

Here is an exercise for clients to feel less depressed, happier and maybe to become addicted to this exercise six months from now. Invite them to set aside ten minutes before they go asleep every night for the next week. Ask them to write down three things that went well that day and why they went well. They may use a journal or their computer to write about the events, but it is important that they have a physical record of what they wrote. The three things need not be earthshaking in importance. Next to each positive event ask them to answer the question: Why did this happen? Writing about why the positive events happened may seem awkward at first, but ask them to stick with it for one week: it will get easier (Seligman, 2011, p. 33).

The History of Positive Psychology

The notion of a PP movement began at a moment in time after Seligman was elected president of the American Psychological Association (in 1997). While he was weeding his garden, his five-year old daughter Nikki was throwing weeds into the air and dancing around. He yelled at her. Nikki walked away, came back, and said, "Daddy, I want to talk to you. Do you remember before my fifth birthday? From the time I was three to the time I was five, I was a whiner. I whined every day. When I turned five, I decided not to whine anymore. That was the hardest thing I've ever done. And if I can stop whining, you can stop being such a grouch" (Seligman, as cited in Snyder & Lopez, 2005, p. 3).

Seligman learned from Nikki something about raising kids, about himself, and about his profession. He realized that raising children is more than fixing what is wrong with them. It is about identifying and nurturing their strongest qualities, recognizing what they own and are best at, and helping them find niches in which they can best live out these positive qualities. He acknowledged that he was a grouch and decided to change. The broadest implication, however, was in the science and practice of psychology. After World War II, psychologists had discovered that they could make a living treating mental illness and academics had found out that they could get grants if their research was about pathology. This has brought many benefits: At least fourteen disorders can now be cured or considerably relieved. But the downside was that making the lives of all people more productive and fulfilling and identifying and nurturing high talent were forgotten. As mentioned previously, psychology thus became a victimology and psychologists became pathologizers. Psychology's empirical focus shifted to assessing and curing individual suffering. There was an explosion in research on psychological disorders and the negative effects of environmental stressors such as parental divorce, death, and physical and sexual abuse. Practitioners went about treating mental illness within the disease-patient framework of repairing damage.

STORY 11. *The Grant Study*

The focus on (mental) health did not start with Seligman and his daughter Nikki. In 1937, an entrepreneur and philanthropist, Grant, met with the director of the Harvard University Health Service, Dr. Bock, and together they decided that medical research was too weighted in the direction of disease. They agreed that large endowments had been given for the study of the mentally and physically ill, but very few had thought it pertinent to make a systematic inquiry into the kinds of people who are well and do well. As a result, Grant and his colleagues selected a healthy sample of several consecutive college classes (268 Harvard graduates from the classes of 1939 to 1944) for intensive medical and psychological study, and the now-famous Grant study was born. The Grant study is the longest longitudinal study of adult development ever conducted. For sixty-eight years, men have been studied (they forgot to include women!) from adolescence into late life to identify the predictors of healthy aging
—Vaillant, 1995

Well-Being Theory

The original PP theory was that happiness could be analyzed and categorized into three different elements: *positive emotion, engagement,* and *meaning*. The first element, positive emotion, is something we feel—pleasure, serenity, ecstasy, warmth, comfort, and so forth—and is called the *pleasant life*. The second element, engagement, is about flow, being one with the music, time stopping, and the loss of self-consciousness that occurs during an absorbing activity, and is called the *engaged life*. The third element, meaning, consists of belonging to and serving something that is bigger than oneself—for example, religion, nature, family, a political party—and is called the *meaningful life*.

In his latest book, Seligman (2011) changed the topic of PP from happiness to well-being. The goal of PP is to increase flourishing by increasing positive emotion (P), engagement (E), positive relationships (R), meaning (M), and accomplishment (A). (A handy mnemonic is PERMA.) Thus, Seligman's well-being theory adds *positive relationships* and *accomplishment* to the three previous elements. The element of positive relationships is added because other people are the best antidote to the downs of life and the single most reliable elevator. Doing a kindness to another person produces the single most reliable momentary increase in well-being of any exercise tested in PP research. Happiness and life satisfaction are all aspects of positive relationships.

The fifth element is accomplishment: People pursue success, accomplishment, winning, achievement, and mastery for their own sake, even when they bring no positive emotion, no meaning, and no positive relationships. The addition of the *achieving life* also emphasizes that the task of PP is to describe, rather than prescribe, what people actually do to get well-being.

Together with Seligman, Peterson surveyed diverse world cultures to create a comprehensive index of character strengths and virtues. In Seligman's former happiness theory, the strengths and virtues are the support only for the second element of engagement. You go into flow when your highest strengths are deployed to meet the highest challenges that come your way. In well-being theory, the twenty-four strengths underpin all five elements, not just engagement. Deploying your highest strengths leads to more positive emotion, to more meaning, to more accomplishment and to better relationships.

The strengths perspective argues that people and the systems they live in usually do not embrace change well under conditions of fear, trauma, or any kind of manufactured urgency. It might be the opposite. Humans might well become more resilient and capable of realizing their potentials the more they engage not the negative emotions, but the positive emotions, for example, hope, inspiration, and joy. In contrast to anger or fear, which constricts cognition, positive emotions tend to open thought-action repertoires, whereby we are able to see the best in the world (Fredrickson, 2009).

Peterson developed the Values in Action (VIA) Survey of Character Strengths test (Peterson, 2006) to reliably classify people on the basis of twenty-four character strengths. More information and applications can be found in Chapter 6.

SOLUTION-FOCUSED BRIEF THERAPY

Problem-solving certainly has a place in psychotherapy and in other areas. The main limitation, however, is that we may put much too defi-

---

Exercise 7. PRACTICE YOUR STRENGTHS

The key to building a new habit is to practice the behavior over and over. The famous aikido master Ueshiba stated that instructors can impart only a small portion of the teaching; only through ceaseless training can people obtain the necessary experience. His advice is not to chase after many techniques but, one by one, to make each technique your own. This works for character strengths as well. Ask clients to find ways that they can comfortably practice using their strengths. Here are a few ways that resonate with many people:

- *Conversation.* Talk with others about your strengths; tell stories about how your strengths have helped you and were at play when you were at your best. Use your strengths as you converse with others; for example, if you want to build your curiosity, ask questions with a sense of genuine interest.
- *Journaling.* Write about your strengths; explore them in this intrapersonal way. For example, if you want to build your prudence, consider a situation you are conflicted about and write about the costs and benefits of both sides.
- *Self-monitoring.* Set up a tracking system to monitor your experiences throughout the day. Track one or more of the strengths you are using hour by hour; you might need an alarm or another external cue to remind yourself to monitor when you use your strengths. This strategy involves using your strength of self-regulation

---

nite a view on what we believe the solution should be before we have really done our thinking about the matter. As soon as we say "this is the problem," we have defined the sort of solution we expect. In *designing a positive outcome*—instead of problem-solving—we set out to design something: There is an output, there is something to achieve. It is not just a matter of removing a problem; there is a designed something that was not there before. In this design, the focus shifts from problem analysis to outcome analysis or goal analysis, in which clients are invited to give a detailed description of their preferred future.

De Bono (1985) stated that with design there is a sense of purpose and a sense of fit. Problem analysis is always looking back at what is already there; design is always looking forward at what might be created.

> I do not even like saying design solutions because this implies that there is a problem. Even when we cannot find a cause, or, after finding it, cannot remove it, we can always attempt to design an outcome. The main point about the design idiom is that it is open ended. We set out to achieve an outcome. (p. 42)

SFBT is an approach to psychotherapy based on solution-building rather than problem-solving. It explores current resources and future hopes rather than present problems and past causes and typically involves only three to five sessions. It has great value as a preliminary and often sufficient intervention and can be used safely as an adjunct to other treatments. It is a structured process for understanding how to capitalize on change, whereby problems are acknowledged but not analyzed. SFBT is about useful interaction that leaves the client changed, with more hope, more creative ideas, a feeling of competence, and a clearer view on possibilities (Bakker, Bannink, and Macdonald, 2010). What clients (and their therapists) focus their attention on tends to increase and expand in both their awareness and their life. When someone is having problems, it is usually because he or she is attending to the same thing over and over again. The statement "Insanity is doing the same thing over and over again and expecting different results" is generally attributed to Einstein. Clients and therapists are invited to shift their attention from analysis, explanations, and problems to descriptions, thoughts, actions, and feelings that can help clients flourish. Therapists listen for openings in problem-focused conversations. These openings can be about what clients would like to see different in their lives, about exceptions to the problem or about the goal, about competencies and resources, or about who and what might be helpful for the client in taking next steps. Improvement is often realized by redirecting attention from dissatisfaction about a status quo to a positive goal and by starting to take steps in the direction of that goal. In this sense, SFBT uses the same concept of designing (preferred) outcomes described by De Bono (see above).

This process of shifting attention often uses three steps:

1. Acknowledge the problem of the client. ("This must be hard for you.")
2. Suggest a desire for change. ("So I guess you like things to be different?")
3. Ask about the desired outcome. ("How would you like things to be different?")

The History of Solution-Focused Brief Therapy

De Shazer, Berg, and colleagues at the Brief Family Therapy Center in Milwaukee developed the solution-focused model of psychotherapy during the 1980s. They expanded on the findings of Watzlawick, Weakland, and Fisch (1974), who had found that the attempted solution would sometimes perpetuate the problem and that an understanding of the origins of the problem was not (always) necessary. De Shazer (1985) proposed that:

- The development of a solution is not necessarily related to the problem. An analysis of the problem itself is not useful in finding solutions, whereas an analysis of exceptions to the problem is.
- The clients are the experts. They are the ones who determine the goal and the road to achieving it.
- If it isn't broken, don't fix it.
- If something works (better), continue with it, even though it may be something completely different from what was expected to work.
- If something does not work, do something else. More of the same leads nowhere.

De Shazer (1985) stated that the most useful way to decide which door can be opened to get a solution is to get a description of what the client will be doing differently and/or what sorts of things will be happening that are different when the problem is solved, thus creating the expectation of beneficial change. With possible alternative futures in mind, the client can join the therapist in constructing a viable set of solutions.

Useful books describing use of the SF approach with trauma survivors have been written by Dolan (1991, 1998); Furman (1998); O'Hanlon and Bertolino (1998); and Henden (2011).

STORY 12. *Do Something Different*

A Japanese legend provides an example of doing something different if what you're currently doing isn't working. A coastal village was threatened by a tidal wave, but the wave was sighted in advance, far out on the horizon, by a lone farmer in the rice fields on the hillside above the village. There was no use in shouting and there was no time for him to go home to warn his people. At once the farmer set fire to the field, and the villagers who came swarming up to save their crops were saved from the flood

—Author unknown

Positive Differences

SFBT is the pragmatic application of a set of principles and tools, probably best described as *finding the direct route to what works* (see Chapter 6). The nature of SFBT is nonacademic; its pursuit is to find what works for this client at this moment in this context. The emphasis is on constructing solutions as a counterweight to the traditional emphasis on the analysis of problems. "Interventions can initiate change without the therapist's first understanding, in any detail, what has been going on' (De Shazer, 1985, p. 119). SFBT does not claim to solve peoples' problems or to cure their disorders. However, it claims to help clients achieve their preferred future, so classification or diagnosis of problems is often irrelevant. Of course, when clients achieve their preferred future, their apparent problem might have gone away. Or it might not have gone away.

SFBT is a competency-based model that minimizes emphasis on past failings and problems and instead focuses on clients' strengths and previous successes. SFBT utilizes already existing resources to create forward movement toward desired improvements in ways sensitive to time, costs, and local conditions. It seeds improvements that can grow, flourish, and be maintained with ordinary effort.

SFBT is an approach to change that puts *positive differences* to work, which invites conversations about what clients like to see different in their lives, what is working, and what might constitute progress.

Neither the client nor the therapist necessarily directly relates the clients' solutions to any identified problem. Franklin, Trepper, Gingerich, and McCollum (2012) stated that the conversational skills required of the therapist in inviting clients to build solutions are different from those needed to diagnose and treat client problems.

When are clients able to see glimpses of the future they desire? If these positive exceptions have manifested themselves, the therapist can solicit more information about them. If they have not yet appeared but a goal can be formulated, the therapist can inquire about that. If that is not the case, the problem can be analyzed. It is only necessary to shift to problem analysis if no improvement has occurred before the first session, if no exceptions can be found, and if no goal can be formulated in behavioral terms by means of, say, the "miracle question" (see Chapter 5) or other goal-formulation questions. In most cases, one can immediately begin working toward a solution without elaborately mapping the problem first (De Shazer, 1985).

SFBT is applied to psychotherapy (Bannink, 2007, 2010a, 2012a, 2103; De Jong & Berg 2002), coaching, mediation and conflict management (Bannink 2008b, 2009b, 2010b), management and leadership (Bannink, 2010c), strategic planning, education, and sports.

Is it possible to solve problems without even talking about them? The answer is yes. Ask clients to "suppose there is a solution," and then invite them to think about:

- what difference that would make in their lives and in the lives of important others
- what they would be doing (or thinking and feeling) differently
- who would be the first to notice
- what would be the first small sign that a solution is under way
- who would be least surprised
- what else would be better

Solution-Focused Questions

We live in worlds our questions create. The questions we ask determine what we find, and what we find determines our behavior as professionals. Asking questions is an important technique in SFBT. Solution-

Exercise 8. DON'T DEPEND ON KNOWING THE PROBLEM

Do this exercise with a colleague to find out that you don't need to know the problem to examine the goal and solutions. Have the other person say, "I feel too embarrassed to talk about my problem, but I need help now, because it can't go on like this any longer!" You respond, "Suppose there is a solution. What difference will that make for you and for other people around you? How will you know? How will that help you?" Practice asking the questions outlined in the "Positive Differences" section.

Exercise 9. PROBLEM FOCUS VERSUS SOLUTION FOCUS

Here is an exercise to help you notice the differences between a problem-focused and a solution-focused approach. Sit comfortably, close your eyes, and repeat the following sentence ten times: "I have a big problem!" Observe closely what you are experiencing physically and emotionally. Notice carefully the effect that this sentence has on your body and your emotions.

Stretch a little, get up, and do the exercise again, this time using a different statement. Sit comfortably again, close your eyes, and then repeat the following sentence ten times: "I have a great opportunity." Once again, observe the effects that this sentence has on your physical and emotional state.

focused (SF) therapists are *not knowing* (they ask questions to elicit clients' expertise instead of giving advice) and *lead from one step behind* (see Chapter 4).

Dolan (1991) stated that with SF questions, therapists ask clients to describe the smallest signs of progress one by one and then encourage them to carry out the smallest and easiest of these. This enables clients to experience control over the symptoms in a safe and gradual manner, without becoming afraid or feeling overwhelmed by tasks that they are not yet ready for. These small changes may pave the way for increasingly large changes, but in such a way as to prevent relapse. SF questions are very effective in encouraging clients to participate in and develop their own treatment plan, and a context of hope is implicitly created. Clients find that this way of looking at their recovery process influences many aspects of their lives positively, since they are invited to see that what they do is good, healthy, and effective. Four basic SF questions (Bannink, 2010a) are:

1. What are your best hopes?
2. What difference will that make?
3. What works?
4. What will be next signs of progress? (Or, what will your next step be?)

The *first basic SF question* is "What are your best hopes?"

Hope is one of the most powerful attitudes, emotions, thoughts, beliefs, and motivators. It is vital to human beings; it keeps many people alive. It gets people out of bed in the morning. Hope keeps us going, even in the face of severe adversity. Hope whispers, "Try it one more time" when the world says, "Give up."

Hope is one of the major constructs of PP. *Hope theory* states that hope is like a journey: A destination (goal), a road map (pathway thinking), and a means of transport (agency thinking) are needed. Research on the subject of hope (Snyder, 2002) has shown that it is important to have a goal and ways to reach that goal. Hopeful people have a clearer goal (destination) than non-hopeful people. They also have a clearer image of the route via which they can reach their goal: They have a mental map. In addition, they believe that they themselves can do something to get closer to their goal (they are their own means of transport). And should the route to the goal be blocked, high-hope persons will think of an alternative more easily and will continue to feel better than low-hope persons. Therefore, the first question in SFBT, after establishing rapport, is "What are your best hopes?" or "What is your hoped-for outcome of this therapy?" In systems or group therapy, the therapist makes sure to invite all participants to think and talk about their best hopes for a better future (see also Chapter 4). This may result in "positive contagion," like an electrical arc sparking across a gap.

Helping clients to see for themselves that change is possible and that there are new and better ways to deal with the situation is important in therapy. SFBT fits well with this value, because solution-building is about the development of a well-formed goal through asking about the client's best hopes and about the differences that realizing those hopes would make. These questions encourage clients to develop a detailed vision of what their lives might be when their problems are over. By listening for openings in sometimes problem-focused conversations, therapists find opportunities to invite clients to create that vision by drawing on their own frames of reference. This approach relies less on therapists' suggestions than do problem-solving approaches. It fosters hope and motivation in clients and promotes self-determination. SFBT also counters any tendency to raise false hope in clients. They define their own vision for change and, as experts about their situation, clarify what parts of their preferred future can and cannot happen. They think about and explain what is realistic and what is not.

Questions about hope are different from questions about expectations. The question "What do you expect from this therapy?" invites clients to look at the therapist for solutions to their problems. The risk is that they will see the therapist, rather than themselves, as the only means of transport for reaching their goal.

The second basic SF question is "What difference will that make?" Asking this question invites clients to describe their preferred future in positive, concrete, and realistic terms. Many will say that in their preferred future, they will feel relieved, at rest, relaxed, or happy. The therapist can elicit further details: How will they react, and how will they interact? What will their day look like? What will they be doing differently so that others will know that they have reached their preferred future? Questions about differences are always asked in the future tense, since hope can only ever be about the future. Clients usually describe their preferred future as being without the problem that brought them to therapy, although for some clients the problem is still present but doesn't bother them so much anymore.

De Shazer (1991) stated that difference itself is an important tool for professionals and clients. In and of themselves, however, differences are just differences; they do not work spontaneously. Only when recognized can they be put to work. "In the language game of therapy, the client's story makes the therapist see things one way: the therapist's revision (a difference) makes the client see things another way" (p. 56). The therapist needs to find a point or element in the client's story that allows a different perspective to be put to work. There are many possible points where a distinction can be noted, and any of these differences can be employed in helping clients to view life as more satisfactory.

Change is happening all the time, and the role of the therapist is to find useful change and amplify it. Since SFBT is about change and about helping clients make a better future, questions about positive differences are considered very important. "What difference will it make when your best hopes become reality? How will your future look? What will you be doing differently? How will your relationship with the other person(s) differ? What will they be doing differently?"

Asking about exceptions to the problem in the present or in the past is another way of asking about differences: "When the problem is (was) there to a lesser extent, what is (was) different then? What are (were) you doing differently? What are (were) other people doing differently? How is (was) your relationship different?" Or you can ask about exceptions pertaining to the goal: "When is (was) there already a glimpse of your preferred future (the goal)?" Questions about exceptions can be very useful, since they may reveal what is or was working in better times. Some things that were helpful in the past may be used anew to improve the life of the client. Also, *scaling questions* (see Chapter 6) may be useful in finding *differences that make a difference*. Scaling questions can be asked in regard to clients' progress, but they can also be used to find out about pretreatment change, hope, motivation, and clients' confidence that they can reach their goal.

Exercise 10. SUPPOSE THINGS COULD CHANGE

Invite your clients to think of something in their life they would like to see changed. Tell them, "Suppose things could change. What difference will that make? What else will be different? What else?" They will probably come up with more things than you or they imagined they would. (This is called the *upward arrow technique* and is described in more detail in my book *Practicing Positive CBT* [Bannink, 2012a] and the article *Positive CBT* [Bannink, 2013]).

CASE 4. *Hearing "Yes, But"*

The therapist compliments her client about her coping strategies: "I am very impressed with the way that you have been coping recently, given that things have been so tough." The client looks rather puzzled and responds by saying, "Yes, but you should have seen me yesterday." By hearing *yes, but,* the therapist understands that she needs to slow down and that the client does not see the world as the therapist is presenting it. Therefore, she asks a solution-focused question: "So what will it take to convince you that you are coping, even just a little bit, with all the difficulties that you are facing?" The therapist notices and accepts the client's difference in position and works without retracting the compliment.

CASE 5. *What Difference Will It Make?*

A client, a survivor of sexual abuse, says she might feel happier if she could sleep better, without having nightmares. The therapist asks, "What difference will being able to sleep better make in your life?" The woman replies that she might feel slightly more fit and that she would cautiously begin to believe that better sleep without disturbances is possible. The therapist then asks her what difference that slightly better feeling and that bit of hope will make in her life. The client says that she would go outside more and would also be nicer to her children and her husband, because her mood would improve. Thus, in answering the question, the client's vision of her preferred future is further magnified, which increases hope even more and enhances the likelihood that she will take the first step.

The third basic SF question is "What works?"

Therapists may start by inquiring about pretreatment change (see Chapter 6). Most clients have tried other ideas before seeing a therapist. The therapist can determine whether changes already occurred before the first session. It is still a common assumption that clients begin to change when the therapist starts to help them with their problem. But change is happening in all clients' lives. When asked, two-thirds of clients in psychotherapy report positive change between the time they made the appointment and the first session (Miller, Duncan, & Hubble, 1997). Shining a spotlight on change illuminates existing client strengths and resources and allows their enlistment. Of special interest is what clients have done to bring about this change. The therapist may say, "Many clients notice that, between the time they call for an appointment and the first session, things already seem different. What have you noticed about your situation?"

Exploration of pretreatment change can reveal new and useful information. When clients report that some things are already better, even just a little bit, the therapist may ask competence questions like, "How did you do that? How did you decide to do that? Where did you get this good idea?"

When asking about what is working, *exception-finding questions* are frequently used (see Chapter 6). Those questions are new to many clients, who are more accustomed to problem-focused questions. When clients are asked about exceptions, which are the keys to solutions, they may start noticing them for the first time. Solutions are often built from formerly unrecognized differences. The Austrian-British philosopher Wittgenstein (1889–1951) (1968) stated that exceptions lie on the surface and you don't have to dig for them. The aspects of things that are most important for us are hidden because of their simplicity and familiarity. We may be unable to notice something because it is always before our eyes. According to Wittgenstein, therapists should not excavate, speculate, or complicate. That is why, in SFBT, therapists stay on the surface and resist the temptation to categorize or to look for the *essence* of the problem (from an SFBT point of view, there is no essence of the problem). Exploration of exceptions is similar to other aspects of SFBT in that it respects the clients' frame of reference. After hearing about and exploring exceptions, the therapist compliments the client for all the things he or she has done (see Chapter 6).

Scaling questions can be used to help clients discover what is working: "On a scale from ten to zero, where ten means that you have reached your preferred future and zero is the worst situation you can imagine, where would you say you are right now?" By means of scaling questions, therapists can help clients to express complex, intuitive observations about their past experiences and estimates of future possibilities. Scaling questions can also be used to invite clients to evaluate their observations, impressions, and predictions. For example, you might say, "On a scale from ten to zero, where ten means you are confident that you can reach your goal and zero means you are not confident at all, where would you say you are now?" More information about the use of scaling questions can be found in Chapter 6.

CASE 6. *Scaling Questions*

The therapist says to the client, "Here is a different kind of question, called a *scaling question*, which puts things on a scale from ten to zero. Let's say that ten equals how your life will be when all is going very well and zero equals how bad things were when you made the appointment to see me. Where are you on that scale today? And where would you like to be at the end of this therapy? What will be different in your life then?"

The fourth basic SF question is either "What will be the next signs of progress?" or "What will be *your* next step?" By asking "What will be your next step," the therapist invites clients—maybe for the first time—to actually think about what they themselves can do to ameliorate the situation instead of waiting for the therapist or someone else to do something.

This fourth question is only asked when clients want or need to go up further on the scale of progress. When the current state is the best possible state at the moment, then the therapist can continue the conversation by asking the client how he or she can maintain the status quo. The question about next signs of progress is open as to who will be active in making progress. This can be the client or someone else or both. A sign of progress may also be something that could happen without the client's taking action.

The four basic SF questions can be seen as *skeleton keys*: keys that fit in many different locks. You don't have to explore and analyze each lock (i.e., each problem) before you can use these keys. The keys can

---

Exercise 11. BEIGE AND BLUE

This is an exercise I use to explain to colleagues, clients, and students the difference between working with a *problem focus* and working with a *solution focus*. I invite them to look around and find five beige objects. Then, before they list them, I quickly invite them to say which blue objects they just saw. They probably did not see many blue objects and will have to refocus to find them.

This exercise makes clear how clients see their negative situation. They describe it as *beige*: They don't want beige, and they suffer from it. By answering questions about what they would like to have instead of beige (e.g., blue, or their favorite color), they can begin to focus on that color as a better alternative to beige. "What does a blue life look like? When are there or have there already been pieces of blue (exceptions to the problem)? On a scale of ten to zero, where ten indicates a totally blue life and zero indicates a totally beige life, where are you now?"

One last question I ask is: "What do you need to know about beige to be able to start focusing more on blue?" The answer to this question—often to my colleagues', students', and clients' amazement—is *nothing*.

be used for all Axis I and Axis II disorders in the DSM-5, including PTSD.

The chapters in Part II are based on these four questions. Chapter 4 is about creating a context for change, Chapter 5 is about focusing on goals (questions 1 and 2), Chapter 6 is about focusing on what works (question 3), and Chapter 7 is about focusing on progress (question 4). In Appendix A, two protocols for the first session are described.

CASE 7. *Working From the Future Back*

A colleague described the therapy of a fourteen-year-old girl who had experienced abuse. She had refused to attend school for two years. She walked into my colleague's office with shaved hair and tattoos on her head. She had been to many therapists, social workers, psychologists, and school counselors because she was so angry. My colleague said to her, "You've talked to everybody about your past; now let's talk about your dreams for the future." Her face lit up when she said her dream was to become a princess. My colleague asked what the concept of princess meant to her. She talked about being a people's princess who would be caring and generous. She described the princess as slender and well dressed. They started talking about what this princess would be doing.

The princess the girl described was a social worker. My colleague then said, "Okay, it's now ten years' from now and you've trained as a social worker. What university did you go to?" She mentioned one, and my colleague asked, "What books did you read? What did you study?" She said, "Psychology and sociology and a few other things" Then my colleague asked, "Remember when you were fourteen? You'd been out of school for two years. Remember how you got back in school?" She said, "I had this psychiatrist who helped me." And then my colleague asked an important question: "How did she help you?" The girl talked about how she made a phone call to the school. My colleague asked, "Who spoke? Did you or she?" She replied, "The psychiatrist spoke, but she arranged a meeting for us to go to the school." My colleague asked, "Do you remember how you shook hands with that teacher when you went in? How you looked and what you wore?" They went into detail about what that meeting was like, looking from the future back. The girl described the conversations they'd had, how confident she had been, and how well she had spoken.

A month later, the girl told my colleague, "I think it's about time we went to school. Can you ring and make an appointment?" When they went to the school, she was just brilliant.

My colleague met that same girl some time later. Now she's a qualified social worker: She has fulfilled her dream.

A SHORT COMPARISON OF PP AND SF

Bannink and Jackson (2013a) compared and contrasted PP and working with a solutions focus (SF). They concluded that both fields could benefit from each other: SF from PP research and practice and PP from SF research and the use of *SF language*. SF may be more art than science, and PP more science than art, but they overlap fruitfully in any practical quest for human flourishing.

Both PP and SFBT are evidence-based forms of psychotherapy. For information on the empircal evidence-based practice, see Fredrickson (2009) and Seligman (2011). Research in PP uses the same scientific methods as traditional research, but for the most part refocuses on the measurement, understanding, and building of those characteristics that make life most worth living.

For information on the evidence-based practice of SFBT, see Macdonald (2011) and Franklin et al. (2012). Meta-analytic reviews of the outcomes research have shown SFBT to have a small to moderate positive outcome for a broad range of topics and populations. When SFBT has been compared with established treatments in recent, well-designed studies, it has been shown to be equivalent to other evidence-based approaches, producing results in substantially less time and at less cost. Gingerich and Peterson (2013) reviewed forty-three studies. Thirty-two (74 percent) of the studies reported significant positive benefit from SFBT; ten (23 percent) reported positive trends. The strongest evidence of effectiveness came in the treatment of depression in adults, where four separate studies found SFBT to be comparable to well-established alternative treatments. Three studies examined length of treatment, and all found that SFBT used fewer sessions than alternative therapies. Gingerich and Peterson concluded that the studies reviewed provide strong evidence that SFBT is an effective treatment for a wide variety of behavioral and psychological outcomes and, in addition, may be briefer and therefore less costly than alternative approaches.

DIFFERENCES IN THERAPEUTIC APPROACHES TO TRAUMA

What clients (and their therapists) focus their attention on tends to increase and expand in both their awareness and in their life. Table 1 is a comparison between the two therapeutic approaches to trauma. This comparison shows how the paradigm shift from the problem-solving approach to the strengths-and solutions-building approach is applied in helping clients to survive and patients thrive.

Table 1. Differences in therapeutic approaches to trauma.

A problem-focused approach to trauma . . .	A strengths-and-solutions-focused approach to trauma . . .
Focuses on the past or present and on problems	Focuses on the preferred future and on solutions
Focuses on negative emotions	Focuses on positive emotions while acknowledging negative ones
Uses the cause and effect model: Focuses on causes of patients' problems (problem analysis)	Does not use the cause and effect model: Focuses on what clients want different in their lives (goal analysis)
Identifies precipitating, predisposing, and perpetuating factors	Identifies what works (exceptions and previous successes)
Uses the term patient (medical model)	Uses the term client (nonmedical model)
Uses the therapist's theory of change	Uses the client's theory of change
Involves conversations about what the patient does not want (the problem)	Involves conversations about what the client wants (instead of the problem)
Views the patient as damaged and asks how the patient has been affected by traumatic experiences (deficit model)	Views the client as having been influenced by experiences but not as damaged and as having strengths and resources; asks how the client responded to traumatic experiences (resource model)

Looks for weaknesses and problems	Looks for strengths and solutions
(Sometimes) views patients as not motivated (concept of resistance)	Views clients as always motivated (although their goal may differ from that of the therapist)
Regards remembering and expressing a negative affect as goals of treatment	Individualizes goals for each client and does not necessarily involve remembering and expressing a negative affect
May involve confrontation by the therapist	Involves the therapist's acceptance of the client's view (the therapist asks, "How is that helpful?")
Involves interpretation of and conversations about impossibilities	Involves acknowledgement of, validation of, and conversations about possibilities
Regards the therapist as the expert and as having special knowledge regarding trauma, to which the patient submits; the therapist gives advice to the patient	Regards the client and therapist as both having particular areas of expertise; the therapist asks questions to elicit the client's expertise
Sees the problem as always there	Sees that exceptions to the problem are always there
Involves long-term treatment	Involves a variable, individualized term of treatment
Views coping mechanisms as needing to be learned	Views coping mechanisms as already present
Requires big changes	Sees that small changes are often enough
Views insight or understanding as a precondition to treatment	Allows insight or understanding to come during or after treatment
Involves conversations that focus on insight and working through the problem	Involves conversations that focus on accountability and action

(Sometimes) elicits feedback from the patient at the end of therapy	Elicits feedback from the client after every session
Authorizes the therapist to define the end of treatment	Invites the client to define the end of treatment

In Part I (Chapters 1, 2 and 3), we have looked at theory and research in helping clients move toward post traumatic success. Now it is time to turn to Part II and look at the many applications of theory and research in working with adults and children.

SUMMARY

- In traditional psychotherapies, the medical problem-solving model is used. The focus is predominantly on analyzing problems and how to reduce them. Client assessments often mention few or no client strengths, resources, and abilities. It is, however, the clients' abilities, strengths, resources, and solutions that are most important in helping to bring about change.
- Positive psychology focuses mainly on strengths; solution-focused brief therapy focuses mainly on what works.
- Both solution-focused therapy and positive psychology can benefit from each other: SF from PP research and practice and PP from SF research and the use of SF language. SF may be more art than science, and PP more science than art, but they overlap fruitfully in any practical quest for human flourishing.
- Differences between the problem-focused approach and the strengths-and-solutions-focused approach to trauma are described. The problem-focused approach focuses on insight and working through the trauma, the strengths-and-solutions-focused approach involves conversations of what clients want to have instead of the trauma and on accountability and action.

PART TWO

....··········

APPLICATIONS

CHAPTER 4

Creating a Context for Change

Frankl (1963), an Austrian psychiatrist and Holocaust survivor, stated that when we are no longer able to change a situation, we are challenged to change ourselves. This chapter focuses on creating a context for change to help clients move on from the aftereffects of trauma to recovery and perhaps post traumatic growth or to being (more) resilient. This chapter starts with how to build rapport with clients and create a positive therapeutic alliance, a necessary condition of change across all forms of psychotherapy.

Acknowledgment and validation of clients' experiences are other prerequisites of the therapeutic process. It is important to let clients know that their experiences, their points of view, and their actions have been heard and noted and to *normalize* their experiences. They are not bad, weird, or crazy, and their reactions have been experienced by many others too. Building hope and optimism are important, because many trauma survivors go through very difficult times before they come to see a therapist and may feel hopeless and pessimistic about possibilities for change and their future.

THE THERAPEUTIC ALLIANCE

Therapy starts with building *rapport*—a positive working relationship—with clients. The concept of the *therapeutic alliance* has a long history. There is probably no psychotherapy book written in the past decades that has not referred to the alliance. Although it emerged as a contribution from the psychoanalytic tradition, it now stands as a necessary condition of change across all forms of psychotherapy. The therapeutic alliance has been defined in many ways, and despite this diversity of definitions, the consensus is that the alliance represents a positive attachment between therapist and client as well as active and collaborative engagement of all of those involved in the therapeutic tasks designed to help the client. Here are just a few facts from the research on alliance (Constantino, Castonguay, & Schut, 2002):

- The alliance is significantly related to client improvement and a robust predictor of outcome.
- Both the client and therapist contribute substantially to the quality of the alliance.
- Client and therapist relationship histories have an impact on the therapeutic relationship.
- The quality of the alliance is determined by complementary transactions between the client and the therapist, rather than by the separate action of either of these participants.

Clinical researchers have been focusing on the one aspect of psychotherapy that seems to make little difference: the type of therapy delivered. Psychologist contributions to outcome overwhelm treatment differences; the person of the psychologist is critical. The most researched common factor—the *alliance* between the psychologist and the client—has been found to be a robust predictor of outcome, even when measured early in therapy (Wampold, 2001). Regardless of theoretical orientation or professional discipline, the strength of the relationship between therapist and client is consistently associated with an effective treatment outcome. This is particularly true in regard to the client's assessment of the relationship; clients' ratings of the alliance have a stronger correlation with outcome than the ratings of therapists. Moreover, ratings at early stages of treatment are more predictive of outcome than ratings taken later in the process.

Nevertheless, only a few studies have been designed to assess psychological effects, despite the fact that ignoring them biases the results. The evidence-based treatment movement emphasizes treatments, even though it has been found that the type of treatment accounts for very little of the variability in outcomes, and aspects of treatment that are valued by psychologists and clients and that have been shown to account for variability in outcome have been ignored. Research shows that alliance is particularly predictive of outcome when measured early in treatment, and poor early alliance predicts client dropout. The implication is that attention must be paid to the alliance as soon as therapy begins.

Therefore, therapists should make explicit efforts to facilitate the creation of a positive and strong alliance in treatment. They should also systematically monitor the alliance with one of the instruments now available, rather than relying only on their clinical impression (see Chapter 9). It is important to keep in mind that the client's view of the alliance (and not the therapist's!) is the best-known predictor of outcome, and clients should be asked to fill out alliance measures early in therapy.

From an SF point of view (De Shazer, 1991), the therapeutic relationship is a negotiated, consensual, and cooperative endeavor in which the therapist and client jointly focus on (a) exceptions, (b) goals, and (c) solutions. In doing so, the therapist and client jointly assign meaning to aspects of the client's life and justify actions intended to develop a solution.

Visitor-, Complainant-, or Customer–Relationship

SFBT uses the following terms to assess the alliance between client and therapist: Does it involve a visitor relationship, a complainant relationship, or a customer relationship? For convenience, the terms are shortened to *visitor*, *complainant*, and *customer*, although they do not refer to a quality of clients as such, but to the type of relationship between the therapist and each individual client. The challenge for all psychotherapists is to invite each client to become (or remain) a customer. It often happens that clients will start therapy from a visitor or complainant position in their relationship with the therapist. Early assessment of each client's level of motivation is essential in devising a strategy and in making homework suggestions.

In a *visitor relationship*, therapy is mandated (by a doctor, partner, insurance company, employer). The involuntary client has no problem personally; others have a problem with her or see her as the problem. Naturally, she not motivated to change her behavior. Often the mandated client's goal is to maintain the relationship with the person referring her or to free herself from this person as soon as possible.

Therapists should create a climate in which a call for help is possible. What does the client want to achieve through her relationship with the therapist? What would the person referring her like to see changed in her behavior as a result of therapy, and to what extent is the client prepared to cooperate in this? Here are some tips:

- Assume that clients have good reasons for thinking and behaving the way they do.
- Do not be judgmental, and inquire into the perceptions of clients that make their—often defensive—attitude understandable.
- Ask what clients think the person(s) referring them would like to see changed at the end of the therapy.
- Ask clients their opinion on this and what their minimum input might be.

Exercise 12. IDENTIFY INVOLUNTARY CLIENTS

See who in your caseload may have been referred. Think about which of your clients have indicated that they want something out of their sessions with you. Do the clients want to achieve something by coming to you? Or are there others (e.g., family, parents, an employer) who want something from the client and see him as having a problem or being the problem? If the answer to the first question is no, your client has no goal (except maybe that of pleasing or shaking off the referrer). If your client says someone else is forcing him to come, you have an involuntary client, a *visitor*.

In a *complainant relationship*, the client has a problem and is suffering from it, but he does not see himself as part of that problem or the solution. He does not feel the need to change his own behavior; he thinks someone or something else is to blame for the problem and should change.

The therapist gives acknowledgment and asks about the client's strengths and competencies (e.g., "How do you cope?"). The therapist invites clients to talk about exceptions to the problem: moments when the problem is or was present to a lesser extent, or moments when there is already a sign or small part of what the client does want instead of what he does not want. Thus, the clients are invited to think and talk about their preferred future (without the problem) rather than focusing on the problem.

When having a client in a complainant relationship there are several ways in transforming their problems with someone else or with their situation into workable goals (Walter & Peller, 1992). The therapist may point out to the client that he or she cannot change the other person or their situation. "I wish I could help you with this, but I'm not a magician. How else might I help you?" Or, "In what way is this problem a problem for you?"

A second way is to explore a positive scenario and find exceptions to the problem. "Imagine [the other person or the situation] changing in the direction you want. What would you notice different about him or her? What would you notice different about yourself? What difference will that make to your relationship with him or her? At what moment is (or was) this already occurring?"

Yet another way is to explore a less positive, but sometimes more realistic scenario, a future without a change in the other person or the situation. The therapist may ask, "What can you still do yourself to make the situation better?" Or the therapist may explore the goal of the client. "What are you hoping your solution will achieve?"

STORY 13. *Oh, Misery, I Love You!*

Ellis, one of the founders of CBT, was a well-known writer of rational humorous songs. In some of these songs we can find the stance of clients in a complainant relationship. One of the songs is titled "Oh, Misery, I Love You!"

Exercise 13. COMPLAIN ABOUT A THIRD PERSON

Choose a colleague or partner for doing this exercise. Ask your partner to complain about someone else, a third person (not you!) whom she would like to change. Ask her to talk about the same complaint every time so that you can practice the four different strategies described above. Notice the differences brought about by each strategy. Then change roles. In the role of the client, you can learn a lot from the different types of questions that are asked of you.

In a *customer relationship*, the client sees herself as part of the problem and/or the solution and is motivated to change. In her request for help, the word I or we is present: "What can I do to solve this problem?" or "How can we ensure that we reestablish a good relationship?"

Therapy with customers is often the icing on the cake (and gives therapists much-needed positive reinforcement, reassuring them that they are competent and are doing something that works).

In the first session, it is common to find that clients are "complainants" and think that someone else needs to change. Notice that the trichotomy between visitor, complainant, and customer is a value-free continuum: Each position of the client is validated and accepted; the fact that he has shown up makes him already a visitor, because he could also have chosen not to come. Cialdini (1984) stated that the rule of reciprocation and the client's liking of the therapist are strong *weapons of influence*. Giving compliments to clients for showing up helps in establishing a good relationship (see Chapter 6).

Resistance

Traditional therapies use the concepts of *resistance* and *noncompliance*. However, it is more helpful to see clients as always cooperating. They are showing their therapists how they think change takes place. As therapists understand clients' thinking and act accordingly, there will always be cooperation. If therapists see resistance in the other person, they cannot see her efforts to cooperate; if, on the other hand, they see her unique way of cooperating, they cannot see her resistance.

De Shazer (1984) stated that what therapists see as signs of resistance are in fact the unique ways in which clients choose to cooperate. For example, clients who do not carry out assigned homework are not demonstrating resistance, but are actually cooperating because in that way they are indicating that this homework is not in accordance with their way of doing things. De Shazer assumes that clients are competent in figuring out what they want and in which way they can achieve it. It is the therapist's task to assist clients in discovering these competencies and in using them to create their preferred future.

> With resistance as a central concept, therapist and client are like opposing tennis players. They are engaged in fighting against each other, and the therapist needs to win in order for the therapy to succeed. With cooperation as a central concept, therapist and client are like tennis players on the same side of the net. Cooperating is a necessity, although sometimes it becomes necessary to fight alongside your partner so that you can cooperatively defeat your mutual opponent. (p. 13)

In this case, the opponent is the problem. This view relates to the narrative approach (White & Epston, 1990), in which *externalizing the problem*—turning the problem into the enemy—is a much-used intervention (see Chapter 7). Also in Erickson's view (as cited in Rossi, 1980), resistance is cooperative: It is one of the possible responses people can make to interventions.

If therapists feel that they are becoming irritated, insecure, or demoralized, *counter-transference*—the negative reaction of therapists to the behavior of their clients—is taking place. This may happen when therapists—wrongly—consider the client a customer when there is still a visitor or a complainant relationship.

When clients are angry or seem unmotivated with regard to a particular topic, it is useful for therapists to remind themselves that clients are competent and that they have to look for a (better) way to cooperate with them. From this perspective, resistance becomes a signal that they need to formulate a question about what the resistance suggests is important to the client, instead of concluding that the client is resistant or unmotivated. This applies equally to voluntary and involuntary clients.

Focus on Change

Prochaska, Norcross, and DiClemente (1994) developed a theory about the stages of behavior change, which can be broadly compared to the terms mentioned above. When clients adopt an *indifferent or unknowing attitude* (the attitude of clients in a visitor relationship), the emphasis is on providing information and on establishing a link between the behavior to be changed and the worries or problems that others experience. In the next stage, with clients who are *contemplating change* (as clients in a complainant relationship may be), the emphasis is on deciding on and initiating the desired behavior. This is followed by the stages of *change action* (working toward one's goal, as clients in a customer relationship are doing), *behavior maintenance*, and (possibly) *relapse*.

One of the principles of *motivational interviewing* (Miller & Rollnick, 2002) is unconditional acceptance of the client's position. Therapists build a relationship that is based on collaboration, individual responsibility, and autonomy. Miller and Rollnick stated that the necessity of approaching clients in a nonmoralizing way is impeded if therapists are unprepared or unable to defer their own (mistaken) ideas about problem behavior and label their clients' behavior.

Effective therapists react with empathy, avoid discussions, and strengthen their clients' self-efficacy. Miller and Rollnick (2002) described the term *change talk*. This is a method of SF communication used for enhancing clients' intrinsic motivation to change by stressing the advantages of behavior change. Change talk assists clients in preparing for change. To elicit change talk, Miller and Rollnick suggest asking open-ended questions, such as, "How would you like to see things change? How would you want your life to look in five years' time?"

By inviting clients to talk about their preferred futures (their goals), their competencies, and their successes and to look for exceptions (moments in which they were or are successful), therapists can encourage visitors and complainants to transform into customers. Asking competence questions stimulates clients to talk about successes and to give self-compliments, which feeds their feeling of self-worth. Focusing on the preferred future facilitates change in the desired direction (see Chapter 5).

The Changing Role of Therapists

Therapists are constantly reminding their clients that they cannot change other people, only themselves. How ironic, therefore, that therapists are typically trained to develop a treatment plan and enter sessions with the intention of changing their clients! Fortunately, the role of therapists is also changing. Instead of being the only expert in the room, the one who explores and analyzes the problem and then gives advice to clients on how to solve their problems, as in traditional forms of therapy, the therapist is now taking on the role of someone who neither pushes nor pulls. The therapist remains one step behind his or her clients and looks in the same direction they do (toward their preferred future). This stance is called *leading from one step behind*. Clients are seen as co-experts, and therapists are "not-knowing"; they invite their clients—by asking SF questions (Bannink, 2007, 2008a, 2010a)—to share their knowledge and expertise in order to reach their preferred future. After thirty years of clinical practice, it is my conviction that the solutions are always in the room.

Therapists also change their focus of attention in using, wherever and whenever possible, the positive reinforcement of *strengths-and-solution- talk* (reinforcement of conversations about goals, exceptions, possibilities, strengths, and resources) and in using the negative punishment of *problem-talk* (nonreinforcement of conversations about problems, causes, impossibilities, and weaknesses). This does not mean that clients are not allowed to talk about their problems or that this approach is *problem-phobic*. The difference is that therapists do not seek any details about the presented problem and thus do not reinforce problem-talk. They do, however, ask for a detailed description of goals, solutions, exceptions, strengths, and competencies, thus reinforcing solutions-talk.

The Start of the First Session

Therapists may make a positive start by asking questions about the daily life of the client, such as, "What kind of work do you do?" or, if the client is a child, "What grade are you in?" This may be followed by questions like "What do you like about your work? What are you good at? What hobbies do you have?" or "What is your best subject in school? Who is your favorite teacher?" These questions can be seen as icebreakers, but they may also be the start for uncovering useful information about strengths and solutions already present in the client's life. They set the tone for a more lighthearted conversation than clients may have been expecting.

After these questions, therapists may ask clients about their goals in coming to therapy or about the concerns they want to address in therapy. A good way to start this part of the session is to ask, "What will be the best outcome of you coming to see me?"

Many clients like to have the opportunity to talk about their problems, not least because they think that is the intent of the therapy. Therapists may listen respectfully to their stories but will not ask for details of the problem, so there is no positive reinforcement of problem-talk (see Chapter 7). With the question "How is this a problem for you?" clients can often begin to talk about the problem in a different way. It may also be helpful to provide information about the way the therapist works, because it makes clear that nowadays there is a different kind of therapy possible: strengths-and-solutions-focused therapy. This therapy is about possibilities instead of impossibilities and strengths instead of weaknesses. Therapists may ask clients who adhere to a problem-focused conversation, "How many sessions do you think you need to tell about your problems and what is wrong with you before we can start looking at your preferred future and what is right with you?" The four basic solution-focused questions used in the first session are described in detail in Chapter 3.

Normalizing and Reframing

The therapist's skill of normalizing is used to depathologize clients' concerns and present them instead as normal life difficulties. This helps people to calm down in regard to their problem. It helps them to realize that they're not abnormal for having this problem. Thinking it's not normal to have a problem causes a further problem. People are more compassionate with themselves and experience lower negative affect when they see that others have the same problems they have.

It is advisable, whenever possible, to normalize and neutralize both the problem itself and the ways in which the client and his or her environment respond to it. For example, the therapist may say, "Of course you were angry when you heard that," or "It is understandable that you thought this way." Neutral language is essential; accusations, threats, hurtful speech, and other words with negative emotional connotations must be avoided. Normalization puts the client at ease, changes the moral judgment of and by the other person, and encourages greater understanding from and of the other.

It is important to always keep in mind that clients *are* not the problem, but that they are individuals who *have* a problem. Labels like *depressed* or *borderline* are best avoided. After all, clients are much more than their problem or diagnosis. A diagnosis should not be a label. It should lead to support, allowing clients to reach their potential. Instead of saying, "Henry is depressed," one might say, "Henry suffers from depressive episodes." O'Hanlon and Rowan (2003) also emphasized the importance of *distinguishing between the person and the illness* and of examining the effects of the illness on the person. Ask not what disease the person has, but rather what person the disease has. Reframing traumatic events in terms of survivorship and heroism rather than victimization is often helpful.

ACKNOWLEDGMENT AND VALIDATION

Therapy with trauma survivors will be impossible if the negative impact a problem has on the client goes unacknowledged. Clients are often in great distress and generally want to make that known during the session. The therapist respectfully listens to their story and shifts to a more positive conversation as soon as possible. It is, however, a misconception that there can only be sufficient acknowledgment if the problem is wholly dissected and analyzed or if the client is afforded every opportunity to expatiate on his or her view of the problem. Utterances by the therapist such as "I understand that this must be a very unpleasant situation for you, and I can imagine how difficult it must be to get out of this impasse" offer that acknowledgment just as well and take up considerably less time than having a client describe the entire problem.

Furthermore, the mood of the session can remain positive if the focus is on what clients want to have instead of their problems. Asking clients what they have tried so far to solve their problems also offers acknowledgment, since most clients have taken some steps to address their problems before therapy. However, a more positive question, "What have you tried so far that has been helpful, even just a little bit?" invites clients to talk about their successes (however small) instead of their failures. The therapist may present the client with the option by asking, "Would you like to conduct these sessions in a strengths-and-solutions-focused or in a problem-focused way?" after explaining both to the client. It has been my experience that clients who are motivated to change choose the strengths-and-solutions-focused approach. Clients who do not (yet) see themselves as part of the problem and/or the solution often choose problem-focused sessions. I surmise that they make that choice because it does not require them to take action yet. After all, in the problem-focused approach, before any behavioral change is attempted, the problem must first be analyzed and explored, or insight must be gained into the source of the problem or the reason for its perpetuation. Thus, this question also gives the therapist some insight into which clients are motivated to change their behavior and which clients are not. Questions that offer acknowledgment include:

- "How do you cope? How do you keep your head above water?"
- "How do you ensure that the situation isn't worse than it is? How do you do that? Which personal strengths and which resources do you use?"
- "I can tell that this is a problem for you, and I understand that this is an unpleasant situation for you. What would you like to see different?"
- "How is this a problem for you?"
- "I see what's important to you. What solutions would fulfill your wishes?"
- "Suppose you were given one opportunity to say what absolutely needs to be said before we proceed. What would you say?"

When clients (or their therapists) think that they (or their clients) need to work through past trauma or need to talk extensively about what happened, they are telling us that they have a theory of change about what will help and what will make a difference. When a therapist accepts an invitation into these often problem-saturated conversations, he or she may look for and initiate opportunities to help clients identify what changes they hope will result from talking about these past experiences (in terms of solutions and goals). Questions that may cast some doubt on the client's theory of change are:

- "How do you suppose talking about these experiences will be helpful to you in making the changes you want?"
- "How will you know (what will be the signs that tell you) that we have talked enough about these experiences so that we can concentrate more on where you would like to go rather than where you've been?"
- "What will be the first signs that will tell you that you're putting the past behind you?"

Clients can regain control when therapists give them some choices. The therapist may say, "Some people I have worked with were able to make some of the changes you want without going back and trying to understand what happened in the past. Other people tell me it's helpful to explore the past. Some have made the changes they wanted first, and then we looked at the possible roots of the trouble later. What do you suppose will be most helpful for you?"

Validation of the client's point of view is important: "I am sure you must have a good reason for all this; please tell me more." In this way, therapists show that they respect their clients' opinions and ideas. At the beginning of the first session, therapists may give clients one opportunity *to say what definitively needs to be said* before switching to what clients want different in their lives. This has become a proven method in solution-focused conflict management (Bannink, 2008b, 2009b, 2010b).

O'Hanlon (1999) proposed a solution-focused way of working in the present toward the future to resolve trauma (see Chapter 7). First of all, this involves acknowledgment of the facts along with the present and former inner experience of the trauma. Next it focuses on helping clients value, own, and associate with dissociated aspects of themselves. Finally, it helps clients develop a clear sense of a future with possibilities.

STORY 14. *Acknowledge the Problem*

Long ago, the inhabitants of a village were starving because they were afraid of a dragon in their fields. One day a traveler came to the village and asked for food. The villagers explained that they did not dare to harvest their crops because they were afraid of the dragon. When the traveler heard their story, he offered to slay the dragon, but arriving at the fields he saw only a large watermelon. He said to the villagers that they had nothing to fear because there was no dragon, only a watermelon. The villagers were angry at his refusal to understand their fear and hacked him to pieces.

Another traveler came passing by the village, and he, too, offered to slay the dragon, much to the relief of the villagers. But he also told them they were mistaken about the dragon, and they hacked him to pieces as well.

In the meantime, the villagers were becoming desperate, but then a third traveler came to the village. He too promised to kill the dragon so that they could go to their fields to harvest their crops. He saw the giant watermelon, reflected for a moment, and then drew his sword and hacked the watermelon to pieces. He returned to the village and told the people he had killed their dragon. The villagers were very pleased. The traveler stayed in the village for a long time, long enough to teach the villagers the difference between dragons and watermelons

—Author unknown

CASE 8. *Nobody Understands What I've Been Through*

A client suffered sexual abuse as a child by her father. Later in life she developed symptoms of PTSD: numbness, nightmares, and sexual problems with her boyfriend. She never talked about her traumatic experiences and claims that "nobody understands what I've been through." The therapist asks her a solution-focused question: "Suppose someone could understand; what difference would that make for you? What would be different in your life then? What else would be different?" The client replies that she would feel less alone and more connected to the world. She would go out more and try to talk with her boyfriend about what happened to her. At this point she realizes that, although her boyfriend may not understand completely what she has been through, she could start sharing her experiences with him just the same.

BUILDING HOPE AND OPTIMISM

There are two situations that may lead to feelings of hopelessness: You may feel insecure because you fear that things will change in an undesired way, or you may feel that change is exactly what is needed, but be afraid that nothing will ever change. In both situations, there is an overarching sense that you have lost control over the future. According to Fredrickson (2009), there are two basic responses to hardship: *despair* and *hope*. In despair, negativity is multiplied. Fear and uncertainty can turn into stress, which can change into hopeless sadness or shame. Despair smothers all forms of positivity, and all possibilities for genuine connections with others are lost. Despair opens the gate to a downward spiral. Hope, however, is different. It is not the mirror reflection of despair. Hope acknowledges negativity with clear eyes and kindles further positivity, allowing an individual to connect with others. Hope opens the gateway to an upward spiral that empowers one to bounce back from hardship and emerge even stronger and more resourceful than before.

Hope is the belief that the future will be better than today (this belief is the same as in optimism) and the belief that an individual can influence this view (pathway thinking and agency thinking; see below). Hope is one of the twenty-four character strengths in the domain of *transcendence* (see Chapter 6). The five strengths that enable one to forge connections to the larger universe and provide meaning are (a) appreciation of beauty, (b) gratitude, (c) hope, (d) humor and playfulness, and (e) spirituality.

Hope Theory

Since the 1950s, doctors and psychologists have pointed to the role of hope in people's health and well-being. In his address to the American Psychiatric Association, Menninger (1959) said that hope was an untapped source of power and healing. Menninger believed that hope is an indispensable factor in psychiatric treatments and psychiatric training. The interest in hope in psychotherapy was initially aimed at reducing despair rather than increasing hopeful thoughts. Given the link between despair and suicide, Beck, Weissman, Lester, and Trexles (1974) focused on combating hopelessness. Their definition of hopelessness is "a system of cognitive schemas whose common denomination is negative expectations about the future" (p. 864).

In the 1990s, Snyder (2002) developed *hope theory*, in which he proposed a two-factor cognitive model of hope that similarly focuses on goal attainment. Snyder focused not only on expectancies, but also on the motivation and planning that are necessary to attain goals. He defined hope as a positive emotional state based on an interactively derived sense of successful (a) agency and (b) pathways (planning to meet goals). Based on this definition, hope's agency or *willpower* component provides the determination to achieve goals, whereas its pathways or *waypower* component promotes the creation of alternative paths to replace those that may have been blocked in the process of pursuing those goals. Hope has been shown to be applicable to performance in various domains, including the workplace (Youssef & Luthans, 2007).

The above definitions tie hopeful thinking expressly to goals. By focusing on goal objects, people are able to respond effectively to their environment. Snyder, Michael, and Cheavens (1998) made the distinction between high-hope people and low-hope people. Compared to low-hope people, who have vague and ambiguous goals, high-hope persons are more likely to clearly conceptualize their goals.

In addition to setting goals, hope theory encourages therapists and clients to set goals that *stretch* clients (Snyder, 2002). In hope theory, goals that are difficult enough to be challenging but easy enough to be accomplished are called *stretch goals*. Such goals encourage clients not only to "patch up" problems, but also to grow as an individual. For example, a stretch goal might be to increase well-being or connectedness, instead of just solving the problem. Continuously setting and meeting stretch goals is a way to move oneself toward a more positive, strengths-based stance. Hopeful thought reflects the belief that one can find pathways to desired goals and become motivated to use those pathways. Hope serves to drive emotions and the well-being of people.

Hope and Coping

The protection hope gives in coping with political turmoil, forced immigration, social injustice, and trauma has been exemplified by various spiritual models throughout human history, from Moses, Jesus, and Muhammad to Martin Luther King Jr. A study on post-9/11 mental health linked faith and perceived spiritual support with hope in American students with diverse beliefs, and this hope in turn was associated with better mental health in these students with diverse beliefs (Ai, Cascio, Santangelo, & Evans-Campbell, 2005). Another current structural equation model demonstrated the importance of hope in the connection between positive religious coping and postoperative adjustment in American cardiac patients, predominantly Christians (Affleck et al., 1987). The cross-cultural evidence implies that hope as a positive psychological virtue may be a universal resource for positive adaptations and changes, which can also be enhanced in various spiritual beliefs. Cognitive coping involves processing and comparing information, which may direct attention from the present trauma to alternatives. It may shift negative counterfactual rumination, which focuses on regret for not being able to avoid trauma, to a more positive orientation and to setting new physical and psychological goals for adapting to the new situation. Hope can be enhanced in clients by finding out what they are most excited about and then asking them to spend time with the most hopeful person(s) they know. Other ways to enhance hope are to tell clients stories about people in similar situations who have overcome hardship, to help clients identify and focus on the positive steps that have been taken so far, and to encourage clients to see the positive aspects of their situation. We can also explain to our clients that focusing on what we want in life can in fact create the life we want.

Questions about hope and how hope may increase include:

- "What are your best hopes? What difference will realizing those hopes make?"
- "What has kept your hope alive during this prolonged period of difficulty?"
- "How has your hope influenced your decisions recently?"
- "Suppose you had a bit more hope. How would your life (or your relationship) change?"
- "How would (more) hope help you reach your goal?"
- "What is the smallest difference that will increase your hope?"
- "How will you be able to tell that you have enough hope?"
- "When *did* you feel hopeful, and how did you manage that?"
- "When you think of hope, what does it conjure up?"
- "If you had a painting on your wall that reminded you of hope when you looked at it every morning, what would that painting look like?"
- "What smell, color, song, or sound reminds you of hope?"
- "What rating do you give yourself on a scale of ten to zero, where ten equals lots of hope and zero equals no hope?"

- "How do you manage to be at that number?"
- "What will one point higher on the hope scale look like?"
- "How could you move up one point?"
- "Can you tell me about a period in your life when you had a lot of (or more) hope?"
- "If you were to examine your problem, which aspects of the problem would give you more or less hope?"
- "What would someone who *did* have (more) hope do in your situation?"
- "What occurrence or person can make your hope increase or decrease?"
- "What can you do to make hope visible at a time when you see no hope?"
- "If you wanted your hope to increase by the next session, what would you do or like me to do before we see each other again?"
- "What in our conversation today has given you more hope, even if only a little?"
- "What indicates that you are on the right track to solving this problem?"
- "Suppose the positive moments were to last longer. What difference would that make for you?"
- "How has going up one point on the scale given you hope?"
- "Which good things need to happen in your life to give you hope that you can leave the bad things that happened behind?"

Because there are multiple ways of gaining hope, clients may experiment. What works for one person may not be suitable for another person. It helps if there is room for humor, because laughter can reduce tension and often puts things into perspective. Clients may also come up with something that reminds them of times of hope, so that they can think about or look at it every now and then.

Hope usually grows slowly. Clients might predict their behavior for the following day and discover that exceptions to the problem can be found and that more control can be exerted than they thought. Therapists can augment their clients' hope by asking questions about it and by stimulating their clients' creativity.

STORY 15. *Positive Changes in Kosovar War Refugees*

Research on war trauma has been dominated by a pathological focus for decades. However, researchers have now counterbalanced previous studies of trauma with a new focus: positive changes following crisis. Ai, Tice, Whitsett, Ishisaka, and Chim (2007) examined how specific psychological factors influenced postwar adaptive outcomes in a sample of fifty Kosovar war refugees. The Kosovars in this study were not soldiers. Rather, they were victims of the severe sociopolitical and economic consequences of war. Having abruptly relocated directly from the war zone, leaving everything behind, they brought fresh wounds from brutal experiences in relation to the Serbian–Albanian conflict, NATO bombing, retributive persecution, and ethnic cleansing. The researchers explored individual differences in attitude and coping strategies. Hope during resettlement and cognitive coping strategies employed between resettlement and follow-up were associated with PTG, after controlling for war-related trauma and baseline symptoms. PTG and symptoms were unrelated. Ai and colleagues (2007) concluded that future mental health practice with refugees should address both positive and negative aspects of their experience.

Crisis Situations

In *crisis situations*, the available time does not usually lend itself to an elaborate diagnosis and, besides this, clients in crisis benefit from regaining confidence in their personal competencies and a future-oriented approach. Think of questions such as, "How do you manage to carry on? What has helped you in the past weeks, even if only slightly?" Commonly, clients relinquish competencies to the therapist ("You tell me what I should do")—a pitfall that can be avoided using this approach (Bakker et al., 2010).

The mere willingness to take part in a conversation with a therapist generates hope and positive expectancy. These are strengthened when the client's attention is directed toward his options rather than his limitations. When the therapist steers the client's attention to his previous successes instead of his failures, a further positive expectancy is generated. It allows the client to see himself and his situation in a more positive light. The notion of the client's personal control is emphasized, and problems are placed outside the client, which serves to remove blame from him.

Most of the time, no extensive diagnosis is needed. Therapists may choose to commence treatment immediately and if necessary pay attention to diagnostics at a later stage. Severe psychiatric disorders or a suspicion thereof justifies the decision to conduct a thorough diagnosis, since tracing of the underlying organic pathology, for instance, has direct therapeutic consequences. During the first or follow-up conversation, it will automatically become clear whether an advanced diagnosis will be necessary—for example, if there is visible deterioration in the client's condition or if the treatment fails to give positive results. Analogous to *stepped care*, one may think of *stepped diagnosis*.

If, however, therapists have no confidence in their own ability to help clients reach their goals and have lost the hope of a favorable outcome, they should examine what is needed for them to regain hope. They may also halt the sessions and turn their clients over to a more hopeful colleague. Miller and colleagues (1997) and Duncan, Miller, and Sparks (2004) also stressed the importance of offering hope and creating a positive expectancy of change during interactions with clients. According to them, it is often the assumptions, attitude, and behavior of therapists themselves that lead to "hopeless cases." They have identified four ways in which therapists may bring about failure, which are described in Chapter 9.

Many therapists feel anxiety when they talk with clients who are thinking of committing suicide. Their initial impulse may be to persuade clients that suicide is not the right option for them. However, by contradicting them, they may further isolate their clients. Another reaction of therapists may be to minimize or refuse to believe what may be the client's desperate cry for help. Or they may think all suicidal clients should be hospitalized and use medication.

The best way not to feel hopeless about clients' prospects is to tell ourselves that there is always another side and then set about exploring it. Keep in mind that clients who are talking about suicide are still alive for some reason, and invite them to think about how they are still surviving. There is a saying: "Just when the caterpillar thought the world was over . . . it became a butterfly." If clients want to (re)gain a glimmer of hope, even in crisis situations, the following questions may be useful:

- "What helped in the past, even if only marginally?"
- "How do you cope with everything that is going on and all you have gone through?"
- "How do you succeed in getting from one moment to the next?"
- "How will you get through the rest of the day?"
- "How did you survive long enough to get here?"
- "How often do you have these (suicidal) thoughts?" (Look for exceptions.)

- "Could the situation be worse than it is? Why is it not worse?"
- "Is there anyone else who shares this with you? How is that helpful?"
- "What do your friends or family say you do well, even in very bad times?"
- "Imagine that in ten or fifteen years, when things are going better, you look back on today. What helped you to improve things?"
- "Suppose there is a solution. What difference would that make? What would be different? What would be better?"
- "Some trauma survivors depend on others for hope, because they feel hopeless and must rely on borrowed hope—hope that others hold out for them. What are important people in your life hoping for? What are their best hopes for you?"

STORY 16. *A Helpful Diagnosis*

A severely ill man was in the hospital. The doctors had given up any hope of his recovery. They were unable to ascertain what the man was suffering from. Fortunately, a doctor famous for his diagnostic skills was due to visit the hospital. The hospital doctors said that maybe they could cure him if this famous doctor was able to diagnose him. When the doctor arrived, the man was almost dead. The doctor looked at him briefly, mumbled "moribundus" (Latin for "dying"), and walked over to the next patient. A few years later, the man—who did not know a word of Latin—succeeded in finding the famous doctor. "I would like to thank you for your diagnosis. The doctors had said that if you were able to diagnose me, I would get better."

—Bannink, 2010

CASE 9. *Giving Up All Hope of Having a Better Past*

Hope is always future oriented; one cannot hope for something to happen in the past. However, sometimes people keep on hoping that the past were different. For example, clients who have experienced a difficult childhood or have been in a car crash may ruminate upon how they would have liked things to be different. One client kept on saying how he wished his mother had been a warm and caring person instead of the cold person she actually had been. The therapist acknowledged his feelings and asked him how he would know when he was ready and able to *give up all hope of having a better past.*

Exercise 14. PREVIOUS SUCCESSES

Invite clients to describe one or more of their previous successes in handling a difficult situation in the past. Be curious and inquire, "How did you manage to do that? What exactly did you do? Where did you get these good ideas? What talents, strengths, and resources did you use? What could you perhaps use in the difficult situation you are in now?"

Optimism

Seligman (2002) observed that exposure to uncontrollable negative events leads to helplessness. In a series of famous experiments in the 1970s, Seligman demonstrated that dogs subjected to painful electric shocks that they had no control over became passive, developed symptoms resembling depression, and became more prone to physical ailments. This passivity or helplessness persisted even if later they did have the power to control the situation and escape the shock.

Additional studies have demonstrated that this phenomenon of *learned helplessness* also applies to humans. To explain these findings, Seligman proposed that individuals develop expectancies about the occurrence of adversity in their lives. These expectancies are powerful predictors of behavior. The expectancy that adversity will continue and that one will be powerless in its wake leads to helplessness, passivity, withdrawal, anxiety, depression, and even physical illness. In contrast, expectations of control engender persistence, the ability to cope, and resilience to depression and physical health problems. Seligman's experiments focused on the group of dogs who became anxious, passive, and depressive, with some even dying, when their cage was subjected to an electric charge. Only later attention was given to the dogs that, although unable to escape, had continued looking for a way out. What had caused these dogs to persevere and survive?

Seligman therefore shifted his attention from learned helplessness to *learned optimism*. He undertook research into the factors that lead people to perceive an event as positive or negative and their reasoning behind this. Pessimistic people attribute negative events particularly to stable, global, and internal factors. They say, "Things never go right with me [stable], I will never be happy again [global], and I am good for nothing [internal]." They attribute positive events to temporary, specific, and external factors. If something positive happens, they say, "That was only luck, which had nothing to do with me."

Optimistic people think in the opposite way. They attribute positive events to stable, global, and internal factors. If something positive happens, they believe that it does say something about them, for example, "I really am valuable." Optimists attribute negative events particularly to temporary, specific, and external factors. They might say, "I couldn't do anything about it, because he threatened me."

Einstein said, "I would rather be an optimist and a fool than a pessimist who is right." And Churchill said, "The pessimist sees difficulty in every opportunity; the optimist sees the opportunity in every difficulty." A. T. Beck (1967) similarly underscored the importance of optimistic cognitive styles in protecting people from depression. According to the cognitive perspective, people with optimistic cognitive styles are at lower risk for depression than people with pessimistic cognitive styles. However, a little pessimism at times cannot hurt. It forces people to confront reality, and depressed people tend to have a more realistic view of the world. Every day could be your last; you could be involved in a traffic accident or catch a fatal disease. Depressed people harbor few illusions about how safe and predictable the world and life actually are. Yet it turns out that we feel better and happier if we do hold these illusions and are able to preserve them.

Optimism and pessimism are relatively stable personality traits, but they can be influenced by the way one acts and by what one focuses on. Optimism contributes to more adaptive survival strategies, namely, more positive reappraisal, better coping abilities, and more use of positive distractions (hobbies and exercise).

Seligman's research (2002) showed that even people with a pessimistic nature felt happier if over the course of week they (a) made notes of when in the past they had been at their best, (b) every day noted something about their strengths or expressed gratitude to someone they had not yet properly thanked, or (c) made a note of three good things that were happening in their lives (see Exercise 6). Six months late these people were still feeling happier, even though the exercise had taken place over a period of only one week. Research has also shown that happy people are optimistic about their future and that optimistic people are in better health than pessimistic people. Four positive elements significantly contribute to a happy life: Happy people (a) like themselves, (b) are mostly extroverted, (c) have the idea that they are in control, and (d) are optimistic. The question relevant to all four is, does optimism make people happier (A), or are happy people more optimistic (B)? It turns out that A leads to B and B leads to A. Some questions you can ask your clients to help them enhance their optimism are:

- "What makes you optimistic that you will reach the desired outcome?"
- "Which indications do you have that you will reach your goal?
- "What fuels your hope?"
- "Which good arguments do you have to be optimistic?"
- "What will be the first signs that things are going to work out well?"

STORY 17. I Will Prevail

More than thirty Vietnam war veterans, who had been held as prisoners of war for six to eight years, tortured, and kept in solitary confinement, were interviewed and tested. Unlike many fellow veterans, they did not develop depression or PTSD after their release, even though they endured extreme stress. What was their secret? Ten characteristics set them apart, the foremost being optimism ("I am in a tough spot, but I will prevail"). Other characteristics included having strong social support (they used a tapping system on the walls to keep in contact with each other), altruism, humor, and feeling that life had meaning and that there was something to live for.

—Charney, 2012

In the next chapter, we will look at setting well-defined goals. Setting goals begins to focus clients on future possibilities rather than on current symptoms and problems and emphasizes the possibility.

SUMMARY

- Therapy starts by creating a context for change, a positive therapeutic alliance being a necessary condition for change.
- There are three types of therapeutic alliances: a visitor relationship, a complainant relationship, and a customer-relationship.
- In Post Traumatic Success, the role of therapists is a solution-focused one in which they take the position of not-knowing and leading from one step behind.
- The start of the first session should be positive, with the therapist using his or her normalizing and reframing skills.
- Acknowledgment and validation are important. However, this does not mean that problems need to be fully analyzed or that clients need to talk extensively about what has gone wrong in their lives.
- Building hope and optimism is important, because many clients feel hopeless or pessimistic about their future. Research about and applications in building hope and optimism are described.

CHAPTER 5

. . . .

Focus on Goals

There is a saying: "Seeing yourself as you want to be is the key to personal growth."

And Eliot, an English novelist (1819–1880), wrote, "It is never too late to be who you might have been" (as quoted in Baker & Ross, 2002).

How people see their future influences how they behave today. Therefore, investing in the future pays off today. The good news is that people can edit the stories about their future selves. Setting goals begins to focus clients on these future possibilities rather than on current symptoms and problems and emphasizes the possibility of change. It also reinforces the notion that clients are active members of the therapeutic relationship, and that involvement is required; clients will not be "done" to. Defined goals help to impose structure on treatment. Setting goals also prepares clients for discharge, making explicit that therapy will be terminated when goals are achieved, or that therapy will be discontinued if there is little or no progress toward them. This is not to say that goals cannot be renegotiated during treatment, but that this should be done explicitly, together with the client, thus reducing the risk that the client and the therapist are pursuing different agendas. Finally, setting goals provides the opportunity for an evaluation of outcome related directly to the individual's presented problems.

This chapter explains how to set well-defined goals, and future-oriented therapy techniques are described. As the fantasy realization theory shows, goals should be realistic, not mere fantasies or dreams.

Differences between approach and avoidance goals and motivation are explained, and an example of SFBT for trauma survivors is described.

STORY 18. *The Cheshire Cat*

The Cheshire Cat, known for its mischievous grin, is depicted in Carroll's *Alice's Adventures in Wonderland* (1865, p. 43). The following conversation between Alice and the Cheshire Cat illustrates that when the destination is not clear, clients might not reach it and might possibly end up somewhere else.

> **Alice:** "Would you tell me, please, which way I ought to go from here?"
>
> **The Cat:** "That depends a good deal on where you want to get to."
>
> **Alice:** "I don't much care where."
>
> **The Cat:** "Then it doesn't much matter which way you go."

SETTING GOALS

Happiness is different for each person, but researchers have discovered that one factor virtually guarantees a boost in happiness: *working toward a goal*. Lyubomirsky (2008), one of the PP researchers on happiness, found that people who strive for something personally significant, whether it be learning a new craft, changing careers, or raising moral children, are far happier than those who do not have strong dreams or aspirations. Find a happy person, and you will find a project. Pursuing a goal provides our lives with six benefits: (a) greater feelings of purpose and control, (b) increased self-esteem and confidence, (c) greater structure and meaning, (d) sharper planning and prioritizing skills, (e) increased ability to cope with problems, and (f) opportunities to engage with others.

A worthwhile goal should be personally meaningful and rewarding. It should be one an individual freely chooses rather than one that is imposed on him or her. For example, you are less likely to find lasting happiness being a doctor to please your parents than being an architect to please yourself. The goal should move an individual toward doing something (such as learning a new skill) rather than acquiring something that improves his or her circumstances (such as moving to a bigger house). People soon get used to improvements in their circumstances and no longer get the same degree of pleasure from them, whereas *activity goals* produce a steady inflow of positive feelings and experiences. Setting goals helps people channel their energy into action. Aiming for achieving a desired outcome rather than avoiding an undesired outcome is advisable. Research by Beijebach and colleagues (2000) showed that setting clear goals in therapy predicted a twofold increase in success.

Previous studies showed the effects of the neurotransmitter dopamine on short-term goals. Dopamine neurons show brief bursts of activity when animals receive an unexpected reward. These dopamine signals are believed to be important for reinforcement learning, the process by which an individual learns to perform actions that lead to reward. A recent study (Howe, Tierney, Sandberg, Phillips, & Grabyiel, 2013) suggests that dopamine also influences long-term goals and plays a part in how the brain signals the value of long-term rewards. The level of dopamine increases steadily, peaking as the animal approaches its goal—as if in anticipation of a reward. Such prolonged dopamine signaling could provide sustained motivational drive in humans, a control mechanism that may be important for normal behavior and that can be impaired in a range of neurologic and neuropsychiatric disorders (see also Chapter 2).

In problem-focused therapies, it is assumed that the problem is blocking clients from being able to move forward toward their goal. Therefore, it is assumed that if the problem is solved, clients will be able to move forward in a more productive direction in their life. Clients and therapists typically agree that the problem will be solved when it is reduced or gone: The client is no longer depressed, no longer argues with her partner, and no longer does drugs or alcohol. Thus, a successful therapy tracks the gradual reduction of the problem in the client's life.

However, if the therapy focuses solely on the reduction of the nondesired situation, then the client might not replace it with a specified desired situation. The danger of finishing therapy at a point where something is not happening rather than at a point where the preferred future is happening lies in the lesser stability of the vacuum option. It is easier to continue seeing friends, going to the gym, attending a language class, and meditating than it is to continue not doing drugs. Continuing *not* to do things is tough, as most of us know from our own experience (see Chapter 3).

The client's goal achievement signals to the client and the therapist alike that a solution is developing or has developed. The majority of a therapeutic SF conversation is focused on three interrelated activities (De Shazer, 1991):

1. Producing exceptions and/or prototypes (examples of the goal[s] in client's lives that point to desired changes)
2. Imagining and describing the client's preferred new life
3. Confirming that change is occurring (i.e., that the client's new life has indeed started)

If therapists do not know where they are heading with their clients, they will probably end up in the wrong place (as shown in the excerpt about the Cheshire Cat). The task of therapists is to look for a realistic goal together with their clients. There should be mutual agreement on what the overall goal of therapy is and what will constitute a successful outcome. Often therapists have taken on the responsibility of setting goals for clients that the world assumes are feasible rather than allowing clients to sort out goals for themselves. In SFBT, it is always the goal of the clients, not that of their therapists, that is aimed for.

Ten Suggestions for Setting Goals

Well-defined goals should be (a) positively framed, (b) formulated as a process, (c) stated in the here and now (i.e., clients can start the solution immediately), (d) as specific as possible, (e) within the client's control, and (f) phrased in the client's language. Ten suggestions for setting well-defined goals are listed below.

1. Specific questioning may help to focus clients on *positive targets*. For example, if a client says that she wants to "stop being irritable all the time," the therapist might ask, "What would you do that is different if you were not irritable?" or "What would you like to be instead of being irritable?"
   If you go to the supermarket, do you make a list of the things you want to buy or a list of the things you don't want to buy? If you chose the latter, that would mean making a list of about 5,000 things you didn't want to buy. Of course you'll make a list of what you do want. For that same reason, ask clients what they want instead of what they don't want.
2. Failing to plan is planning to fail. Goals should also be *as specific* as possible. Clients are often aware in general terms of how they would like to be. For example, a client might reply that she

wants "to be normal." The therapist might then respond, "Being normal means different things to different people. If you feel normal, how will you be different from how you are now? What will tell you that you are more like you used to be? What will you be doing that you are not doing now?" To a client lacking in self-confidence, the therapist might say, "How will you know if your self-confidence improved? What will you be doing that you are not doing now?" If possible, goals should be phrased so that more than one person can agree that the goal has been achieved, as this is likely to increase the reliability of measures related to goal achievement.

3. It is important that therapists obtain from their clients a detailed, *videotaped description* of what life will look like and what they will be doing (differently) when they have reached their goal.

4. Problems can be solved; facts or disabilities cannot be solved. Therefore, it is important to differentiate between problems and disabilities. A solution can be found for problems; with disabilities (e.g., autism or intellectual disabilities), individuals and their environment have to learn how to adapt in the best possible way.

5. Whenever possible, wishes and complaints should be phrased as goals, that is, as something about which something can be done.

6. Goals are not fixed or static but can be seen as a desired situation. They develop during the process, and they are refined and can even change as the process proceeds. Goals are not set to achieve an ideal state, but instead to reach a situation that is "good enough" from the client's perspective.

7. It is not only the client herself who may define the changes she seeks to achieve in her life. Her partner, children, colleagues, and referrer can be asked the same kinds of questions about their goals and/or what they see as the goal for the client (see Appendix G).

8. Setting an agenda is commonly used in (CBT) therapy. In positive CBT, an agenda is set, but a question about goal formulation for each item is added before the agenda is addressed, such as "What will be the best result of discussing this item?" or "How will we know we can stop discussing this item?" (Bannink, 2012a).

9. Whenever possible, invite clients to formulate *stretch goals*. Stretch goals, as described in Chapter 4, are defined as goals that are beyond the client's current performance level (clients have to stretch to reach them). Stretch goals energize, and clients who reach for what appears to be impossible often actually do the im-

possible. Even when clients do not quite make it, they will probably wind up doing better than they would have done otherwise.
On this point, it should be noted that individuals reporting high
levels of hope often prefer stretch goals that are slightly more difficult than previously attained goals.

10. Chapter 4 discusses a method of assessing the client's motivation
to change and how this change can be encouraged to promote a
positive outcome of therapy. In this process, the therapist assesses
the type of relationship he or she has with the client to optimize
cooperation: Is it a visitor relationship, a complainant relationship, or a customer relationship?

A further suggestion is to just get started. Break up the goal into
manageable subgoals and enlist the support of others. Check from
time to time to see whether clients have to modify their goal or aban-
don it when it no longer servers them, and celebrate progress (see
Chapter 9).

Questions for Setting Goals

Specific questions for setting goals include:

- "What is the purpose of your visit?"
- "What would you like to see instead of the problem?"
- "What are your best hopes? What difference will it make when
  these hopes are met?"
- "What will be the best outcome of you coming to see me?"
- "What would you need to have accomplished by the end of this
  session (or these sessions) in order to say that it was a success
  or that it has been meaningful and useful?"
- The *miracle question*: "Suppose a miracle happens tonight and
  the problem that brings you here today has been solved (to a
  sufficient degree), but you are unaware of it because you are
  asleep. What will be the first thing you notice tomorrow morning that will tell you that this miracle has happened?"
- "What will be different (in your relationship) when the problem
  has been solved (or when you have reached your goal)?"
- "What would you like to see different as a result of these
  sessions?"
- "How will we know we can stop meeting with each other? •
  What should have changed?"

- "What would you like to accomplish here regarding your life (your relationship, your children)?"
- "Who would you be without the problem(s)?"
- "What would you do if you were not depressed/anxious/angry?"
- "What *impossible* goal could you reach if you completely ignored your limitations?"

If more than one person is present—for example, in couples therapy, family therapy, and some forms of group therapy—it is important that a collective goal be formulated. The goal is often framed as a situation in which the personal relationship has been mended. The shared goal may also be that a relationship be terminated in as positive a way as possible.

CASE 10. *A Taxi Driver*

I may explain to clients and colleagues that my work is comparable to that of a taxi driver. Clients define the destination of the taxi ride (the goal), and it is my responsibility to drive them safely there. It is also my responsibility to see to it that the route is as short as possible and that the ride is as comfortable as possible. Therefore, my first question—being a taxi driver—is: "Where to?" not "Where from?" If the client answers, "I don't want to go to the airport" (i.e., "I don't want to have these problems"), I ask where he or she would like to go instead (his or her preferred future or goal).

FUTURE-ORIENTED TECHNIQUES

"I am not what happened to me. I am what I choose to become" (Jung, 1965). From an SF perspective, therapy always starts with the end: the client's preferred future and what he or she chooses to become. Clients may be invited to do some therapeutic *time traveling*. How will clients know they can stop therapy? How will important others in their life notice this? What will be the best outcome? What will clients be thinking/doing/feeling differently? And how will important others react differently? In this respect, SFBT (moving from B to A) is different from PP (moving from A to B). Clients may also like to answer the question of how they will look back on their past when therapy has been successful. These future-oriented techniques use the inner wisdom of clients:

They usually already know the solution(s) to their problem, but they do not know (yet) that they know. Exercises such as Best Possible Self, Letter From Your Future, Older and Wiser Self, and Life Summary are described.

Erickson (Rossi, 1980) was one of the first professionals to use future-oriented techniques. He used the hypnotic technique of *pseudo-orientation in time*. During hypnosis, he had his clients imagine running into him in six months and telling him that their problem had been solved and how they had achieved that success. He ended the hypnosis by suggesting that the clients *forget* what had happened during the hypnosis. Even though Erickson's clients did not always apply the same solutions they had put forward under hypnosis, it turned out that many of them reported doing better six months later.

Exercise 15. BEST POSSIBLE SELF

Invite clients to take a moment to imagine a future in which they are bringing their best possible self forward. Ask them to visualize a best possible self who is very pleasing to them and whom they are interested in. Also ask them to imagine that they have worked hard and succeeded in accomplishing their life goals. You might think of this as the realization of their life dreams and of their own best potential. The point is not to think of unrealistic fantasies, but rather things that are positive, attainable, and within reason. After they get a fairly clear image, invite them to write down the details. Writing down thoughts and hopes will help them to create a logical structure and to move from the realm of foggy ideas and fragmented thoughts to concrete, real possibilities.

Imagining the Future Self

Imagining a *best possible self* has proved to be useful in goal-setting and in building hope and optimism. For a few minutes on four consecutive days, participants in a study done by King (2001) were asked to write down their ideal future in which all had gone well and they had met their desired hopes and goals (see Exercise 15). One of the control groups was asked to write about a traumatic event that had happened to them for those same few minutes on the four consecutive days. Another control group was asked to write about life goals as well as a

Exercise 16. LETTER FROM YOUR FUTURE

A great future-oriented technique is to have clients write a "letter from their future." Invite clients to write a letter to their current self *from* their future self X years from now (six months, one year, five years, or maybe ten years, whichever is a relevant period of time for them). Ask them to describe how they are doing fine and tell about where they are, what they are doing, what they have gone through to get there, and so on. Ask them to tell themselves the crucial things they realized or did to get there. Finally, ask them to give their present selves some sage and compassionate advice from the future (Dolan, 1991, 1998).

A variation is used in PP, and here the exercise is to write a letter *to* your future, which shows one of the differences between PP and SFBT (see Chapter 3).

trauma for the four days. Still another control group was asked to just write about their plans for the day.

The results were that the future-oriented group, who wrote down their ideal future, reported more subjective well-being after the experiment than the controls. The trauma and the future-oriented group both had less illness when followed up five months later.

Another SF technique is to invite clients to imagine that many years later they are an *older and wiser version of themselves* (Dolan, 1998). They are still healthy and have all intellectual capabilities. They may ask this older and wiser version of themselves questions like:

- "If you look back on your life, what advice would you give your younger version?"
- "If you look back on your life, what do you like most about the life you have lived?"
- "Is there anything you would rather have done differently?"
- "What do you hope your children would like to remember about their lives with you?"
- "On a scale from ten to zero, to what extent have you achieved these wishes in your present life?"
- "What would be the smallest step you can take to reach a higher mark?"

Clients can also go for a walk with the older and wiser version of themselves and ask for advice regarding their problem, as in Exercise 17.

In PP, this exercise is known as "entering the aging booth," in which clients are invited to imagine that they are ten to twenty years older, living the life they want to live. "Spending time with an older you" is another way of phrasing therapeutic time travel.

Exercise 17. OLDER AND WISER SELF

Invite your clients to imagine that they have become an *older and wiser person* and that they are looking back on this difficult period of their life. What do they think this old and wise person would advise them to do in order to get through the present phase of their life? What would this person say they should be thinking about? What would this person say that would help them to recover from the past? How would this person say they can console themselves? And how, from this person's view, could therapy (if needed) be most useful to them?

Exercise 18. POSITIVE VISUALIZATION

Positive visualization refers to the practice of seeking to affect the outer world by changing one's thoughts and expectations. Positive or creative visualization is the technique underlying positive thinking and is frequently used by athletes to enhance their performance. Some celebrities have endorsed the use of visualization and claimed that it had a significant role in their success. Such celebrities include Oprah, Tiger Woods, Arnold Schwarzenegger, Anthony Robbins, and Bill Gates. Actor Will Smith used visualization to overcome challenges and, in fact, visualized his success years before he became successful. Another example is actor Jim Carrey, who wrote a check to himself in 1987 in the sum of $10 million. He dated it "Thanksgiving 1995" and added the notation "for acting services rendered." He visualized it for years, and in 1994 he received $10 million for his role in *Dumb and Dumber*.

Clients may profit from positive visualization of their preferred future as much as athletes and celebrities do. Have them give it a try.

Wanting and Liking

A future-oriented question frequently asked in therapy is "What do you want (in your life)?" This question activates the limbic system in the brain, which is linked to feelings, motivation, and memory. There are two subsystems to distinguish: *wanting* and *liking*. To engage in *wanting* is to ensure that we will continue to want things. Wanting inclines us toward doing things for a reward. *Liking* indicates that we will become happy or fortunate in what we do and in what happens to us. If everything works out, then these two systems can correlate with and learn from each other. However, sometimes we want to do things that do not make us happy at all, like become addicted or learn bad habits or avoid difficult social situations that we had every intention of confronting. Therefore, the question "What do I want?" is not a useful question for our clients or ourselves, because then we focus only on wanting. It would be better to pose the question "What makes you [or me] happy?" To answer that, previous experiences are important: "What has made you [me] happy in the past?" Then liking and wanting make a better match, and you will want and do more of the things that make you happy (Litt, 2010).

FANTASY REALIZATION

In Exercise 15, it was stressed that clients should not think of unrealistic fantasies, but of things that are attainable and within reason. Lao Tzu (Chinese philosopher, 604–531 AD) said, "Vision without action is but a dream. Action without vision is a waste of energy. But a vision with action can move mountains." Oettingen and Stephens (as cited in Moskowitz & Grant, 2009) stated that the self-help industry would have

---

Exercise 19. DESIRED FUTURE

Ask your clients questions about their desired future: "How will you know you don't have to come here anymore?" or "How will we know we can stop meeting like this?" Then, as a follow-up question, ask, "How confident are you that you are on track to getting what you want?" The responses to these questions will give you some hints about the next step. Are your clients saying they are on track? What personal strengths and solutions do they use? What else may be helpful in overcoming the obstacles down the road?

Exercise 20. CREATING DESIRED BELIEFS

The following exercise is about *creating desired beliefs* by selecting a specific time and place in the future where the client would like to have a certain belief. It is derived from NLP (*neurolinguistic programming*). Ask clients to follow these steps:

1. Think of something you want to believe about yourself, but that your aren't quite sure is true.
2. State your desired belief in a positive form. Make sure it's truly yours, something you can do something about.
3. Ask yourself: What would a person with this desired belief naturally do? Imagine many different actions and list them.
4. Select a specific time and place in your future where you would like to have your desired belief.
5. Select an action from your list that is evidence of your desired belief and is appropriate for that specific future time and place.
6. See yourself in your selected future time and place doing the action. Watch the scene (as though it were a movie) of that *future you* completing the actions of your desired belief. Revise the scene if necessary so that it is positive and appropriate.
7. Rewind that scene to the beginning. Step into it and go through this future time as if you are living it now. See the scene around you. Feel the feelings. Hear yourself state your belief with conviction. Go through the scene to the end.

Repeat steps 4 through 7 three more times. Each time, select a different action from your list of appropriate actions for your desired belief, each with another future time and place..

us believe that to *think positive* is the most effective means of getting what we want. And although empirical research does consistently find that optimistic beliefs foster motivation and successful performance, recent research reveals that alternate forms of positively thinking about the future (e.g., positive fantasies, wishful thinking, and other avoidant coping styles) are less beneficial in producing effortful action, performance, and well-being. Whether an individual indulges in a desired future (has positive fantasies about a desired future) or actually judges a desired future as within reach (has positive expectations about a desired future) has very different implications for effortful action and successful performance.

Oettingen proposes a model of fantasy realization that serve to turn free fantasies about a desired future into binding goals. The model assumes that mentally contrasting aspects of the future and reality activates expectations about attaining a desired future that in turn lead to persistent goal pursuit and effective goal attainment in the case of high expectations.

Fantasy realization theory (Oettingen, 1999; Oettingen, Hönig, & Gollwitzer, 2000) elucidates three routes to goal-setting that result from how people elaborate their fantasies about desired futures. One route leads to expectancy-based goal commitment, whereas the other two routes lead to goal commitment independent of expectations.

1. *Mental contrasting* is the expectancy-based route and rests on mentally contrasting fantasies about a desired future with aspects of the present reality. When people use the self-regulatory strategy of mental contrasting, they first imagine a desired future and then reflect on the respective negative reality, emphasizing a necessity to change the present reality to achieve the desired future. This necessity to act should activate relevant expectations of success, which then informs goal commitment.

   When engaging in mental contrasting, individuals first elaborate a desired future, establishing the positive future as their reference point, and only thereafter elaborate aspects of the present reality, thereby perceiving the negative aspects as obstacles standing in the way of attaining the future. Reversing this order (i.e., reverse mental contrasting), by first elaborating the negative reality and then elaborating the desired future, thwarts reconstrual of the present standing in the way of the future and thus fails to elicit goal commitment congruent with expectations of success (Oettingen, Pak, & Schnetter, 2001).

2. *Indulging* consists of solely fantasizing about a positive future. There are no reflections on the present reality that would point to the fact that the positive future is not yet realized. A necessity to act is not induced and expectations of success are not activated and used.

3. *Dwelling* consists of merely reflecting on the negative reality, producing continual ruminations, as no fantasies about a posi-

tive future designate the direction to act. A necessity to act is not included and expectations are not activated and used.

Numerous studies have now shown that mental contrasting turns free fantasies into binding goals by activating expectations, thus influencing subsequent goal commitment and goal-directed behavior. Mental contrasting enables people to commit to their desired future and is effective in promoting commitment to goals that are initially hard to commit to. It can be used as a metacognitive strategy to help people manage and improve their everyday lives. "Making fantasies come true is not merely the stuff of daydreams or fairy tales. To make our fantasies come true, a person need the appropriate thought processes to activate expectations and commitment" (Oettingen & Stephens, 2009, p. 174).

In summary, inviting clients to design their preferred future is important as a first step and is useful when it is followed by mentally contrasting this outcome with the present reality to help overcome the obstacles in the present.

Exercise 21. MENTAL CONTRASTING

Invite clients to imagine that they will achieve their goal. Then have them focus on obstacles that are in their way. Ask clients to write down a wish or concern they currently have. Ask them to think about what a happy ending would look like for this wish or concern and to write down one positive aspect of this happy ending. Next, ask them to think about an obstacle that stands in the way between where they are now and their happy ending. Now have them list another positive aspect of the happy ending. And another obstacle. And another positive aspect. And another obstacle. After this exercise, invite clients to reflect on whether it was useful for them and, if so, how it was useful.

APPROACH AND AVOIDANCE GOALS

We can only move toward or away from things, so approach and avoidance capture a lot of what we do in life. *Approach motivation* may be defined as the energization of behavior by, or the direction of behavior toward, positive stimuli (objects, events, possibilities); whereas *avoidance motivation* may be defined as the energization of behavior by, or

Exercise 22. LIFE SUMMARY

This is another future-oriented intervention using mental contrasting. Invite clients to write a short description of how they would like to have their life relayed to their grandchildren (or a young child they care about). A few days later, ask them to review the summary and take stock of what is missing in their life and the changes that would be necessary to make the summary a reality.

A variation of Life Summary is to invite clients to write a *eulogy*: "How do I want to be remembered?" A eulogy is a piece written in praise of a person who recently died or retired. Covey (1989) used a similar technique. He stated that one of the habits of highly effective people is *to begin with the end in mind*. This means starting with a clear understanding of your destination. If you know where you are going, you can better understand where you are now and so that the steps you take are always in the right direction. One of the ways to do so is to imagine attending your own funeral in three years' time. What would you like your family, friends, and colleagues to say about you at your funeral?.

the direction of behavior away from, negative stimuli (objects, events, possibilities) (A. J. Elliot, 2008). For example, weight control behavior is typically motivated by a desire to reach a positive goal, characterized by improvements in one's appearance and physical comfort, whereas smoking cessation is typically motivated by a desire to avoid the health threats associated with smoking.

Goals in therapy can be stated as increasing strengths or positive values (approach goal: be more considerate) as well as reducing distress (avoidance goal: feel less anxious) (Kuyken et al., 2009). Both approach and avoidance motivation are integral to successful adaptation: Avoidance motivation facilitates *protection and survival*, while approach motivation facilitates *growth and thriving*.

From a positive CBT point of view (Bannink, 2012a, 2013), therapists should routinely ask about goals and aspirations in early sessions and add these to the client's list of presenting issues. Discussions of positive areas of a client's life often reveal alternative coping strategies to those used in problem areas. These coping strategies, which are often more adaptive, can be recognized as part of the same process that identifies triggers and maintenance factors for problems. When it is time to alter maintenance circles, the client can practice alternative coping responses drawn from more successful areas of life.

De Shazer (1991) stated that too often clients (and therapists) are willing to accept the absence of the problem as *goal enough*, but the absence can never be proved and, therefore, success or failure cannot be known by either therapist or client. Unless clearly established beforehand, even the presence of significant changes is not enough to prove the absence of the problem.

Walter and Peller (2000) stated that clients sometimes speak only of what they do not want or what they want to eliminate from their lives (avoidance goal). In interactional situations, clients often speak of what they want the other person not to do. Their only course of action has been to try to get the other person to stop doing what they consider to be problematic behavior. The other person is also in a strange position, in that the options are either to defend the present behavior or to stop what the other finds so problematic. He or she is still in the dark as to what the client does want to happen. Talking about what the client does want (approach goal) may open up the conversation in a more positive direction.

From a functional point of view, both approach and avoidance goals are necessary for successful adaptation. Tamir and Diener (2008) stated that although it is beneficial to pursue at least some degree of both approach and avoidance goals, pursuing such goals may carry different implications for well-being. The pursuit of approach goals is more manageable than that of avoidance goals. According to cybernetic control models (Carver & Scheier, 1998), the pursuit of approach goals involves diminishing the discrepancy between a current state and a desired state. On the other hand, the pursuit of avoidance goals involves enlarging the discrepancy between a current state and an undesired state. From this conceptual viewpoint, the pursuit of approach goals should be more manageable than the pursuit of avoidance goals, because progress is more tangible and easier to monitor (A. J. Elliot & Church, 1997).

In addition, the pursuits of approach and avoidance goals differ in the cognitions they give rise to. If goal pursuits involve constant comparisons of a current state to an end state, the pursuit of approach goals involves constant monitoring of positive outcomes, making them more accessible during goal pursuit. On the other hand, the pursuit of avoidance goals involves constant monitoring of negative outcomes, making them more accessible during goal pursuit. Thus, the pursuit of approach goals maintains positive cognitions, whereas the pursuit of avoidance goals maintains negative cognitions (A. J. Elliot & Sheldon, 1998).

CASE 11. Avoidance Goals

If a young man marries a woman just because he cannot bear his loneliness any longer, we would not be surprised to find that his marriage does not bring him much happiness. Marrying somebody simply to avoid being alone does not guarantee marital happiness. Common interests, personal well-being, and mutual understanding and growth, to name just a few, are approach goals neglected by the young man in the example.

Avoidance goals, even when perfectly accomplished, facilitate the termination or prevention of aversive states but do not necessarily promote the satisfaction of needs. Instead, avoidance motivation is associated with reduced subjective well-being, impaired subjective competence, and increased physical symptoms (A. J. Elliot & Sheldon, 1998).

STORY 19. How to Be (Not Un)Happy

The ancient Greeks also faced the choice between approach and avoidance goals: how to be happy versus how not to be unhappy. The Stoics (third century BC: Zeno, and later Seneca and Epictetus) practiced discomfort and difficulty; their aim was not to be unhappy (an avoidance goal). Today the word *stoic* commonly refers to someone indifferent to pain, pleasure, grief, or joy.

Epicurus was another ancient Greek philosopher (second century BC) and the founder of the school of philosophy called Epicureanism. For the Epicurists, the objective was to attain a happy, tranquil life, surrounded by friends and living self-sufficiently. Their aim was to be happy (an approach goal).

Although research shows that we generally benefit more from approach goals than from avoidance goals, there is considerable evidence that most people try harder to avoid losses than to obtain comparable gains. The effects of punishment and negative reinforcers on behavior are generally stronger than the effects of reward and comparable positive reinforcers, and people report more often trying to get out of bad moods than to get into or prolong good moods (Baumeister, Bratlavsky, Finkenauer, & Vohs, 2001). This means that therapists should invite clients to change their focus to thinking and doing something that is probably contrary to what they would be thinking and doing automatically—that is, to focus on obtaining gains instead of on avoiding losses.

CASE 12. *Approach and Avoidance Goals*

Client A is depressed, and her goal is to have more positive feelings (approach goal). Client B is depressed, and her goal is to avoid becoming even more depressed (avoidance goal). Client A can monitor her progress toward her goal. If she fails to feel better, she knows that she is not making progress toward her desired outcome. If, however, she is feeling better, she knows that she is getting closer to obtaining her goal. Client A can monitor success and failure in her goal pursuit and experience pleasant or unpleasant affect as a result.

Client B may have a harder time monitoring her progress. If she is not feeling better, she knows that she is failing to obtain her goal of keeping things as they are. What would indicate to her that she is succeeding in her goal pursuit? Finding indications of success in pursuing avoidance goals is often challenging. Thus, Client B may be likely to detect more failures than successes in her goal pursuit, making it more likely that she will experience unpleasant affect.

In addition, the pursuits of approach and avoidance goals tend to differ in the cognitions they give rise to. Clients A and B may have different thoughts accessible to them in their daily lives. Client A may think of what it would be like to be feeling better, and such thoughts may engender pleasant affect. Client B, on the other hand, may think of what it would be like if things don't get better, and such thoughts may engender unpleasant affect.

Overall, the process of pursuing approach goals is different from the process of pursuing avoidance goals. Approach goals appear to be easier to monitor and more manageable than avoidance goals. In addition, whereas approach goals elicit positive cognitions by leading individuals to focus on desirable outcomes, avoidance goals elicit negative cognitions by leading individuals to focus on undesirable outcomes. Therefore, the pursuit of approach goals promotes more well-being than the pursuit of avoidance goals. Greater well-being results from experiencing a pleasant affect more frequently and an unpleasant affect less frequently, and from having personally meaningful experiences in life.

More information about approach and avoidance goals can be found in Bannink (2012a).

STORY 20. *Top Performers*

How do top performers set goals? Barrell, a performance improvement expert working with baseball players from the San Francisco 49ers and the Atlanta Braves, stated that there are "toward goals" and "away goals" (Barrell & Ryback, 2008). Which ones you use have quite an impact on performance. Toward goals have you visualize and create connections around where you are going. You are creating new connections in your brain. What is interesting is that you start to feel good at lower levels with toward goals. There are benefits earlier. Away goals have you visualize what can go wrong, which reactivates the negative emotions involved.

SFBT WITH TRAUMA SURVIVORS

As an example of SFBT with trauma survivors, O'Hanlon (1999) gave the following guidelines for therapy. To start with, therapists should find out what their clients are seeking to gain from therapy. How will they know their therapy has been successful? Therapists should stay focused on the goal of treatment rather than get lost in the gory details. Another guideline is that, when starting therapy, clients should be safe. If not, steps to ensure this should be taken. If necessary provisions for safety from suicide, homicide and other potentially dangerous situations should be made (mutually if possible).

It is important to remember that it is not always necessary to go back and work through traumatic memories, some clients will and some won't. It is also important to look for clients' strengths and resources. Therapists should pay attention to what clients did to survive the traumatic events and how they coped so far. Do clients have healthy relationships and role models? What other competencies and skills do they have? Each part of the clients' experiences and selves should be validated and supported and self-blaming or invalidating identity stories clients may have should be gently challenged. Therapists should always remember that clients might be affected by what happened to them, but that their future is not determined by these events

---

CASE 13. *Once and for All*

A client asked, "How will I know I have *once and for all* resolved the trauma of being raped when I was fourteen years old?" The therapist answered, "You can say you have resolved the trauma when you can continue with your life, without suffering from symptoms such as depression, flashbacks, or nightmares, *and* when you have a sufficient level of well-being. Having resolved the trauma in a good way, however, is not the same as *finally* having resolved the trauma. If later in life you have to go through a similar experience, chances "

Maybe this suggestion will be helpful to your clients: "Take a moment to think of the metaphor of your brain as a library. The books close to the entrance contain the pleasant and unpleasant things that have happened to you recently. Books containing what happened earlier in your life are placed on the shelves that are more to the back of the library (and they may even have gathered some dust). Now imagine you are the librarian. You can move the books according to what you think is wise and helpful. If a book containing an unpleasant event shows up every time at the front of the library, move the book to the shelves at the back and put some books with pleasant events in front. Repeat this a couple of times. In this way, you can become the director of your thoughts."

DEFINING SUCCESS

Different people define success in different ways. More and more, it has become synonymous with money and status. Real success, however, is less about results or a bottom line, and more about the process of achieving goals and dreams. In *Winnie-the-Pooh on Success* (Allen & Allen, 1997, p. 17), the wise Stranger tells the animals how they can become successful, which they consider to be "the most important subject of all." He writes the following acronym on a sheet of paper and shows it to his friends:

- **S**elect a Dream
- **U**se your dreams to set a Goal
- **C**reate a Plan
- **C**onsider Resources
- **E**nhance Skills and Abilities
- **S**pend time Wisely
- **S**tart! Get Organized and Go

Every client is unique. In the next chapter, we will take a closer look at finding what works for a particular client in a certain situation at a specific time. Basic SF principles are: If something works (better), do more of it; if something does not work, do something else.

SUMMARY

- Working toward a goal boosts happiness.
- Well-defined goals should be created early in therapy and be stated as specifically as possible, in a positive manner, and in the here and now. They should be actionable, within the client's control, and phrased in the clients' language.
- Useful future-oriented techniques include Best Possible Self, Letter From Your Future, and Older and Wiser Self, among others.
- It is preferable to ask clients what they *like* in life rather than what they *want*.
- According to fantasy realization theory, goals should be realistic and, instead of indulging in dreams or dwelling on the negataive reality, should be contrasted mentally with the current situation.
- Approach motivation and approach goals are preferable to avoidance motivation and avoidance goals.
- When using SFBT with trauma survivors, start by finding out what clients are seeking to gain from therapy and how they will know when the therapy has been successful.

....

CHAPTER 6

Focus on What Works

In the previous chapter, SFBT was defined as a negotiated, consensual, and cooperative endeavor in which therapists and clients focus on exceptions, goals, and solutions. SF conversations focus on finding out what works for this client at this moment in this context. A guiding SF principle is: If something works (better), do more of it; if something does not work, do something else. Solution-focused conversations are different from conversations where positive psychology applications are used. One difference is that in PP conversations, the focus in not on what works, but on personal strengths and how to use these to bring about positive change. However, the combination of both is a very fruitful one in helping trauma survivors survive and thrive, enhancing hope and optimism along the way.

Assessing strengths and resources is the first way of finding out what works. These resources can be found within clients or in their environment (partner, children, family, friends, colleagues etc.). Assessing hope, motivation, and confidence is another way of knowing where clients stand and what they want to see different in their lives. Asking about pretreatment change is important, because many clients experience positive treatment-related gains prior to the formal initiation of therapy. Finding exceptions to the problem is another great way of creating an inventory of what works. Most clients have been through difficult times before, and these previous successes may be highlighted, together with cataloging what works (even just a little bit) in the current situation. It is the task of therapists to reinforce everything that works for their clients and to not reinforce what isn't working. As American philosopher and psychologist William James (1842–1910) stated, "The art of being wise is the art of knowing what to overlook."

STORY 21. *Solzhenitsyn*

As a political dissident, Solzhenitsyn (1973) was for many years banished to a Russian labor camp. In discussing the corruption of prisoners in the camps, he said he was not going to explain the cases of corruption. He asked why people would worry about explaining why a house in subzero weather loses its warmth. What needs to be explained is why there are houses that retain their warmth even in subzero weather.

Exercise 23. WHAT WOULD YOU LIKE TO KEEP THE WAY IT IS?

Invite your clients to keep a diary for a week (or longer) to examine what is (already and/or still) working. Ask them to pay attention to the things in their lives that *they would like to keep the way they are* and write them down. Ask them to pay themselves a compliment at the end of every day, based on their diary, and write it down.

ASSESSING STRENGTHS AND RESOURCES

Research shows that successful therapists focus on their clients' strengths, abilities, and available support from the very start of a therapy session. They create an environment in which clients feel they are perceived as well-functioning persons. Successful therapists also make sure they end sessions by returning to their clients' strengths (Gassman & Grawe, 2006), enhancing the therapeutic alliance along the way.

Clients are often not aware of the strengths and resources they use to recover, to be resilient, and even to grow, and highlighting these increases the likelihood that clients will consider their use during future challenges. Noticing the strategies a person employs to manage adversity is often an easy first step toward conceptualizing resilience. These strategies may be behavioral (e.g., persisting in efforts), cognitive (e.g., acceptance), emotional (e.g., humor, reassurance), social (e.g., seeking help), spiritual (e.g. finding meaning in suffering), or even physical (e.g., sleeping and eating well).

As stated in Chapter 3, Peterson (2006) developed the Values in Action (VIA) Survey of Character Strengths, which is available at www. authentichappiness.org. This survey has been developed to reliably classify people on the basis of twenty-four character strengths. Together with Seligman, Peterson surveyed diverse world cultures to create a comprehensive index of character strengths and virtues. This taxonomy of strengths and virtues is meant as a positive alternative to the DSM taxonomy of psychiatric disorders (and can also be used in combination with the DSM-5).

The key to extracting more than a temporary high out of listing these strengths, however, is to invite clients to reshape their lives in such a way that they are able to apply their strengths more often. Seligman, Steen, Park, and Peterson (2005) discovered that the boost in positivity that comes from learning about one's strengths is significant but temporary. By contrast, the boost in positivity that comes from finding new ways to apply these strengths is significant and lasting.

Anyone can register at the Authentic Happiness website and take all the tests for free. The website is intended as a public service (more than 2 million people have already registered at the website and taken the tests, among them the VIA test). Tests include emotion questionnaires, engagement questionnaires (among which is the Brief Strengths Test, measuring the twenty-four character strengths), meaning questionnaires, and life satisfaction questionnaires.

Assessment may take the form of inviting clients to take the test online at home and bring the printed outcome with them to the next session. The therapist and client may then pay attention to the rank order of the client's strengths. Then clients can take a closer look at the top five strengths as measured by the survey, or list their own five highest strengths and provide some examples of how they have used these strengths, either lately or in the past. Not surprisingly, the atmosphere in the session becomes more positive when clients are invited to talk about their successes and strengths. The organization of the 6 *values and 24 character strengths* is as follows. The first value is wisdom and knowledge. The five strengths that involve the acquisition and use of wisdom and knowledge are: creativity, curiosity, open-mindedness, love of learning, perspective and wisdom. The second value is courage. The four strengths that allow one to accomplish goals in the face of opposition are: bravery, persistence, integrity and vitality. The third value is humanity. The three strengths of tending and befriending others are: love, kindness and social intelligence. The fourth value is justice. The three strengths that build a healthy community are: social responsibility and loyalty, fairness and leadership. The fifth value is temperance. The four strengths that protect against excess are: forgiveness and mercy, humility, prudence, self-regulation and self-control. And the sixth value is transcendence. The five strengths that forge connections to the larger universe and provide meaning are: appreciation of beauty, gratitude, hope, humor and playfulness and spirituality.

More PP questionnaires include the Positive and Negative Affect Schedule (PANAS), the Gratitude Questionnaire (GQ-6), the Hope Scale (HS), the Inspiration Scale (IS), the Meaning in Life Questionnaire (MLQ), the Mindful Attention Awareness Scale (MAAS), the Quality of Life Inventory (QOLI), and the Personal Growth Initiative Scale (PGIS). They can be found at www.ppc.sas.upenn.edu/ppquestionnaires.htm.

Exercise 24. EXERCISE YOUR SIGNATURE STRENGTHS

After you have completed the VIA test, create a designated time in your schedule when you will exercise one or more of your signature strengths in a new way, either at work, at home, or while you are at leisure. Just make sure that you create a clearly defined opportunity to use it. For example, if one of your strengths is creativity, you might begin working on writing a book or play. Then evaluate yourself: How did you feel before, during, and after engaging in the activity? Was the activity challenging or easy? Did time pass quickly? Do you plan to repeat the exercise?

You may also invite your clients to complete this activity

Exercise 25. EVIDENCE OF COMPETENCIES

Ask clients how you as their therapist can collect the best evidence of their competencies. What should you as their therapist especially look for? How can you address these competencies in a way that is meaningful for them? What is the best way to give them feedback?

Exercise 26. STRENGTHS, QUALITIES, SKILLS AND RESOURCES

Invite clients to answer the following questions:

- "What strengths, qualities, skills and resources do you have?"
- "How have you used these strengths, qualities, skills, and resources up till now?"
- "How will these strengths, qualities, skills, and resources be helpful to you in the future?"

Exercise 27. RESOURCE AWARENESS

This exercise for a group of therapists emphasizes resources. Someone in the group is invited to tell the others about a recent pleasant or successful event, something he or she is proud of or happy about. The others are asked to respond by giving as many compliments as possible. The individual is then asked which compliments he or she liked best. Then the same person or someone else in the group tells about a recent unpleasant or unsuccessful event, something he or she is ashamed of or unhappy about. The others are asked again to react with as many compliments as possible. The individual is again asked which compliments felt really good.

This is an exercise in noticing how difficult it often is to pay compliments to people who tell unhappy stories. The group can also discuss who they think needs the compliments the most: the person who tells a pleasant story or the person who tells an unpleasant story.

Exercise 28. DEFINING MOMENTS

This exercise builds on research done on the You at Your Best exercise (see Exercise 32). The purpose of this exercise is to invite clients to facilitate exploration of their character strengths, to build a bridge between past critical experiences and future possibilities, and to link positive identity formation with character strengths. There are three steps:

1. Name the defining moment; tell your story (e.g., passing an important exam).
2. List the character strengths involved in the story.
3. Reflect on how this story has shaped who you are (your identity) and how it has impacted you to the present day.

When it comes to studying or trying to cultivate psychological strengths, people tend to focus on just one strength at a time rather than seeking to understand the multidimensional interdependence of strengths. For example, two strengths together appear to reduce the risk of suicide. Kleiman, Adams, Kashdan, and Riskind (2013) found that adults who were both *grateful* and *gritty* experienced near-zero suicidal thoughts over a period of a month. This may be due to the fact that gratitude is about being attentive and attuned to the outside world (the cool breeze you feel upon exiting a building) and to both past and present experiences (the kindness of friends and family), whereas grit is about internal determination to persevere in the face of life's obstacles while orienting oneself to the future and accepting the pain associated with following through with meaningful goals. According to the researchers, a person with this pair of strengths, both grit and gratitude, may have a healthy orientation toward the past, present, and future, and may as a consequence be very resilient where suicide is concerned.

Gratitude

Thankfulness, gratefulness, and appreciation are feelings or attitudes one experiences in acknowledgment of a benefit that one has received or will receive from a person who gave, or gives, spontaneously of his

Exercise 29. POSITIVE REMINISCENCE

The essence of positive reminiscence is to spend time recalling a positive event from the past. This could be an experience that brings forth pleasant memories, such as a birthday, a wedding, a job interview, or a time when you accomplished something important in your life. You might find benefit from doing this exercise with physical memorabilia—photo albums, trinkets collected from a vacation, trophies or awards, meaningful letters or printed emails, or college diplomas. After recalling the event, take a few minutes to simply bask in the past success and pleasant feelings this experience brings forth in you. This experience of stretching out and extending a moment is one example of savoring. Bring your attention to the details and your positive emotions. Don't analyze the experience by picking it apart and trying to figure out why certain things happened; this is often counterproductive in the case of positive experiences and is not truly savoring. Instead, focus on the replaying of the experience. This exercise has been shown to build positive emotions and confidence.

Exercise 30. YOUR STRENGTHS AS A THERAPIST

In your work as a therapist, you are using your strengths, too. Think about which three character strengths have brought you to where you are in your profession today. Discuss this with a colleague and ask what three strengths he or she would say you have used. Now reverse roles: Which three strengths does your colleague use, and which would you say have brought your colleague to where he or she is today?

Consider how you can use these strengths even more than you do now, or how you can use them in a new area of your life. Consider which other strengths you might use (more) in your work in the future.

or her own free will. Gratitude is one of the twenty-four character strengths in the domain of *transcendence*.

The experience of gratitude has historically been a focus of several world religions and has been considered extensively by moral philosophers. The systematic study of gratitude within psychology began around the year 2000, possibly because psychology has traditionally been focused more on understanding distress than on understanding positive emotions. However, with the advent of PP, gratitude has become a mainstream focus of psychological research. The study of gratitude has focused on the understanding of the short-term experience of the emotion of gratitude (*state gratitude*), individual differences in how frequently people feel gratitude (*trait gratitude*), and the relationship between these aspects. Gratitude is probably a considerable *protective factor* against the development of PTSD.

Gratitude is distinct from *indebtedness*. While both emotions occur following help, indebtedness occurs when a person perceives that he or she is under obligation to make some repayment or compensation for the aid. These two emotions lead to very different actions: Indebtedness can motivate the recipient of the aid to avoid the person who has helped him or her, whereas gratitude can motivate the recipient to seek out the benefactor and to improve his or her relationship with that person.

Research on gratitude has shown the following results. In an experimental comparison, people who kept gratitude journals on a weekly basis exercised more regularly, reported fewer physical symptoms, felt better about their lives as a whole, and were more optimistic about the upcoming week compared to those who recorded hassles or neutral life events (Emmons & McCullough, 2003). A related benefit was observed in the realm of personal goal attainment: Participants who kept gratitude lists were more likely to have made progress toward important personal (academic, interpersonal, and health-based) goals over a two-month period compared to subjects in the other experimental conditions.

A daily gratitude intervention (a self-guided exercise) with young adults resulted in higher reported levels of alertness, enthusiasm, determination, attentiveness, and energy compared to focusing on hassles and downward social comparison (i.e., finding ways in which you think you are better off than others). There was no difference in levels of unpleasant emotions reported among the three groups. Participants in the daily gratitude group were more likely to report having helped someone with a personal problem or having offered emotional support to another, relative to the hassles and social comparison groups (Froh, Sefick, & Emmons, 2008).

In a sample of adults with neuromuscular disease, a twenty-one-day gratitude intervention resulted in more positive emotions. It also resulted in a greater sense of feeling connected to others, more optimistic ratings of one's life, and better sleep duration and sleep quality, relative to a control group. The researchers also found that people with an "attitude of gratitude" have lower levels of stress hormones in their blood (McCraty, Barrios-Choplin, Rozman, Atkinson, & Watkins, 1998), and undo the cardiovascular aftereffects of negative emotions (Branigan, Fredrickson, Mancuso, and Tugade, 2000). Also, children who practice grateful thinking have more positive attitudes toward school and their families (Froh et al., 2008).

CASE 14. *What Was Good About This Experience?*

A client with a history of sexual abuse by her brother wanted help with not feeling anxious anymore, sleeping better, and focusing on her work again. The therapist acknowledged her problems and feelings and said, "This must have been very bad for you, but allow me to ask you a very strange question. Tell me, what was *good* about this experience?"

The client listed things she had done that had been helpful. For one thing, she had found the courage to have her brother tried, as a result of which he was spending time in jail. Talking about what was good about the experience gave the client and therapist an opportunity to compliment her and emphasize her resources for coping with the bad experience.

Exercise 31. GIVE THANKS FOR THE ORDINARY AND THE EXTRAORDINARY

Invite clients to give thanks for the ordinary and the extraordinary. Invite them to note, each morning after waking up, at least twenty things for which they are *grateful*. This may seem daunting, but once they get into the habit and find the right frame of mind, it may become easier. Here are examples of things they could note and appreciate: "I have hot and cold running water. I have a roof over my head. I have clean clothes. I am alive. I have friends."

Now invite your clients to experiment to find what works best: writing down the appreciations, saying them out loud to their partner or a family member, or silently noting them to themselves. Let them do this activity for a week and notice what difference it makes. Then ask them to decide whether they would like to continue this habit or not.

Courage

The virtue *courage* is composed of the four character strengths that allow people to accomplish goals in the face of opposition: bravery, persistence, integrity, and vitality. For clients suffering from (symptoms of) PTSD in particular, courage is an important virtue; it can be hard to be brave and persistent in surviving and in working on progress.

History is full of stories about courage. However, there has not yet been much research done on courage. According to many researchers, it is difficult to give an accurate definition of courage. You may find yourself courageous because you have been skydiving, but courage mainly takes place in interpersonal relationships. "Being deeply loved by someone gives you strength, while loving someone deeply gives you courage" (Lao Tzu).

One study examined to what extent positive personality variables are associated with courage and kindness. A distinction was made between people who had played an active and courageous role in helping Jews during their persecution in World War II and people who had stood by passively. The courageous group showed a much greater degree of empathy, social responsibility, and altruism, and were prepared to take far more risks (Fagin-Jones & Midlarsky, 2007).

Self-Compassion

Recovering and resilient people build a gentle relationship with their emotions and have a healthy way of relating to themselves; they go easy on themselves. While we cannot change the gut-level feelings and reactions that our minds and bodies produce, we can change how we respond to these feelings. Most of us are taught that vulnerable feelings are signs of weakness, to be hidden from others at all cost. However, if properly managed, expressing your vulnerability can be a source of strength and confidence. Being kind to yourself is not only about providing comfort in the moment; it is also about committing, whenever possible, to reducing future instances of suffering. Compassion is sensitivity to the suffering of oneself and of others and a commitment to doing something about it (Gilbert, 2010). Self-compassion encourages a person's drive while also giving it focus and healthy, wholesome boundaries. The soothing system, as Gilbert put it, gives the context for the striving. According to Neff (2011), self-compassion revolves around three things:

1. Compassion instead of judgment toward oneself. People who are kind to themselves are tolerant and loving toward themselves when faced with pain or failure. Self-judging people are tough on and intolerant of themselves.
2. A "common humanity" stance instead of isolation. A *common humanity* perspective sees our failings and feelings of inadequacy as part of the human condition shared by nearly everyone. By contract, people who isolate tend to feel alone in their failure.
3. Emotional regulation instead of overidentification. People who can regulate their emotions take a balanced view and keep their emotions in perspective. They neither ignore nor ruminate on elements of their lives that they dislike. By contrast, overidentified people tend to obsess about failure and view it as evidence of personal inadequacy.

Increasing self-compassion creates positive effects, such as satisfaction with one's own life, wisdom, optimism, curiosity, goal-setting, social connectedness, personal responsibility, and emotional resilience. Gilbert (2010) refers to PP for a number of exercises, including You at Your Best (Exercise 32) and Loving-Kindness Meditation (Exercise 77).

Exercise 32. YOU AT YOUR BEST

Invite clients to think of a specific time, recently or a while back, when they were at their best—whey they were really feeling and acting at a high level and feeling as if they were being authentic and true to who they are. Ask them to develop a story for that experience or that moment in time and give the story a beginning, middle, and end. They might take the approach of replaying and reliving the positive experience, just as if they were watching a movie of it.

Reexperiencing and savoring moments like this in your mind can lead to greater happiness and a greater chance that you'll savor future moments as they happen in the present. Research has shown that it is most beneficial to keep this exercise a mental one; however, clients might find it useful to jot down a few highlights

Exercise 33. SPARKLING MEMORIES

This is another exercise for inviting clients to think of a time they were at their best. Have your clients think about a *sparkling moment* in their life during the past few weeks—a moment when they really felt at their best. How did it come about? What was it that made the moment sparkle for them? Now invite your clients to reflect for a while on their excellent qualities, skills, and resources. What small step might they take to increase the prospect of (even more) sparkling moments?

CASE 15. *A Little Bit of Self-Compassion*

A client told her therapist that her youth had been awful. Her parents, both of them psychiatric patients and autistic, had treated each other terribly. Later in life, the client and her own family had been seriously wounded in a plane crash. To add to this, the client's youngest daughter was experiencing an unwanted pregnancy. The client explained that she cried a lot because she felt she was losing her usual perseverance and courage. She found it difficult to do anything nice for herself and asked how she could become better at self-soothing.

The therapist acknowledged the client's feelings and normalized the fact that she had difficulty in being kind to herself, acknowledging that her parents had never been able to model this kind of behavior when she was a child. "Without this model as a child," the therapist asked, "how do you succeed in comforting your own children when they need you? Where have your learned how to show compassion for others?" The therapist also asked exception-finding questions: "When did you succeed in showing a little bit of self-compassion? What exactly did you do then? How can you do more of it in the future? What will be your next (small) step?" The therapist also invited the client to do more *acts of kindness* (see Exercise 106) for other people, because this was something she was very good at.

Self-compassion is distinct from *self-esteem*. According to research (Neff & Vonk, 2009), self-esteem has been associated with a steady rise in narcissism over the last forty-five years. High self-esteem is associated with the need to feel superior to others in order to feel OK about oneself. High self-esteem encourages us to maintain an unrealistically high view of ourselves in comparison to others. This has a particularly devastating effect when we face failure. People with high self-esteem tend to dismiss negative feedback, trivialize their failures, and take less accountability for their own harmful actions. In short, self-esteem can create distance between others and us. Self-kindness, also referred to as self-compassion, comes from Buddhist cultures and is less intentionally cultivated in the West. Self-kindness does not require that we feel superior to others and may be a healthier alternative to self-esteem. Self-kindness is not an evaluation of ourselves at all, but is an attitude we adopt toward our own failure and suffering. It is a positive, proactive attitude toward oneself, not simply the absence of negative attitudes. For instance, the absence of self-judgment does not necessarily mean that one is compassionate toward oneself. We often become our own worst critic because we believe it's necessary to keep ourselves motivated, but in fact research shows that healthy self-compassion increases our inner drive, our resilience to setbacks, and our ability to excel at work and in every aspect of life. Self-compassion may well be the most important life skill, imparting resilience, courage, energy, and creativity.

Feeling cared for and accepted and having a sense of belonging and affiliation with others are fundamental to our physiological maturation and well-being (Siegel, 2001). They are linked to particular types of positive affect that in turn are associated with wellness and a neurohormonal profile of increased endorphins and oxytocin (Panksepp,

1998). They can be seen as part of the twenty-four character strengths (humanity and temperance).

Self-compassion is also distinct from *self-pity*. People who engage in self-pity generally feel disconnected from others while exaggerating their own problems. Self-kindness directs us toward the universality of our condition and allows us to adopt an objective perspective toward our own suffering. People who are kind toward themselves are more able to admit mistakes, change unproductive behavior, and accept new challenges.

Most of us are already good at being kind to others. Self-kindness turns this practice inward, so that we treat ourselves as kindly as we would treat a good friend. Self-kindness allows us to embrace our basic, imperfect humanity.

Exercise 34. SELF-COMPASSION

Invite clients to think of some moments in their life when they were able to be kinder to themselves, even just a little bit (finding exceptions). What exactly did they do? How come they were able to do that? What were the positive consequences of these moments? Then ask them what small step(s) they may take to increase their prospects of having more self-compassionate moments

---

Exercise 35. SELF-APPRECIATION

Invite clients to follow these instructions:

• Find five things you like about yourself.
• Find five things you do that add value to the world around you.
• Tell about your proudest achievement in the last twelve months.

Compassion-Focused Therapy

Compassion-focused therapy (CFT) originated from combining CBT and emotion work with a compassion (kindness) focus. CFT was developed in working with people with high shame and self-criticism. These people can find experiencing positive, affiliative emotions (accepting compassion from others and being self-compassionate) difficult. CFT is process- rather than disorder-focused, because shame and self-criticism are transdiagnostic processes that have been linked to a range of psychological disorders. CFT aims to develop care- and affiliative-focused motivation, attention, emotion, behavior, and thinking. Key skills include using compassion-focused imagery, building the compassionate self, and using the sense of a compassionate self to engage with areas of personal difficulty. As an example of this *compassionate rescripting*, a client who is trained in the compassionate self can hold the compassionate position as he approaches a difficult memory and watches the scene unfold. Then, gradually, using his compassionate self, he might bring new things into the scene (e.g., helpers) and begin to decide on new endings. The compassionate self can offer any support to the client that he sees in his memory, and together they can make up the most fantastic, fresh endings (Brewin et al., 2009).

Compassion-focused exercises can be oriented in four ways:

1. Development of the inner compassionate self
2. Compassion flowing out from you to others
3. Compassion flowing into you
3. Compassion toward yourself

Gilbert (2010, p. 11) stated, "There is increasing evidence that the kind of *self* we try to become will influence our well-being and social relationships, and compassionate rather than self-focused self-identities are associated with the better outcomes."

As mentioned before, feeling compassion for others is usually easy enough, but feeling self-compassion is often more difficult for many clients (and therapists). Not all clients think highly of themselves; some even may tell you that they do not have any strength or any resources. Often these clients are very strict and set high standards for themselves; they tend to look at what should have been better. Their self-compassion is often low. Self-compassion means that you are able to look at yourself in a kind rather than a critical way. As Buddha said, "You, as much as anyone else in the entire universe, deserve your love."

If clients cannot find any strengths or resources, you may invite them to look at themselves through a more positive lens:

- "What would your best friend(s) say what your strengths and resources are?"
- "What qualities and skills do they know you have?"

- "What would your kids (parents, colleagues) say that your strengths and resources are?"
- "Where do you get the courage to change if you want to?"
- "How can you make change easier for yourself?"
- "Where do you get those good ideas?"
- "How do you manage to be so determined?"
- "When was your last success, and what did you do to make that happen?"
- "If you go back in time, when did you become aware that you had those qualities?"
- "When were others aware that you had those qualities?"
- "How can you use these qualities and skills again now?"
- "How will others notice that you are using these qualities in this situation?"
- "What things are easy for you to do that others may find difficult?"
- "What was easy for you when you were a child?"
- "If _____ [e.g., a deceased person] could see you now, what would he or she be proud of?"
- "What would that person say about you, if that were possible?"
- "What would he or she say about how you have achieved this?"
- "How does change in your life usually take place?"
- "What's going well in your life, even just a little bit?"
- "What are you satisfied with in your life and want to keep as it is?"

CASE 16. *Left and Right*

A client with a long history of physical and sexual abuse finds it very difficult to name something she is good at or pleased about. The therapist invites her to make a list of everything she is not happy about. The client lists these points on the left side of a sheet of paper after the therapist has drawn a vertical line down the middle of the paper. The therapist then asks the client what she would like to see instead of each point on the left side as well as what (small) exceptions there have been. The client notes these on the right side of the paper. Then the therapist cuts the paper in half, and the client suggests that they throw the left side into the wastebasket. From then onward, the therapist and client work only with her goals and the exceptions to the problems.

Fredrickson (2009), a researcher in the field of PP, mentioned another compassion-focused intervention, called *loving-kindness meditation*. It aims directly to evoke positive emotions, especially within the context of relationships. It is a technique used to increase feelings of warmth and caring for oneself and others. Like mindfulness, loving-kindness evolved from ancient Buddhist mind-training practices. In a guided imagery exercise (see Chapter 8), clients direct these warm and tender feelings first to themselves, and then to an ever-widening circle of others (nice people they know, then to strangers, and finally sometimes even to people with whom they have a negative relationship). Fredrickson (2009, p. 89) stated that meditation produced more positivity regardless of whether people were alone or with others, yet the boosts in positivity were especially large during social interactions. "Meditation brings out not only the best in you, but in others as well. At the very least, it helps you more fully enjoy their company."

Mindfulness

Mindfulness practices for cultivating well-being and transforming suffering have a long lineage, dating back at least 2000 years. Kabat-Zinn (1994) began systematically teaching mindfulness to people with chronic health problems in medical and psychiatric settings in the 1970s. He called his work *mindfulness-based* stress reduction (MBSR). He defines mindfulness as paying attention in a particular way, on purpose, in the present moment, and nonjudgmentally.

Siegel (2010) stated that mindfulness is a form of mental activity that trains the mind to become aware of awareness itself and to pay attention to one's own intentions. Mindfulness requires one to pay attention to the present moment from a stance that is nonjudgmental and nonreactive. It teaches self-observation; practitioners are able to describe with words the internal seascape of the mind. At the heart of this process is a form of internal *tuning in* to oneself that enables people to become *their own best friend*. This also promotes a foundation for resilience and flexibility.

Mindfulness-based cognitive therapy (MBCT) has been developed as an approach that combines the mindfulness mediation rooted in Buddhist thought and the Western tradition of CBT. It is an intervention that promotes a wide, open awareness as well as focused attention and reduces automatic responding. The power of mindfulness is that it can literally sever the link between negative thoughts and negative emotions. As such, mindfulness is used in combination with exposure to traumatic memories.

Research has shown that among clients with recurrent depression, MBCT halves the rate of relapse accompanying usual care and is equivalent to staying on an antidepressant long-term. It has also proved useful in the treatment of children and adolescents with ADHD.

The important thing to remember is that mindfulness involves paying attention to our changing, moment-to-moment experience, whether it be pleasant, unpleasant, or neutral. To do this, we employ the character strengths of self-regulation (of our attention) and curiosity (being open to the present moment). Mindfulness can be practiced formally, through regular sitting/walking/eating meditation, or informally, through bringing deliberate focus to what we are doing (e.g., feeling the softness of the cloth as we make our bed; listening to the sound of the food hitting the ceramic bowl as we feed our cat).

Science has documented that mindfulness training leaves a lasting mark on the brain. It alters the basic metabolisms in brain circuits known to underlie emotional responding, reducing activity in circuits linked with negativity and increasing activity in circuits linked with positivity (Davidson et al., 2003). Siegel (2010) stated that experience creates the repeated neural firing that leads to gene expression, protein production, and changes in both the genetic regulation of neurons and the structural connections in the brain. By harnessing the power of awareness to strategically stimulate the brain's *firing*, mindsight (focused attention that allows us to see the internal workings of our own minds) enables us to voluntarily change a firing pattern that was laid down involuntarily. When we focus our attention, we create neural firing patterns that permit previously separated areas to become linked and integrated. The synaptic linkages are strengthened, the brain becomes more interconnected, and the mind becomes more adaptive.

ASSESSING PROGRESS, MOTIVATION, HOPE, AND CONFIDENCE

The Greek philosopher Heraclitus (540–480 BC) is often credited with saying that nothing is permanent but change: *Panta rhei*. Exploring what is different about better versus worse days, times without the problem versus times when the problem seems to get the best of clients, can help therapists to use the description of such fluctuations as a guide to activity.

Exercise 36. 5-4-3-2-1

This is a short mindfulness exercise. Invite your clients to look successively at five objects and see if they can be grateful for them, joyful about them, or simply accept them as they are. Then invite them to do the same with four different objects; then with three; with two; with one.

Next invite them to hear five sounds; then four; then three; then two; then one. And invite them to do the same with five tactile or bodily sensations; then four; then three; then two; then one.

Exercise 37. VALUE TIME

Ask your clients to imagine that time is a bank account and that each morning they are credited with 86,400 seconds. If, by the end of that day, they haven't spent any of their credits, they will instantly be deducted from their account. Given such a scenario, what would they do? Probably they would try to use every one of those seconds. So invite your clients to enjoy each second of every minute or every hour of every day, because the moment is something that we can never recover.

Therapists may view their clients through a change-focused lens. As noted in Chapter 3, shining a spotlight on change illuminates existing client resources and allows their enlistment. A change focus requires the therapist to believe, like Heraclitus, in the certainty of change, and creates a context in which new or different perspectives and behaviors can be welcomed, explored, and developed. Of special interest is what the client has done to bring about this change and how the client makes sense of it all.

Walter and Peller (2000, p. 7) described their own development as therapists:

> As we weighed the frequency of problem patterns versus exception patterns, we asked, even more radically, how useful it was to interpret clients' experiences as stable patterns. Perhaps the notion of stable patterns was just a construct that

was limiting our ability to observe change. Perhaps it would be more productive to think of change as constant and randomness of behavior as the norm, rather than enduring interactional patterns as the norm. We began to think that the assumption *change is occurring all the time* might be a more useful starting point than *behavior is constant and repetitious*.

Scaling Questions

By means of scaling questions, therapists can help clients to express complex, intuitive observations about their past experiences and estimates of future possibilities. Scaling questions invite clients to put their observations, impressions, and predictions on a scale from ten to zero. For example, therapists may ask, "On a scale from ten to zero, where ten means you are confident that you can reach your goal and zero means you are not confident at all, where would you say you are today?"

Scaling questions can be used to assess progress, motivation, hope, and confidence. When progress is being assessed, clients may be invited to indicate to what degree their goal has already been achieved on a scale of ten to zero, with ten being the most desirable outcome and zero being the worst things have ever been. "Where would you say you are right now on this scale? What did you do to (already) reach this score? How come it is not lower than it is? How did you do that? What would one point higher on the scale look like? What would you then be doing differently? What point on the scale do you want to reach for you to consider the goal (sufficiently) achieved? At what number would you deem yourself ready to conclude therapy?"

Scaling questions can also make clear which part of the road has already been traveled. Most clients are not at a complete zero when they come in for therapy (although sometimes they are, in which case the therapist may extend the scale a bit and ask, "How do you manage?" or "How come it is not lower than zero?"). Scaling questions can be the starting point for an operant conditioning technique called *successive approximation* (or *shaping*) of desired behavior.

Usually, when clients have a clear sense of what they want to achieve and when they have already been able to achieve to some extent what they want, it will be relatively easy for them to choose the next steps forward. Scaling can also be done as a physical exercise in which the client and the therapist literally walk along a ten to zero scale that has been constructed inside or outside the therapy office.

> ## Exercise 38. SCALING WELL-BEING
>
> Scaling questions are a useful tool in therapy. On the scale of psycho-logical well-being (see Figure 1 in Chapter 2), the point –10 indicates the worst possible psychological situation while +10 indicates perfect personal thriving. Solution-focused questions include:
>
> - "Where on the scale is the ideal situation?" or "When your best hopes are met, where on the scale will you be?"
> - "What will be a realistic aim? What does that look like?"
> - "Where are you now on the scale (and why are you not lower)?"
> - "What will be next signs of progress? What will be your next step(s)?"
> - "At what point would you consider therapy successful enough that we can stop meeting with each other?"

Scaling questions are used in traditional therapies, too. However, in problem-focused therapies like CBT, the scales are about the problem: a depression scale, an anxiety scale, or a SUD (Subjective Units of Distress) scale in EMDR. On these scales, the highest point is where the depression or stress is at its peak and the zero is where the negative feeling is absent. But the absence of negative feelings does not say anything about the presence of positive feelings or well-being (see Chapter 1).

CASE 17. *Scaling Control*

In a clinical setting for adolescents with drug or alcohol addiction, (problem-focused) therapists frequently ask their clients scaling questions about their craving: "How high are you now on this scale, where ten stands for the craving being at its worst and zero stands for no craving?" Often their clients answer, "My craving was rather low until you brought it up, but now that you mention it, I feel it right away!" A better scaling question, in which the problem is ex-ternalized, would be, "Where are you now in having control over your addiction, where ten indicates 'I have every control over the addiction' and zero indicates 'I have no control at all'?"

Assessing Motivation to Change
It would be nice if both clients and therapists could always begin with the assumption that therapy is being used as intended: to find solutions or to

put something behind them. However, commitment to therapy and the motivation to make changes are not synonymous. If a client is willing to come to therapy (commitment), this does not necessarily signify that she is also willing to change her behavior. Often clients will (silently) hope that the therapist will solve the problem or will see the other person as the one who is to blame for the problem. Assessment of the client's motivation to change and how this change can be encouraged to promote a positive outcome of therapy starts with the therapeutic alliance (see Chapter 4). In this process, the therapist assesses the type of relationship he has with each client to optimize cooperation: is it *a visitor relationship*, a *complainant relationship*, or a *customer relationship*?

Therapists may also ask scaling questions about motivation, for example, "On a scale from ten to zero, where ten means you will do everything possible to achieve your preferred future and zero means that you will only hope and pray, where would you say you are today? How come you are at that point (and not lower)? What will one point higher look like? What will be different in your life? What will you be doing differently? Who and/or what might help you to get to one point higher on that scale?"

PRETREATMENT CHANGE

Studies done by Miller and colleagues (1997) show that 15 to 66 percent of clients experience positive treatment-related gains prior to the formal initiation of treatment (*pretreatment change*). Simply scheduling an appointment may help set the wheel of change in motion and present the possibility for an emergent story of competence and mastery.

Shining a spotlight on change illuminates existing client resources and allows their enlistment. A change-focus requires that the therapist believes in the certainty of change and creates a context in which to welcome, explore, and develop new or different perspectives and behaviors. Of special interest is what clients have done to bring about this change and how clients make sense of it all. Questions about pretreatment change include:

- "Between the time you made the appointment for this therapy and our first session today, what has gotten better (even just a little bit)?"
- "Between the time you made the appointment and our first session today, what have you noticed about your situation that is already different?"

- "How were you able to do that?"
- "What will help you to experience more of that?"
- "As you continue to do these things, what difference will that make to you (or important others)? How will your day go better?"
- "What are these positive changes saying about you as a person?"

FINDING EXCEPTIONS

As noted above, SF therapists Walter and Peller (2000) began to think that "the assumption *change is occurring all the time* might be a more useful starting point than *behavior is constant and repetitious.*"

Also, as mentioned in Chapter 3, Wittgenstein (1968) stated that the aspects of things that are most important for us are hidden because of their simplicity and familiarity. Consequently, one does not need to dig deep to find exceptions: They lie at the surface, but clients tend to pass them over, because they feel the problem *is always happening.* It is the task of therapists to help their clients find these exceptions and to amplify them, so that these exceptions may start to make a difference in their lives. Therefore, *exception-finding questions* are another useful way to focus on what works. These kinds of questions are new to many clients (not to mention therapists), and they may start noticing the exceptions for the first time. Solutions are often built from formerly unrecognized *positive differences*. One can distinguish between exceptions pertaining to the desired outcome (the goal) and exceptions pertaining to the problem (see Appendix B).

- *Questions to find exceptions pertaining to the goal:* "When have you already seen glimpses of what you would like to be different in your life? When was the last time you noticed this? What was it like? What was different then?"
- *Questions to find exceptions pertaining to the problem:* "When was the problem less severe? When was the problem not there for a short period of time? When was there a moment you were able to cope a little bit better?"

STORY 22. *Positive Differences*

A small boy was picking something up and gently throwing it into the ocean. A man approached the boy and asked, "What are you doing?" The boy replied, "I am saving the starfish that have been stranded on the beach. The tide is going out and if I don't throw them back they will die."

The man noticed that there were miles and miles of beach and thousands of starfish. He looked at the beach again and then at the boy and said, "Well, you won't make much of a difference, will you?"

After listening politely, the little boy bent down, picked up another starfish, and threw it back into the sea. Then, looking up, he smiled and said to the man, "I made a difference for that one!"

—Author unknown

Exceptions to the problem can be found in any symptom within the four clusters of the PTSD spectrum in the DSM-5: reexperiencing of the traumatic event, avoidance of stimuli associated with the trauma, negative cognitions and mood, and symptoms of increased arousal. Pertinent exception-finding questions include:

- "When was there a situation where you did not reexperience a part of the traumatic event, even though you expected you would?"
- "When have you felt somewhat better lately?"
- "Which nights in the past few weeks were somewhat better (you slept better, had fewer nightmares, etc.)?"
- "When were you able to feel more relaxed, even just a little bit?"
- In the case of self-mutilation: "When in the last few weeks did you not hurt yourself, even though you thought you would?"
- "When do you feel a bit more connected to others and the world?"

Exceptions to the problem can be either deliberate or spontaneous. If the exceptions are deliberate, clients can make them happen again. If the exceptions are spontaneous, clients can discover more about them by, for example, monitoring them or trying to predict them.

Having heard and explored these exceptions, therapists can then compliment their clients for all the things they have already done and ask competence questions, inviting their clients to *relate their success stories*:

1. "How did you do that?"
2. "How did you decide to do that?"
3. "How did you manage to do that?"

The first question assumes that clients have done something and therefore supposes action, competence, and responsibility. The second question assumes that clients have taken an active decision, affording them the opportunity to write a new life story that will influence their own future. The third question invites clients to relate their successes.

Lamarre and Gregoire (1999) described a technique called *competence transference* in which they invited clients to talk about other areas of competence in their lives, such as a sport or a hobby or a special talent. They then asked clients to bring those abilities to bear in order to reach their goals. For instance, they described how a client suffering from a panic disorder learned to relax by applying his knowledge of deep-sea diving whenever he experienced anxiety.

CASE 18. *Competence Transference*

Here is an example of competence transference. A client had for years suffered from the severe mood swings of her husband, a war veteran with PTSD. She had tried everything but without success. As a horse trainer, she had a special talent for training supposedly untamable horses. When asked the secret of her success, she replied that she always rewarded the horse for its achievements, even if the results were minimal. She also explained that she resisted disciplining the horse or becoming angry and abandoning it. At that point she would stop for the day, offer the horse a sugar cube, and try again the next day. In answering the question, the client realized that she could use her talent in precisely the same way when dealing with her husband's mood swings.

More questions for finding exceptions (Bannink, 2010a) include:

- "What has changed since you made an appointment for this session?"
- "What has already been going better since you made this appointment?"
- "What is better already?"
- "What is working?"
- "What have you tried, and which of those things helped, even if only a little bit?"
- "Of all the things you did, what helped the most?"

- "What else has helped so far?"
- "At what times do you already see parts of your preferred future?"
- "What is different about those times?"
- "What successes have you had in the past?"
- "In what situations do you feel somewhat better?"
- "How is that new for you?"
- "When was the last time you had a good day?"
- "When did you manage to behave in a way that was consistent with how you would like to be?"
- "Think back to a moment in the past week (month, year) when the problem was absent or was less of a problem. What was that moment? What are you doing differently then?"
- "When is the problem not a problem? What are you doing differently then?"
- "When is the problem not a problem for other people? What are they doing differently then? What is different then?"
- "When is the problem still there, but you manage to suffer less from it? What is different then?"
- "Suppose you *could* think of an exception. What might it be?"
- "What happens when the issue starts to become less of a problem or when things are going a little better?"

Appendix D offers an Exceptions Journal.

STORY 23. *The Bright Spots*

Vietnam invited Save the Children to fight malnutrition, result of huge problems: poverty, ignorance, poor sanitation, and lack of clean water. According to StC, these problems were "TBU": True But Useless. The kids couldn't wait for those problems to be solved.

StC met with local mothers in rural villages, measured their children and found kids who were healthier. They searched for bright spots: people whose behavior created better results, using the same resources. "Bright spot" mothers fed kids more meals per day (using the same amount of food). Healthy kids were actively fed, while unhealthy kids ate on their own. These mothers collected shrimps from the rice fields (adult food) and sweet potato greens (low-class food), making their kids' meal more nutritious.

StC ensured that the solution was native: the mothers spread the

Exercise 39. WHAT HAVE YOU DONE TODAY THAT IS GOOD FOR YOU?

Most clients will tell you about things they have done that are not good for them, like drinking too much alcohol, ruminating, or quarreling with their partner. For a change, ask clients what they have done today that is good for them. Invite them to come up with at least four things:

- "What have you done (so far) today that is good for you?"
- "What else have you done that is good for you?"
- "What else?"
- "What else?"

These questions can also be asked at the end of the session ("What have you done in this session that is good for you?"). Other questions are "What will you do during the rest of the day that is good for you?" and "What have you done today (or what will you do today) that is good for the relationship with important others: your partner, kids, family, or friends?" This exercise can also be part of a homework assignment: Invite clients to keep a journal in which every day they write down four things they have done that are good for them (and/or others).

Exercise 40. FIFTY POSITIVE THINGS TO PROMOTE WELL-BEING

Do you remember the song "Fifty Ways to Leave Your Lover" by Paul Simon? For many clients, making lists is fun and challenging at the same time. Below are fifty (5 x 10) positive things that promote well-being. It's also nice to hear which fifty positive things important others come up with when they do the exercise.

1. Name ten positive characteristics of yourself.
2. Name ten successes in your life.
3. Name ten ways you are kind to others.
4. Name ten windfalls in your life.
5. Name ten ways in which you are supported by others.

new behaviors to other villages. After six months, 65 percent of the kids were better nourished; the program reached 2.2 million people. StC didn't have the answers when they started, but they had a deep faith in finding the bright spots.

—Heath and Heath, 2010, pp. 27–32

REINFORCING WHAT WORKS

Clients have personal qualities and past experiences that, if drawn upon, can be of great use in resolving difficulties and creating more satisfying lives. These qualities, such as a sense of humor, resilience, and caring for others, are your clients' strengths. Useful past experiences are those in which the clients thought about or actually did something that might be put to use in therapy. These experiences are your clients' past successes.

Giving compliments to clients for their strengths, qualities, and past successes—a means of positive reinforcement—is a powerful tool and is widely used in positive CBT. Cialdini (1984) stated that giving compliments relates to two *weapons of influence*: reciprocation and liking. If you give compliments, chances are that the other person will be nicer too, because people who provide praise are liked better and because the rule of reciprocation will oblige the other person to do so. Cialdini cited a study done on men in North Carolina. The men in the study received comments about themselves from another person who needed a favor from them. Some of the men received only positive comments, some received only negative comments, and some received both. There were three interesting findings: First, the men liked the evaluator who provided only praise best. Second, this was the case even though the men fully realized that the man who provided praise stood to gain from their liking him. Finally, unlike the other types of comments, pure praise did not have to be accurate to work. That is, positive comments produced just as much liking for the person who provided praise when they were untrue as when they were true.

Research by Arts, Hoogduin, Keijsers, Severeijnen, and Schaap (1994) showed that systematic use of compliments in therapy not only ensured a positive alliance between therapists and clients but also enhanced the outcome of psychotherapy no less than 30 percent compared to psychotherapy in which compliments were not given.

There are three different types of compliments. A *direct* compliment is a positive evaluation or reaction by the therapist in response to the client. It can be about something the client has said, done, or made or about his or her appearance. A compliment can also be about the client's strengths or resources: "You must be a really caring mother to _____; tell me more about that" or "You must be a very determined person; please tell me more about this determination of yours."

An indirect compliment is a question that implies something positive about the client. One way to indirectly compliment is to ask for more information about a desired outcome stated by the client. These kinds of questions invite clients to tell a success story about themselves: "How did you do this? How were you able to do it? Where did you get this great idea?" Indirect complimenting is preferable to direct complimenting because its questioning format leads clients to discover and state their own strengths and resources.

A *positive character interpretation* is a question that implies that clients have a positive character trait (e.g., are caring, courageous, or determined).

When working with several people at once, it is very important to give everyone an equal share of the compliments. Compliments can be given to each person individually or to everyone together, such as, "Apparently you all succeeded in the past to work together in a pleasant way. Please tell me how you were able to do that." This form of indirect complimenting is often preferable to direct complimenting because its questioning format leads clients to discover and state their own strengths and resources.

Many clients accept compliments easily, while others downplay or even reject them. But remember that the first goal in giving compliments is for clients to notice positive changes, strengths, and resources; it is not necessary for them to openly accept the compliments. Author and psychotherapist Yalom (2008) posed a question about what it is that clients remember when they look back on their therapy years later. Generally, it is not the insights they had or the analyses the therapist made. According to Yalom, clients remember the positive and supportive remarks of the therapist the most.

From an SF point of view, clients are invited to do more of what works and to stop doing what does not work and do something else instead. Therapists should do the same: They should give positive reinforcement of everything that is working for the client and stop reinforcing what is not working by ceasing to pay attention to what was not helpful. In learning theory terms, this implies that they should give verbal and nonverbal positive reinforcement for what works and verbal and nonverbal negative punishment (or nonreward) for what is not working—for example, by reinforcing solutions-talk and not rewarding problem-talk (see Chapter 7).

In the next chapter we will look at ways to work on the progress made by clients. The role of therapists is to find useful change and amplify it, whether in thoughts, behaviors, or feelings.

Exercise 41. THREE COMPLIMENTS

At the next session, give your client at least three compliments and notice how the atmosphere of the conversation changes. Give your client a *direct compliment* about something he said, made, or did, or about his appearance. Or give your client an *indirect compliment* by asking a competence question like "How did you manage to do this?" Competence questions are aimed at eliciting a success story. Your compliment may also take the form of a *positive character interpretation*, such as "From what you told me, I get the impression that you must be a very caring person; is that correct?"

SUMMARY

- From a solution-building point of view, the focus is on what works for this client at this moment in this context.
- The focus on what works may start with the assessment of strengths and resources. The VIA test is a good way to assess personal values and strengths.
- Gratitude, self-compassion, and mindfulness are important qualities to enhance.
- Another useful way of finding out what works is by assessing progress, motivation, hope, and confidence, using scaling questions to invite clients to put their observations, impressions, and predictions on a scale from ten to zero.
- Questions about pretreatment change and exception-finding questions are useful.
- Therapists should reinforce what works for their clients by paying them compliments and asking competence questions.

CHAPTER 7

●●●●●●●●●●●●

Focus on Progress

It is said that change happens from desperation or inspiration. Most people would rather move toward change and growth out of inspiration than out of desperation, but times of desperation can motivate people to start working on the changes needed to increase their well-being. But working on progress is not easy. Many clients feel pessimistic or believe that their problems are insurmountable. Some stay stuck in the *victim mode*; others want effortless change or accept negative events, as they believe they are fated to experience them. Some clients may think that insight is sufficient to promote change, even though it is their willingness to find ways to reach their goals and their perseverance to continue despite setbacks that allows them to see themselves as stronger than they previously imagined themselves to be. Edison (1847–1931) stated that our greatest weakness lies in giving up, and that the most certain way to succeed is always to try just one more time (as cited in Clark, 1977).

According to Darwin, it is not the strongest of the species that survives, nor the most intelligent, but rather the one most adaptable to change. Indeed, change is happening all the time; stability is an illusion. The role of therapists is *to find useful change and amplify it*.

In this chapter, methods of changing clients' viewpoints, behaviors, and feelings are described in detail, using strengths-and-solutions-talk instead of problem-talk. The importance of language is stressed. Progress in therapy can be made through inviting clients to rewrite their negative stories into positive ones or to use positive imagery. There are many ways to help clients change their perspective. Shifting repetitive patterns or noticing what clients do when things are going better brings about behavior change. Feelings can be changed by reducing negative emotions and building positive ones; this also works in the medical setting.

Exercise 42. WORKING ON PROGRESS

Invite clients to answer these two simple questions. Progress in therapy may occur sooner and be more effective than you and your clients thought possible.

1. "How can you continue using what is already working for you?"
2. "How can you do more of this?"

—Author unknown

PROBLEM-TALK VERSUS STRENGTHS-AND-SOLUTIONS-TALK

Clients often want to talk about their problems. Many clients (and therapists) still assume that therapists need to know about the problem before they can help solve it. Some models in psychotherapy say clients need to talk about their problems as a way of discharging their strong negative feelings. However, the SF approach argues that when clients are enabled to talk about their best hopes for the future and their successes in dealing with things in the past and present, their apparent need to talk about their problems and discharge their negative emotions often disappears. If they wish to talk more about their problems, therapists can listen some more until clients are ready to shift from *problem-talk* to *strengths-and-solutions-talk* (see Table 3). The simplest way to assess their readiness is by giving them a brief acknowledgment of what they are going through and then asking an SF question. For example, the therapist might say, "So you've been having this terrible time lately. I'm wondering how you've managed to survive it and still get to this session?" If the client responds constructively to this question, the therapist and client can proceed with a solution-focused dialogue. Otherwise, the therapist needs to persevere with more acknowledgment. A relevant question might be, "How long (or how many sessions) do you think you will need to talk about your trauma or problem before you are ready to talk about your preferred future and solutions?"

As stated before, asking about *exceptions* in the present or in the past is a useful way of asking about positive differences and enhances strengths-and-solutions-talk. Scaling questions (e.g., "What is different between a four and five on the scale of progress?") can also be used to find *differences that make a difference*.

TABLE 3. Differences Between Problem-Talk and Strengths-and-Solutions-Talk.	
Problem-Talk . . .	**Strengths-and-Solutions-talk . . .**
Focuses on problems, what the person does not want, the causes of problems, negative affect, disadvantages, risks, deficits and weaknesses, failures, and the feared future	Focuses on what the person wants, exceptions to problems, positive affect, advantages, chances, strengths and resources, successes, and the preferred future
Ergo: less creativity, flexibility, and empathy	Ergo: more creativity, flexibility, and empathy

---

STORY 24. *The Dog I Feed Most*

A Native American elder once described his own inner struggle. "Inside of me there are two dogs. One of the dogs is mean and evil; the other dog is good. The mean dog fights the good dog all the time." When his grandson asked him which dog wins, he reflected for a moment and then replied, "The dog I feed most."

—Author unknown

When clients have a clear sense of what they want to achieve (their goal), and when they have already been able to achieve to what they want (the exceptions) to some extent, it will usually be relatively easy for them to choose the next steps forward. Rothman (2000) found that the decision criteria that lead people to *initiate a change* in their behavior are different from those that lead them to *maintain that behavior* (see Chapter 9). Decisions regarding behavioral initiation depend on favorable expectations regarding future outcomes, whereas decisions regarding behavioral maintenance depend on perceived satisfaction with received outcomes. Also, a comparison with the preferred situation is particularly beneficial and motivating at the start of the therapy, but during the therapy the client will become more motivated to continue when making regular comparisons between his or her current state and what was going on in the past before changes were initiated. As shown in Story 25, people find it more motivating to be partly finished with a longer journey than to be at the starting gate of a shorter one.

STORY 25. *At the Car Wash*

A carwash ran a promotion featuring loyalty cards. Eight stamps got customers a free wash. Others needed to collect ten stamps, but were given a "head start" of two. The goal was the same, but the psychology was different: In one case, you're 20 percent of the way; in the other case, you're starting from scratch. Some months later, 19 percent of the eight-stamp customers earned a free wash versus 34 percent of the head-start group (and this group earned the free wash faster).

—Heath and Heath, 2010, pp. 126–127

This experiment shows that people find it more motivating to be partly finished with a longer journey than to be at the starting point of a shorter one. To motivate action is to make people feel as though they're closer to the finish line than they might have thought.

Exercise 43. WHAT DIFFERENCE WILL THAT MAKE?

Invite clients to think of something they would like to change. Then ask, "Supposing things could change, what difference would that make? What else will be different? What else? What will be different for others who are important to you? How will your reactions to these people who are important to you be different?" Asking these questions about *positive differences* ensures that clients will come up with more things than you and they imagined they would.

THE IMPORTANCE OF LANGUAGE

Communication is the tool of therapy just as physical instruments are the tools of surgery, and it is incumbent on us to treat therapeutic communication equally carefully and precisely (Bavelas, Coates, & Johnson, 2000). *Microanalysis* of dialogue aims for a detailed and replicable examination of observable communication sequences between therapists and clients as they proceed, moment by moment, in a dialogue, with an emphasis on the function of these sequences within the dialogue. Two tools are observed in analysis of video recordings of the dialogues: analysis of *formulations* and analysis of *questions*. Formulations are a way for therapists to display their understanding of what a client has said:

- The client presents information ("I don't know what to do anymore").
- The therapist displays his understanding with a formulation ("Do you mean you are at your wit's end?").
- The client acknowledges, explicitly or implicitly, that the formulation is a correct understanding (or not) ("Yes, that's right").

Another tool is the analysis of how questions function (intentionally or not) as therapeutic interventions. The impact of a question begins with its (often implicit) presuppositions, assumptions that form the background of the question. Questions from different therapeutic approaches demonstrate how the therapist's story shapes these presuppositions. In a problem-focused (CBT) conversation, the question might be, "Could you please tell me more about the problem you want to address today?" whereas in an SF conversation the question might be, "What will be the best result of our meeting today?"

The content of each question or formulation could be positive, negative, or neutral.

Bavelas and colleagues (2000) used microanalysis to analyze expert sessions on SFBT and client-centered therapy (De Shazer and Berg for SFBT; Rogers and Raskin for CCT). Results showed that the SF- and client-centered experts differed in how they structured the sessions. The client-centered therapists used formulations almost exclusively; that is, they responded to clients' contributions. SF experts used both formulations and questions; that is, they both initiated and responded to client contributions. The experts also differed in the tenor of their contributions: The SF therapists' questions and formulations were primarily positive, whereas those of the client-centered therapists were primarily negative and rarely neutral or positive.

Positive therapist content includes question, statements, formulations, or suggestions by therapists that focus their clients on some positive aspect of the client's life (e.g., a relationship, trait, or experience in the past, present, or future). Positive client content includes questions, statements, formulations, or suggestions by clients that focus on some positive aspect of their life. Negative therapist or client content is the opposite of positive content.

Another finding is that when therapists' utterances are positive, clients are more likely to say something positive, whereas when therapists' utterances are negative, clients are more likely to say something negative.

Smock, Froerer, and Bavelas (in press) compared positive versus negative content in three SFBT and three CBT expert sessions (one of the CBT therapists was Meichenbaum). The content of the SFBT therapists was significantly more positive and less negative that that of the CBT therapists. Across all of the therapists, the clients responded in kind; that is, positive talk led to more positive talk and negative talk led to more negative talk. Thus, a therapist's use of positive content seems to contribute to the co-construction of a positive session overall, whereas negative content does the reverse. The third finding was that, as a group, the SFBT experts were all consistently more positive than negative, whereas the CBT experts differed widely among themselves (Franklin et al., 2012).

Exercise 44. OPENING SENTENCE

Think about what opening sentence you usually start a first session with. You may opt for a problem-focused question: "What is the problem?" or "What is bothering you?" You may choose a neutral question: "What brings you here?" You may opt for a question that implies that you will work hard: "What can I do for you?" Or you may choose an SF question: "What is the purpose of you visit?" or "What needs to be accomplished by the end of this session (or this therapy) so that you can say that coming to see me was useful?" Or, "What would you like to see different in your life?" Or, "What would you like to see instead of the problem?" Or you may ask the *miracle question* (see Chapter 5). Try out all these possibilities and note the differences in your clients' reactions and the differences in the mood of the sessions.

Microanalysis can complement outcomes research by providing evidence of what therapists do in their sessions and how the co-constructive nature of language is important in dialogues. Co-constructing a dialogue may even be compared to a dance, or a duet between therapist and client. Some useful ideas for paying more attention to language are:

- Change *if* into *when*: "If I get out of this depression, I will be able to do what I want" > "When I get out of this depression, I will be able to do what I want."
- Change *can't* into *not yet*: "I can't stop drinking" > "I haven't stopped drinking yet."
- Move problems from internal to external: "I am depressed" > "Depression has been visiting me for a while," or "I am a negative person" > "Negativity speaks to me regularly, and mostly I listen to what it says."
- Use the past tense when talking about problems and the future tense when talking about what clients want to be different in their lives: "So until now you have not been able to have a steady relationship. How will your life look like when you have a girlfriend?"

CHANGING POINT OF VIEW

If clients are not happy or are not getting the results they want, they will need to do something different. In changing the point of view, therapists need to focus on *changing how clients think and what they pay attention to.*

According to O'Hanlon (2000) this may involve five things. Feelings and the past need to be acknowledged without letting them determine what clients can do. Clients may change what they are paying attention to in a problem situation. Directing their attention to past or present successes instead of their failures generates a positive expectation of change and clients can begin to see themselves or the situation in a more positive light. The clients' attention may be directed to what they like to see different in the future, rather than on what they do not like in the present or the past. Their unhelpful beliefs about themselves and the situation may be challenged; the meaning of what happened to them may be changed, using different perspectives. Clients may start rewriting their negative stories into (more) positive ones. Also a spiritual perspective to help clients transcend their troubles and to draw on resources beyond their usual abilities may be helpful

Rewriting Stories

There are three *narratives* (stories) available to people describing and evaluating their own and other people's lives. These narratives are:

1. *Progressive narratives* that justify the conclusion that people and situations are progressing toward the person's goals.
2. *Stability narratives* that justify the conclusion that life is unchanging.
3. *Digressive narratives* that justify the conclusion that life is moving away from the person's goals.

Progressive and solution-determined narratives are more likely than complaint-centered narratives to produce transformations and discontinuities (De Shazer, 1991).

Although people cannot turn back the hands of time, they can, fortunately, edit the narratives or stories about their future self. Therapists can help clients change their negative stories to positive stories by first acknowledging the impact of the problem and the facts of the situation instead of evaluating, judging, or explaining. They can then invite clients to find evidence that contradicts the unhelpful problem stories, and clients can be reminded that whatever story they have, that story is not all there is to them. Creating compassionate and helpful stories and finding a kinder, gentler view of oneself, the other, and/or the situation is very helpful for clients, especially trauma survivors (Gilbert, 2010; O'Hanlon, 1999).

According to O'Hanlon (1999) there are four types of negative stories that can be changed to *positive stories*. These negative stories are:

- *Blame stories:* someone is bad or wrong, has bad intentions, or gets the blame for the problem.
- *Impossibility stories:* change is seen as impossible.
- *Invalidation stories:* someone's feelings, thoughts, or actions are seen as wrong or unacceptable.
- *Unaccountability stories:* people claim that they are under the control of other people or some other factor beyond their control.

Exercise 45. POSITIVE BLAME

This exercise is an example of how negative stories can be changed to positive ones. Most clients talk about blame in a negative sense. They have probably never heard of the concept of positive blame and are surprised when their therapist asks what they are to blame for in a positive way. When therapists ask clients for exceptions to the problem, past successes, or present solutions, they are using a form of positive blame. How were you able to do that? How did you decide to do that? How did you come up with that great idea? The hidden message behind these competence questions is that clients have achieved a degree of capability and that—if appropriate—this success may be repeated.

Exercise 46. FIRST SMALL CHANGE IN FEELING GUILTY

Invite clients who feel guilty to answer the following question: "You're feeling very guilty, but what do you think will be the first small change in your thinking—that maybe, just maybe, this wasn't entirely your fault? That you did the best you could do under the circumstances?"

Or ask, "Could someone else have acted the same way?" This is a good question for helping clients to stop second-guessing and criticizing themselves for something that has happened and is spilled milk anyway.

CASE 19. *February Man*

Erickson described the story of Mary in his and Rossi's book *February Man* (1989). Using hypnosis, Mary was regressed to the age of six, when a traumatic incident had happened. Her little sister had climbed fully clothed into a bathtub filled with water. Mary had tried to pull her sister out, with the result that her sister rolled under the water and nearly drowned. Mary shouted for her mother, who came running and grabbed the little girl, who was already turning blue. Mary still felt guilty and anxious when these memories were evoked.

Mary told Erickson this story with tears in her eyes. Erickson started by affirming Mary's actions: "You saw that your sister was in danger and you tried to get your mother to come to rescue her. You could not help losing your grip because you did not have enough strength to pull her out, but you acted cleverly in quickly calling your mother for help." Little Mary felt better as soon as she saw the incident with new eyes, and her *blame story* changed. Erickson used several of these kinds of encounters with Mary at different stages of her life, comforting her and sympathizing with her various painful childhood experiences.

The present and future determine how we look at our past. It is said that "it is never too late to have a happy childhood." Furman (1998), an SF psychiatrist, asked readers of several Finnish magazines who had endured difficult childhoods to reply to three questions related to their experiences:

1. "What helped you survive your difficult childhood?"
2. "What have you learned from your difficult childhood?"
3. "In what way have you managed in later life to have the kind of experiences that you were deprived of as a child?"

The nature of the replies convinced Furman of the ability of human beings to survive almost any trauma. This gave him the belief that people can view their past—including even the most extreme suffering—as a source of strength rather than of weakness.

> Our past is a story we can tell ourselves in many different ways. By paying attention to methods that have helped us survive, we can start respecting ourselves and reminisce about our difficult past with feelings of pride rather than regret. (Furman, 1998, p. 56)

Asking clients questions about how they survived and what strengths, resources, and competencies they used sometimes renders exposure to the negative past unnecessary.

According to Furman (1998), it's natural to think that our past has an effect on how our future will turn out, but we rarely look at it the other way around. When we've seen and enjoyed a movie but our friends later criticize it, our friends' opinion is likely to influence our perception of the film. Similarly, the present and our hopes for the future determine what our past looks like. This means that if we are depressed, the past appears darker, whereas if we are in love, it appears brighter. Therefore, it might be helpful for clients to ask their therapist the following question prior to therapy: "How will I view my past once we are finished here?"

CASE 20. *What Helped You Survive?*

A client told his therapist in a weary voice that, because of his depressive moods, she was the fourth therapist he had consulted over a period of about fifteen years. He had seen a psychoanalytic therapist for three years, he had been in client-centered group therapy for two years, and he had done extensive bodywork. But despite taking antidepressant medication, which had proved to be of little help, he was still suffering from severe depressive episodes.

The therapist asked him, "What do you think helped you survive your difficult childhood?" The client answered that he had never thought of it this way. He had always seen himself as a victim of his aggressive and abusive father, with no control over the situation. He discovered that he actually *had* done something active: He had tried to stay away from home as long and as much as possible, and he had found refuge with the parents of his school friend. For the first time in the client's life, the realization that he had actually achieved something in staying safe and escaping his father transformed his vision of himself from victim to (partly) successful survivor. This change in vision enhanced his self-efficacy and generated further positive emotions.

Clients who have gone through terrible events may see themselves as a *victim* or as a *survivor* (or even a *thriver*). If they see themselves as a victim, it becomes more difficult to play an active role in shaping their life. Clients who seem themselves as victims feel that they were unable to do anything about what has happened to them, and they expect that they cannot change much about the way the rest of their life pans out. They probably feel powerless and feel that they have lost control. However, when clients see themselves as survivors, the possibility of a more active role becomes apparent, offering them the opportunity to organize and take control of their life despite what they have experienced. This initiates a spiral of positivity and more control.

Rubin (1996) interviewed people who as children had endured traumatic experiences. In looking at their inner strengths and the qualities that had enabled them to overcome these experiences and also at the strategies and adaptations they had used to that effect, Rubin found that the survivors had actually changed very little. Still present was their ability to cope with pain, which prevented it from becoming overwhelming, as was their ability to withdraw when the outside pressure became too high. Proficiency in finding other sources of support was still present in their later lives, as was their ability to feel involved in something beyond them, which was reflected in their need to feel useful—for example, by helping others who were having similar experiences. The determination and resilience with which they had overcome obstacles as children persisted as they worked toward their goals as adults. This was particularly visible in their refusal to perceive themselves as victims, despite the hardships of their lives. They rejected the culture of victimization, because they saw it as a trap for those who believe in it. Although traumatic events might have determined their pasts, these survivors refused to let them dominate the present: "This is what has *happened* to me, not what I *am*."

Exercise 47. VICTIM OR SURVIVOR

There is a saying: "This is the first day of the rest of your life." The following four-step exercise can help clients to find out which role they want to play in the rest of their lives, that of victim or that of survivor (or thriver).

1. "How would you like to see your life in a month's time? The same people and circumstances are still present, but you feel a little less influenced by what you have experienced."
2. "If you think about your answer to the previous question— that is, your goal in a month's time—how will you think and feel and behave in order to reach your goal if you see yourself as a victim?"
3. "Answer the same question, but now from the perspective of a survivor (or even thriver)."
4. "What differences do you notice? Which attitude is the most helpful to you?"

Dolan (1998) stated that overcoming the immediate effects of abuse, loss, or other trauma and viewing oneself as a survivor rather than as a victim are helpful steps, but are ultimately not sufficient to help people fully regain the ability to live a life that is as compelling, joyous, and fulfilling as it used to be. People who remain at the survivor stage see life through the window of their survivorhood rather than enjoying the more immediate and unobstructed vision of the world around them that they previously held. All experiences are evaluated in terms of how they resemble, differ from, mitigate, or compound the effects of past events. This diminishes their ability to fully experience and enjoy life and is responsible for the flatness and depression reported by many people who categorize themselves as survivors. In this vein, a third position may be added to Exercise 47: the position of a *thriver*. This position signifies that the trauma doesn't define the person any longer and has just become one part of who he or she is. For this purpose, Dolan's *therapeutic resolving letters* may be useful (see Chapter 8).

As mentioned previously, it is helpful for clients to ask their therapists the following question at the start of the therapy: "How will I view my past once we are finished here?" Another way to stabilize a new direction in clients' lives opens up when therapists invite their clients to *construct the history of their solutions*—before the change actually takes place (George, 2010). This change of affairs often takes a shorter route than talking about the past is likely to take.

To facilitate this new direction, therapists may ask their clients, "What has it taken to make the changes that you have made in your life?" When the client responds by identifying personal qualities that he or she has drawn on, the therapist may inquire, "When else in the past have you seen yourself drawing on those qualities in a way that is useful to you?" Beyond this, therapists can invite clients to adopt the wisdom of *hindsight*: "Having made these changes, looking back to the time before the change, what tells you that you always did have the capacity to make these changes?" The changes can be rooted into the client's history through the eyes of supportive others: "Of all those who have known you in your past, who would be least surprised by the changes that you have made? And what is it that those people knew that others perhaps did not about you and your possibilities?"

Positive Imagery
Positive imagery can be created or enhanced in therapy. The use of imagery has a long history, and there is evidence of the significance of

imagery in a number of psychological disorders. Since its inception, cognitive therapy has emphasized the role of *mental imagery* (Beck, 1967). Contending that mental activity may take the form of words and phrases or images, Beck observed that affective distress can be directly linked to visual cognitions—as well as to verbal cognitions—and that modifying upsetting visual cognitions can lead to significant cognitive and emotional shifts. Imagery plays an important role in CBT interventions like systematic desensitization (SD) and flooding.

Imagery can be either positive or negative. From a problem-focused perspective, negative imagery can be removed or transformed, whereas from an SF perspective, positive imagery can be created or enhanced. Until recently, imagery in CBT was based on the problem-focused paradigm, but lately more positive forms of imagery are being developed. For example, research done by Vasquez and Buehler (2007) showed that imagining future success (*positive imagery*) enhances people's motivation to achieve it. Research shows that a positive image of oneself in the future motivates action by helping people to articulate their goals clearly and develop behaviors that will allow them to fulfill those goals. The very act of imagining future events not only makes those events seem more likely, but also helps to bring them about.

Intrusive images are very common in psychological disorders such as PTSD and are therefore an obvious target for imagery-based interventions. Additionally, clients often experience an absence of positive, adaptive imagery. For example, happy, predictive images of the future are often lacking in depression and generalized anxiety disorder (Hackmann, Bennett-Levy, & Holmes, 2011). A sound body of theory suggests the potential value of positive imagery interventions, and a growing empirical base derived from neuroscience, cognitive science, and sports psychology also supports this. For example, generating positive images has a powerful and positive impact on emotion and enhances goal-setting and skill development.

Hackmann and colleagues (2011) stated that positive imagery is one of the main psychological interventions in sports psychology, with an evidence base spanning several decades of research. Currently, there is little overlap between the sports psychology and traditional CBT imagery literature. In contrast to the CBT literature, imagery research in sports psychology has focused on positive imagery and paid little attention to negative imagery. The impression within the sports psychology literature is that negative imagery is an irritant to be circumvented; in contrast, CBT has paid little attention to the deliberate construction of positive images until recently. Maybe the reason for this difference is that sports psychology, in attempting to help athletes build better performances, never adopted a medical model from the outset.

Imagery rescripting (ImRs) is an imagery technique in which a distressing image is modified in some way to change associated negative thoughts, feelings, and behaviors. Arntz and Weertman (1999) described the use of imagery rescripting to treat psychological problems such as nightmares, PTSD, bereavement, intrusive images, and eating disorders.

One set of instructions for imagery rescripting in the treatment of nightmares is as follows: Choose a nightmare and modify it in *a positive way*; rehearse the modified nightmare for at least several minutes daily; and modify additional nightmares as necessary every three to seven days, rehearsing no more than one or two new dreams per week. Imagery rescripting is used not only to overcome problems but also to enable clients with a *positive* view of themselves and of their strengths to overcome other difficulties and to promote self-determination and well-being.

CASE 21. *Imagine the Scene Again*

A client who used imagery rescripting said that she imagined the scene again, just as it occurs in her flashbacks. Only this time, her adult self goes right over to the little girl (her), picks her up, and takes her away, saying soothing, kind words and holding her gently but firmly close. She is protecting her from her aggressive mother. She said that using imagery may sound crazy, but it feels great.

CASE 22. *Control Over Nightmares*

A client told her therapist that she had worked with another therapist to get over sexual abuse by using EMDR, writing letters to herself, and even having a conversation with her abuser. She and her therapist had thought she was doing fine, but then she started having nightmares, which she had never had before. The recurring nightmares were about something she had left behind in the abuser's home, but it was not clear to her what it was. In her dreams she was afraid that when the man found it, she would be very vulnerable and he could blackmail her.

The therapist complimented the client for noticing everything she had already done that had been helpful and for having the courage to talk with the man who had abused her. The therapist also reassured the client that all her work had not been done in vain. The therapist told her of a technique where more control over nightmares could be gained by modifying them in a positive way. Nightmares always stop at the scene that is most traumatic, because that is the moment when the person wakes up. The client was invited to rehearse the modified nightmare a couple of times a day, resulting in the nightmares gradually disappearing.

In CBT, *core beliefs* are challenged. These are central, absolute beliefs about oneself, others, and the world. People develop both positive and negative beliefs. Automatic thoughts and their underlying assumptions lead therapists and clients toward relevant core beliefs. The *downward arrow technique*, used in traditional CBT, is one of the ways to identify beliefs that underpin negative reactions to a given situation. Questions used in the downward arrow technique are:

- What does that matter?
- What is so bad about _____?
- What would be the worst-case scenario here?

The questions are repeated in response to each answer the client provides.

The *upward arrow technique*, which I introduced in *Practicing Positive CBT* and *Positive CBT* (Bannink, 2012a, 2013), is different in that the focus is on positive reactions to a given situation, or on exceptions to the problem. Questions used in the upward arrow technique are:

- "How would you like the situation (yourself, others) to be different?"
- "What will be the best outcome? What will be the *best-case scenario* here?"
- "Supposing that happens, what difference will that make to you? What difference will it make to others?"

These questions are repeated in response to each answer the client provides.

Exercise 48. THE UPWARD-ARROW TECHNIQUE

With a colleague, do the following exercise to experience the different effects of the downward and upward arrow techniques. Think about problems or worries in your life that are causing you concern. Invite your partner to spend some time posing a range of questions relating firstly to the downward arrow technique and then to the upward arrow technique. Discuss the differences you have noticed, both as an interviewer and as an interviewee. Now change roles. Which technique do you prefer?

Exercise 49. WORST CASE SCENARIO

Ask very pessimistic clients to imagine the worst-case scenario before a dreaded event takes place (e.g., your client is a soldier who is afraid to revisit the country where his best friend died from a bomb blast) and then compare what actually happens to this scenario to see if the two views even come close to each other (most of the time they don't).

Exercise 50. RAPID-FIRE FACTS

Rapid-Fire Facts is a CBT exercise designed to *challenge unhelpful beliefs*. In this exercise, clients rapidly fire contradicting positive facts at their negative thoughts as quickly as possible. Give them a pile of index cards and invite them to write down negative thoughts that pop into their mind, such as, "I can't do this" and "Nobody likes me." These negative sentences represent their inner critic that tries to undermine them. After they have written several of their regular negative thoughts on the cards, ask them to pick one up at random and read it out loud. Then invite them to rapidly dispute the negative belief with every argument they can come up with. When they run out of facts, ask them to pick another card and repeat the exercise. Coming up with contradictory facts will get easier and easier with each card. With this tool, clients become quick at contradicting their negative thoughts.

CHANGING PERSPECTIVE

According to Nietzsche, "being happy doesn't mean that everything is perfect. It means that you've decided to look beyond the imperfections." Inviting clients to change their perspective can be done in several ways. Clients may be invited to change the meaning of what happened to them. Another way is to construct descriptions of interactional events and their meaning by asking your clients relationship questions using different perspectives (see Appendix F). Yet another way to change the meaning of events is by inviting clients to look at themselves and the situation from the third-person perspective. Actions viewed from the third-person perspective are generally construed at a relatively high level of abstraction—in a manner that highlights their larger meaning and significance—which heightens their motivational impact. The fourth way to change perspectives is to *externalize the problem*. Clients are invited to see the problem as something separate from themselves that affects them but does not always control every aspect of their lives. The fifth way to change perspectives is to use a *spiritual perspective*, in which there are three sources of resilience: connection, compassion, and contribution. These five perspectives are described in detail below.

Changing the Meaning

In SFBT, the focus is on the preferred future (the goal of the clients), without therapists even having to know what the problem is (see Exercise 11). The solution is often not related to the problem. For that reason, some professionals don't talk about solutions, because this implies there is a problem. They use terms like *preferences* and *possibilities* instead (De Bono, 1985; O'Hanlon, 1999; Walter & Peller, 2000).

Dealing with the past without discussing it seems to many therapists to be just wrong. However, it is generally accepted that the events of the past cannot change, whatever clients may do in therapy. So all that can change is the *meaning* that the events have for the clients in the present and the expectation of the meaning that those events will hold for them in the future (the view of the problem). This struggle in *finding meaning* is the crucible of growth at the core of cognitive-emotional processing after trauma (Joseph & Linley, 2005).

One way to shift meaning is to talk with your clients about the events themselves. For example, in reference to sexual abuse, the shift from the idea that the abuse happened and that it was the client's fault to the idea that the abuse happened and that it was not the client's fault, has in itself had a major impact on the lives of many clients. However, a dramatic shift of meaning can often be achieved without talking about the trauma or the problem (George, 2010). As the client and therapist move forward together in therapy, the client develops a firm confidence that the future will continue to be satisfactory. In making this shift, the meaning of the trauma changes from something that determines the client's life minute by minute to an event that happened, should not have happened, and yet is no longer controlling the client. In the best possible way, the event has been marginalized; it has been *detoxified*. Two questions for inviting clients in this direction are:

1. "How will you know that what happened is no longer holding you back in your life?"
2. "How will you know that you are doing justice to yourself and your possibilities despite what was done to you?"

Exercise 51. DETOXIFY TRAUMATIC EVENTS

This is an exercise to *detoxify* traumatic events. When clients suffering from (symptoms of) PTSD are invited to draw a circle and then to draw a point that represents the most traumatic event in their life, they often draw this point right in the middle of the circle, symbolic of the central place of the event in their lives. Therapists may ask clients if they think putting the event in this central place is helpful, or if they think that, in a better future, the point would not be quite so central or would even be outside the circle.

For each point the client chooses, the therapist asks what difference that point makes for him or her and for important others. The therapist may also ask about helpful exceptions and how the client is or was able to bring them about.

Relationship Questions

Relationship questions invite clients to construct descriptions of interactional events as well as their meanings. Therapists find out who are their clients' significant others and weave them into the questions so as to encourage their clients to describe their situations and what they want to be different in interactional terms. These questions are a good way to invite clients to amplify their solutions. A relationship question might be: "Supposing the two of you got along a little bit better in the future, what would he notice that you do instead of losing your temper?" Or, "What will your children say is different when things are somewhat better?"

Walter and Peller (1992) introduced the *interactional matrix*. This matrix is a tool for facilitating the building of solutions from an interactional view and for inviting clients into areas of difference. Across the top of the matrix are the frames of "Goal," "Hypothetical Solution/ Miracle Question," and "Exception." Along the left side of the matrix are the different reporting positions for the question and response. The first is the *for-oneself* position. Questions from this position invite clients to answer using their own point of view. The next position is *for the other*. Questions from this position invite clients to answer questions as if they were listening and reporting for someone else. For example, in couples therapy, each partner is asked what he or she thinks the other partner will say about certain topics. To answer this question, clients have to suspend their own way of thinking for the moment and imagine the other's answer to the question. They have to put themselves in the other's shoes briefly or at least think of what the other person might say if he or she were responding to the question. This usually induces a search for new and perhaps different information.

Questions in the third row of the matrix originate from a *detached position*, that is, from someone who is detached from the problem and is merely observing. As an alternative, therapists might say, "If I were a

---

Exercise 52. INTERACTIONAL MATRIX

Do this exercise with a colleague or partner. Think of a situation in which you have a problem with another person (not your colleague/ partner!). Ask yourself every question from the interactional matrix, or let your partner ask you these questions. Keep the same order as in the matrix: from goals to hypothetical solutions to exceptions. Notice the differences in your reactions and how this changes your personal movie. Then choose the next row with another viewpoint and notice again how this changes your reaction. What differences do you notice in your personal movie? Which questions are most useful to you?

fly on the wall observing you, what will I see you doing differently when things are better?" Each row of the matrix invites clients into an area of experience different from their usual way of thinking.

CASE 23. *Suppose There Might Be Some Way Forward*

Following a traumatic incident at work in which a colleague was killed, the client, who works in an iron factory, expresses his belief that his work is too dangerous and that after the incident the working atmosphere is failing and beyond repair. He has no plans to return to work. Because of the situation, he has decided to stay at home, claiming sickness benefits. The therapist says, "Suppose there might still be some way forward for you. What might be the first small step that you could take or that you think others should take?"

The therapist also asks some questions from the interactional matrix:

- "What would you like to see different at your workplace [self-position]?"
- What will your wife say about what you will be doing differently that will allow her to say you are making progress [other position]?
- If I were a fly on the wall and I could see that there still remained a faint hope of the possibility of your returning to work, what differences in your behavior would I see [detached position]?

A Third-Person Perspective

Another useful perspective in therapy is the third-person perspective. A common goal of therapy is to change the self, so clients who visit a therapist should be particularly interested in assessing how they have changed since beginning treatment. Assessing change matters because it constitutes critical determinants of satisfaction and well-being (Carver & Scheier, 1998) and also guides future courses of action: "Am I getting any thinner?" or "Are we getting over the problems in our relationship?"

Self-change influences people's memory perspective. Third-person recall produces judgments of greater self-change when people are inclined to look for evidence of change, but lesser self-change when they are inclined to look for evidence of continuity. Research by Ross and Wilson (2002) shows that recalling an old, pre-change self from the third-person perspective helps to deal with the challenge of maintaining personal change. Greater perceived change leads to greater satisfaction with one's efforts thus far and therefore makes it easier to summon the resources necessary to maintain one's efforts. In sum, psychologically distancing oneself from negative past selves and remaining close to positive past selves promotes well-being.

Libby, Eibach, and Gilovich (2005) found that there are two ways of seeing oneself as successful: from the first-person perspective and from the third-person perspective. Libby and colleagues found that there is a much greater chance of continuing with desired behavior when one considers oneself from a third-person perspective. This theory builds on the research finding that we have a tendency to interpret the behavior of others as being indicative of their personality, whereas we tend to interpret our own behavior as being indicative of the situation we are in. Therefore, seeing ourselves from the third-person perspective, as an observer would, allows us to see that we are the sort of person who engages in that sort of behavior. Seeing oneself as the type of person who would engage in a desired behavior increases the likelihood of engaging in that behavior.

Vasquez and Buehler (2007) found that people feel more motivated to succeed on a future task when they visualize its successful completion from a third-person perspective rather than a first-person perspective. Actions viewed from the third-person perspective are generally construed at a relatively high level of abstraction—in a manner that highlights their larger meaning and significance—which heightens their motivational impact. They found that students experience a greater increase in achievement motivation when they imagine their successful task completion from a third-person perspective rather than from a first-person perspective. Moreover, research shows that third-person imagery boosts motivation by prompting students to construe their success abstractly and to perceive it as important.

Externalization of the Problem

Externalization of the problem can help clients change their perspective and see the problem as something separate from themselves that affects them, but does not always control every aspect of their lives. This intervention is retrieved from narrative therapy (White and Epston, 1990) and grants clients the freedom to separate themselves from their problematic self-image. In asking how the problem has affected their clients' lives and relationships, therapists offer their clients the opportunity to gain more control. The problem can be seen as something that lies outside the clients and usually has a negative influence on them. The problem is then seen as an *enemy* by both clients and the therapist and can be fought jointly. De Shazer (1984) stated that therapists and clients should be like tennis players on the same side of the net, with the problem as the opponent.

Externalizing the problem can also be brought about by drawing it or designing a symbol for it. Clients first give a name to the problem, like *Depression* or *Tension* or *Trauma*. A noun (*X*) is best for this. The question to the client is "How would you name the problem that bothers you?" Then questions are asked about the times when *X* is not there or is present to a lesser degree (exceptions) and what clients do to bring that about. Clients can also be asked to talk about the times when *X* is present and how they deal with it. Depending on the needs of the client, more or less time can be spent on finding out how *X* controls their lives. The competence of the clients can be highlighted, thereby increasing their confidence that more control is possible. Also, the tendency to blame someone else for the problem can be minimized as clients reap the benefits of collaboration in gaining control over *X*.

During each meeting, clients can indicate on a scale of ten to zero the extent to which the problem (X) has control over them: Ten means the problem has complete control over them and zero means they have complete control over the problem. It is apparent that in most cases the problem will more or less disappear as the control of the clients increases. Scaling questions for externalizing the problem include:

- "At what point of the ten to zero scale are you today?"
- "What point were you at least session?"
- (If the point this session is higher than it was last session) "How did you succeed in doing that?"
- (If the point this session is the same as it was last session) "How did you manage to maintain the same point? How come it is not lower?"
- (If the point is lower this session than it was last session) "What did you do earlier on to go ahead again? What have you done in the past in a similar situation that has been successful?"
- "What have significant others in your life noticed about you in the last week? How did that influence their behavior toward you?"
- "What are you doing together (as a couple, as a family) when X has control over you?"
- "How does X manage to do that?"
- "What do you do (differently) when you have control over X?"
- "What do you do when you are planning to attack X?"
- "How are you able to fool X?"

(See also Appendix E.)

Exercise 54. EXTERNALIZING THE PROBLEM

Invite clients to think of a current personal problem. What name would they give the problem? Discover what their realistic aim is. Where would they like to end up on the scale of control? Ask them where they are today: What is already working? Then ask what a higher point on the scale would look like. Finally, ask them how they think they can reach that higher point on the scale.

A Spiritual Perspective

As previously mentioned, the fifth way to change one's perspective is to use a *spiritual perspective*. O'Hanlon (1999) described the "three C's" of spirituality as sources of resilience. *Connection* means moving beyond your little, isolated ego or personality into connection with something bigger, within or outside yourself. *Compassion* means softening your attitude toward yourself or others by feeling yourself to be with rather than against yourself, others, or the world. *Contribution* means being of unselfish service to others or the world.

One of the twenty-four character strengths mentioned in Chapter 6 is spirituality (sense of purpose, faith, religiousness). (You have strong and coherent beliefs about the higher purpose and meaning of the universe. You know where you fit in the larger scheme. Your beliefs shape your actions and are a source of comfort to you.) Seligman (2011) stated that after a half-century of neglect, psychologists are again studying spirituality and religiosity in earnest, no longer able to ignore their importance to people of faith. Do you have an articulate philosophy of life, religious or secular, that locates your being in the larger universe? Does life have meaning for you by virtue of attachment to something larger than you are? There is now considerable evidence that a higher level of spirituality goes hand in hand with greater well-being, less mental illness, less substance abuse, and more stable marriages (Myers, 2000).

CHANGING BEHAVIOR

We know that constructive action is an antidote to despair. In changing behavior, instead of analyzing why the problem arose, clients can change what they are doing to solve it by determining the problem pattern and beginning to experiment with doing something different (breaking the pattern). Einstein (1954) said that *insanity is doing the same thing over and over again while expecting different results*.

Doing more of what is already working is another way of changing behavior. Remember: If something works (better), do more of it; if it does not work, do something else. Therefore, in changing the *doing of the problem*, the focus in therapy is on concrete actions that clients can take. Therapists help clients make these changes by doing two things:

- Paying attention to repetitive patterns that clients are caught up in or that others are caught up in with them and inviting

them to change anything possible about these patterns.
- Noticing what clients are doing when things are going better and inviting them to do more of that.

STORY 26. *For a Change, Do Something Different*

If you always do what you have always done,
You will always get what you've always got.
So for a change, do something different,
And do something different for a change.

Changing Repetitive Patterns

O'Hanlon (1999) states that most therapists have the idea that it takes years to make a significant change, especially with serious, long-standing problems, but that the SF approach has shown that people can make changes rapidly. The SF approach focuses on the present and the future and encourages clients to take action and change their viewpoint. The past is important in the sense that it has influenced clients and has brought them to where they are today, but letting it determine their future is a mistake. Instead, this approach suggests acknowledging the past and then getting on with changing things.

O'Hanlon offered three keys for breaking repetitive problem patterns. These keys are: (1) changing the doing of the problem; (2) using paradox; and (3) linking new actions to the problem pattern.

In changing the doing of the problem, any part of regularly repeated actions may be changed. Clients are invited to pay attention to what they usually do when the problem is present and do something else instead. For example, when clients feel depressed, instead of staying in bed, they might go outside and take a short walk.

In using paradox, invite clients to go with the problem or try to make it worse (more intense or more frequent), or ask them to try to deliberately make the problem happen. Or instead embrace the problem and allow it to happen. Invite clients to stop trying to fix the problem or make the situation better. This works best for emotional or bodily problems like insomnia, anxiety, phobias, panic, and sexual problems. For example, when clients are feeling anxious, instead of avoiding the situation, invite them to stay and use a mindfulness exercise instead and watch their anxiety come and go.

In linking new actions to the problem pattern, invite clients to do something they can do every time the problem is present—something that is good for them. Ask them to find something that they usually avoid or put off. When they feel the urge to do the problem, ask them to do this avoided action first. If they are not able to do that, do the avoided action for the same amount of time as the problem action, after the problem is over. Ask them to make the problem an ordeal by linking it to something that they find unpleasant. For example, when clients have had a few drinks too many, ask them to do some extra fitness exercises the next day.

Insight and Understanding

Instead of focusing on the inner life of clients and why the problems arose, invite clients to move into action. Research by Grant and O'Connor (2010) shows that problem-focused questions (e.g., "What exactly is your problem? What went wrong, and how is that affecting you?") reduce negative affect and increase self-efficacy, but do not increase understanding of the nature of the problem or enhance positive affect. SF questions (e.g., "What can you do to change the situation? How have you managed before?") increase positive affect, decrease negative affect, increase self-efficacy, and surprisingly increase participants' insight and understanding of the nature of the problem.

One of the differences between traditional approaches to trauma and the approach to trauma described in this book (see Table 1) is that in traditional forms of therapy, insight or understanding is often a precondition for change, whereas in reality insight or understanding may come during or after change and is not necessary for therapy to be successful (Klaver & Bannink, 2010). Therefore, *why questions* lead therapists and their clients in the wrong direction, seeking explanations and going over the same problem again and again. *What, how,* and *when* questions are often more productive.

STORY 27. Sail Away From the Safe Harbor

Twenty years from now, you will be more disappointed by the things that you did not do than by the ones you did do. So throw off the bowlines. Sail away from the safe harbor. Catch the trade winds in your sails. Explore. Dream. Discover.
—Twain, as quoted in Burns, Duncan, and Ward, 2001

Positive Addictions

We know that the key to building a new healthy habit is to practice the behavior, over and over. Aristotle (trans. 1998) stated, "We are what we repeatedly do. Excellence, then, is not an act but a habit." This works for building character strengths as well. Habits are those behaviors that have become automatic, triggered by a cue in the environment rather than by conscious will. When we think of habits, most of the time we think of bad ones: biting our fingernails, procrastinating, eating sweets when we are anxious, and so on. But of course we also have good habits: jogging or brushing our teeth. Therapists want to assist clients not only in breaking the repetitive pattern of unhealthy habits and negative addictions, but also in helping them building healthy habits and *positive addictions* instead.

How long does it take to build a healthy habit? Research on healthy habit formation (Lally, Jaarsveld, Potts, & Wardle, 2010) showed that early repetitions of the chosen behavior commonly produced the largest increases in its automaticity. Examples of healthy behavior or positive addictions include going for a fifteen-minute run before dinner, eating a piece of fruit with lunch, or doing fifty sit-ups after morning coffee. The average time to reach maximum automaticity was sixty-six days, much longer than most previous estimates of the time taken to acquire a new habit. Participants who chose exercise behaviors took about one and a half times as long to reach their automaticity plateau as participants who adopted new eating or drinking behaviors. Contrary to what was thought earlier, a single missed day had little impact on later automaticity gains.

Action Triggers

Gollwitzer (1999) found that making a *mental plan* is quite effective in motivating action. Setting *action triggers* implies that you have made the decision to execute a certain action (go jogging) when you encounter a certain situational trigger (tomorrow morning; coming home after work). Noticing in advance exactly when and where you intend to execute the action makes a huge difference. Gollwitzer argues that the value of action triggers resides in the fact that we are preloading a decision. Action triggers protect goals from tempting distractions, bad habits, or competing goals. In essence, action triggers create an *instant habit*. One study showed that the single biggest predictor of whether women gave themselves a monthly breast examination was whether

Invite clients who want to change their behavior to participate in an if-then training, based on *mental contrasting* (see Chapter 5). Ask them to write down three *if-then* assumptions:

- One to *overcome an obstacle*: If I feel exhausted after work, *then* I will put on my running shoes and go for a jog around the block.
- One to *prevent the obstacle*: If I hear the clock chime five, then I will pack my things and leave the office to go for a run.
- One to *identify a good opportunity to act*: *If* the sun is shining, *then* I will go for a thirty-minute jog in the park.

they had a habit of doing so. When another group of women who didn't have such a habit were asked to set action triggers, they ended up doing just as well as the women with longtime habits. By preloading a decision, they created an instant habit.

People can delegate the initiation of goal-directed behavior to environmental stimuli by forming *implementation intentions* (*if-then plans* of the format "If situation *X* is encountered, then I will perform behavior *Y*). Forming implementation intentions facilitates detecting, attending to, and recalling the critical situation. Moreover, in the presence of the critical situation, initiation of the specified goal-directed behavior is immediate and efficient and does not need conscious intent.

Noticing What Clients Are Doing When Things Are Going Better

According to Thomas Edison, "If we did all the things we are capable of doing, we would literally astound ourselves." It is the task of therapists to move their clients' attention away from their problems and symptoms and to invite them to astound themselves. In Chapter 4, we discussed the concept of setting *stretch goals*: goals that encourage clients not only to "patch up" problems, but also to grow as individuals. For example, a stretch goal might be to increase well-being or connectedness, rather than just solving the problem. Continuously setting and meeting stretch goals is a way to invite clients to move themselves toward a more positive, strengths-based stance.

O'Hanlon (1999) offered four keys to finding and using solution patterns. These keys are: (1) finding exceptions; (2) noticing what happens when the problem starts or ends; (3) importing solution patterns from other situations; and (4) finding out why the problem isn't worse.

Invite clients to find out when the problem didn't happen after they expected it would. Invite them to find exceptions to the usual problem pattern and look for changes they can make by repeating whatever action worked. For example, when was there a moment when they expected to have another fight with their partner, but somehow it didn't happen? What did they do differently and what difference did that make in their relationship?

Clients may also be invited to notice what happens as the problem ends or starts to end. Ask them to do some of the helpful actions earlier in the problem situation. For example, how do their fights usually end?

Invite clients to import solution patterns from other situations in which they feel competent. Ask them to examine their patterns at work, in hobbies, with friends, and in other contexts to find something they can use in the problem situation (see *competence transference* in Chapter 6). For example, which of their areas of competence will be helpful now in changing the problem?

Or invite clients to find out why the problem isn't worse. Then use their natural abilities (that they have been using without noticing) to limit the severity of the problem. For example, invite clients to think about what they have done and what they do to prevent the problem from getting worse. Or, when the problem is more or less stable, invite clients to ask themselves how they managed to do that. Most of the time, clients know often better than their therapists do what works and what doesn't, and that for a change they will have to do something different from what they are currently doing.

Enhancing Self-Control

One of the six virtues in the organization of the twenty-four character strengths is *temperance* (see Chapter 6). The four strengths that protect against excess are (a) forgiveness and mercy, (b) humility, (c) prudence, and (d) *self-regulation and self-control*.

Self-regulation is an extremely important executive function of the brain. A lack of self-control and self-regulation is found in a large number of psychological disorders, including ADHD, antisocial personality disorder, borderline personality disorder, addictions, eating disorders, and impulse control disorders.

Self-control is defined as a set of responses that can be taught; learning and using those responses reduces the need to depend on external control by others. Self-control is also known as *impulse control* or *self-regulation*. Some psychologists prefer the term *impulse control* because it may be more precise. The term *self-regulation* is used to refer to the many processes individuals use to manage drives and emotions. Therefore, self-regulation also embodies the concept of *willpower*. When psychologists isolate the personal qualities that predict positive outcomes in life, they consistently find two traits: intelligence and self-control (Baumeister, & Tierney 2011). Self-control is a vital strength and key to success in life. Willpower, like a muscle, becomes fatigued from overuse, but can also be strengthened over the long term through exercises. According to Baumeister and Tierney, the first major step in self-control is to set a clear goal (see Chapter 5); the second major step is to monitor behavior (see Chapter 8). Useful questions are:

- "What would you like to do instead of the undesired behavior?"
- "When didn't you experience the problem after you expected you would?"
- "What do you do when you overcome the urge to _____?"
- "What do you know about how others overcome the urge to _____?"
- "How much confidence do you have that you can do this (again)?"

Beginning in the late 1960s and early 1970s, Mischel and colleagues pioneered work illuminating the ability to delay gratification and to exert self-control in the face of strong situational pressures and emotionally "hot" temptations. His studies with preschoolers (four-year-old children) in the late 1960s, often referred to as the "marshmallow experiment," examined the processes and mental mechanisms that enable a young child to forego immediate gratification (one marshmallow) and wait fifteen minutes for a larger but delayed reward (two marshmallows). Continuing research with these original participants has examined how preschool delay of gratification ability is linked to development over the life course, may predict a variety of important outcomes (e.g., social and cognitive competence, educational attainment, drug use), and can have significant protective effects against a variety of potential vulnerabilities. This work also opened a route to research on temporal discounting in decision-making, and most importantly into the mental mechanisms that enable cognitive and emotional self-control, thereby helping to demystify the concept of willpower (Mischel & Ayduk, 2004; Mischel, Shoda & Rodriquez, 1989). The researchers concluded that self-control is correlated with various positive life outcomes such as happiness, adjustment, and various positive psychological factors. Great films about the marshmallow experiment can be found on the Internet.

STORY 28. *Chocolate-Chip Cookies*

Baumeister, Bratlavsky, Muraven, and Tice (1998) showed that self-control is not synonymous with willpower, but rather an exhaustible resource. College students participated in a study about food perception (or so they were told). They had been asked not to eat for three hours beforehand and were led to a room that smelled great: The researchers had baked chocolate-chip cookies. On a table were two bowls: One held the chocolate-chip cookies and the other held radishes.

The researchers told the students they had selected the cookies and radishes because of their highly distinctive tastes. The students were informed that they would be contacted the next day and asked about their memory of their taste sensations. Half the participants were asked to eat two or three cookies but no radishes. The other half were asked to eat two or three radishes but no cookies. Despite the temptation, all participants ate what they were asked to eat, and none of the radish-eaters sneaked a cookie.

At that point, the experiment was "officially" over, and a new group of researchers entered with a supposedly unrelated study: They wanted to find who was better at solving problems, college students or high school students. The college students, of course, wanted to show that they did better. They were presented with puzzles that required them to trace a geometric shape without retracing any lines and without lifting their pencils from the paper. In reality, the puzzles were unsolvable. The researchers wanted to see how long the students would persist in a frustrating task before giving up. The students who had not had to resist eating the chocolate-chip cookies spent nineteen minutes on the task and made thirty-four attempts. The radish-eaters gave up after eight minutes—less than half the time—and they managed only nineteen solution attempts.

Baby Steps

In changing behavior, only a small change is needed, because small steps may lead to big changes. Ideally, the focus is always on small steps forward instead of a big leap, even in situations with big problems. When problems are large, taking small steps may be even more powerful. Small steps are often the only way to start tackling overwhelming problems. Small steps (*baby steps*) have the following advantages: There is a low threshold, there is low risk, chances of successes are bigger, and there can be a positive snowball effect of bigger changes.

Research on hope theory (see Chapter 4) has shown that high-hope people naturally break big goals into small subgoals. Small steps can lead to big changes, so setting frequent short-term *stepping-stone goals* is important. Clients, who often lack hope at the beginning of therapy, are invited to design and choose their own small steps forward. Suggestions by therapists are often not necessary because of the clients' need for autonomy and their expertise on what might be working.

If clients do not (yet) have any ideas about which step forward they might take, an observation suggestion might be useful:

- "Between now and the next time we meet, could you observe when things are just a little bit better and what you did to make that happen?"
- "Do you think it might be useful to observe situations when the problem is there to a lesser extent, even just a little bit?"

Exercise 56. HOW DID YOU MANAGE TO BRING ABOUT THIS CHANGE?

Ask clients to consider a particular skill in which they are now proficient but which in the past they had not yet developed. Ask them to explain how they managed to bring about this change

---

Exercise 57. IN LINE WITH YOUR VALUES

Ask clients the following two questions:

1. "How can you live (even) more in line with your values?"
2, "What could be better if you made some changes in your life?"

In many traditional therapies, therapists advise clients on the procedures for changing behavior. Their role is that of the expert. This approach is different: Clients, whose role is that of co-expert on what works for them, in this context and at this moment, are competent to make changes and have made changes before. Also, there are always exceptions to the problem. Therefore, the procedures may be the same as those advised by therapists, with the difference that now clients themselves come up with these procedures, which have helped before and may be repeated. In this vein, I replaced the term *learning new behavior* with the term *becoming better at*. This term is also more positive to many clients, who may feel that the word *learn* has a negative connotation. The French mathematician Pascal (1623–1662) stated that people are generally better persuaded by the reasons which they have themselves discovered than by those which have come into the mind of others.

CHANGING FEELINGS

To create and sustain change, therapists have to embrace a growth mindset instead of a fixed one and instill it in their clients (Dweck, 2006; see Chapter 9). This brings up the question whether feelings can be changed. Some people (therapists as well as clients) believe emotions are fixed (entity theorists), whereas others believe that everyone can change their emotions (incremental theorists). It may come as no surprise that from a post traumatic success viewpoint, feelings can be changed. Entity beliefs are associated with lower well-being and increased psychological distress. Beliefs are linked with well-being or distress via cognitive reappraisal (reinterpreting the meaning of the emotional stimulus), and these beliefs may have important consequences for psychological health (De Castella et al., 2013).

In traditional forms of therapy, many questions are about feelings: "How do you feel about having these nightmares? How did you feel when your children were taken away from you? How do you feel when you start drinking?" It is widely believed that getting clients to explore and express their negative emotions is important in helping them. But reducing negative emotions does not automatically increase positive emotions. So far, little attention has been paid to theories of (building) positive emotions in psychology and psychotherapy. This may well reflect the spirit of the age in which most disciplines have focused on problems, and it may also reflect the nature of emotions themselves. The literature in psychology between 1970 and 2000 contains 46,000 papers about depression and only 400 papers about joy (Myers, 2000).

Positive emotions are fewer in number than negative emotions; generally, a ratio of three to four negative emotions to one positive emotion is identified. Positive emotions are less differentiated than negative emotions, and this imbalance is also reflected in the number of words in most languages that describe emotions.

By changing thoughts and/or behavior, chances are that feelings will also change. Instead of focusing only on negative feelings, the focus in psychotherapy is slowly shifting to include and enhance positive emotions and their broadening and building effect (Fredrickson, 2009).

Reducing Negative Emotions

In traditional therapy, the therapist's job is to minimize negative affect by dispensing drugs or instigating psychological interventions, thereby rendering people less anxious, angry, or depressed. For example, in CBT, therapists aim to obtain a clear picture of situations that are distressing to clients. They help clients to clearly differentiate thoughts from emotions, empathize with their emotions throughout the process, and evaluate the dysfunctional thinking that has influenced their mood. Seligman, however, describes some disappointing results with this approach (2011, p. 54):

> As a therapist, once in a while I would help a patient get rid of all of his anger and anxiety and sadness. I thought I would then get a happy patient. But I never did. I got an empty patient.

Research by Lieberman and colleagues (2007) shows different results. They found that putting feelings into words—simply putting a name to the emotion—diminishes the response in the amygdala, the portion of the brain that handles fear, panic, and other strong emotions. What lights up instead is the right ventrolateral prefrontal cortex, the part of the brain that controls impulses. That is why talking to a therapist—or even a sympathetic bartender—often makes people feel better. The same strategy of putting feelings into words is seen in *mindfulness meditation* practice. This involves the regular practice of stepping back and observing the flow of experience. Labeling is a tool that can help in this process.

Lieberman and colleagues conducted four studies examining the effect of affect labeling on self-reported emotional experience. In study one, self-reported distress was lower during affect labeling compared to passive watching of negative emotional pictures. Studies 2 and 3 added reappraisal and distraction conditions, respectively. Affect labeling showed similar effects on self-reported distress as both of these intentional emotion regulation strategies. In each of these three studies, however, participant predictions about the effects of affect labeling suggest that, unlike reappraisal and distraction, people do not believe affect labeling to be an effective emotion regulation strategy. Even after experiencing the lowered distress brought about by affect labeling, participants predicted that affect labeling would increase distress in the future. Finally, study four employed positive emotional pictures, and here affect labeling was associated with diminished self-reported pleasure relative to passive watching. This suggests that affect labeling tends to dampen affective responses in general, rather than specifically alleviating negative affect.

These findings may be in line with the disappointing results of research showing that unexplained positivity lasts longer than positivity that we analyze until we fully understand it (Wilson, Centerbar, Kerme, & Gilbert, 2005). The researchers found that the cognitive processes used in making sense of positive events reduces the pleasure people derive from them.

STORY 29. *Venting Anger Feeds the Flame*

Selective attention theory indicates that what you focus on expands. This theory has obvious applications in relation to emotions. If you focus on anger, for example, your anger will increase. If you focus on sadness, you will feel sadder.

The psychoanalytical catharsis method involves the assumption that negative emotions must be aired to activate a purifying process. Therefore, whacking a punching bag or attacking a pillow is advised as a way for clients to express their anger. Catharsis theory predicts that venting anger should get rid of it and should therefore reduce subsequent aggression.

However, there is no scientific evidence to support this theory. Research has shown that expressing anger, even against inanimate objects, does not make people less angry at all. It actually seems to increase anger, not tame it. These findings directly contradict catharsis theory (Bushman, Baumeister, and Stack, 1999). For reducing anger and aggression, the worst possible advice to give people is to tell them to imagine their provocateur's face on a pillow or punching bag as they wallop it. Yet this is precisely what many therapists advise people to do. If followed, such advice will only make people angrier and more aggressive.

A possible explanation for this increase in anger is that people are training their brains to associate anger with controlled aggression rather than compassion and reconciliation. In other words, people create bad habits. So if clients are feeling angry, instead of encouraging them to express negative emotions in a dramatic way, invite them to act the way they wish they felt by finding a calm way to express their feelings, to practice mindful meditation, or to take steps to distract themselves.

Building Positive Emotions

Although building a positive cooperative relationship with clients does not require that emotions be singled out for special conversation, a demonstration of natural, empathic understanding is necessary and helpful when clients are describing what they find difficult and painful in a given problem. Empathic affirmation of the client's perspective ("I understand that things have been getting worse lately") is useful. Then therapists can move on to explore what clients want to be different in their lives or what the clients are doing to keep their heads above water. In dealing with emotions, it is useful on the one hand to acknowledge negative emotions like anger, frustration, or sadness, and on the other hand to look for possibilities by saying something like "I see that your feelings are very strong about this topic. What would you like to feel instead in the future?" From a PP point of view, moving from –10 (e.g., feeling very depressed) to 0 (not feeling depressed anymore) requires different strategies than moving from 0 (not feeling depressed anymore) to +10 (feeling great and flourishing). SFBT does not make this distinction. It assumes that people can go from minus to plus using the same SF techniques.

The transparency of this method can also ensure that the potential emotional charge of the focus is reduced. The therapist announces that, together with the client, he or she will focus on all positive elements that can replace the problem: what is desirable rather than what is undesirable. This proposal meets with the approval of most clients. The focus is on positive emotions and on balancing positive and negative affect: "How will you feel when your hoped-for outcome is reached? What will you be thinking, doing, and feeling differently when you notice that the steps you are taking are in the right direction?" Also, bringing back the best from the past by asking questions about previous successes and competencies triggers positive emotions. The broaden-and-build theory of positive emotions suggests that negative emotions narrow our thought-action repertoires, whereas positive emotions broaden our awareness and encourage novel, varied, and exploratory thoughts and actions (see Chapter 1).

The power of asking open questions ("How will you know this session has been useful? How will you know the problem has been solved? What has been working well? What is better?") is in widening the array of thoughts and actions available to us. Using imagination, as in the "miracle question" (see Chapter 5), also creates positive emotions and has a powerful impact on our capacity to expand our ideas and activities. While this is highly speculative, it is possible that the miracle question, by engaging our imagery, which is consistent with right hemisphere processing, also engages the global processing capacities of the hemisphere, enabling us to expand our thinking. The right hemisphere sees the forest; the left hemisphere sees the trees. Compliments and competence questions ("How did you manage to do that? How did you decide to do that?") also elicit positive emotions. The focus is on noticing the skills and resources of clients and on playing those resources back to them.

In sum, focusing on positive goals, focusing on hope and optimism and on positive differences, and focusing on exceptions to the problem and on the abilities of clients, all help to create an atmosphere in which positive feelings can flourish and problems can be transformed into something positive: the preferred future of our clients. As Fredrickson (2009, p. 16) stated, "Downward spiral or upward spiral, as I see it, that's your choice."

Isen (2005) stated that a growing body of research indicates that positive emotions facilitate a broad range of important social behaviors and thought processes. For example, work from approximately the past decade shows that positive affect leads to greater creativity, improved negotiation processes and outcomes, and more thorough,

Exercise 58. USE DRAWINGS

Ask your clients to draw some happy events from their lives and invite them to explain them to you. Or ask your clients to draw themselves while they are doing something they are proud of. You can also invite clients to draw their preferred future, or to draw a circle and point out where they would prefer to place the traumatic event in the future as opposed to the central position in the circle where they might draw this event now (see Exercise 51).

open-minded, flexible thinking and problem-solving. And this is in addition to earlier work showing that positive affect promotes generosity and social responsibility in interpersonal interactions.

In a negotiation study, positive affect induced by a small gift (a pad of paper) and a few cartoons significantly increased the tendency of bargainers who were face to face to reach agreement and to obtain the optimal outcome possible for both of them in the negotiation. According to Isen (2005) relative to control groups, people in positive-affect conditions have better negotiation outcomes and enjoy the task more, and they can take the other person's perspective.

The literature indicates that under most circumstances, people who are feeling happy are more likely to do what they want to do, to want to do what is socially responsible and helpful and what needs to be done, to enjoy what they are doing more, to be more motivated to accomplish their goals, and to be more open to information and think more clearly. In the case of positive emotions, one of the clearest and most distinctive cognitive effects observed has been increased flexibility and creativity. This may be mediated by release of the neurotransmitter dopamine. Dopamine may play a role in the effects of positive affect on cognition that have been observed. This *dopamine hypothesis* arose from the observation, at behavioral and cognitive levels, that positive affect fosters cognitive flexibility and the ability to switch perspectives (together with the understanding that dopamine in the anterior cingulate region of the brain enables flexible perspective-taking or set-switching).

Another type of research was done by Isen and Reeve (2005), showing that positive emotions foster *intrinsic motivation*, as reflected by choice of activity in a free-choice situation and by rated amount of enjoyment of a novel and challenging task, but also promote responsible behavior in a situation where uninteresting tasks need to be done. This has implications for the relationship between positive affect and aspects of self-regulation, such as self-control. The *undoing effect* of positive emotions on negative emotions is described in Chapter 1.

Questions for enhancing positive emotions in clients who have experienced traumatic events (Bannink, 2010a) include:

- "How can I help you?"
- "How have you managed to survive?"
- "How have you maybe helped others survive?"
- "What helps you deal with what you've experienced?"
- "Is this the worst thing you've ever experienced? On a scale of

ten to zero, where ten equals the worst and zero equals not bad at all, indicate how bad it was."
- "What else have you been through that was difficult, and what helped you then?"
- "Which of the things that helped you then could be useful to you again now?"
- "Do you know anyone else who has been through the same ordeal? What has helped that person deal with it?"
- "What does it mean for you to have survived these traumatic events?"
- "If a miracle were to happen in the middle of the night, and you overcame the consequences of the traumatic events well enough that you didn't have to come to therapy anymore and were (relatively) satisfied with your life, what would be different then?"
- "What will you be doing differently when these traumatic events are less of a problem in your daily life? How will you use your time differently?"
- "What will you think about and what will you do instead of thinking about the past?"
- "How will you know that you're doing that, and how will you know that you'll be able to keep doing it?"
- "How do you manage to make those moments happen?"
- "What will others say is different then, and how will they say you manage that?"
- "What difference will those healing changes make in your life when they have lasted for a longer period of time (days, weeks, months, years)? What difference will they make in relationships with important people in your life?"
- "What difference will the changes that you've accomplished make for future generations of your family?"
- "How will you be able to tell that you're handling this problem a little better or that things are a little easier for you?"
- "What will be the smallest sign that things are going better? What difference will that make for you and others?"
- "How can you regain hope that life can get easier in the future?"
- "What do you think your next step could be? When you've taken that step, what difference will that make for you?"
- "What did the traumatic event not change, and how did you manage that?"

- "What things in your life do you wish to maintain, despite what has happened?"
- "What would you like your life to look like a month from now, with the same people and with the same circumstances still in place, when your behavior is less influenced by the traumatic event?"
- "Imagine you're a wise old person looking back on your life. What advice would the wise old you give the present-day you to help you get though the current phase of your life? According to the wise old you, what should you be thinking about? What would be most helpful to you as you heal? What would the wise old you say to comfort you? What advice does the wise old you have about how the treatment could be most useful and could help the most?"
- "What helps you keep traumatic images (intrusions) and memories under control?"
"On a scale of ten to zero, where ten means that you are handling what's happened very well and zero means that you can't handle what's happened at all, where are you now?"
- "What would you have done differently had you known about the trauma that the other person has experienced? What difference could that have made in your relationship? What can you do in your relationship now to compensate for what you couldn't do then?"
- "With whom did you used to feel safe as a child? Which experience of safety or comfort from the past could you make use of now?"
- "What symbol for that safety or comfort could you use to help with this?"
- "How do you now manage to sometimes feel safe and to have control of your life?"
- "How can you comfort yourself now? How do you do that?"
- "Who can comfort you now, even if only a little bit?"
- (In cases of, for example, dissociation or self-mutilation) "You must have a good reason to_____. Please tell me more. How does this help you? How do you manage to come out of the dissociation into the here and now (or how do you manage to stop hurting yourself)? What else helps in this respect?"
- "How will you celebrate your victory over these problems?"

The Positivity Ratio

Fredrickson's positivity ratio (see Chapter 1)—comparing positive and negative thoughts, emotions, and activities during our day-to-day lives—shows a tipping point at around the 3:1 mark where people experience transformed lives through positivity. For those with positivity ratios below 3:1, positivity is inert and useless; for those with ratios exceeding 3:1, positivity forecasts both openness and growth. "Only those people truly enjoyed the sweet fruits of positivity" (2009, p. 135). Although Fredrickson's research on the positivity ratio lately has been criticized, it remains obvious that positivity is helping people to survive and flourish.

Gottman (1994) developed a way to compute the positivity ratio of a marriage. He divided marriages in two groups: One group was made up of so-called "flourishing" marriages that had lasted and that both partners found to be satisfying. The other group was made up of marriages that had fallen apart; the partners had become dissatisfied, estranged, separated, or divorced. He found that among flourishing marriages, positivity ratios were about 5:1. By sharp contrast, languishing and failed marriages had positivity ratios lower than 1:1.

Gottman stated that in order for a relationship to flourish, there must be five positive remarks or signals for every disapproving remark or negative signal. In relationships where the partners separated, the ratio often fell to 1:1 or even lower. Gottman was able to predict with 94-percent accuracy which of the 700 couples who participated in his research would still be together after ten years and which would separate based on his observations of a fifteen-minute film of each couple, from which he scored the ratio of their positive and negative interactions.

Fredrickson (2009) stated that for individuals, marriages, and business teams as well, flourishing, or doing remarkably well, comes with positivity ratios above 3:1. By contrast, individuals who don't overcome their depression, couples who fail in their marriages, and business teams that are unpopular and unprofitable all have ratios in the gutter, below 1:1. Below 3:1, positivity may be inert, swamped as it is by the greater potency of negativity. Positivity needs to accumulate and compound to a certain degree before it reaches the crucial tipping point. Only then will the broaden-and-build effects of positivity emerge. Only then will people see the astonishing benefits of positivity blossom in their own lives, relationships, and work. In the United States, the upper bound for flourishing is around 11:1; this is probably different in other cultures.

STORY 30. *Consider a Sailboat*

Rising from a sail-boat is an enormous mast that allows the sail to catch the wind. Below the waterline is the keel, which can weigh tons. You can take the mast going up as positivity, and the keel down below as negativity. If you've ever sailed, you know that you can't get anywhere without the keel. If you tried, at best you'd slide aimlessly across the water, or at worst you'd capsize. Although it is the sail hanging on the mast of positivity that catches the wind and gives you fuel, it is the keel of negativity that keeps the boat on course and manageable. And just as the keel matters most when you're going upwind, appropriate negativity matters most in hard times.

—Fredrickson, 2009, p. 137

Exercise 59. POSITIVE MOOD BOARD

Invite clients to make their own *positive mood board*. Designers frequently use mood boards to help them illustrate the kind of style they are pursuing. However, mood boards can also be used to visually explain a certain style of writing, or an imaginary setting for a storyline. In short, mood boards are not limited to visual subjects, but serve as a visual tool to quickly inform others of the overall *feel* that a designer is trying to achieve. Creating mood boards in a digital form may be easier and quicker, but physical objects tend to have a higher impact on people because of the more complete palette of sensations they offer.

Exercise 60. SAVORING YOUR DAY

Invite clients to reflect on their day for a couple of minutes, and in particular on two pleasurable experiences or moments. Ask them to allow the pleasure to last as long as possible. This taps into the intensification or elongation of positive emotions through focused attention on the present moment.

STORY 31. *The Nun Study*

Handwritten autobiographies from 180 Catholic nuns, composed when participants were a mean age of twenty-two years, were scored for emotional content and related to survival during ages seventy-five to ninety-five. A strong inverse association was found between positive emotional content in these writings and risk of mortality in late life. As the quartile ranking of positive emotion in early life increased, there was a stepwise decrease in risk of mortality, resulting in a two-and-half-fold difference between the lowest and highest quartiles. Positive emotional content in early-life autobiographies was strongly associated with longevity six decades later

—Danner, Snowdon, & Friesen, 2001

Positive Affect in the Medical Setting

Below, some studies showing that positive affect also matters in medical settings are described.

Are all psychiatrists equally effective when prescribing medication? This question led to research done by McKay, Imel, and Wampold (2006), showing that both psychiatrists and treatments contributed to positive outcomes in the treatment of depression. Given that psychiatrists were responsible for more of the variance in outcomes, it can be concluded that effective psychiatrists can augment the effects of antidepressant medications as well as placebos.

In another study, Ankarberg and Falkenstrom (2008) argued that available empirical evidence indicates that depression treatment using antidepressants is primarily a psychological treatment. This conclusion has far-reaching consequences for the scientific status of contemporary treatments for depression. It also affects what the doctor should focus on in a treatment with antidepressants and how to act when the patient is treatment resistant. To achieve the results obtained in clinical trials, the quantity and quality of support from the doctor is more important than pharmacological concerns, such as adequate doses of medicine. When faced with a treatment-resistant patient, relationship factors rather than pharmacological factors should be in focus.

The risk of being sued for malpractice seems to have very little to do with how many mistakes a professional makes. Analysis of malpractice lawsuits show that there are highly skilled doctors who get sued a lot, and doctors who make lots of mistakes and never get sued.

In other words, patients do not file lawsuits because they have been harmed by shoddy medical care. Patients file lawsuits because shoddy medical care and *something else* happening to them have harmed them. The medical researcher Levinson (as cited in Gladwell, 2005) recorded hundreds of conversations between a group of physicians and their patients. Roughly half of the doctors had never been sued. The other half had been sued at least twice, and Levinson found that just on the basis of those conversations, she could find clear differences between the two groups. The surgeons who had never been sued spent more than three minutes longer with each patient than those who had been sued did (18.3 minutes versus 15 minutes). They were more likely to make orienting comments, such as, "First I will examine you, and then we will talk the problem over," which helps patients get a sense of what the visit is supposed to accomplish and when they ought to ask questions. These doctors were more likely to engage in active listening, saying things like, "Go on, tell me more about that." And they were far more likely to laugh and be funny during the visit. Interestingly, there was no difference in the amount or quality of information they gave their patients; they did not provide more details about medication or the patient's condition. The difference was entirely in that they talked to their patients.

A colleague listened to Levinson's tapes, zeroing in on the conversations that had been recorded between surgeons and patients. For each surgeon, she picked two conversations. Then, from each conversation, she selected two 10-second clips of the doctor talking, so she had a total of forty seconds. Then she removed the high-frequency sounds from speech that enable us to recognize individual words. What is left is a kind of garble that preserves intonation, pitch, and rhythm but erases context. She found that by using only those ratings, she could predict which surgeons got sued and which ones didn't.

The judges of the tapes knew nothing about the skill level of the surgeons or how experienced they were, what kind of training they had, or what kind of procedures they tended to do. They did not even know what the doctors were saying to their patients. All they were using for their prediction was their analysis of the surgeon's tone of voice. In fact, it was even more basic than that: if the surgeon's voice was judged to sound dominant, the surgeon tended to be in the sued group. If the voice sounded less dominant and more concerned, the surgeon tended to be in the nonsued group. Malpractice sounds like one of those complicated and multidimensional problems. But in the end it comes down to a matter of *respect*, and the simplest way that respect is communicated is through tone of voice, and the most corrosive tone of voice that a doctor can assume is a dominant tone.

A study done by Estrada, Isen, and Young (1994) investigated whether creative problem-solving and reported sources of satisfaction from the practice of medicine are influenced by the induction of positive affect among physicians. Physicians (internists) randomly assigned to the positive affect group received a small package of candy; the control group received nothing. The physicians were told that the reason for the study was to analyze how an internist solves a clinical case. The positive affect group was told that the bag of candy was a small token of appreciation for their willingness to volunteer for the study.

The affect group scored better on the creativity measure than did the control group. Regarding practice satisfaction, all physicians perceived humanism as more important than extrinsic motivation as a source of satisfaction from the practice of medicine. However, a significant interaction between affect and source of satisfaction revealed that the affect group attributed more importance to humanism and less relative importance to extrinsic motivation compared with the control group. In contrast, physicians in a third condition, in which they read phrases reflective of humanistic satisfaction from the practice of medicine, did not differ from the control group in the creativity test or in the practice satisfaction questionnaire. The researchers concluded:

- Induction of positive affect among physicians improves their creative problem-solving and influences which source of practice satisfaction they report.
- Induction of positive affect in clinical settings seems possible, despite the serious nature of the work that takes place in these settings. Feelings of success and competence, pleasant interactions with co-workers and patients, a sense of helping people and being appreciated, and the everyday events that sustain enjoyment in many work settings are only a few of the ways in which positive affect may be introduced in clinical settings;
- In facilitating creativity, positive affect promotes the clinician's ability to see relatedness among concepts, ideas, and symptoms, enabling him or her to formulate an appropriate diagnostic list and thus enhancing medical diagnosis and decision-making.
- Induction of positive affect sensitizes physicians to humanistic concerns.

Rakel et al. (2009) found that clinician empathy, as perceived by patients with the common cold, significantly predicts subsequent duration and severity of illness and is associated with immune system changes. Hershberger (2005), a family physician, also promoted mental and emotional well-being. As part of health promotion or primary prevention, a family physician may frequently encourage patients to be physically active. Although not currently part of the culture of family medicine, it is reasonable to think about mental health promotion and the development of life satisfaction in a similar vein. While some of the most common physician–patient communication strategies appropriately emphasize eliciting negative emotions, similar strategies can be used for helping patients share good experiences and the associated positive emotions. Happy people have better quality of life. Research in the behavioral, social, and medical sciences is continuing to identify other benefits of happiness, including better health. The promotion of mental and emotional well-being can legitimately be viewed as synergistic with the promotion of physical health. One of the identified, and perhaps most influential, pathways between positive outlooks/moods and better physical health is health behavior. This has been found in the relationship between optimism and health and also in longitudinal research demonstrating that individuals with positive views of aging tend to live longer. Perhaps family physicians who begin to give more attention to their own happiness, satisfaction, and meaning in life will be most likely to promote the same in patient care. Family medicine educators in particular are in an excellent position to emphasize the promotion of emotional well-being as an important part of comprehensive care. The starting point is adoption of the perspective that such an endeavor can (and arguably should) be a part of family medicine.

PUTTING IT ALL TOGETHER

In sum, in order to help clients reach recovery, growth, and resilience in the face of adverse events, it may help to invite them to:

- Think about the personal strengths that they showed to survive the traumatic events. Even if they made some mistakes or did things they regret, they did what they had to do to survive, and that is something to be proud of.
- Think about the things that they have put in their life currently that make it meaningful, be they relationships, work, faith, or

taking care of their family. Invite them to find everyday happiness in the life they have now.

- Think about what they have gained from going through these difficulties, and about how they might use this to help themselves and others or create something of personal or societal value.
- Know that growth and hope can coexist with grief and that there will be ups and downs. Invite them to become better at anticipating and managing these and to be compassionate with themselves on days when it is too difficult to see the positive.

In the next chapter, we will take a closer look at homework suggestions intended to direct clients' attention to those aspects of their experiences and situations that are most useful in reaching their goals.

SUMMARY

- When clients have a clear sense of what they want to achieve (their goal) and when they have already been able to achieve to some extent what they want (the exceptions to the problem), it will be relatively easy for them to choose the next steps forward.
- A strengths-and-solutions perspective is often more helpful for clients and therapists than a perspective on weakness and problems.
- Language is important, since it is the main vehicle used in psychotherapy.
- In helping clients to change their point of view, the focus is on changing how they think and what they pay attention to.
- Progress in therapy can be made through inviting clients to rewrite their negative stories into positive ones or to use positive imagery.
- Changing clients' perspective can be done in five different ways.
- Changing repetitive patterns and noticing what clients do when things are going better bring about behavior change.
- Reducing clients' negative emotions and building positive ones—enhancing their positivity ratio—can promote well-being. This also applies to the medical setting.

CHAPTER 8

■■■■■■■■■■■■■

Homework Suggestions

Many forms of psychotherapy consider homework to be important. For example, *self-monitoring* is the most widely used adjunct to CBT and is almost invariably used both at the initial assessment stage and to monitor subsequent change. However, from an SF perspective, self-monitoring and other homework assignments are important only if clients think they are useful. Some clients struggle with the terms *homework* and *task*, because not everyone has positive memories of doing homework at school. Therefore, the term *suggestions* may be a better alternative. Presenting homework suggestions as a (small) experiment may also make it easier for clients to try them, because this alleviates the pressure to be successful at accomplishing the task. Before coming up with these suggestions, it is useful to ask clients whether they want to do homework in the first place. If clients say they don't have any need for it, they probably have a good reason. Perhaps they don't consider it necessary or useful, or maybe they don't have time before the next session. In these instances, therapists needn't offer homework suggestions.

The importance of homework as seen in traditional psychotherapies is no longer deemed useful in SFBT. De Shazer (1985) stated that he could get as much information when clients did not perform the homework task as when clients did perform the task. He also found that accepting nonperformance as a message about the clients' way of doing things (rather than as a sign of resistance; see Chapter 4) allowed him to develop a cooperative relationship with clients that might not include homework assignments. This was a shock to him, because he had assumed that tasks were almost always necessary to achieve behavioral change.

In this chapter, general homework suggestions, based on the working alliance between the therapist and client, are described. Four positive homework suggestions are explained. Several forms of self-monitoring and many behavioral experiments are described in detail. Therapeutic rituals may help clients to move on with their lives or build new habits.

GENERAL HOMEWORK SUGGESTIONS

At the end of each session, therapists have the option of offering their clients homework suggestions. These are intended to direct clients' attention to those aspects of their experiences and situations that are most useful in reaching their goals. In offering these suggestions, it is important for therapists to keep the following three questions in mind:

1. Does the client have a well-defined goal?
2. Do I have a visitor, a complainant, or a customer relationship with this client? (see Chapter 4). Remember, as long as someone is not part of the solution, he or she is part of the problem.
3. Are there spontaneous or deliberate exceptions related to the client's goal?

In a *visitor relationship*, in which therapy is mandated, no suggestions are given. After all, the problem has not yet been defined, nor is there any talk of a goal or related exceptions. It may be that people in clients' environment have a problem with them or feel concern. In that case, there is often a complainant relationship with those people. Therapists go along with their clients' worldview, extend acknowledgement, and compliment clients on their personal strengths and resources and for coming to the therapist's office. They propose another appointment for continuing to find out, together with their clients, what would be the best thing for them to do.

In a *complainant relationship*, in which clients do not see themselves as part of the problem and/or the solution but think that someone else or something else has to change, only observational suggestions are assigned. To clients in a complainant relationship, who cannot name exceptions or a goal or have vague complaints, therapists may assign one of the following suggestions:

- "Pay attention to what happens in your life that gives you the sense that this problem can be solved."
- "Reflect on what you would like to accomplish with these sessions."
- "Pay attention to what is going well and should stay the same. Pay attention to what happens in your life that you would like to continue to happen."
- "Observe the positive moments in your life so that you can talk about them next time we meet."
- "Pay attention to the times when things are going better so that you can talk about them next time."
- (If a scaling question [see Chapter 6] has been used) "Observe when you are one point higher on the scale and what you and/or (significant) others are doing differently then."
- "Pay attention to what gives you hope that your problem can be solved."

The use of an observation suggestion implies that the exceptions can occur again and can contribute to the clients' feeling more hopeful. Observation tasks also indicate that useful information is to be found within the clients' own realm of experience (De Jong & Berg, 2002).

De Shazer (1988) added an element of prediction to his suggestions. He believed that the value of such suggestions derives from their suggestive power. If there are exceptions, a *prediction task* suggests that they will occur again, maybe even sooner than clients imagine. If clients predict a better day, they will be more inclined to look for signs of confirmation (a *positive self-fulfilling prophecy*). Clients in a complainant relationship who are able to describe spontaneous exceptions may benefit from such a prediction task.

In a *customer relationship*, in which clients see themselves as part of the problem and/or the solution *and* are motivated to change, behavioral and observational suggestions may be given. If clients in a customer relationship are able to clearly formulate their goal and find exceptions, therapists can offer them the following suggestions:

- Continue with what works, and pay attention to what else you are doing that is helpful that you haven't noticed before (a combination behavioral and observational task).

Exercise 61. PREDICTION SUGGESTIONS

This task is intended to supply information about what works. Prediction suggestions (also in crisis situations) imply that exceptions may occur again. Invite clients to:

- make a prediction of what the following day will look like.
- find an explanation for why the day turned out the way it did at the end of that day and make a new prediction for the following day.
- if the prediction became true: How did they know this would happen? What contributed to this outcome?
- if the prediction didn't become true: what was different and what contribute to this outcome?

- Continue to find out what works best for you (a combination behavioral and observational task).
- Do more of what works.
- Do the easiest thing that works.
- Think about what else might help.
- Do a piece of the miracle or the goal.
- Discover more about seemingly coincidental exceptions.
- Predict the seemingly coincidental exceptions and explain the result.

If clients in a customer relationship seem motivated but do not (yet) have a clear picture of the miracle or the goal and are unable to find exceptions, or if there is a power struggle between two or more clients, suggest that the clients do something else, preferably something unexpected, and note the difference it makes. If clients in a customer relationship do have a clear picture of the miracle or goal but are unable to find exceptions, therapists can give the following suggestions:

- "Pretend the miracle has happened. In the coming week, pretend for a day (or part of a day) that the miracle has happened and pay attention to the differences it makes."
- "In the coming week, pretend for one day that you are one or two points higher on the scale of progress. Pay attention to the

difference this makes. Pay special attention to the reactions of people who are important to you."

As a result, unnecessary battles between therapists and clients (referred to as *resistance* or *noncompliance*) can be prevented (see Chapter 4). If clients have not done the agreed-upon homework, many problem-focused therapists will talk to their clients about the importance of doing the homework and will want to know why they failed to do so.

However, cooperation with clients increases when therapists are curious and validating toward their clients. A good strategy is to invite clients to explain what *good reasons* they had for not doing the homework. In my thirty years as a therapist, I have noticed that one of the best ways to ruin the working alliance is to leave an ongoing visitor or complainant relationship unaddressed and give clients homework tasks or suggestions that they are not yet, or not any longer, motivated to carry out.

It is important that homework suggestions be doable and realistic. The key is to keep it simple. Offering one or at most two suggestions is sufficient. In order to remember what the suggestions are, clients may want to write them down before the end of the session. The homework suggestion is often concluded with the phrase "so that you can tell me what's going better next time" (for clients in a customer relationship) or "so that you can tell me something about it next time" (for clients in a complainant relationship). In this way, therapists imply that clients will have something to relate at the next session.

FOUR POSITIVE HOMEWORK SUGGESTIONS

Walter and Peller (1992) described four positive homework suggestions. These suggestions show some overlap with the general suggestions mentioned earlier.

The first suggestion is to invite clients to observe for positives and notice, between now and the next session, what is going on in their life (marriage, family, work, etc.) that they like to see continue. Or invite clients to do more of the positives or exceptions, when these are within the clients' control. Invite them to keep up what they are doing that is helpful, and take notice of what they are doing that is helpful.

Or invite clients to find out how spontaneous exceptions happen. Invite them to pretend to feel different on the odd-numbered days of the week and see what happens, even if they feel the same old way. Ask them to do as they normally do on the even-numbered days and notice the differences. Or invite clients to do a small piece of the hypothetical solution and notice what difference it makes.

Walter and Peller urge therapists to suggest that clients *observe* rather than *do* something when they feel hesitant about change (e.g., when there is a complainant relationship). The thought of doing something might seem too big a step for them. The observational task might not seem as threatening. Therapists might ask, "I would like to suggest that between now and the next time you come in, you notice what you are doing or what is different when you are acting even the slightest bit more the way you want to act. Make mental notes, if not written ones, so you can tell me about it next time." This task assumes that clients are already doing some of what they want and does not require them to do anything in the areas where they might be fearful. Since clients do not have the pressure to do anything different, they may be more likely to observe what they are already doing. By doing this, they will find more exceptions to enumerate in the next sessions. This observational task is also a good fit for clients who like to think about changes before they take action.

CASE 24. *What Do You Want to Continue to Happen?*

This is what is known in SFBT as the *first session task*. The therapist suggests to the client that he *observe for positives*: "Between now and the next time we meet, I would like you to observe what happens in your life that you want to continue to happen."

This intervention is used to define therapy as dealing with the present and the future rather than the past. The assignment lets the client know that the therapist expects change and that the therapist is confident that change will occur. That is, the therapist expects something worthwhile to happen, and this is opposite what clients may expect. This assignment is an easy task for clients to cooperate with, since it does not call for anything different: only observations are required. Observation is something clients will do anyway, and the assignment directs the focus of their observations

---

CASE 25. *At Least Ten Things*

A client has been severely wounded in a car accident and is suffering from flashbacks and intrusive thoughts.. The therapist offers the following suggestion: "Observe at least ten things that take you in the right direction so that you can tell me about them next time."

Completing this exercise will help the client to become calm and think straight again. Should the client not be able to find ten things, he may ask his family members what they think is moving him in the right direction. Observing at least ten things that work is challenging (and often fun), and clients typically come up with more creative ideas than they thought they would.

Exercise 62. START AT CHAPTER TWO

Invite clients to do this homework exercise. Say to them, "A book is made up of many chapters. You can see your own life in this way. If you were to write the story of your life as an exercise, then you could begin with the second chapter instead of beginning at chapter one. Any problems that you are currently experiencing can be omitted. What positive differences will there be in your life description? How will you feel differently? Which persons will you omit, and which persons will you include to make them part of chapter two? Which strengths and resources do you have in chapter two? Which good ideas from chapter two could you use now?"

SELF-MONITORING

Self-monitoring can be seen as a form of the observational experiments described above. In psychotherapies like CBT, self-monitoring of symptoms is used to gain a more accurate description of behaviors as opposed to relying on recall. It helps tie the intervention in to the client's progress and provides clients with feedback about their progress. It is a means of helping clients to become active, collaborative participants in their therapy by identifying and appraising how they react to events (in terms of their own physiological reactions, cognitions, behaviors, and feelings). Self-monitoring is often integrated into therapy, both in the sessions and as part of homework assignments.

Self-monitoring in post traumatic success, however, is not about clients' symptoms and problems, but about clients' strengths and about exceptions to the problem. When clients use this form of self-monitoring, they often feel more competent and can choose to do more of what works to change their situation for the better. If the self-monitoring pertains to *frequency*, it concerns how often the desired situation or be-

Exercise 63. THERAPEUTIC RESOLVING LETTERS

To help clients to go beyond being merely survivors (see Chapter 7), Dolan's *therapeutic resolving letters* can be useful (Dolan, 1991). Invite clients to write four letters as homework and bring them to the next session. *Letter one* will include all the unresolved feelings that clients have toward someone or something that has happened to them. *Letter two* is something that clients fear, this being a response from either their attacker or someone who has no good intentions toward the them. *Letter three* is the letter that clients hope they would get. It includes the acknowledgment the clients seek and, in the case of an attacker, also includes an apology. Letter three should be written straight after letter two, in order not to deepen the trauma but to ease it. *Letter four* can be written whenever clients feel like it, and it represents the hope clients have for a better future—a future in which the trauma is genuinely in the past and the clients have gone beyond surviving it and have become *thrivers*.

havior (cognitions or feelings) occurs. For instance, how often does the client manage to remain calm or even just a little bit calmer in stressful situations that would otherwise elicit a panic attack? How does the client already manage to have (more) helping cognitions in these situations? This may be followed by additional *competence questions*, for example, "How did you succeed in doing that?" In other words, the objective is to find exceptions. If the self-monitoring pertains to *intensity*, the client is asked to rate positive emotions associated with the desired situation or behavior/cognition instead of the negative emotion associated with the undesired behavior/cognition.

Baumeister and Tierney (2011) did research on self-control (see Chapter 7). They found that there are two major steps in self-control. The first step is to set *a clear goal*. Making a plan makes a difference. Self-control without goals would be nothing more than aimless change, like trying to diet without knowing which foods are fattening. The second step is to *monitor behavior*. Keeping track is more than just knowing where things are. It means knowing where things are in relation to where they should be. People who adjust their actions to meet certain standards fare better than those who are oblivious to their own social mistakes. In self-monitoring behavior, clients focus on how far they have come (i.e., focus on what works; see Chapter 6), which generates contentment, or focus on how much remains to be done (i.e., focus on progress; see Chapter 7), which generates motivation and ambition.

The first method of self-monitoring is through the use of a *thought record*, as seen in Figure 2. In problem-focused therapies like CBT, this thought record is used to help clients understand which automatic thoughts (thoughts that occur automatically in response to a given situation) or images trigger their problem behavior, whereas now it is used to help clients understand which thoughts and images trigger their desired behavior. Therapists working with a combination of a problem focus and a solution focus may invite their clients to fill in both problem-focused and strengths-and-solutions-focused records.

Figure 2. THOUGHT RECORD			
Situation	Feelings (10–0)	Thoughts (images)	Behavior

The second method of changing the focus from negative to positive in self-monitoring is *observation of positive changes*. Clients are invited to answer the following questions:

- "Indicate an area in your life in which you desire change the most."
- "Suppose that someday things will change and everything in this area of your life will be the way you want it to be (your goal). Describe how you and others will know that everything is going well."
- "Evaluate the current situation on a scale of ten to zero (ten meaning very good, zero meaning very bad)."

- "Describe briefly what is happening in this area that prompted you to choose this point and not a lower one. What is working?"
- "Think what you can do in the near future for your evaluation on the scale to increase by at least one point (indicating that your situation has become a little bit better). Make the actions as specific as you can."
- "When you take these actions, what will change in this area of your life? How will this be helpful for you and/or others in your life?"

The third method of self-monitoring is the *monitoring of exceptions* to the problem (see Figure 3). In using this method, special attention should be paid to the ways in which this exception was different from problem times. Whereas in traditional psychotherapy, therapists explore the who, what, when, and where of client problems, therapists are now interested in exploring the who, what, when, and where of exceptions. Exception-finding questions include:

- "When didn't you experience the problem after expecting that you would?"
- "What happens as the problem ends or start to end?"
- "Could the problem be worse? Why isn't the problem worse?"
- "When was the problem less of a problem (even just a little bit)?"
- "What is better already?"

More exception-finding questions are described by Bannink (2010a). Appendix D contains a journal for the monitoring of exceptions.

Notice that exceptions are either deliberate or random. To find out about the how of an exception, therapists inquire about who did what and when to make that happen. If clients are able to describe how an exception happened, the exception is deliberate. If, however, clients respond by shrugging their shoulders and saying they don't know, this is a random exception. The importance of this distinction is explained in Chapter 6, because it plays a key role in determining which homework suggestions are given to the client.

Exercises 64–68 for self-monitoring appear on pp. 201–202. See also Exercise 6 and Exercise 16.

Figure 3. OBSERVATION FORM FOR FINDING EXCEPTIONS TO THE PROBLEM.						
Date	Event	What changed in the desired direction?	What did you do to make this change?	What thoughts or emotions did this raise?	Further possible actions

Exercise 64. SELF-MONITORING OF STRENGTHS

As described in Chapter 3, invite clients to set up a tracking system to monitor their experiences throughout the day. Ask them to track one or more of the strengths they are using hour by hour (see Chapter 6 for an overview of the twenty-four character strengths); they may need an alarm or another external cue to remind themselves to closely track the strengths they use.

Exercise 65. FIRST-SESSION FORMULA TASK

This is known as the *first-session formula task*. This homework suggestion is used to shift clients' attention from the past to the present and the future, and to increase the expectancy of change. This suggestion also implies that therapists have positive expectations. Invite clients to keep a diary for a week. Ask them to pay attention between this and subsequent sessions to what happens in their life (e.g., in their family, marriage, work) that they would like to continue to see happening. Ask them to pay themselves a compliment at the end of every day based on the things written in their diary, and to write it down as well.

Exercise 66. POSITIVE JOURNALING

Each day for a week, invite clients to write down three good things that happened that day. These three things can be small in importance ("I went to bed early tonight as I had planned") or big ("The guy I've liked for months asked me out"). Next to each positive event, ask them to write about one of the following: "How is it that this good thing happened? What does this mean to me? How can I have more of this good thing in the future?"

Exercise 67. JOURNALING GRATITUDE

Invite clients to buy a handsome blank book to be their *gratitude journal*. Ask them to describe the things for which they are grateful each day. Beyond simply listing good things in their life, one effective strategy is to describe why each good thing happened, in a few sentences. Doing so will draw their eye to the precursors of good events

Exercise 68. REFLECTED BEST SELF

Invite clients to ask ten to twenty people in their life to give them three written stories that describe what worked when they made a contribution in some way. Ask clients to collect all the stories and bring them together, looking for common themes, surprises, and insights. Then ask clients to synthesize all the different contributions into a *best self-portrait*, summarize their findings, or create a project based on the synthesis and share the results with important people in their life. People often combine this exercise with their VIA survey results to get a clear picture of their character strengths in action, as well as to see how closely the strengths they perceive they have line up with the strengths others perceive them to have.

Note that twenty people may sound like a daunting number, but think of the impact this might have. Clients will be having meaningful conversations with twenty people in their life; they will be soliciting positive, engaging comments from these people; and they will probably be connecting with people across numerous domains of their life—personal, social, work, and spiritual. Consider how transformative this can be for them, for the people they talk to, and for these relationships

A forty-year-old client tells her therapist how four years ago she lost her husband in a car accident in which she herself was also involved. Eighteen months ago her house went up in flames, containing her dog and many personal belongings. She is depressed and apathetic, and sometimes she thinks about putting an end to her life. She can barely take care of her two children, ages seven and nine, who spend most of their time with their grandmother, who lives in the same city. Her friends have tried to help in any way they can and have attempted to cheer her up and distract her, but when she goes back home the sadness falls over her like a blanket. Her family doctor, who has referred her for therapy, prescribed antidepressants, which she soon stopped because of the side effects.

The therapist listens to her story, acknowledges the impact of everything that has happened to her, and then asks her how she will know that she does not have to come to therapy anymore. She describes her preferred future: She will be working as a secretary again and enjoying it (she is now on sick leave), her children will be living with her again, and she will perhaps have obtained a new dog from the animal shelter. The therapist asks her how she has managed to get through her days, how it is that she is still alive, and who had helped her so far. She says that her family, friends, and neighbors have done their best to take care of her. The therapist asks what positive things those people saw in her that made them willing to help her. Surprised, she mentions that others have found her an easygoing person and that she has always been there for them when they needed someone. The therapist asks her to write a "letter from her future" (see Exercise 16).

When she comes in for the next appointment, she looks better, and she is wearing makeup for the first time. She says she cried a lot while writing the letter and realized that she wanted to stay alive for her two children. A week later, her children come to live with her again during the week, which leaves her the weekends free to go out with her friends. She also takes the difficult step of going to the grave of her husband for the first time, and later she takes her children there too. After several sessions, she is able to find meaning in life again, using her strengths, resources, and the help of significant others. The wise and compassionate advice she gave herself at the end of the letter from her future—"Be grateful for what you have."—has become reality. She tells her therapist how much clearer it has become to her how grateful she is that her children survived the fire. The therapist compliments her on her strengths, her progress, her discoveries, and her courage. In a follow-up session four months later, she tells her therapist that she is doing fine and that she is organizing a dinner to thank her family, friends, and neighbors for their ongoing support.

BEHAVIORAL EXPERIMENTS

According to Bennett-Levy and colleagues (2004), *behavioral experiments* are planned experiential activities, based on experimentation or observation, that are undertaken by clients in or between therapy sessions. Their primary purpose is to obtain information that may help to test the validity of the clients' existing beliefs about themselves, others, and the world. They also help construct or test new, more adaptive beliefs and contribute to the development and verification of the cognitive formulation.

There are three types of behavioral experiments:

1. *Experimental manipulation of the environment.* This necessitates doing something that is different from what clients would usually do in a particular situation (i.e., "do something different for a change").
2. *For example, clients may try to answer this question:* "If I go to the supermarket alone and do not take my usual precautions, will I faint (as my existing belief would predict), or will I just feel anxious (the prediction of an alternative theory)?"
3. *Observational experiments,* in that it is either not possible or not necessary to manipulate key variables. Instead, clients set out to observe and gather evidence that is relevant to their specific negative thoughts or beliefs. Observational experiments are a form of self-monitoring. For example, clients may try to answer this question: "Will people think I am stupid if I sweat in social situations?"
4. *Discovery-oriented experiments,* in which clients have little or no idea what will happen when they undertake a behavioral experiment and need to collect data systematically in order to build a theory. For example, clients may try to answer this question: "What would happen if I acted as if others valued me?" Or clients

may be encouraged to try out different ways of behaving in order to collect data. For example, they may try to find out, "How might a valued person act in these circumstances?"

However, when a positive focus is used, these experiments are different:

1. *Experimental manipulation of the environment.* Clients are invited to explore exceptions to the problem: What have they done—even slightly—differently before? How has that been helpful? Do clients think it might be a good idea to use this solution again?
2. *Observational experiments.* Clients are invited to observe and gather evidence that is relevant to their specific *positive* cognitions and beliefs. For example, clients may try to answer this question: "Will people think I am likable if I go to this party?" When clients pay attention to their positive cognitions or beliefs, chances are that they will find evidence for them, and when they pay attention to their negative thoughts or beliefs, chances are that they will find evidence for them as well. What you focus on expands.
3. *Discovery-oriented experiments.* Clients are invited to act as if the miracle has happened (when the miracle question is posed), as if (part of) their preferred future has already arrived, or as if they are one or two points higher on the scale of progress. During the session, individuals, couples, or families may be invited to pretend things are going better and show their therapists (for several minutes) how their life or relationships will be different and how this will appear.

SKELETON KEYS

De Shazer (1985) developed the idea of skeleton keys, keys that fit different locks. Skeleton keys are based on the three types of behavior experiments. Having a different key (solution) for each lock (both Axis I and II problems in the DSM-5) is unnecessary, and there is no need for the lock to be analyzed first; interventions can initiate change even when therapists do not know in detail what the problem is. The only thing the interventions need to ensure is that a new behavioral pattern can emerge. The key to building a new habit or positive addiction (see Chapter 7) is to practice the behavior over and over. A number of "skeleton keys" are described in Exercises 69 through 89.

Exercise 69. WRITE, READ, AND BURN

This suggestion can be used if clients are plagued by obsessive or depressive thoughts. De Shazer (1985, p. 120) described a client who was obsessed with her ex-partner months after breaking off the relationship. She felt guilty and kept asking herself what she had done wrong. The thoughts had even grown into nightmares. After normalizing the problem, De Shazer gave the client the following suggestion to help her move on with her life. At the same time every day, she was to retire to a comfortable place for at least an hour and no more than an hour and a half. During that time, on all odd-numbered days, she was to focus on and write down all her good and bad memories of her ex-partner. She was to keep writing the entire time, even if it meant that she ended up writing some things down more than once. On even-numbered days, she was to read her notes from the previous day and then burn them. If the unwanted thoughts came to her at times other than during the scheduled hour, she was to tell herself, "I have other things to do now, and I will think about it when the scheduled hour has arrived," or she was to make a note to remind herself to think about her ex-partner at the scheduled time. After just a few days, the thoughts had largely disappeared.

Exercise 70. STEP BACK AND ASK WHY

Wilson (2011) suggested a writing exercise for "being happy after the bad stuff" and for rendering setbacks in life more understandable and predictable: the *step-back-and-ask-why approach*. It is simple, anyone has the tools to do it, and, according to Wilson's research, it works. This exercise requires two conditions. First, enough time must have passed between the bad experience and the present that clients can think about it without being overwhelmed with negative emotions. Next, clients must be able to analyze why the event occurred instead of ruminating over the fact that it did occur.

Invite clients to write about their experience for at least fifteen minutes on three to four consecutive days. Importantly, ask them to write about the experience *as a dispassionate observer* reporting on the experience, rather than rationalizing the case for their feelings. Ask them not to recount the event but to take a step back, reconstruct it, and explain it.

Exercise 71. STRUCTURED FIGHT

This task can be used if two clients complain that their arguments never lead anywhere. This task consists of three steps:

1. A coin is flipped to determine who gets to go first.
2. The winner may berate the other person for ten minutes, without interruption.
3. The other person may do the same, also without interruption.

Ten minutes of silence follow before the next round is begun with another coin toss.

Exercise 72. DO SOMETHING DIFFERENT

This task can be used if clients complain about another person and claim to have already tried everything. The solution may involve doing something different from what didn't work before. De Shazer (1985, p. 124) offered the following example: A ten-year-old boy was apprehended for prowling around his school. He had broken in to get his homework, which he'd forgotten; however, he refused to answer the police officer's questions. Once the police officer had tried everything to get him to talk, he threatened to hold his own breath until the boy explained why he had broken into the school. This proved too much for the boy. He revealed that he had broken in to retrieve his homework so as not to get a failing grade.

Exercise 73. THANKS FROM YOUR FUTURE SELF

Invite clients to do something each day *that their future self will thank them for*. Ask them to take good care of themselves and search for things they can do today, such as taking a walk, eating healthy food, or doing an act of kindness for someone else.

Exercise 74. FIND MEANING AND PURPOSE

Having something to look forward to every day, something that is meaningful to oneself or others, fulfills the human need to make a meaningful contribution to one's life and the lives of others. Invite clients to do something simple every day, such as expressing appreciation of others with a smile, a touch, or a compliment; making something for the volunteer gift shop; or just calling someone to say hello.

Exercise 75. PAY ATTENTION TO WHAT YOU DO WHEN YOU OVERCOME THE URGE

This task can be used as an alternative to Exercise 72. Although clients will often say that the problematic behavior (e.g., alcohol or drug use, gambling, nail-biting) always occurs, there are often circumstances under which the problematic behavior does not manifest itself. These are exceptions on which clients can build, because they are already part of their repertoire. This task presupposes that clients definitely conquer the urge every now and then and that they may be doing something different to overcome the urge. The clients' attention is directed to their behavior, not to any interior sensation. In some cases, it may also be useful to draw attention to what other people do in comparable situations.

Exercise 76. MULTIPLE OPTIONS

If clients have multiple options and are unable to choose, an observation task may be useful. Every night before going to sleep, the client flips a coin, and the next day he carries out what has been agreed upon on the basis of the coin toss. Heads may mean that the client pretends to have made decision A, for example, to stay with his wife. Tails may mean he pretends to have made decision B, that is, to leave his wife. This may bring clients more clarity so that they can reach a decision.

With problems of choice, *future-oriented techniques* (see Chapter 5) are useful: Clients imagine how they will be doing in the future (in six months, one year, five years, or even ten years) if they decide to do A or B (or even C). Clients can also look back from the future to the present and examine what helped them make a decision (see Chapter 7)

Exercise 77. LOVING-KINDNESS MEDITATION

This is a *mindfulness* exercise. Invite clients to find a quiet place where they can sit comfortably without being disturbed. Ask them to rest their hands lightly on their lap, palms up. Ask them to close their eyes and take a few deep breaths and then breath normally. Say to them, "Just let it be, and just continue to observe your breath. The goal in attending to your breath is to practice being present, here and now. There is no need to suppress your thoughts; just let them be and become aware of them as they come and fade away again."

Mindfulness exercises (see Chapter 6) are used to cultivate *loving-kindness*. This is like guided imagery in which clients reflect on positive feelings for others around them. Invite them to first reflect on a person (or animal) for whom they feel warm and compassionate feelings. Once these feelings take hold, creating positivity in them, ask them to gently let go of the image and simply hold the feeling. Then ask them to extend that feeling to themselves, cherishing themselves as deeply and purely as they would cherish their own newborn child. Next, ask them to radiate their warm and compassionate feelings to others, first to someone they know well, then gradually calling to mind other friends and family members, and then all people with whom they are connected, even remotely. Ultimately, ask them to extend their feelings of love and kindness to all people and creatures of the earth: May they all be happy (Fredrickson, 2009, p. 209).

Exercise 78. COMPASSION EXERCISE

This is an exercise in developing *compassion*. An important way of compassionately engaging with different and problematic parts of the self is in imagery (see Chapter 6). When clients have practiced this a little, they can focus on their compassionate self. Say to clients, "Suppose you are very anxious about something. Sit quietly and engage with your breathing, and then imagine yourself as a compassionate person. When you can feel this compassion expanding and growing inside you, then imagine you can see your anxious self in front of you. Look at her (or his) facial expression; note the feelings rushing through her. Just sit and feel compassion, and send compassionate feelings out to that anxious self. Try to surround that anxious self in compassion and understanding of the torment of anxiety. For now, you are not trying to do anything other than experience compassion and acceptance for your anxiety. Imagine giving as much compassion and understanding as that anxious part needs. You may want to imagine what happens to the anxious part when it actually has all of the understanding and support it needs" (Gilbert, 2010).

Exercise 79. RAINY DAY LETTER

When clients most need comfort, it is often most difficult for them to re-member or figure out what will help. The rainy day letter (Dolan, 1998) provides consolation when clients most need it. They can carry the letter with them wherever they are. It offers wisdom from the person who knows them best: the client himself or herself. Invite clients to set aside some time when they are feeling calm and write this letter to themselves. Give them the following instructions for writing the letter:

- List activities you find comforting.
- Record the names and phone numbers of supportive friends or family members.
- Remind yourself of your strengths and virtues.
- Remind yourself of your special talents, abilities, and interests.
- Remind yourself of your hopes for the future.
- Give yourself special advice or other reminders that are important to you.

Exercise 80. RELAXATION EXERCISE

This is a *relaxation* exercise. Invite clients to take their mind off their stress and replace it with an image that evokes a sense of calm. The more realistic the daydream in terms of colors, sights, sounds, and touch, the more relax-ation they will experience. Ask clients to visualize a peaceful situation or *dreamscape*. This could be a favorite vacation spot, a fantasy island, a pent-house in New York City, or something touchable, like the feel of a favorite sweater.

Exercise 81. SAFE PLACE

lients may be invited to visualize a *safe place*. This exercise, also used in hypnosis and EMDR, is an excellent way to reduce stress and anxiety. Invite clients to select a place they have been at at any time in their life or a place they make up in fantasy that evokes a sense of peacefulness, calm, seren-ity, safety, and security. For example, this might be their own bed, a fantasy island where nobody can come unless they are invited, or a vault in a bank.

Ask them to take two to three minutes per day to connect as closely as they can with their safe place. Ask them to think of all the details they like about it and how it makes them feel. Clients may do this exercise with their eyes open or closed, and they may disclose what their safe place is or keep it to themselves.

Exercise 82. A RIVER CROSSED

Surviving a traumatic event is like crossing a river: While fending for yourself, you develop new skills that can help you in the future. Invite clients to set aside one hour for this exercise. Ask them to think about a painful experience that they have survived and answer the following questions:

- "What did you learn from surviving this experience?"
- "What strengths or talents did you draw on then or develop later to survive the experience?"
- "How can these strengths or talents be used to your best advantage now?"

Exercise 83. DESIGN YOURSELF A BEAUTIFUL DAY

Invite clients to set aside next Saturday and design themselves a beautiful day. Ask them to plan the enjoyable things they will be doing that day, where they will be and with whom. Ask them to design the beautiful day or even beautiful half-day in a way that uses their personal strengths and talents. If, for example, one of their main strengths is curiosity and love of learning, their day might include a trip to the museum or simply reading a book that they have been meaning to read. When their beautiful day arrives, ask them to employ their savoring and mindfulness skills to enhance these pleasures. A variation of this exercise is *Set a strengths date* for couples, in which both partners use their top five character strengths during the date (see Chapter 11).

Exercise 84. GRATITIDE VISIT

Say to clients, "Close your eyes. Call up the face of someone still alive who years ago did something or said something that changed your life for the better—someone you never properly thanked, someone you could meet face to face. Got a face? Write a letter of gratitude to this person and deliver it in person. The letter should be concrete and about 300 words: Be specific about what the person did for you and how it affected your life. Let this person know what you are doing now, and mention how you often remember what he (or she) did. Once you have written the testimonial, call the person and tell him you'd like to visit him, but be vague about the purpose of the meeting; this exercise is much more fun when it is a surprise. When you meet him, take your time reading your letter. Notice his reactions as well as yours. If he interrupts you as you read, say that you really want him to listen until you are done. After you have read the letter (every word), discuss the content and your feelings for each other. Research shows that you will be happier and less depressed one month from now." (Seligman, 2011, p. 30)

The gratitude visit can also be done in a "virtual" way. This may be of particular use if the person is no longer alive or is too far away to visit.

Exercise 85. GRATITIDE IN FOUR STEPS

Here is another gratitude exercise. By doing this exercise, clients will experience more satisfaction and well-being. The four steps are as follows:
1. Focus on some of your nongrateful thoughts.
2. Formulate some grateful thoughts instead.
3. Replace your nongrateful thoughts with your grateful thoughts.
4. Translate the inner positive feeling into action: Do something with it.

Exercise 86. LEARN AND APPLY YOUR STRENGTHS

Invite clients to take the online VIA survey of their character strengths at the website www.authentichappiness.org. After completing the survey, they will receive a report that ranks the twenty-four strengths by the degree to which they characterize them. The report also features their top five strengths and encourages them to reflect on which ones truly resonate for them (see Chapter 6). (This exercise may be combined with Exercise 68.) Once clients have learned their strengths, ask them to redesign their job and life so that they can use them every day.

Exercise 87. TALK ABOUT YOUR STRENGTHS

Invite clients to talk with others about their strengths, telling stories about how their strengths have helped them and were at play when they were at their best. Ask them to use their strengths while they are in conversation. For example, if they want to build on their curiosity, they can ask questions with a sense of genuine interest.

Research on *capitalization*—telling others about positive events in one's life—shows that this generates additional affect, over and above the positive affect associated with the event itself. There are several possible mechanisms for such an effect. First, sharing a positive event with others requires retelling the event, which creates an opportunity for reliving and reexperiencing the event. Furthermore, the communicative act may involve rehearsal and elaboration, both of which seem likely to prolong and enhance the experience by increasing its salience and accessibility in memory. In this way, capitalization builds personal and social resources (Gable, Reis, Impett, & Asher, 2004).

Exercise 88. OPTIMISM TRAINING

Seligman (2011) shifted his research from *learned helplessness* to *learned optimism*. Clients can learn to have more optimistic thoughts, even when they are pessimistic. Seligman battled with his own pessimistic outlook. He described himself as a dyed-in-the-wool pessimist and believed that only pessimists could write sober and sensible books about optimism. He uses the techniques that he wrote about in *Learned Optimism* every day. He takes his own medicine, and it works for him.

Invite your clients, every night before going to bed, to write down a sentence about *the most pleasant event* of that day, as if the event was brought about by something general, global, and within their control (e.g., "Today my colleague offered to help me out, because I am someone who would help another person if needed and he knows that").

Also ask them to write down a sentence every night about *the most unpleasant event* of the day, as if that event was brought about by something specific, temporary, and outside their control (e.g., "Because the bus was delayed, I was not able to get to the appointment with my dentist on time").

Exercise 89. THREE QUESTIONS FOR A HAPPY LIFEL

Invite clients to take a few minutes every evening, or whenever they feel like it, to reflect on these three questions:

1. What did I do today that I feel good about?
2. What has someone else done that I am happy with? Did I react in such a way that this person will perhaps do something like that again?
3. What do I see, hear, feel, smell, taste that I like? (Isebaert, 2007)

THERAPEUTIC RITUALS

Performing *therapeutic rituals* can be one of the exercises therapists suggest as part of any homework. Rituals of various kinds are a feature of almost all known human societies, past or present. They include not only the worship rites of religions and cults, but also the rites of passage of certain societies, purification rites, oaths of allegiance, dedication ceremonies, coronations, marriages and funerals, school graduations, club meetings, sports events, veterans parades, Christmas shopping, and more. The performance of rituals creates a theaterlike frame around the activities, symbols, and events that shape participants' experience and cognitive ordering of the world. This frame helps to simplify the chaos of life and imposes on it a more or less coherent system of categories of meaning.

Sometimes the healing of clients is inhibited by a lack of rituals to facilitate life cycle transitions. Therapeutic rituals can be used in this instance to help clients mobilize their resources for healing, growth, and change. A therapeutic ritual can also help in resolving conflicts and resentments, in negotiating new roles and relational boundaries, and in developing new shared meanings of life with significant others. There are two distinct types of rituals: rites of passage and rites of stability. *Rites of passage* are rituals that mark a person's transition from one status to another, including birth, coming of age, marriage, and death. This type of ritual is specific and temporary and helps people because they are invited to become active instead of passively ruminating. Often a symbol related to a traumatic event is chosen, such as a photograph of the deceased or a piece of the car after the incident. During the therapeutic ritual, designed by the client and therapist together, this symbol is used, for example, by burning or burying it. *Rites of stability* often become habits, and are intended to prevent problems and promote stability and connection after a traumatic life event or change has occurred. These rituals can be performed alone or together with important others and connect people in a positive way. Examples of stability rituals include writing in a diary or going for an evening walk together (see Exercise 90).

More homework suggestions for children and their families are described in Chapter 10. In the next chapter, we will look at follow-up sessions, in which clients and therapists carefully explore what has improved. The therapists ask for a detailed description of the positive dif-

Exercise 90. STABILITY RITUAL

Invite clients to think of a recurring activity that they used to do alone or with a partner or family member. Maybe they went to the movies together every week, read a book to each other, went out for an evening stroll, or massaged each other.

Given the circumstances currently in their life, ask them what ritual they could perform now. Ask them to write that down and invite the other(s) to participate. Ask clients to check after one month to see whether this ritual is a good one for them and the others involved. If not, ask them to adjust the ritual so that it feels good, or to create another ritual with their partner(s). Ask them to check again after one month to see whether the ritual is a good one.

ferences, give compliments and emphasize the clients' personal input in finding solutions.

SUMMARY

- General homework suggestions are described, based on the three types of alliances. These are intended to direct clients' attention to those aspects of their experiences and situations that are most useful in reaching their goals.
- Four positive homework tasks are explained: (a) observe for positives (notice what is going on in your life that you would like to see continue); (b) do more of the positives or exceptions, (c) find out how the spontaneous exceptions are happening, and (d) do a small piece of the hypothetical solution.
- Self-monitoring in post traumatic success is not about clients' symptoms and problems, but about clients' strengths and about exceptions to the problem. There are three forms of self-monitoring: (a) the use of a thought record, (b) observation of positive changes, and (c) monitoring of exceptions to the problem.
- Three forms of behavioral experiments are described: (a) experimental manipulation of the environment, (b) observational experiments, and (c) discovery-oriented experiments.
- The concept of *skeleton keys* is explained. These are keys that

fit different locks. Having a different key (solution) for each lock is unnecessary, and there is no need for the lock to be analyzed first; interventions can initiate change even when therapists do not know in detail what the problem is.

• Therapeutic rituals may help clients move on with their lives or build new habits.

CHAPTER 9

•••••••••••••

Follow-Up Sessions

In follow-up sessions, clients and therapists carefully explore what has improved. Therapists ask for a detailed explanation of the positive exceptions, give compliments, and emphasize clients' personal input in finding solutions. At the end of every session, clients are asked whether they think another meeting is still necessary or useful, and if so, when they would like to return. In many cases, clients feel it is not necessary to return or schedule an appointment further into the future such as is typical in other forms of psychotherapy.

In this chapter, the goals of each follow-up session are described, as well as how to measure progress and how the term *behavior maintenance* seems more appropriate than the term *relapse prevention*. Pathways to failure in psychotherapy are discussed, as well as how therapy can be concluded and successes can be celebrated.

By reflecting on past sessions and inviting clients to give feedback, therapists can find out what clients think about the sessions and gain understanding about what can be done differently or better next session.

An explanation is given of how to become a "supertherapist" and how to make therapy more enjoyable. Musician Miles Davis once said that he doesn't lead his musicians, but that they lead him. His advice was to carefully listen to the musicians you work with and learn what they do best. Therapists should do the same in working with their clients.

THE GOAL OF FOLLOW-UP SESSIONS

According to De Shazer (1994), the goal of each follow-up session is:

- To ask questions about the time between sessions in such a way as to definitely discern some progress. If one looks carefully and creatively, one can (virtually) always find improvements.
- To see whether clients feel that what the therapist and the client did in the previous session has been useful and has given them the sense that things are going better.
- To help clients find out what they are doing or what has happened that has led to improvements so that they will know what to do more of.
- To help clients work out whether the improvements have caused things to go well enough that further sessions are not necessary.
- To ensure that the therapist and the client will not do more of what doesn't work, if clients do not see any improvement, and to find a new approach.

MEASURING PROGRESS

The opening question in each follow-up session is one about progress: "What is (going) better?" The question implicitly suggests that something is better and that one only need pay attention to *what* is better. Therefore, the question is fundamentally different from "Is anything better? How are you today?" or "How have things been since our last session?" With this opening question about progress, therapists determine—to some extent—the answer they receive.

At the beginning of therapy, clients usually react to the question with surprise, because they don't expect it. Sometimes clients initially respond by saying "Nothing," because that is in fact what they are experiencing from their point of view; they have not yet given any thought to anything better. In that case, therapists can ask questions about the recent past and look for times when the problem was absent or was less of a problem. Working on the assumption that one can always find exceptions if one only looks for them, therapists ask questions not about *whether* there are exceptions but about *when* there are or have been exceptions. It has been my experience that if therapists open every session with this question, clients begin to anticipate it and start to reflect on the answer prior to the session.

In each follow-up session, therapists may also ask the four basic SF questions presented in Chapter 3. These questions may pertain to each individual session (e.g., "What are your best hopes for this session?"), to the entire therapy, or even to clients' entire life.

De Jong and Berg (2002) developed the acronym *EARS* to distinguish the activities in follow-up sessions. *E* stands for *eliciting* (drawing out stories about progress and exceptions). *A* stands for *amplifying*. First, clients are asked to describe in detail the differences between the moment when the exception took place and problematic moments. Afterward, therapists and clients examine how the exception took place, and especially what role the clients played in it. *R* stands for *reinforcing*. Therapists reinforce the successes and the factors that led to the exceptions through meticulous exploration of the exceptions and by complimenting their clients. *S*, finally, stands for *start again*. Therapists continue by asking the question "What else is better?"

Exercise 91. WHAT IS BETTER?

Start the next ten or twenty follow-up sessions with the question "What is better?" Dare to ask that question! You will notice that clients will start anticipating the question and prior to the next session will reflect on what has improved so that they can tell you about it. And if—unfortunately—the answer is that nothing is better or things are even worse, just acknowledge their disappointment, take a look at the possibilities under "Four Responses Patterns," and find out how you can stay on a positive track.

FOUR RESPONSE PATTERNS

Clients may have four different response patterns in answering the question "What is better?" How well clients are doing and whether the homework suits them determine whether therapists should continue on the same path or should do something else. Therapists must always carefully tailor their questions and homework assignments to the relationship they have with the client (i.e., whether it is a visitor, complainant, or customer relationship; see Chapter 8). It is important to keep in mind that clients want their problem solved, however pessimistic or skeptical they may be. For that reason, it is important to listen closely and to examine how clients want to change. In follow-up sessions, it is vital to optimize the relationship with clients and to retain the progress already made and build on it. In addition, therapists need to verify whether the homework has been useful and meaningful, and any possible regression must be caught. The four responses are (a) "Things are better," (b) "We disagree" (if there is more than one client), (c) "Things are the same," and (d) "Things are worse."

When *things are going better*, therapists can generally tell by clients' appearance. They usually look better and often identify many things that have changed. Therapists would do well to ask for details about the improvements, to emphasize the difference between how things are and how they were before, and to pay compliments. Questions for clients who report that things are better include:

- "How did you make that happen?"
- "How do you manage to _____?"
- "How did you manage to take such a big step?"
- "How did you come up with that great idea?"
- "What did you tell yourself to help you do it that way?"
- "What do you have to keep doing so that that will happen again?"
- "How is that different for you?"
"Suppose we see each other again in a month. What additional changes will you be able to tell me about then?"
- "How do I know that you have enough confidence to stop the sessions now?"
- "What ideas do you now have (e.g., about yourself) that are different from the ideas you had before?"
- "What would you have to do to go back to square one?"
- "Can you indicate on a scale of ten to zero, where ten indicates that things are fine the way they are, where you are today?"
- "How will you celebrate your victory over the problem?"
- "Who will you invite to this party?"
- "What will you say in the speech that you give at the party?"

At the end of every session, therapists may ask, "Do you think it is useful for you to come back?" If so, "When would you like to come back?" If clients do not have a preference, therapists can gradually increase the time between sessions to indicate their confidence that clients will work things out themselves. Homework suggestions for clients who report that things are better include:

- Go on with what works.
- Do more of what works.

If there is more than one client and they *disagree about the progress* they have made or are concerned that they have not made enough progress, it is wise to normalize matters. Therapists can make it clear that clients often make progress by taking three steps forward and then taking one or two steps back. In any case, it is a good idea to begin by taking a look, together with the clients, at what is going better, even if it is only going better to a very small degree. Those times when it is better can be amplified, and therapists can pay compliments. Moreover, they can point out that small differences may lead to significant changes later on.

A useful question for clients who disagree is: "Supposing we see each other again in four weeks, what changes would you like to have achieved by then?" If any of the clients remain concerned, therapists may ask competence questions, such as:

- "Could the situation be worse?"
- "How come things aren't worse?"
- "What steps have you taken to ensure that things don't get worse?"
- "What else helps to ensure that things don't get worse?"
- "What difference does that make?"

Therapists can ask themselves the following questions:

- Do I have a customer, complainant, or visitor relationship with these clients?
- Is there a goal, and has it been formulated well?
- What homework suggestions would suit these clients best?
- Can I present the clients with a number of homework suggestions to choose from?

Here are some homework suggestions for clients who disagree:

- If a client tries to undermine another client's attempts to achieve a desired behavior, therapists can suggest an observation exercise. For a week or longer, each of the clients observes what desired behavior the other client displays and makes a note of it. Clients bring their notes to the next session. They are not allowed to go over the notes together before the session.

- If the homework suggestion was helpful, but if one or both of the clients did not find it a pleasant or useful exercise, therapists can examine together with the clients how the suggestion may be improved.

- If more exceptions are needed, therapists may propose the *surprise task*, a playful way to challenge a person's fixed ideas. All clients agree that they will do something (either subtle or highly noticeable) to surprise the other(s) in a positive way. What that might be is left to each client. The other(s) may then guess what the surprise was and talk about it at the next session. Children and adolescents in particular take great pleasure in these surprise tasks.

- If both clients are stuck in a pattern of negative interaction, the therapist may also propose a *do-something-different* task. Here, too, clients themselves decide what they will do differently in the upcoming period. What they do is immaterial; the purpose is to break a fixed pattern. For example, during a course of family therapy, there was frequent mention of serious arguments because the adolescent son and daughter did not follow the parents' rules. During the next argument, both parents lay down on the floor and stopped speaking. The children were so shocked that they came along to subsequent sessions because they were worried about their parents.

- Another possibility is the *pretend-the-miracle-has-happened task*. All clients are instructed to pretend for a day or two (or for a shorter period of time if that proves too ambitious, e.g., part of a day or an hour) that the miracle has happened. None of the clients know which day the others have chosen. Each person is asked to pay attention to the difference that the pretending makes. Everyone may guess on what days the others chose to pretend that the miracle had happened. They keep their findings to themselves and do not share them until the next session with the professional. As it turns out, they may well guess the wrong day.

- Therapists may suggest the *prediction* task: Every day, the clients predict what the following day will look like. This task is intended to supply information about what works. Afterward, the clients examine whether the prediction has come true and what contributed to this. In a variant of this homework suggestion, the clients predict each morning whether or not they will be successful at fulfilling the prediction.

It is important to distinguish between tasks for clients in a customer relationship and tasks for clients in a complainant relationship. The do-something-different task and the pretend-the-miracle-has-happened task are tasks in which clients have to do something different, whereas the prediction task is an observational task. Thus, the prediction task is useful for clients in a complainant relationship, since they do not (yet) have to change their behavior.

Some clients may feel that *things are the same* and that nothing about the situation has changed. In that case, it is useful to find out when small improvements in the situation have been noticeable nonetheless. Clients can use every exception that is found and continue the small improvement by making that exception happen again. Sometimes remaining stable is a great result in itself; progress is not always attainable.

Questions for clients who report that things are the same include:

- "How did you manage to remain stable?"
- "Suppose I were to ask someone who knows you well what is going a little better. What would that person say?"
- "On a scale of ten to zero, how would you rate your current situation?"
- "What is needed for you to maintain that point on the scale in the time to come?"
- "Who among the most important people in your life is most worried about you?"
- "On a scale of ten to zero, how worried is that person?"

It may be useful to expand the sessions to include an important person from the client's life to help find solutions to the problem. If clients stay negative and fail to name exceptions, therapists can ask more competence questions, such as, "How do you cope? How do you manage to go on with these sessions?" Therapists may ask themselves the following questions:

- Do I have a customer, complainant, or visitor relationship with this client?
- Do we need to revisit the goal?

Following are homework suggestions for clients who report that things are the same:

- If the do-something-different task has not yet been assigned, it can be introduced as an experiment, especially if clients are stuck in a rut.
- The pattern of interaction can be changed through the addition of a new element or through deliberate exaggeration of the pattern.
- If clients indicate that they cannot exert any control over the problem, they can be asked to *externalize* the problem (see Chapter 7 and Appendix E).

Clients who say that *things are going worse* often have a long history of failure or have contended with big problems for years. If therapists are too optimistic, they will usually be unable to help such clients. These clients often need a lot of space to tell the story of the problem, including any (negative) experiences with previous therapists. In that case, therapists may apply the *Greek chorus* technique (Papp, 1983). The Greek chorus warns of potential dangers between scenes. With the Greek chorus technique, the therapist adopts an attitude in favor of change, whereas his or her team of colleagues adopts an attitude against change. If therapists work alone, they can apply the technique by introducing a pessimistic supervisor. Clients are invited to work with the therapist to prove the team or the supervisor wrong.

Therapists may ask *pessimistic questions* of clients who report that things are going worse:

- "How do you manage under these circumstances?"
- "How come you haven't given up by now?"
- "How come things aren't worse than they are?"
- "What is the smallest thing you could do to make a minimal difference?"
- "How can you make the same thing happen to a very small extent right now?"
- "What used to help that you could try again now?"
- "What would most help you to face these difficulties?"
- "How did you manage to get out of bed this morning and make it here?"

It is useful to put these clients in an expert position and ask them, as *consultants*, what their treatment should look like. Questions for expert clients are:

- "What did therapists you worked with previously miss?"
- "Of all the things that these therapists did, what did you find most disagreeable?"
- "How could I be of greater assistance?"
- "What qualities would your ideal therapist have, and what would he or she do?"
- "What questions would your ideal therapist ask you, and what, in your opinion, would be the best course for him or her to follow?"
- "If I worked with other clients who were in the same situation as you, what advice would you give me that would allow me to help them?"
- "What question can you think of that would allow me to help you the most?"

Here again, therapists may ask themselves the following questions:

- Do I have a customer, complainant, or visitor relationship with this client?
- Do we need to revisit the goal?

Here are some homework suggestions for clients who report that things are going worse:

- It may help to have the exceedingly pessimistic client *predict in detail when and how the next crisis will take place*. As a result, the crisis may fail to occur, or the client may discover better ways to deal with it.
- The client can also be asked to *exaggerate the problem*. This is a paradoxical assignment: As a result, the gravity of the problem may immediately decrease, because clients do not feel like carrying out such an assignment. If clients do exaggerate the problem, they will likely experience more control than they first thought.

- Therapists may examine clients' earlier successes in solving problems to see what strategies they may try again.

With this group of clients, therapists may deploy the same strategies as with clients who report that nothing is going better. If therapists work alone, it may be useful to invite a colleague to sit in and give feedback. With this group of clients, therapists might also apply the technique of externalizing the problem (see Chapter 7 and Appendix E). Last, therapists may discharge themselves in a final rescue attempt if all other strategies have failed. They can explain to their clients that they apparently do not understand the client or do not have the expertise to help him or her. They might say that it would be best for the client to enlist the help of another therapist, who may have fresh ideas. Clients may agree with this proposition, or they may begin to formulate more realistic expectations, after which cooperation may be possible.

For more homework suggestions, see Chapter 8. For a protocol for follow-up sessions, see Appendix C.

CASE 27. *The Greek Chorus*

This is an example of the use of the *Greek chorus*. A twenty-five-year-old client, a military veteran who returned home from combat a year ago, smokes several joints every day. He says he would like to break the habit because he can't see himself finding work if he doesn't. The therapist introduces a pessimistic colleague into her team; the colleague predicts that the client will undoubtedly relapse if he stops smoking marijuana, because this has happened to others. This is upsetting for the client; he explains to the therapist that he knows what he is getting into, and that once he has made his decision he will certainly stick to it! At the next session, he reports having barely touched a joint. The therapist offers compliments: He must be a truly determined person! The client blossoms as he shares, in response to the therapist's questioning, that this is not the first time in his life that he has shown such determination.

Duncan, Hubble, and Miller (1997) described *therapy veterans of impossibility*. Veterans of impossibility are clients who have had many negative experiences in psychotherapy. Often these clients are blamed or their therapists are criticized. Veterans of impossibility may sometimes be overwhelming in their presentations of problems. These problems seem, at times, to fill the sessions so full that the therapist feels smothered, gasping for air. Much-needed oxygen for both client and therapist comes when the problem is connected to a description that states or implies that the presenting problem is changeable and that positive outcomes are achievable.

Treatment failures taught Duncan and colleagues (1997) three lessons:

1. All theoretical models have limited applicability.
2. The therapeutic relationship is more valuable than expert interventions.
3. What clients know, think, feel, and want has far more relevance to problem resolution than favored academic conceptualizations.

BEHAVIOR MAINTENANCE

How do we help clients to design sustainable change and flourishing? In traditional psychotherapies, *relapse prevention* is a standard intervention toward the end of therapy. But what are therapists suggesting or even predicting when they talk with clients about relapses? You guessed it—that they are bound to happen! A good question is whether it is always necessary to bring this subject up, or whether, instead, it is only useful to discuss relapse prevention if clients think it is useful. The answer to this question is that it is best to ask clients if they are interested in finding out how to maintain the changes they made in therapy.

Of course, maintaining hard-won changes isn't always easy, and clients have to work hard and show determination to do so. Therefore, instead of talking about relapses and how to prevent them, it is preferable to talk about the progress made and how to maintain these positive changes. In this vein, relapse prevention becomes *behavior maintenance*.

Focusing on what clients (and others) have done to help recovery or prevention in past experiences may be useful (O'Hanlon & Rowan, 2003). When prevention plans fail or are not put into practice, therapists may map out a *recovery plan*—especially with clients who have severe mental problems, like psychosis, major depression, or suicidal thoughts. This can usually be derived from asking about what happened as the person regained equilibrium after a previous crisis. Further useful questions include:

- "What did you do when you started to feel better again?"
- "What usually happens when you begin to emerge from one of your depressive episodes?"
- "What did you learn from your previous hospitalizations that may be helpful in this situation?"

A Growth Mindset

To create and sustain change, therapists have to embrace a growth mindset instead of a fixed one and instill it in their clients (Dweck, 2006). People (including therapists) who have a fixed mindset believe that their abilities are basically static. They believe that they may get a little bit better or worse at different skills, but that basically their abilities reflect the way they are wired. People with a fixed mindset tend to avoid challenges, because if they fail, they fear that others will see their failure as an indication of their true ability and see them as a loser. They feel threatened by negative feedback, because it seems as if the critics are saying they are better than them, positioning themselves at a level of natural ability higher than theirs.

In contrast, people who have a growth mindset believe that abilities are like muscles—they can be built up with practice. People with a growth mindset tend to accept more challenges despite the risk of failure. They seek out more challenging assignments and are more inclined to accept criticism, because ultimately it makes them better. Dweck stated that if you want to reach your full potential and be more successful at almost anything, you need a growth mindset.

If failure is a necessary part of change, then the way clients understand failure is critical. The paradox of the growth mindset is that, although it seems to draw attention to failure, and in fact encourages people to seek out failure, it is optimistic, because in the end people will succeed.

Research by Dweck (2006) showed that students who have a fixed mindset have stronger and more depressive complaints than students who have a growth mindset. The students with a fixed mindset stagnated when encountering their failures and in dealing with their mistakes, and the more depressed they became, the more they gave up, making no further attempts to solve their problems. On the contrary, students with a growth mindset, suffering from depressive complaints, displayed different behavior. The more depressed they reported themselves as being, the more action they undertook to solve their problems, the harder they worked, and the more active they became in structuring their lives. To sum up: When people believe that their personal qualities can be further developed, then, despite the pain of failure, they do not become pessimistic, because they are not being defined by their failures. Change and growth remain a possibility, opening up pathways to success.

Questions that may be used when asking about a *growth mindset* are:

- "How did you do this?"
- "What did you do to make that happen?"
- "How is this different from how you used to do this?"
- "What could you do (even) better next time?"
- "What do you like about it?"
- "What do you already understand and what do you not understand (yet)?"

According to Menninger (1959), anticipation is the best defense. But what should be anticipated? He surely was talking about anticipation of the danger of relapses and setbacks. But anticipation using a positive focus is done by analyzing and predicting what may go well and what clients should do to flourish and thrive; anticipation using a negative focus is done by analyzing and predicting what may go wrong and what clients should do to avoid relapse, and cope and survive. By doing the latter, chances are that there will be an increase in negative cognitions and feelings, because this concerns an avoidance goal (see Chapter 5). Clients will focus on what they fear most, trying to keep the distance between their present situation and the feared outcome as large as possible. In contrast, in behavior maintenance—an approach goal—clients will notice an increase in positive cognitions and feelings. Clients will focus on what they want most, trying to make the distance between their present situation and their preferred future as small as possible.

During therapy, clients are encouraged to think about ways to maintain the gains of the therapy, thereby contributing to the client's *mental road map*. Therapists may ask clients to imagine a better future and consider how their strengths and resources can be used to make this future come true. Snyder's research (see Chapter 4) showed that hopeful people are able to come up with more alternative routes than non-hopeful people if the original route is blocked. Discussing ways to tackle possible future obstacles serves as a means of developing alternative solutions before these difficulties even present themselves. This builds coping strategies and enhances *pathway thinking*, which further diminishes the risk of relapse or, better, augments the chances of behavior maintenance.

If a setback occurs, therapists would do well to normalize it: Progress often means taking three steps forward and one or two steps back (and it would be a shame to give up even a single step). Therapists may also give a positive slant to the setback; after all, a setback offers an opportunity to practice getting back on one's feet. "If you fall on your face, at least you are heading in the right direction" (Erickson, as quoted in O'Hanlon, 2000).

Furthermore, it is not always necessary to dwell on the cause of the relapse and its consequences. Therapists would do well to offer acknowledgment to their clients by showing that they understand how frustrating the relapse is. Following this, it is most important to explore how clients have managed on previous occasions to get back on the right track after a relapse. If clients remain disconcerted in the wake of the recent relapse, they and their therapists can consider what steps they can take to get back on the right track.

The session can also deal with relapse in a lighter, more playful manner. Therapists may ask, "What would it take for you to obtain a low rating on the scale or to go back to square one as quickly as possible?" This immediately indicates what the wrong approach is and often lends the conversation a lighthearted tone.

Consolidating Questions

Selekman (1993) described the use of consolidating questions at the conclusion of the sessions as an effective means of getting clients to talk about positive differences. A few of these questions, which can ensure that the achieved results become permanent, are:

- "What would you have to do to go backward?"
- "What would you have to do to prevent a relapse?"
- "What do you have to keep doing to make sure that these changes keep happening?"

Selekman (1993) invited clients to use what he described as his *imaginary crystal ball* to tell him what changes they saw themselves making in the future. He expressed disbelief in the psychoanalytic hypothesis that clients are subject to a *flight into health* if they terminate treatment following rapid changes at the beginning of the therapy. He thinks that clients must determine not only the goal of the therapy but also when to end it:

> As a solution-oriented therapist, I do not believe my job is to cure people, but instead, to help clients have more satisfactory life situations. If clients call to cancel future scheduled appointments because they feel things are better for the time being, I always let them know that I have an open door policy and if they need to schedule a future tune-up session, they may feel free to call me (p. 156).

When clients reenter therapy, a useful question is "How did you succeed in staying away as long as you did?"

Many therapists have a much loftier goal in mind than most clients do. If therapists were more in tune with their clients' goals, treatments would become shorter and probably more successful. It is customary in problem-focused therapies to make several appointments for sessions concerning relapse prevention and follow-up. It often seems that the point of these sessions is to reassure the therapists rather than to meet a need on the client's part.

Rothman (2000) found that the decision criteria that lead people to initiate a change in their behavior are different from those that lead them to maintain that behavior. Decisions regarding behavioral initiation depend on favorable expectations regarding future outcomes. This can be conceptualized as an approach-based self-regulatory system in which people's progress toward their goals is indicated by a reduction in the discrepancy between their current state and a desired reference state. Decisions regarding behavioral maintenance depend on *perceived satisfaction with received outcomes*. This can be conceptualized as an avoidance-based self-regulatory system in which progress is indicated by a sustained discrepancy between a current state and an undesired reference state. Other research (Ross & Wilson, 2002) has shown that recalling an old, pre-change self from the *third-person perspective* (see Chapter 7) helps to deal with the challenge of maintaining personal change. Greater perceived change—as exists when people adopt a third person perspective—leads to greater satisfaction with one's efforts thus far and therefore makes it easier to summon the resources necessary to maintain one's efforts. Psychologically distancing oneself from negative past selves and remaining close to positive past selves promotes well-being. Questions that may be useful are:

- "How did you succeed in making lasting changes in other parts of your life? Which of those strategies might be useful now?"
- "How satisfied are you with the positive changes you made on a scale from ten to zero?"
- "What will one point higher on the scale look like?"
- "What can you do to get to one point higher on the scale?"
- "Predict what tomorrow will be like, and at the end of that day find an explanation for why the day turned out the way it did. If your prediction was correct, ask yourself how you knew. If your prediction wasn't correct, how come?"
- "Find supporters to help you in maintaining these changes. Whom will you invite? How will you keep them updated? How will you thank them for their help?"
- "If, from an observer perspective, you look back to your past self before you made these changes, what would this observer say is going better in your life right now?"

Exercise 92. FIFTY WAYS TO MAINTAIN POSITIVE CHANGE

Invite your clients to follow these instructions:

- Think of fifty *good reasons* to maintain the positive changes you made.
- Think of fifty *ways* to maintain these positive changes.
- Think of fifty *positive consequences* (for yourself, for important others) of maintaining these positive changes.

CASE 28. *Fifty Ways of Coping*

A client sighs heavily and says, "I don't know if I can keep up with everything that is going on in my life." The therapist invites her to write down fifty ways in which she is keeping up right now. "You mean I have to write down five ways of coping?" the client asks wearily. "No, not five, I mean fifty ways," answers the therapist. "Would you like to start here, or would you prefer to do the task at home?" The client looks at her therapist incredulously, but starts anyway. As she continues to find ways that are already working for her (going to bed early once every week, asking her sister to help with bringing the kids to their sports activities, and so on), her posture changes to a more active one. She manages to find forty-three ways during the session, and when she leaves she is quite confident she can find the other seven ways as well. When giving feedback, she states, "This session has made me see that it is not a question of whether I can keep up, but how I can do it."

STAGNATION AND FAILURE

As explained in Chapter 3, the average treated client is better off than about 80 percent of the untreated sample (Duncan, Miller, Wampold, & Hubble, 2010). But unfortunately, dropouts are a significant problem, and although many of our clients profit from therapy, many do not. Sometimes our clients come back and tell us that things are worse instead of better, or that nothing has changed. This may be discouraging for therapists and clients alike, especially when everybody has worked hard in therapy. Clients also may feel embarrassed or ashamed at having to report failure or setbacks. The importance of *saving face* is discussed below.

Another point of concern is the variability among therapists. Some therapists are much better at getting positive results than others. In fact, therapist effectiveness ranges from 20 to 70 percent. Moreover, even very effective clinicians seem to be poor at identifying deteriorating clients (Duncan, 2010).

De Shazer (1994) stated that clients and therapists often are willing to accept the absence of the problem as a good enough goal, but the absence of the problem can never be proved and, therefore, neither clients nor therapists can know success or failure. Unless parameters are clearly established beforehand, even the presence of positive changes is not enough to prove the absence of the problem. Therefore, questions like "What are your best hopes?" followed by "What difference will that make?" are considered essential for establishing well-defined goals in psychotherapy.

Some failures are related to difficulty in shifting from a problem-focused conversation to an SF conversation. The fault here is situated neither on the therapists' side nor on the clients' side: Both are in it together. When this happens, most often therapists have been unable to help clients see exceptions to the problem as "differences that can make a difference" and thus as precursors to fulfilling the clients' goals.

Therapists may also cause failures. Oettingen and colleagues (Oettingen 1999; Oettingen et al., 2000) elucidate the technique of *mental contrasting* in goal setting (see Chapter 5). Mental contrasting is an expectancy-based route and rests on mentally contrasting fantasies about a desired future with negative aspects as obstacles of the present reality, emphasizing a necessity to change the negative present reality to achieve the desired future. This necessity to act activates relevant expectations of success, which then prompt goal commitment. Reversing this order (i.e., reverse mental contrasting) by first elaborating the negative reality and then elaborating the desired future—as is usually done in traditional therapies—fails to elicit goal commitment congruent with expectations of success (Oettingen et al., 2001).

Pathways to Impossibility

Duncan and colleagues (1997) describe four pathways to impossibility. The first pathway arises in the *anticipation of impossibility*. Historically, impossibility has been located in the client. In a well-known experiment, Rosenhan (1973) recruited and trained a group of normal colleagues (one of them was Seligman) to obtain psychiatric hospitalization. To gain admission, they falsified a single psychotic symptom (hearing voices). The clinicians diagnosed the pretend patients as mentally ill and admitted them for stays ranging from seven to fifty-two days. During their hospitalizations, the pseudo-patients showed no signs of psychosis, yet the original diagnosis remained in place. Rosenhan also demonstrated how the clinicians' initial expectations came to serve as confirmatory biases. In one instance, staff took truthful historical information provided by a pseudo-patient and made it conform to prevailing theoretical notions about schizophrenia. Therefore, therapists' expectation of impossibility will probably distort new information to conform to their expectations.

The second pathway to impossibility is *therapists' traditions or conventions*. Therapists are often eager to corroborate their theory with each client, and their theory is often overapplied. Remember the story of the man who bought a hammer and then found that everything needed to be nailed?

Clients have their own theories about their lives and their problems, and when their points of view are ignored or dismissed by the therapist's theory, noncompliance or resistance is a predictable outcome. To therapists, clients begin to look, feel, and act impossible; to clients, therapists come across as uncaring or disinterested. The therapy changes from a helping relationship to a clash of cultures with no winner. Client-directed, outcome-informed therapy, as described later in this chapter, may be the answer to this second pathway to impossibility.

The third pathway to impossibility is *persisting in an approach that is not working*. Watzlawick and colleagues (1974) reasoned that unmanageable problems, those that are often called chronic, couldn't be sufficiently explained on the basis of innate characteristics of the clients. Rather, these authors concluded that the unyielding or impossible nature of a problem arises in the very efforts to solve it. For a difficulty to turn into a problem, only two conditions need to be fulfilled: First, the difficulty must be mishandled; the attempted solutions do not work. Second, when the difficulty proves refractory, more of the same ineffective solutions are applied and the original difficulties become even worse. Over time, a vicious downward spiral ensues, with the original difficulty growing into an impasse, immense in size and importance.

Therapists doing more of the same are sometimes convinced that persistence will eventually win the day, even when all the evidence suggests that the strategy is ineffectual. All theoretical models and strategies are inherently limited and will generate their share of impossibility when repetitively applied. Wampold (2001) found that when there is no improvement after the third session, there is a 75-percent chance that the therapy with fail. This percentage increases to 90 percent when no improvement is found after the sixth session. Research by Lambert and colleagues (2002) indicates that treatment should be brief when little or no progress is being made in the early sessions. Therapy should not be used just to sustain or maintain clients. As long as clients are making documentable progress and are interesting in continuing, however, treatment should be extended.

Research by Piper and colleagues (1999) showed that dropouts could be predicted by treatment process variables, not by client variables. In other words, only what happened in the sessions predicted whether the client failed to return, not who the client was or what the client brought to the process. The Outcome Rating Scale and Session Rating Scale, as described in more detail later in the chapter, are great tools for measuring desired progress and change.

The fourth and last pathway to impossibility is created when the therapist *neglects the client's motivation*. There is no such individual as an unmotivated client. Clients may not share the ideas and goals of their therapists, but they hold strong motivations of their own. An unproductive therapy can come about by mistaking or overlooking what clients want to accomplish, misapprehending clients' readiness for change, or pursuing a personal motivation. Research has established that the critical process outcome in psychotherapy is the quality of the clients' participation in a positive *alliance* (see Chapter 4). The motivation of clients not only for sitting at the therapist's office, but also for achieving their own goals, has to be understood, respected, and actively incorporated into the therapy. To do less or to impose agendas motivated by theoretical prerogatives, personal bias, and perhaps some sense of what would be good for clients invites impossibility.

Top performers review the details of their performance, identifying specific actions and alternate strategies for reaching their goals. Whereas unsuccessful people attribute failure to external and uncontrollable factors ("I just had a bad day"), experts know exactly what they did and more often cite controllable factors ("I should have done this instead of that"). Average therapists are far likelier to spend time hypothesizing about failed strategies—believing perhaps that understanding the reasons why an approach did not work will lead to better outcomes—and less time thinking about strategies that might be more effective. Walter and Peller (1992) offer some questions for therapists in situations where there seems to be no progress:

- Does the client want to change (e.g., is there a customer relationship)?
- What is the client's goal?
- Does the client have a goal and not a wish? Is the goal well-defined and within the control of the client?
- Are you and the client looking for too much too fast? Look for a smaller change.
- Does the client not do the homework that you have been expecting him or her to do? Provide some feedback to think about rather than an action-oriented task.
- If you have gone through all the above steps, is there anything you need to do differently? Sometimes we are too close to the

trees to see the forest and may not recognize a nonproductive pattern between the client and ourselves. A team or consultant may be helpful in providing a more detached frame of reference.

CASE 29. *Deadlock*

Mr. and Mrs. Brown are sitting in the therapist's office. Mr. Brown says, "I don't think that this therapy will succeed; the former therapist didn't help us much. We did make a plan to change things in our relationship, but the implementation of what we agreed has never come off the ground. It has only led to more arguments between us." The (overoptimistic) therapist ignores this remark, and before long therapy reaches a deadlock.

The therapist would have done better to validate the doubts of Mr. Brown by acknowledging them and by asking scaling questions with respect to confidence, hope, and motivation: "Supposing you had a bit more hope, what difference would that make?" Or, "How, despite your previous experience, do you manage to sit here in a therapist office?"

Yes, But and Yes, And

The expression *Yes, but* is often used to indicate that someone disagrees with the other person. When used by clients, it is often interpreted by their therapists as a form of resistance: "Of course you're right, *but* . . ." or "*Yes, but* I see it differently . . ." An utterance like *Yes, but* excludes or dismisses what preceded it, is often perceived as pejorative, and suggests that the first issue is subordinate to the second. It drains energy from the conversation, which soon turns into a discussion that revolves solely around who is right. *Yes, but* is actually an indirect form of *No*.

It is more productive to use *Yes, and*, which expands and includes what preceded it and creates new possibilities and vastly improves co-operation. *Yes, but* excludes others' positions; with *Yes, and*, they complement one another (see Table 4). The alliance with clients who often use *Yes, but* can be classified as a complainant relationship. For therapists, too, it may be useful to practice saying *Yes*, and instead of *Yes, but* to clients and colleagues.

TABLE 4. Differences between *Yes, but* and *Yes, and*	
Yes, but	**Yes, and**
Excludes or dismisses what precedes it	Expands and includes what precedes it
Negates, discounts, or cancels what precedes it	Acknowledges what precedes it
Is often perceived as pejorative	Is often perceived as neutral or positive
Suggests that the first issue is subordinate to the second	Suggests that there are two equal issues to be addressed

---

CASE 30. *Client Worsening*

Is it to be expected that clients will get worse before they get better? Of course not! Considerable clinical lore has built up around the idea that deterioration of the client's situation comes before the situation gets better. This is rarely the road to recovery, and, in fact, it portends a final negative outcome. This idea also allows therapists to ignore, to some degree, client worsening

—Lambert & Ogles, 2004

Saving Face

Duncan and colleagues (2010) stated that the place of saving face should be considered. When clients feel overwhelmed and stuck, they are apt to experience their problems as impossible. Seeking help offers the prospect of something better. Simultaneously, it may signify their failure to resolve the problem on their own. In fact, their feelings of failure may be so acu te that they crowd out any favorable self-evaluation. In these circumstances, going to therapy can represent just one more unpleasant reminder of how badly they have managed their difficulties. Humiliation is added to insult. If therapists then suggest or imply that the clients' point of view is wrong, or somehow invalidate or upstage the client, *resistance* may appear. After all, even if you're not already demoralized, who wants to be reminded of failure, criticized, judged, or made to feel that they must follow orders? What we come to call resistance may sometimes reflect clients' attempt to salvage a small portion of self-respect. As such, some cases become impossible simply because the treatment allows clients no way of saving face or upholding dignity. This is probably what Erickson had in mind when

Exercise 93. COMPLIMENTS IN A COMPLAINANT RELATIONSHIP

During sessions, continue to pay attention to what is going better or what is different and how clients make that happen. Especially in the context of a complainant relationship, give clients at least three compliments in each session and ask them competence questions such as: "How did you do that?" "How were you able to do that?" and "How did you decide to do that?" Notice the difference this makes for clients and for you as a therapist.

he suggested that the art of therapy revolves around helping clients *bow out of their symptoms gracefully*. He recognized that clients simultaneously hold a desire to change and a natural tendency to protect themselves if change (for worse or for better) compromises their personal dignity (Rossi, 1980).

STORY 32. *Ten Million Dollars Lost*

An executive at IBM lost 10 million US dollars. CEO Watson summoned the executive to his office. The executive: "I assume you will fire me." Watson looked surprised. "Of course not. I just spent 10 million educating you."

—Heath and Heath, 2010, p. 173

Spacing Sessions

There is no limit to the possible number of sessions. Sessions are discontinued if clients achieve their goal (to a sufficient degree). After the second session, the time interval between sessions usually increases. One week between the first and the second session is generally a good amount of time (but it can be more or less if clients so wish). Traditional psychotherapy models usually schedule one or more sessions regularly every week or every two weeks. However, in the approach described in this book, each session is scheduled according to:

- The time needed for the performance of some homework assignment
- The promotion of confidence in the solutions
- The promotion of independence from therapy
- The client's responsibility for therapy

Some homework suggestions take more time to do or to reveal a meaningful difference to clients. Spacing out the sessions enables clients to have a longer-term perspective on their construction of solutions and to put setbacks in perspective. The spacing of sessions over longer periods of time, from two weeks to three to six, can also promote confidence in solving the problems, since some clients would otherwise think that the changes in themselves were dependent on therapy and that their therapists were responsible for the changes. The spacing of sessions is determined by the clients and not by the therapists by asking questions like, "Do you think it is useful to schedule another session?" and if so, "When would you like to return?" Clients are responsible for their therapy, and therapists determine with their clients the amount of time they should be spending on homework suggestions and the length of time between the current and the subsequent session, based on the confidence the clients have in their own strengths and solutions.

CONCLUDING THERAPY

De Shazer (1991) stated that if therapists accept clients' statement of their problem at the beginning of treatment, by the same logic they should also accept clients' declaration that they have sufficiently improved as a reason to end the treatment. In principle, each session is viewed as the last session, and just one session may even be enough if the client's goal has become clear. De Shazer (1991) described how the client's goal comes into view if during the session(s) the client and therapist have been attentive to:

- The occurrence of exceptions and the presence of parts of the client's preferred future (the goal), which indicate that desired changes are taking place.
- The client's vision and description of a new life.
- The confirmation that change is taking place and that the client's new life has in fact begun.

Contrary to what happens in most traditional psychotherapies, discussion of ending clients' contact with therapists occurs as soon as the therapy starts. This is evident from the questions clients receive about goal formulation: "What needs to change in your life in order for you to say that these sessions have been worthwhile? What would indicate to you that you're doing well enough that you no longer have to come here?" What therapists wish to elicit here is a description of what clients consider a successful result, in positive, concrete, and measurable terms. A detailed description of the preferred future situation can be of great help: "What are you doing differently that tells me that that's the situation you prefer?"

Discussing the desired outcome from the very beginning of the sessions creates an atmosphere of optimism and gives clients hope that their problem can be solved (to a sufficient degree). Therapists should set aside a fair amount of time for goal formulation: When the goal has been formulated well, half the work is often already done.

The moment when the sessions can be concluded can also be revealed by means of scaling questions. Therapists may ask their clients at what number they need to be in order not to have to come to therapy anymore. Experience shows that most clients are happy with a seven or eight and don't need to reach a nine or ten before they finish treatment. Sometimes treatment can be concluded at a lower point on the scale because clients have enough confidence that they can go without therapy toward the point where they would like to end up. In any case, it should be clear that clients themselves, in close cooperation with their therapists, decide when the treatment can be concluded.

CELEBRATING SUCCESS

At the start of therapy, therapists may already begin asking how clients would like to celebrate when they have reached their goal. Children in particular find this a highly enjoyable way to start. At the last session, therapists come back to this. Some suggestions for celebrating clients' success include the following:

- Therapists ask how their clients will celebrate their victory over the problem.
- Therapists ask whom clients will invite to their victory party.
- Therapists ask what clients will say in the speech that they will give at the party.
- Therapists ask each family member to pay a compliment to the other members of the family.
- Therapists create a Certificate of Success (see Appendix I).
- Therapists write their clients a letter outlining their goal, the steps they have taken toward achieving that goal, and their successes, and compliment the clients.
- Clients make a drawing of the situation at the start of therapy and another of the situation at the conclusion of therapy. Therapists may ask clients whether they would like to save the

drawing of the situation at the start of therapy or, for example, by way of ritual, burn it.

- Clients frame a drawing that they make of their goal (or "miracle," when the miracle question is asked; see Chapter 5).
- Clients make a "recipes for success" booklet filled with descriptions of how they have brought about successes in their life.
- Clients celebrate the conclusion of therapy with cake, flowers, and snacks.
- Therapists give their clients a *transitional object*—for example, a pebble, a mascot, a magic wand—something appropriate for the treatment. Clients may choose one such object from a small assortment.
- Therapists have clients choose a symbol for their victory over the problem and let clients draw or make it.
- Therapists or clients make a small plaque with a maxim or motto on it that symbolizes the clients' success.
- Therapists give clients a mug that says on one side "Stop what doesn't work, do something different" and on the other side "Keep doing what works."
- Clients come up with a magic spell to ensure that things will continue to go well.
- Therapists ask clients to mention the most important tip they have for the next client who experiences the same problems.
- Therapists ask permission to consult their clients as experts if they find themselves at a loss during a similar treatment.
- Therapists ask what clients would have to do to ensure that things will go badly for them again as quickly as possible (*relapse prevention*; see earlier in this chapter).
- Therapists ask clients to mention the thing they have learned about themselves that is most important and therefore worth remembering.
- Therapists ask clients what they will have achieved in one year (five years, ten years) if they continue moving in the right direction.
- Therapists make a follow-up appointment so that clients can come tell them what is going well and what is going better.

REFLECTING ON THE SESSION

Therapists may reflect on sessions, both in the case of successful treatment and in the case of stagnation or failure of treatment: "What

Exercise 94. CERTIFICATE OF POST TRAUMATIC SUCCESS
At the end of treatment, therapists may create a Certificate of Post traumatic Success for their clients. See Appendix I for a certificate format.

worked in these sessions, and what will I do again next time in a comparable situation? What did not work, and what will I do differently next time in a comparable situation?" Reflection may be done alone or take place with colleagues in the form of peer supervision (Bannink, 2012b).

Other questions that can help therapists reflect on their contribution to the session and may also help them develop their skills include:

- Supposing I were to conduct this session again, what would I do differently next time?
- What would my client say I could do differently?
- What difference will that make for him or her?
- What difference will that make for me?
- Supposing I conducted sessions in the future with a client who has comparable problems, which interventions would I use again and which wouldn't I?
- How satisfied do I think my client is with my performance (on a scale of ten to zero)?
- What would my client say about how I've managed to get to that point?
- What would it look like for my client if I were one point higher on the scale?
- How satisfied am I with my performance (on a scale of ten to zero)?
- How did I manage to get to that point?
- What will one point higher on the scale look like?
- What differences will that make for the treatment?
- What positive aspects of this treatment stand out?
- What useful information have I received from my client?
- Which of my client's strengths and competencies and features can I compliment him or her on?
- What does my client want to achieve in meeting with me?
- What strengths and competencies can my client utilize in re-

gard to the problem that brings him or her here?

- What strengths and resources did I fail to capitalize on?
- What kind of resources from my client's environment can help him or her? Which resources are already available?
- What do I see in my client (these partners, this family, this team) that tells me that my client can reach his or her goal?

Questions using different perspectives (see Chapter 7 and Appendix G) can also be helpful.

Berg and Steiner (2003) suggested the following questions if there has been no progress:

- If I were to ask my client how my contribution has helped, even if only a little bit, how would he or she respond?
- What does my client consider to be a sign of a successful outcome?
- How realistic is that outcome?
- What do I myself consider to be a sign of success?
- If my client's and my views differ, what needs to be done so that we can work on the same goal?
- On a scale of ten to zero, where would my client say he or she is right now?
- What needs to happen to bring my client one point closer to ten?

With the second and subsequent sessions, therapists can use the same critical, self-reflective process to closely monitor their clinical thinking and therapeutic actions with each client they work with. A follow-up session a few months after the treatment has ended may provide information not only about the client's current situation, but also about what has worked and what has gotten better since the last session. Moreover, clients generally experience this form of aftercare as solicitous and pleasant. A follow-up session may also take place via telephone, Skype, or email.

Routine Outcome Measurement

The average treated client is better off than about 80 percent of the untreated sample (Duncan et al., 2010). But, unfortunately, dropouts are a significant problem, and although many of our clients profit from therapy, many do not. Another point of concern is the variability among therapists. Some therapists are much better in getting positive results than others (see above). As noted, therapist effectiveness ranges from 20 to 70 percent. Moreover, even very effective clinicians are often poor at identifying deteriorating clients (Duncan, 2010). Hannan and colleagues (2005) found that although therapists knew the purpose of their study, were familiar with the outcome measures, and were informed that the base rate was likely to be 8 percent, they accurately predicted deterioration in only one out of 550 cases. In other words, therapists did not identify thirty-nine out of the forty clients who deteriorated! Other findings included that therapists routinely overestimated their effectiveness; only about 3 percent of therapists routinely tracked their outcomes, and therapists routinely failed to identify clients at risk of deteriorating, dropping out, or experiencing a negative outcome.

The answer to these problems is to use feedback as a compass to successfully navigate a client's unique path to change, something Duncan (2010) calls *practice-based evidence*: delivering what works. Therapy should, according to Duncan, be a discovery-oriented journey, anchored by feedback to manage uncertainty along the way.

To promote the monitoring of clients' progress, the APA Presidential Task Force on Evidence-Based Practice (2006) stated that the application of research evidence to a given patient always involves probability. Therefore, ongoing monitoring of patient progress and adjustment to treatment as needed are essential.

STORY 33. *Brilliant Insights*

During the 1960s Watzlawick (1976) experimented on the nature of feedback and its effect on human activity. Two participants were exposed to pictures of healthy or sick cells. Neither person could see the other and each was given the assignment of distinguishing between the cells through trial and error. Feedback consisted of lights indicating "right" or "wrong."

There was one wrinkle in the experiment, of which the participants were unaware. One of them received accurate feedback. When the light indicated he made the right choice, he indeed guessed correctly. Feedback for the second participant was based on guesses made by the first participant. This person was told he was right if the other person guessed correctly and wrong if the other was incorrect. At the conclusion of the experiment the first participant had learned to distinguish healthy from sick cells with an 80 percent rate of accuracy; the second continued to guess at no better than a chance rate.

The feedback had an interesting impact on the theories of the participants. The participant who received accurate feedback ended with a simple, concrete explanation. The second developed a complicated, subtle and elaborate theory. Something more troubling occurred when the two participants shared their theories with each other. In contrast to what one might hope and expect, the first participant was impressed with the complicated, mysterious, and ultimately unreliable theoretical formulations of his co-participant. The second dismissed the statistically accurate theory of the first as naive and simplistic. In subsequent retests during which both participants received accurate feedback about their guesses, the second continued to guess at little better than a chance rate. However, the performance of the first participant, who was now attempting to put some of the brilliant insights of his co-participant into practice, significantly worsened!

Duncan and colleagues (2004) state that feedback from clients is essential and improves success. Therapists do not need to know in advance what approach to use for a given diagnosis, but rather whether the current relationship is a good fit and is providing benefit. If not, they need to be able to adjust and accommodate early enough to maximize the chances of success.

O'Hanlon and Rowan (2003) add to this the importance of transforming the belief patterns of both therapists and clients to encompass the possibility of change, thus drawing attention away from beliefs in the impossibility of change and from ideas that blame, disempower, or invalidate clients or that see clients as nonaccountable (see Chapter 7).

In traditional psychotherapy, the evaluation of progress is usually carried out only at the end of therapy—if it is carried out at all. Progress is measured by a decrease in problems, and it is usually the therapist who decides when to stop therapy. But session-by-session outcome monitoring appears to be essential. Progress is measured not only by a decrease in the undesired situation, but also by an increase in the desired situation. The Outcome Rating Scale (ORS) and the Session Rating Scale (SRS) are used to obtain feedback from the clients.

Kuyken and colleagues (2009) stated that therapists often consider amelioration of client distress the most important therapy outcome, and they assume that their clients share this view. However, a large survey of people receiving mental health services revealed that the most important outcomes for clients are (a) attaining positive mental health qualities, such as optimism and self-confidence; (b) a return to one's usual, normal self; (c) a return to one's usual level of functioning; and (d) relief from symptoms (Zimmerman et al., 2006).

In the ongoing discussion in psychotherapy between those who advocate empirically supported treatments and those who emphasize the importance of common factors (aspects of psychotherapy that are present in most, if not all, approaches to therapy), monitoring outcomes may hopefully, in the end, provide a common ground for both.

Client-Directed, Outcome-Informed Therapy

Miller, Hubble, and Duncan (1996) collected data from forty years of outcome research in psychotherapy, which provide strong empirical evidence for privileging the client's role in the change process. Clients, not therapists, make therapy work. As a result, therapy should be organized around their resources, their perceptions, their experiences, and their ideas. There need be no a priori assumptions about client problems or solutions, no special questions that are best to ask, and no invariant methodology to follow in order to achieve success. Rather, therapists need only take directions from clients, following their lead; adopting their language, worldview, goals, and ideas about the problem; and acknowledging their experiences with, and inclinations about, the change process. The most potent factor of successful outcome, the client and his or her own propensities for change, is left out of the medical model used in traditional psychotherapy. However, it should be the clients who are the directors of the change endeavor, not the therapists.

Traditionally, the effectiveness of treatment has been left up to the judgment of the provider of this treatment. But proof of effectiveness can emerge from the client's perceptions and experiences as a full partner in the therapy process.

The client's theory of change offers ways of integrating many perspectives on therapy. Trusting the client's theory of change requires a focused effort to conduct therapy within the context of the client's unique ideas and circumstances. Research has shown that all model and technique factors only represent 15 percent of outcome variance at most (Duncan, 2010). They may or may not be useful in the client's circumstances. Therefore, theories should be deemphasized, and instead the focus should be on the client's theories. Exploring clients' ideas has several advantages:

- It puts clients center stage in the conversation.
- It enlists clients' participation.
- It helps ensure that clients' experience of the professional is positive.
- It structures the conversation and directs the change process.

According to research, it is the client that matters: his or her resources, participation, evaluation of the alliance, and perceptions of the problem and the solutions. The therapist's techniques are only helpful if clients see them as relevant and credible. If, for example, it is the client's theory of change that it is useful to talk about who is wrong and who is to blame, therapists may ask:

- "How do you think this will be helpful?"
- "What are your ideas about the positive effects this will have on your preferred future?"
- "How may your relationship with _____ benefit from this?"
- "How will you know this will be helpful for you? What should be better the next time we meet so that we know this has been useful and that we should do more of it?"

Conventional wisdom suggests that competence engenders, if not equals, effectiveness. As a result, there is a continuing education requirement, designed to ensure that therapists stay abreast of developments that enhance positive outcome of therapy. The vast majority of these trainings do not include methods for evaluating the effectiveness of the approach. Emphasis is placed on learning skills or techniques of a particular brand or style of therapy.

But this emphasis on competence versus outcome decreases effectiveness and efficiency. Research has shown that there is no or little relationship between experience level and the effectiveness of professionals (Clement, 1994). The data indicate that increasing the amount and type of training and experience that most professionals receive may even lessen their effectiveness. Researchers distinguished successfully between least and most effective therapists (as determined by outcome; Hiatt & Hargrave, 1995). They found that therapists in the low-effectiveness group tended to have been in practice for more years that those in the high-effectiveness group. They also found that the ineffective therapists were unaware that they were ineffective. Even worse, they considered themselves as effective as the truly helpful therapists in the study.

Miller and colleagues (1997) stated that using client feedback to inform therapists invites clients to be full and equal partners in all aspects of therapy. Giving clients the perspective of the driver's seat instead of the back of the bus may also enable them to gain confidence that a positive outcome is just down the road. Systematic assessment of the client's perceptions of progress and fit are important so that therapists can empirically tailor the therapy to the client's needs and characteristics. Such a process of becoming outcome-informed fits well with how most therapists prefer to think of themselves: sensitive to client feedback and interested in results. Becoming outcome-informed not only amplifies the client's voice but also offers the most viable, research-tested method of improving effectiveness. Miller and colleagues offer the following equation: Client resources and resilience + client theories of change + client feedback about the fit and benefit of service = client perceptions of preferred outcomes.

Building a Culture of Feedback

Apart from asking scaling questions about progress during the sessions, therapists may give clients the Outcome Rating Scale (ORS) at the beginning of each session and the Session Rating Scale (SRS) at the end of each session. At the center of this system is the Outcome Questionnaire 45 (OQ 45), a forty-five-item measure of client functioning along three dimensions (symptom distress, interpersonal functioning, and social role functioning).

The ORS is a clinical tool, a general outcome instrument, and provides no specific content other than ratings of how well clients have been doing in the following areas of their lives: "Individually," "Relationally," "Socially" and "Overall". Administering the ORS at the beginning of each session sets the stage and invites clients into a collaborative partnership.

The SRS, a feedback instrument, is divided into the three areas that decades of research have shown to be the qualities of change-producing relationships:

1. The relationship between therapist and client (the alliance)
2. Goals and topics
3. The approach or method

Clients are asked to place a mark on each 10-cm line, where low estimates are represented to the left and high to the right. The instructions read as follows: "Please rate today's session by placing a mark on the line nearest to the description that best fits your experience."

Each line has a potential of ten, with a grand total possibility of forty. A ruler can be used to measure the mark of the client on each line, and then the marks are added up. There is no specific cutoff score between relationships that have good or bad change potential. Higher scores (above thirty) reflect relationships that have better change potential; lower scores suggest that the relationship may need some extra attention. However, it is always the therapist who asks, "What can I (as the therapist) do differently next time so that you (as the client) will give higher points on the scale?" More information about the ORS and SRS can be found in *On Becoming a Better Therapist* (Duncan, 2010).

The SRS is an engagement instrument; it opens space for the client's voice in regard to the alliance (see Appendix H). It is aimed at starting a conversation with the client, which can be used by the therapist to improve therapy for this particular client. Dropout rates will be higher if the SRS is forgotten. It is helpful to make a graphic of the results of the ORS and SRS over time (for free downloads and instructions, see www.scottdmiller.com). A small decrease (one point) is a signal that therapists should discuss the relationship with their clients.

Duncan (2005, p. 183) stated that monitoring progress is essential and dramatically improves the chances of success. "You don't really need the perfect approach as much as you need to know whether your plan is working—and if it is not, how to quickly adjust your strategy to maximize the possibility of improvement." An absence of early improvement may substantially decrease the chances of achieving what clients want to achieve with the current methods. Research has shown that when no improvement has occurred by the third session, progress is not likely to occur over the entire course of treatment. Moreover, people who did not indicate that therapy was helping by the sixth session were very likely to receive no benefit, despite the length of the therapy. The diagnosis the person had and the type of therapy delivered were not as important in predicting success as knowing whether the treatment that was provided was actually working. Clients whose therapists got feedback about their lack of progress were, at the conclusion of therapy, better off than 65 percent of those whose therapists did not receive any information. Knowing that clients were not benefiting from their therapy allowed these therapists to modify their approaches and promote change. Clients whose therapists had access to progress information, like the SRS, were less likely to get worse with treatment and were twice as likely to achieve a clinically significant change. Nothing else in the history of psychotherapy has been shown to increase effectiveness this much (Duncan, 2005).

Supertherapists

It is obvious that not all therapists are equally successful. Wampold (2001) notes that, just as some lawyers have better results, some artists create more remarkable works of art, and some students perform better with some teachers than with others, some psychotherapists also achieve better results than others. Therefore, most of us, when we recommend a mediator, lawyer, doctor, or psychotherapist to a friend or relative, rely more on the competence and expertise of this person than on his or her theoretical background.

Miller, Hubble, and Duncan (2007) found that recent studies show solid empirical evidence for what distinguishes highly effective therapists (whom they call *supershrinks*) from other therapists. The data show that clients of the best clinicians achieve at least 50 percent more improvement and are at least 50 percent less likely to drop out than those seen by average therapists. Surprisingly, training, certification, supervision, years of experience, and even use of evidence-based practices do not contribute to superior performance. Research conducted over the last thirty years documents that the effectiveness rates of most therapists plateaus very early in training, despite the fact that most therapists believe they improve with time and experience.

Despite the important role played by therapists, it is clear from the research that our knowledge exhibits major gaps. We still know surprisingly little about the variables and qualities that are the characteristics of a competent and effective "supertherapist" and about the interaction of these variables with different approaches in therapy. We know even less about the interaction with clients or client variables.

Wampold (2001) provided an overview of research in psychotherapy. One chapter in his book is about *allegiance*: the faith therapists have in their own treatment model. Faith in the treatment and in the capacity of that treatment to help clients change is an important quality of a competent therapist. When therapists do not invest sufficiently in their treatment, this may endanger the treatment outcome. Allegiance in regard to treatment is based on the idea that if therapists are favorably disposed toward a treatment and experience the positive effects of that treatment, they will execute this treatment with more perseverance, enthusiasm, hope, and competence.

Research on the impact of variables of therapists' characteristics shows that competent, creative, committed therapists can often overcome any restriction based on their age, gender, or color of skin (Beutler et al., 2004). There is a consistent relationship between a positive and friendly attitude of therapists and a positive outcome. A critical and hostile attitude has the opposite effect. Supertherapists seek, obtain, and maintain more consumer engagement. Another consistent finding of research is that it is important that therapists are sufficiently active and directive to ensure that their clients do not simply repeat their dysfunctional patterns, and that they structure the sessions sufficiently to stimulate their clients.

Miller and colleagues (1997) showed that good therapists are much likelier to *ask for and receive negative feedback* about the quality of the work and their contribution to the alliance. The best clinicians, those falling in the top 25 percent of treatment outcomes, consistently achieve lower scores on standardized alliance measures at the outset of therapy—perhaps because they are more persistent or are more believable when assuring clients that they want honest answers—enabling them to address potential problems in the working relationship. Median therapists, by contrast, commonly receive negative feedback later in treatment, at a time when clients have already disengaged and are at heightened risk for dropping out. Supertherapists, therefore, are exceptionally alert to the risk of dropping out and treatment failure.

Most aspects of the style of the therapist are strongly dependent on whether he or she adjusts to the preferences, hopes, and characteristics of clients. They should give fewer directives if clients do not comply, and they should adjust their style to hold a moderate arousal (not too much and not too little), because a moderate arousal promotes change. Flexibility and building rapport are therefore essential qualities of therapists. The specific responses from therapists that are responsible for a positive *alliance* vary from client to client. Good therapists are sensitive to the reactions of their clients and can adjust their interactions on the basis of this feedback (Duncan et al., 2004).

Norcross (2002) and Wampold and Bhati (2004) found that the therapist's personality and his or her alliance with clients are far more powerful determinants of the outcome of the sessions than the choice of methodology. Therapists' high comfort with closeness in interpersonal relationships, low hostility, and high social support predicted higher client ratings of the alliance early in treatment. Additionally, the researchers found that the therapist's experience was not predictive of the strength of any aspect of the therapeutic relationship.

In sum, therapists are in many ways intertwined with change. In most models of change, therapists are central, and how change mechanisms operate in the therapeutic process is dependent on the therapist. The expectation is that this research into the role of therapists also applies to other professionals such as doctors, teachers, lawyers, and mediators (Bannink, 2010b).

"Easy and Fun"

If therapists work harder than their clients, if they think therapy is a difficult endeavor, or if they never laugh during sessions with their clients, they should stop and do something else to make their work more enjoyable. Maybe they should lean back more and start asking more questions. For example, a useful question might be, "What would be the best question I could ask you now?" Maybe therapists want to reach the goal more than their clients do, or maybe the goal of the client is not clear yet. Maybe there is a complainant relationship with their clients but they assume that clients are already motivated to change. Maybe they have a higher or different goal than their clients. Maybe they should make a joke now and then, or ask about their clients' strengths and resources more. If problem-focused therapists are too tired and stressed at the end of a working day to do anything fun, while their clients still can, the strengths-and-solutions approach is a good alternative. The responsibility for a good alliance rests not only with clients but equally with therapists. If no progress is being made, therapists may ask themselves:

- If I asked my client how my contribution has helped so far, even though it may only be a little bit, how would he or she respond?
- What does my client see as a sign (or signs) of a successful result?
- How realistic is this result?
- What do I see as sign(s) of success?
- If my ideas and those of my client differ, what needs to be done in order for me to work toward their goal?
- Where on a scale of ten to zero will my client say that he or she is right now?
- What needs to happen so that my client is able to achieve a score closer to ten?
- How much motivation, hope, or confidence do I have as a therapist that this therapy will be successful? Supposing that I had more motivation, hope, or confidence, what would I be doing differently? What difference would that make to my clients? How would they react differently?

If therapists are no longer motivated, confident, or hopeful that they can help clients reach their preferred future, they should examine what needs to be done to regain motivation, confidence, or hope. If therapists are themselves in a complainant relationship with a client (they have become irritated or discouraged because there is no progress and they think the client has to do something first), and if they are no longer motivated to reestablish a more positive alliance, it is advisable that they stop and reassign the therapy to a colleague.

CASE 31. *Three Compliments*

Because his client has made little or no progress so far, the therapist is starting to feel irritated. He is working hard, while the client is saying "Yes, but" to almost all his explanations and the advice he is giving. The therapist realizes that, since the client does not seem motivated to change, he feels inclined to stop working hard for this client.

Instead, he plans to pay the client at least three compliments in the next sessions. This means he really has to look hard at what the client is doing well to see where he can be complimented. As he focuses on the client's strengths and what works, paying three compliments is easier than he thought. As a bonus, the alliance improves, resulting in the client making some progress.

In the next chapter, we will take a look at post traumatic success in children. Contrary to what therapists may think, children who were traumatized do not have to grow up to be emotionally flawed adults. The idea that what children experience during their youth determines their future is too simplistic. By capitalizing on their strengths and resources and what works in their lives, therapists can help them to create their own positive self-fulfilling prophecies.

SUMMARY

- The goal of follow-up sessions is to explore what has improved and to find out if the previous session has been useful.
- Progress in therapy is measured by asking the question "What is better?" Specific strategies are useful for addressing each of four possible response patterns.
- It may be better to focus on *behavior maintenance* than on *relapse prevention*. Consolidating questions are useful, and it is important for therapists to have a growth mindset.
- Several "pathways to impossibility" exist in therapy.
- It is important to allow clients to save face and to space sessions appropriately.
- Therapy may be concluded when clients think they have reached their goal. There are numerous ways to celebrate clients' successes.
- Reflection on each session is important for therapists. Client-directed, outcome-informed therapy involves building a culture of feedback. Using clients' feedback enables therapists to become "supertherapists" and also renders therapy easier and more fun for both therapists and their clients.

CHAPTER 10

. . . .

Post Traumatic Success in Children

In the past decade, there has been increasing recognition that children who have been exposed to traumatic events can, like trauma-exposed adults, develop PTSD. Furman (1998) stated that children who grow up in troubled circumstances have a statistically higher chance of developing problems at a later stage than children with a normal childhood. However, correlation is not the same as cause. Look at these two generally accepted statements:

- If a child has a difficult youth, he or she will have problems in the future.
- If an adult has problems, it is because he or she had a difficult childhood.

Neither statement is correct. The idea that what a child experiences during his or her youth determines his future is too simplistic. One would then assume that children are passive and that childhood experiences will unavoidably overshadow the rest of their life. Rather, it is the manner in which children deal with these early experiences that determines to a great extent what the outcome will be. The quote by Epictetus in Chapter 2 ("It is not what happens to you, but how you react to it that matters") is equally true for children.

In this chapter, PTSD in children and adolescents is described. PTSD may look different in children of different ages. Many children, however, recover from trauma and may even grow or be resilient. Resilience and growth in children are described, as well as the importance of hope, optimism, and well-being in children.

The role of parents and caregivers is to promote resilience and foster self-compassion in children, using positive reinforcement. A positive working assumption is that all parents and caregivers want what is best for their children—until proven otherwise. Child protection, ensuring the safety of children, is of utmost importance.

Sometimes therapy with children and their families may be necessary. Instead of focusing on what is wrong with the child and the family, therapists would do well to focus on what is right with them and on their strengths and solutions. The homework suggestions for children and families are intended to direct clients' attention to the aspects of their experiences and situations that are most useful for reaching their goals.

As a child once remarked, "When you turn your face to the sun, the shadows will fall behind you."

PTSD IN CHILDREN

Children and teens may develop PTSD if they have lived through an event that could have caused them or someone else to be killed or badly hurt. Such events include sexual or physical abuse or other violent crimes. Disasters such as floods, school shootings, car crashes, or fires may also cause PTSD. Other events that can cause PTSD are war, a friend's suicide, or seeing violence in the area in which one lives.

About 15 to 43 percent of girls and 14 to 43 percent of boys go through at least one trauma. Of children and teens who have had a trauma, 3 to 15 percent of girls and 1 to 6 percent of boys develop PTSD. Rates of PTSD are higher for certain types of trauma survivors.

Three factors have been shown to raise the chances that children will get PTSD: (a) how severe the trauma is, (b) how their parents react to the trauma, and (c) how close or far away the child is from the trauma. Children and teens that go through the most severe traumas tend to have the highest levels of PTSD symptoms. The PTSD symptoms may be less severe if the child has more family support and if the parents are less upset by the trauma. Last, children and teens who are farther away from the event report less distress. Also, the more traumas a child goes through, the higher the risk of getting PTSD.

Another question is whether a child's age at the time of the trauma has an effect on PTSD. Researchers think it may not be that the effects of trauma differ according to the child's age, but rather that PTSD looks different in children of different ages.

Preschool children (ages six and younger) may be exposed to many types of traumatic experiences, placing them at risk for PTSD. These include abuse, witnessing interpersonal violence, motor vehicle accidents, natural disasters, war, dog bites, and invasive medical procedures. The DSM-5 includes a new developmental subtype of PTSD called *post traumatic stress disorder in preschool children*.

Because young children have emerging abstract cognitive and verbal expression capacities, research has shown that the criteria need to be more behaviorally anchored and developmentally sensitive to detect PTSD in preschool children.

The criterion that the child's reactions at the time of the traumatic events must have demonstrated extreme distress has been deleted in the DSM-5. If children were too young to verbalize their acute reactions to traumatic experiences or there were no adults present to witness their reactions, there is no feasible way to know about these reactions. This criterion, which has been shown to lack predictive validity for both adult and preschool populations, has also been deleted from the regular PTSD criteria in the DSM-5.

Because many of the avoidance and negative cognition symptoms are highly internalized phenomena, the most significant changes in the criteria for preschool children are in this section. The major change in the DSM-5 is the requirement of only one symptom in either the avoidance symptoms category or the negative alterations in cognitions and mood category, instead of the DSM-IV threshold of three symptoms.

School-aged children (ages five to twelve) may not have flashbacks or problems remembering parts of the trauma the way adults with PTSD do. Children, though, might put the events of the trauma in the wrong order. They may also think that there were signs that the trauma was going to happen. As a result, they may think that they will see these signs again before another trauma happens. They thus think that if they pay attention, they can avoid future traumas.

Children of this age might show signs of PTSD in their play. They might keep repeating a part of the trauma. These games do not make their worry and distress go away. For example, a child might always want to play shooting games after he sees a school shooting. Children may also fit parts of the trauma into their daily lives. For example, a child might carry a gun to school after seeing a school shooting.

Teens (ages twelve to eighteen) are in between children and adults. Some PTSD symptoms in teens look like those of adults. One difference is that teens are more likely than younger children or adults to show impulsive and aggressive behaviors.

For many children, however, PTSD symptoms go away on their own after a few months. Children often recover or even grow after trauma, or they are resilient and bounce back quickly.

RECOVERY AND RESILIENCE IN CHILDREN

Resilience is a dynamic developmental process for which two conditions must be present: (a) a significant threat to the well-being of the child and (b) positive adjustment of the child (Luthar, Cicchetti, & Becker, 2000). Because it is a reaction pattern, resilience is not something a child is or is not born with, or has or does not have. Resilience is not a personality trait or attribute, nor is it limited to children who possess uncommon, rare characteristics. According to Ungar (2008), it is wrong to identify a child as a *resilient individual*. Children are resilient to the extent that they find the means within their family and community that they need to develop characteristics that are associated with resilience. A broader perspective that takes into account the social context is important when looking at resilience. A common *definition of resilience* is the ability of children to make use of their internal skills (e.g., being easygoing) and external support (e.g., social support) (Ungar, 2008).

STORY 34. *Resilience in Hawaii*

Werner (2004) did a forty-year longitudinal study of 698 infants on the Hawaiian island of Kauai, the island's entire birth cohort for the year 1955. The study supported the conventional wisdom that many children exposed to reproductive and environmental risk factors (for instance, premature birth coupled with an unstable household and a mentally ill mother) go on to experience more delinquency, mental and physical health problems, and family instability than children exposed to fewer such risk factors. However, Werner found that one-third of all high-risk children displayed resilience and developed into caring, competent, and confident adults despite their problematic development histories. She identified a number of protective factors in the lives of these resilient individuals that helped to balance out risk factors at critical periods in their development. Among these factors was a strong bond with a nonparent caretaker (such as an aunt, babysitter, or teacher) and involvement in a church or community group.

Research (Wolin & Wolin, 1993) has shown that, when faced with adversity and stressful life events, many children consistently bounce back quickly and beat the odds. In high-risk children, reared in poverty and high-stress family environments characterized by violence, parental alcoholism and substance abuse, divorce, and parental mental illness, research has found three categories of key *protective factors*. Rutter (1985, p. 600) defined protective factors as follows: "influences that modify, ameliorate or alter a person's response to some environmental hazard that predisposes to a maladaptive outcome." Children and their families should be supported in developing, enhancing, and utilizing all three types of protective factors (McElwee, 2007; Selekman, 2010; Kuiper & Bannink, 2012).

Individual factors are (a) optimistic explanatory style, (b) good sense of humor, (c) self-efficacy, (d) strong social skills, (e) cognitive competence, (f) good-natured temperament, (g) pronounced self-sufficiency, (h) robustness, (i) sense of coherence, (j) perseverance, (k) involvement in creative activities, (l) intelligence, (m) strong problem-solving skills, (n) good management of emotions, and (o) a keen sense of awareness.

Family factors are (a) caring and supportive parents, (b) strong parent–child relationships, (c) low levels of family conflict, and (d) optimistic parenting explanatory styles.

Extrafamilial support factors are (a) a nurturing support system (relatives, friends, teachers, neighbors, and inspirational significant others), (b) church involvement, and (c) successful school experiences (Henderson & Milstein, 1996).

There is some confusion over the terms *resilience* and *protective factors*.

- Some researchers and authors state that resilience (A) and protective factors (B) are the same (A = B).

- Some researchers and authors state that resilience is one of the protective factors (A is part of B).
- Some researchers and authors see protective factors as a way to promote resilience (B promotes A).

The model described by Grotberg (1995), described below, offers practical tools for parents, caregivers, and therapists.

The International Resiliency Project

With resilience, children can triumph over trauma; without it, trauma (adversity) triumphs (Grotberg, 1995).

Grotberg is one of the researchers on resilience in children. In the 1990s, she started the International Resiliency Project. Participants from thirty countries joined the project, and the findings reported here are based on the data submitted in 1993–1994 by fourteen countries (Lithuania, Russia, Costa Rica, the Czech Republic, Brazil, Thailand, Vietnam, Hungary, Taiwan, Namibia, Sudan, Canada, South Africa, and Japan). The international perspective has helped in finding out what different cultures are doing to promote resilience: Do they draw on the same pool of resilience factors? Do they vary in which factors are combined to address adversity? The following instruments were used by the researchers in the different countries: (a) descriptions of fifteen situations of adversity, to which adults and children were asked to respond; (b) a checklist, composed by the researchers, of fifteen reactions that indicate resilience in a child; (c) three standardized tests; and (d) actual experiences of adversity reported by respondents, together with their own reactions to these situations.

A total of 589 children participated, along with their families and caregivers; 48 percent were girls and 52 percent boys. Just over half the children were between nine and eleven years old; the remainder were age six or under.

The findings suggested that every country in the study is drawing on a common set of resilience factors to promote resilience in children. Adults and older children use more resilience-promoting supports, inner strengths, and interpersonal skills than younger children. Overall, less than half of the respondents used resilience-promoting behavior, and even those respondents varied individually in use of the resilience factors, largely depending on the situation. Socioeconomic level contributed very little to variations in responses.

Over the course of the project, it became clear that there are relationships between culture and resilience factors. Some cultures rely more on faith than on problem-solving in facing adversity. Some cultures are more concerned about punishment and guilt, while others discipline and reconcile. Some cultures expect children to be more dependent on others for help in adversity rather than becoming autonomous and more self-reliant. The parents in some countries maintain a close relationship with their children, while others cut off their children at about age five. The resilient children manage this kind of rejection; nonresilient children withdraw, submit, and are depressed.

In the International Resilience Project, the children were not studied independently from their settings. In promoting resilience, any work with children must be done in the context of their families, their schools, their communities, and the larger society. Parents, teachers, communities, and societies are essential to promoting resilience in children, so attention is centered on children, but in their setting.

The results of the International Resilience Project brought forth the categories "I Have," "I Can," and "I Am," which in combination may lead to resilience Each category was divided into five factors. The extent to which children rely on the factors I Have, I Am, and I Can depends on their age. The factors suggest several areas where children and their caregivers can take action to promote resilience.

From a child's perspective, the three resilience factors are reworded as follows:

I Have:
- people around me I trust and who love me, no matter what
- people who set limits for me so I know when to stop before there is danger or trouble
- people who show me how to do things right by the way they do things
- people who want me to learn to do things on my own
- people who help me when I am sick or in danger or need to learn

I Am:
- a person people can like and love
- glad to do nice things for others and show my concern
- respectful of myself and others
- willing to be responsible for what I do
- sure things will be all right

I Can:
- talk to others about things that frighten me or bother me
- find ways to solve problems that I face
- control myself when I feel like doing something not right or dangerous
- figure out when it is a good time to talk to someone or to take action
- find someone to help me when I need it

A resilient child does not need all of these features to be resilient, but one is not enough. Children may be loved (I Have), but if they have no inner strength (I Am) or interpersonal skills (I Can), there can be no resilience. Children may have a great deal of self-esteem (I Am), but if they do not know how to communicate with others or solve problems (I Can) and have no one to help them (I Have), they are not resilient. Children may be very verbal and speak well (I Can), but if they have no empathy (I Am) and do not learn from role models (I Have), there is no resilience. Resilience results from a combination of these features. These features may seem obvious and easy to acquire, but they are not. In fact, many children are not resilient, and many parents and other caregivers do not help children become resilient. Only about 38 percent of the thousands of responses in the International Resilience Project indicated that resilience was being promoted. That is a very small percentage for such a powerful contribution to the development of children. Too many adults crush or impede resilience in children or give mixed messages, and too many children feel helpless, sad, and not fully loved. This is not necessarily the intended situation; it is more the fact that people do not know about resilience or how to promote it in children.

In sum, children need to become resilient to overcome the many adversities they face and will face in life; they cannot do it alone. They need adults who know how to promote resilience and, indeed, are becoming more resilient themselves. The goal of resilience is to recognize adversity, to decide which resilience factors to draw on to deal with the adversity, and to feel stronger and more competent as the adversity is dealt with. To be successful, interventions must focus on enhancing and creating positive environmental contexts—families, schools, and communities—that, in turn, reinforce positive behaviors (see below).

Post Traumatic Growth in Children

All too often a pathology model has been applied to studying how children develop. Although the specialties of psychology dealing with children recognize the serious problems encountered during their development, much of the recent orientation involves moving away from concentrating on the psychological and behavioral deficits resulting from a developmental challenge. Instead, the focus increasingly has become one of perceiving the competence of the child and his or her family and enhancing growth in psychological domains (Roberts, Brown, Johnson, & Reinke, 2005). Still, however, little is known about post traumatic growth in children and adolescents, although younger populations are frequently exposed to varied traumatic events. However, recently the concept of PTG has been explored with children and adolescents. Variables related to PTG in children have been evaluated in adolescents with cancer (Barakat, Alderfer, & Kazak, 2006), those who have experienced the death of a loved one (Ickovics et al., 2006), children who were victims of traffic accidents (Salter & Stallard, 2004), college students exposed to community violence (S. S. Park, 2006), and adolescents exposed to terrorist attacks (Milam, Ritt-Olson, Tan, Unger, & Nezami, 2005). However, there is some debate on whether or not PTG is an appropriate construct to study in children and adolescents. Cohen, Hetter, and Pane (1998) argue that children are less resilient than adults and thus are less likely to experience PTG after suffering a traumatic event. Further, children's cognitive capabilities are less developed than those of adults.

Adults can be instrumental for helping children develop post traumatic growth by teaching resilience skills, such as telling stories, using positive coping skills, seeking support, and helping others who may be hurting. First and foremost, it is important that parents take care of themselves and manage their own distress, not only because they are modeling for their children how to respond to trauma, but also because their own distress can add to their child's. Modeling a sense of security, assuring children of one's love and protection, offering praise when one's children make positive coping statements, and educating children may help reduce their distress and foster post traumatic growth.

Several *measures of PTG for children* have been developed, most of which are adaptations of the PTGI (Tedeschi & Calhoun, 1996). In a study by Milam and colleagues (2004), nearly 30 percent of the 435 adolescent participants reported at least moderate positive outcomes as a result of various negative life events, and there were no significant differences in PTG scores across different events. The researchers found that age was a significant predictor of PTG. This relationship was attributed to a certain level of cognitive maturity necessary to find benefits in the wake of a negative event (Milam et al., 2004). Cryder, Kilmer, Tedeschi, and Calhoun (2006) used a modified version of the PTGI, the Post Traumatic Growth Inventory for Children (PTGI-C), in their study of children and adolescents displaced by flooding caused by Hurricane Floyd. The PTGI-C measured all five of the original domains contained in the PTGI. The results showed that PTGI-C scores were variable. PTG was significantly related to competency beliefs, but not to rumination or social support. The Post Traumatic Growth Inventory for Children Revised (PTGI-C-R) is a ten-item questionnaire that assesses the five domains of post traumatic growth using language and a response style appropriate for preadolescent children.

HOPE, OPTIMISM, AND WELL-BEING IN CHILDREN

Hope and optimism are two constructs that play an important role in understanding how adults and children deal with traumatic events. Building hope and optimism is essential (in therapy), because many adults and children have been through very difficult times before they come to see a therapist and may feel hopeless and pessimistic about possibilities for change and their future.

Exercise 96. VICTORY BOX

Invite children to create a *victory box*. In this exercise, they record on paper any personal triumphs, achievements, and efforts in school, at home, in sports events, or with the creative arts, including the steps they took to achieve those wonderful accomplishments, and then place these slips of paper in the box. Other signs of victory, such as a medal won at a sports event, can be placed in the box as well. The victory box serves as a storehouse for blueprints of success and mastery for the children and their families.

Hope in Children

Hope is an important construct if one wants to understand how children deal with stressful events, how to prevent them from developing problematic behavior, and how they can use past events to lead their lives in a good and effective way. Hope and intelligence are not related: The majority of children have the intellectual capacity to think hopefully and purposefully. Children's capacity for hope has a bearing on their performance at school. Boys and girls equally demonstrate hopefulness. Children's idea of the future is often slightly too positive. However, this is a plus, because this ensures that their thoughts develop in a positive way and that they can retain them, even if the thoughts are not, under the circumstances, realistic.

Research (Seery, Holman, & Silver, 2010) has shown that hopeful children cope better with stressful events. The degree of hope children possess is positively linked to self-reported competence. Hopeful children have higher self-esteem and are less prone to depression. Besides, self-esteem in children is connected to the development of hope. Research into children with sickle-cell disease, a serious genetic form of anemia, showed a positive connection between hope and adaptation within a group of these children. On the other hand, it demonstrated a negative connection between hope and fear. Adolescents who as children had suffered serious burns took part in a questionnaire study to assess their level of hopefulness, as it is a good predictor of the definitive occurrence of behavioral problems. More hope was associated with fewer behavioral problems. On top of that, hope combined with social support contributed to a more substantial feeling of self-worth. Research into the relationship between hope and the level of violence adolescents had been exposed to (where they had good reason to think they would become victims themselves) proved that they were able to maintain a high level of hope so long as they were only witnessing the violence and were not directly involved themselves. Seery and colleagues pleaded for children to be told hopeful stories at school. After reading of these stories, discussions may take place with the children on how hope can be brought into their lives. In this way children can experience increasing feelings of hopefulness.

Optimism in Children

Seligman, Reivich, Jaycox, and Gilham (1995) concluded that optimistic children fare better at schoolwork and in sports than pessimistic children. They also concluded that optimistic adolescents are less angry and less likely to indulge in drug and alcohol abuse. Seligman and colleagues distinguished four factors that influenced the development of optimism in children:

1. The *genetic definition*.
2. The *child's immediate environment*. A child's parents have a strong influence on his or her level of optimism. There is in particular a strong relation between the way the mother deals with events (her interpretations and expectations) and the way her child deals with them. If the mother is optimistic, then the likely outcome is that her child will be too. Children see their parents as role models and imitate their behavior. There also appears to be a correlation between pessimistic mothers and pessimistic children. The same applies to the development of the child's capacity for demonstrating gratitude.
3. The *influence of the environment*, for example, the educational input of both teachers and parents. There is more depression and pessimism among children whose mothers grant less autonomy. The exertion of control does not lead to more optimism in children. Criticism from parents, teachers, coaches, and other adults also plays a part. If an adult criticizes a child's proficiency—for example, by saying, "You will never learn this"—chances are that the child will start to think in a pessimistic way. With increasing maturity, there is a decline in the importance of the role played by the child's upbringing on his or her well-being. The influence of friends and peers will take on greater importance. However, even then, the degree of autonomy provided by parents remains important.
4. The *events the child will experience*. These events present either a feeling of control or an experience of helplessness. Seligman and colleagues state that optimism has its limits. Children must be able to look at themselves realistically if they are to take on life's challenges.

Well-Being in Children

Many factors play a role in well-being, which includes physical and mental health as well as spiritual and social health. In research with adults, well-being has been defined as *quality of life*. Little research has been carried out with children in this field. The quality of the child's early upbringing and especially the bonding between mother and child is related to the child's mental health, well-being, and subsequent development (or lack of development) of psychological problems. Research has shown that adults' well-being is linked to the concern and familiarity expressed by their mothers during their childhood. This outcome was the same for both sons and daughters (Benard, 1991).

The adaptation of the environment to children's needs also plays an important role in the well-being of children. How can a hospital environment, for instance, be adapted in such a way as to help seriously ill children to feel as well as they possibly can? How can doctors and nurses be trained in such a way as to help them focus on the emotional and social needs of children as well as their medical needs? And how can these children be more involved and have more control over their medical treatment?

THE ROLE OF PARENTS AND CAREGIVERS

As mentioned earlier, children need to become resilient to overcome the adversities they face and will face in life, and they cannot do it alone. They need adults who know how to promote resilience, foster self-compassion, use positive reinforcement, and ensure their safety.

Promoting Resilience in Children

Parents and caregivers promote resilience in children when they:

- Provide unconditional love and acceptance
- Express these feelings verbally
- Help the child trust his or her parents and teachers and trust himself or herself
- Model resilient behavior
- Maintain rules and set limits without crushing a child's spirit
- Praise accomplishments
- Encourage independent actions
- Gradually expose the child to adversities and prepare him or her to deal with them
- Encourage the demonstration of empathy
- Help the child learn to assume responsibility

Fostering Self-Compassion in Children

A new field of research suggests that the focus on self-esteem is distracting parents from imparting a far more important life skill: self-compassion. Often misunderstood as self-indulgence, *self-compassion*, as defined by Neff (2011; see Chapter 6), has three aspects: (a) mindfulness of one's own thoughts and feelings, (b) a sense of a common humanity, and (c) treating oneself kindly. While building self-esteem has been linked to a number of mental health problems, including narcissism and emotional fragility, self-compassion is associated with resilience, enhanced energy levels, creativity, and general life success. Here are five ways parents and caregivers can help their children develop this critical life skill:

1. *Teach children the truth about the good life.* There is no state of fulfillment that, once achieved, will eradicate discomforts, hardships, and disappointments. Often suffering—even at the hands of age or illness—is interpreted as some sort of failure. As irrational as this is, labeling suffering as failure gives the illusion that it can be avoided. It is uncomfortable to accept that we can't control everything, but we can't. Children need to have an accurate understanding that life is, and always will be, made up of both highs and lows. Part of growing up is learning how to accept the bad. Good parenting is about giving children opportunities to learn how to deal with their emotions and helping them understand themselves as social beings, according to Gilbert (2010). To be successful adults, children need to learn not only how to care for themselves and others, but also how to ask others for help.

2. *Try self-compassion with training wheels.* Researchers have found that the key to a happy and successful life is resilience. A major key to resilience is self-compassion. Parents should walk children through the steps of compassionate self-treatment by first helping them become mindful of their own emotions and reactions. This involves listening empathetically and helping them to find labels for what they are feeling. Expressions of sympathy are also helpful. Parents and caregivers can point out that these experiences are universal, saying such things as, "It is normal to

feel frustrated and disappointed when you don't get what you want." Finally, they can discuss actions that may help children feel better immediately (a hug or a walk) or in the long run (planning ahead, learning patience, or asking to share).

3. *Judge the behavior, not the child.* The most important job of parents or caregivers is to make children feel intrinsically worthy, no matter their accomplishments or failures. Parents should completely accept their child for who he or she is (rather than whom they want him or her to be). To that end, honestly critiquing a child's behavior, not the child's character, is important. This distinction makes it less likely that children will confuse their actions or accomplishments with their self-worth.

4. *Shape future behavior rather than punishing the past.* How parents or caregivers respond to a child's failures and successes influences the internal model children develop for themselves. Extreme punishment, such as spanking or grounding for two months, teaches children that they should treat themselves harshly when they do something wrong, and offers little instruction on what to do differently when similar difficulties again arise. Children then grow up to be harshly self-critical, which saps energy and motivation levels and undermines their quality of life. Alternatively, compassionate discipline starts by understanding the child's point of view and then helping children change harmful behaviors. The goal is to build healthy habits and social skills that will serve children well in the long run.

5. *Be a good role model.* Modeling self-compassion instead of self-criticism is important, because children watch their parents or caregivers for ways to deal with life. If they see them beating themselves up, that message is stronger than anything parents preach. Being compassionate with yourself will not turn you into a lazy, worthless slob. On the contrary, people who are self-compassionate often have more equanimity, are better liked, work harder, and have higher standards than those who are critical of themselves. It keeps people motivated and in a positive state of mind that greases the wheels of social interaction, which is the mortar for building happy, healthy, and successful lives.

Using Positive Reinforcement

Positive reinforcement is one of the most important tools that parents and caregivers have at their disposal in dealing with children (and adults). It has a very positive effect on everybody irrespective of status, position, or the nature of the problem. Positive reinforcement helps in solving problems, and it also helps in developing the possibilities people have at their disposal to feel better and to maintain agreeable relationships. Positive reinforcements can be material reinforcements, such as sweets or an outing, but they can also be social reinforcements, such as a smile, eye contact, company, compliments, or a pat on the shoulder. This social reinforcement is particularly effective but unfortunately underutilized. A ratio of 5:1 is most effective for positive and negative reinforcements—in other words, five compliments, confirmations, and so forth to one disapproval, criticism, or negative remark (Flora, 2000).

However, there is a difference between positive reinforcement and a positive approach. One does not reinforce the person, only the behavior of that person. (A positive approach to the person is also very useful and produces favorable effects.) Reinforcement of behavior must closely follow that behavior if it is to be effective, and what for one person is reinforcement is not necessarily so for another. It is not expensive, it is inexhaustible, and it works, so long as there is enough variation.

Many things can be positive reinforcers, including consumables (e.g., food, drinks), activities (e.g., a favorite game), objects that can be manipulated, and social reinforcers, which range from being with someone to physical affection. Some reinforcers, such as food and warmth, which are naturally desirable, are called primary reinforcers. Other things, such as money, are called conditioned reinforcers, because they come to function as reinforcers themselves when they have been paired with a primary reinforcer. However, an event or object can be said to be a positive reinforcer only if we see that the behavior immediately preceding it has actually strengthened—increased in frequency, rate, duration, or intensity.

Effective approaches to parenting, teaching, and other guidance tend to emphasize systematic use of positive consequences—positive reinforcement—to shape new and more adaptive behavior. Positive reinforcement is the magic that leads to healthier, happier lives (Plaud, 2001).

CHILD PROTECTION

The working assumption regarding parents is that they want to be good to their children—until proven otherwise (see below). Each year, child protection services in the United States receive around 3 million reports involving 5.5 million children. Of the reported cases, there is proof of abuse in about 30 percent. From these cases, we have an idea of the distribution of different types of abuse: 65 percent neglect, 18 percent physical abuse, 10 percent sexual abuse, and 7 percent psychological (mental) abuse. Also, 3 to 10 million children witness family violence each year; around 40 to 60 percent of those cases involve child physical abuse. (Note: It is thought that two-thirds of child abuse cases are not reported [U.S. Department of Veterans Affairs, n.d.].)

Turnell and Edwards (1999) developed the *Signs of Safety approach* to child protection casework in the 1990s in Western Australia in collaboration with over 150 West Australian child protection professionals. It is currently being used in the United States, Canada, the UK, Sweden, the Netherlands, New Zealand, and Japan. This SF approach focuses on the following question: "How can the professional build partnerships with parents and children in situations of suspected or substantiated child abuse and still deal rigorously with the maltreatment issues?"

Signs of Safety offers a simple yet rigorous assessment format that professionals can use to elicit, in common language, the professionals' and family members' views regarding concerns or dangers, existing strengths and safety, and envisioned safety. The Signs of Safety framework integrates risk assessment with case planning and risk management by incorporating a future focus within the assessment. This format balances the usual problem saturation of most risk assessment. It helps offenders identify any existing signs of safety, which are measurable, and to develop these signs and expand them so that a safe care plan can be put in place. Offenders are helped to do this, but are held accountable for their behavior in the future. However, blame and confrontation are avoided. The role of the professional is one of helping offenders define a goal that is achievable, measurable, and ethical (i.e., within pragmatic and safe limits). Professionals also help offenders find exceptions to their violent behavior and find solution behaviors. Then they amplify, support, and reinforce these behaviors. The six practice principles developed by Turnell and Edwards (1999) are:

1. Understand the position of each family member.
2. Find exceptions to the violence.
3. Discover strengths and resources that can be used in the problem situation.
4. Focus on the goals of everyone involved to ensure the safety of those most vulnerable.
5. Scale safety and progress.
6. Assess willingness, confidence, and capacity to change.

THERAPY WITH CHILDREN AND FAMILIES

Continual and aggressive emotional outbursts in children and adolescents, serious problems at school, preoccupation with the traumatic event, continued and extreme withdrawal, and other signs of intense anxiety or emotional difficulties all point to the need for professional help.

Traditional therapies for PTSD in children and adolescents (e.g., CBT) are—like traditional therapies for adults—based on the medical model of treatment and therefore aim at *recovery* from (symptoms of) PTSD. Recently, however, more positive therapy approaches are being developed, viewing clients' (including children's) difficulties through a strengths-and-solutions-based lens (see Chapter 3). Leckman and Mayes (2007) stated that threats to the well-being of children are commonplace throughout the world. In their opinion, finding ways to enhance resiliency is a major task for child mental health professionals.

De Jong and Berg (2002) gave some advice regarding working with children and their families. They stated that when therapists first meet with a family, it is easy to forget that they care about each other because they seem so angry, hurt, and disappointed with each other. It can help to remember that the other side of anger, hurt, and disappointment with the other person is the wish to be cared about, respected, valued, and loved by that person. It is helpful to be aware of both sides of emotions, not just the side that is showing. Remember that when people truly do not care about another person, they do not get stirred up about the other but coolly walk away from developing conflict. The reason clients become upset with one another is because they care about these other people. Staying aware of both sides makes it easier for therapists to ask the questions that invite clients to construct something more satisfying. The task for therapists is to foster and highlight the signs of car-

Exercise 97. COMIC STRIP

A *comic strip* is a sequence of drawings arranged in interrelated panels to form a narrative. As most children are animal lovers, ask children which animal they would compare themselves with and which animal they would like to be in the future. Ask them to draw a comic with six drawings, first drawing the animal they want to become (drawing six), then drawing the animal they are now (drawing one). Then they can draw the other pictures (drawings two through five) in any order they wish. Finally, ask children which strengths of the animal in the first drawing they want to take with them as they transform into the preferred animal. The therapist can discuss these drawings with the child (and his or her parents) and translate the drawings to his or her life as a child.

Exercise 98. FUTURE-FOCUSED QUESTIONS FOR ADOLESCENTS

Many adolescents come to therapy because others (parents, the school) think they should visit a therapist. Invite adolescents in an involuntary therapy situation to answer the following future-focused questions:

- "Where do you hope to be in ten years' time when all goes well with you?"
- "What will your best friend(s) say you are doing then?"
- "What would they tell me about what you are good at in ten years' time?"
- "Who and what is important to you?"
- "What are you good at doing ten years from now?"
- "What is the next thing you want to become good or better at?"
- "What or who might help you achieve that?"
- "How will that help you (or others)?"
- "How will you (or others) know that you have been able to do what others (parents, the school) think is necessary?"
- "Who of these people believe that you can achieve this?"
- "Who of these people will be the most surprised? Who will be the least surprised?

ing and goodwill between clients to promote hope for the relationship. Inviting families to talk about their past successes, their strengths and resources, and where they would like to be when therapy is not needed anymore (their goal) empowers them to create their own *positive self-fulfilling prophecies*.

Children who see a therapist are often in an involuntary situation or have been mandated to come to therapy. The adults in their lives define their successes and problems. By the time children are sent to a therapist, many concerned adults have already tried many things to help them, usually without success. Understandably, these adults are often frustrated or angry and anxious to have their child change. The children are also often frustrated and discouraged because of all the negative messages they have been getting and the conflicts that have arisen between them and important adults.

To some degree, conflict is an unavoidable part of maturation. Children and adolescents change roles and test the boundaries of relationships with authority figures and peers as they grow and master new skills. Approach emotions will motivate limit-testing behavior, whereas avoidance emotions will deescalate conflict and promote periods of stability where the status quo of relationships and authority is maintained. Although parents, teachers, and sometimes youths will seek therapy for these sorts of developmental conflicts, typically these do not represent psychopathology or emotion dysfunction so much as the inevitable bumps of growing up.

A nice way to start therapy with children (and their families) is to ask them how they would like to celebrate when they have reached their goal and do not have to come to therapy any longer. Children in particular find this highly enjoyable, but parents also like this question, because it generates hope that things can change for the better and that there will be a celebration at the end of therapy (see Chapter 9).

Positive Working Assumptions
Berg, cofounder of SFBT, listed a number of positive working assumptions about children and about parents. These assumptions are helpful for therapists in maintaining a positive focus. Some of the working assumptions about *children* are that, until proven otherwise, all children want to: please their *parents*, be accepted as a part of a social group, learn things, and make choices when given an opportunity. Some of the

Exercise 99. HAPPINESS DETECTIVES

As a way to build resilience in the classroom (or in group therapy), invite a small group of children to become *happiness detectives*. Their mission is to track down all the things they see others doing that lead to the class or group becoming a place with more happiness and well-being. All of the things the children note are listed. After a week, the group gets together again and members share their discoveries. Subsequently, there are regular monthly gatherings at which they discuss what they have seen in the class or group, which promotes well-being. Such a group can be formed as support for a certain child who has difficulties, or it can be started without any specific reason. The groups may swap around from time to time.

Teachers who launched "happiness detectives" at school found that the children who spent some time being happiness detectives acquired better social skills and more self-confidence and showed better cooperative behavior in class (Young, 2010). Happiness detectives can also be introduced to teams at the workplace.

working assumptions about *parents* are that, until proven otherwise, all parents want to: be proud of their child, have a positive influence on their child, give their child a good education, and feel that they are good parents.

Focus on Strengths and Solutions

In therapy with children, the same principles apply as in sessions with adults. The main emphasis is on their strengths and solutions rather than on their weaknesses and impossibilities. As mentioned in Chapter 5, it is important to differentiate between problems and facts or disabilities. A solution can be found for problems, whereas with facts or disabilities (e.g., autism or intellectual disabilities), children and their families have to learn how to adapt; there is no solution for facts or disabilities. Therapists would do well to limit *problem-talk* when talking with children to an even greater degree than when talking with adults. Parents are often so frustrated that therapists should first acknowledge their frustration—but moving on as quickly as possible to *strengths-and-solutions-talk* brings out the best in children. In creating a collaborative and nonblaming atmosphere in working with children and their families, the expertise and knowledge that families have should be given at least as much weight as the expertise of therapists (O'Hanlon & Rowan, 2003). Families know a lot about what works and what doesn't work.

Fredrickson (2009) developed the *broaden-and-build theory of positive emotions* (see Chapter 1). She stated that positivity may well be the greatest resource in times of crisis, because it is important to transform the downward spiral of negative emotions into an upward spiral of positive ones. To this extent, Kuiper and Bannink (2012) offered eight suggestions to therapists working with children and their families.

Therapists should shift their focus from negative to positive. Instead of asking: What is wrong with you, therapists should ask: What is right with you? They should use a strengths- instead of a deficit perspective and use strategies for building hope and optimal functioning. Besides paying attention to risks, they should pay attention to opportunities and possibilities with children and their environment. Kuiper and Bannink recommended to look for opportunities first and then pay attention to risks. If the focus is placed on risks first, it becomes more difficult to see opportunities later (Bannink, 2010c). Paying attention to opportunities creates positive emotions and increases intrinsic motivation (Isen & Reeve, 2005). Questions for finding opportunities and possibilities are:

- What are the best (unexpected) things that can happen?
- What difference will it make if those things would happen?
- What difference will that make for the child/his or her environment?
- What already happened (a bit) in the past?
- How could that happen again?
- Who and what can help?
- How can we as therapists ensure that the chances of such unexpected and positive surprises increase?
- How can we ensure that we discover opportunities we might overlook?
- What opportunities did we see in the past and how did we use them?
- How did we succeed in doing that?

Therapists should not only look at strengths and solutions within the child, but also help in creating a positive environment for the child in the family, the school, and in society. This positive environment reinforces the positive behavior and positive emotions of the child.

A positive focus should also be used in *prevention* programs. A focus on resilience helps children and their therapists discover and encourage the strengths of themselves or their clients. It may have a discouraging effect when the attention is focused on what is not working. Beyond reducing problems and negative emotions, therapists should promote positive emotions, by asking what children and their environment would like to see instead of the problem (their goal), by asking what works and what may constitute progress (see Chapters 5, 6 and 7).

The balance between vulnerability and resilience should be changed, either by reducing exposure to risk factors and stressful events, or by increasing the existing protective factors in the lives of vulnerable children. Therapists should have high expectations and be hopeful that children will survive (and sometimes thrive) in difficult situations. If therapists lose hope or no longer have high expectations of how children and their families cope with difficulties, therapy may not be optimal. Therapists also do well in seeing children and their families as co-experts. They may invite them to discover and use their own expertise. More questionnaires and other diagnostic tools may be devel-

---

Exercise 100. COMPLIMENT BOX

For families who are focused on negative behavior, construction of a compliment box may be a good idea. On a daily basis, family members write on slips of paper one or more compliments for other family members and place them in a (shoe) box with a slit in the top. At dinnertime, they take turns reaching into the box and reading aloud each other's compliments. The compliment box may help to reduce blaming and negativity and create a more positive atmosphere in the home.

A compliment box can also be made during *group therapy* with children—and with grown-ups, too. At the end of the session, each group member puts an anonymous or signed note with a compliment for each of the other group members in the box. These notes are read aloud during the next session.

---

oped and used to measure resilience and growth (for example the VIA Strengths Survey for Children and PTGI for Children: at www.authentichappiness.org).

Another way to assess the strengths of children and their families is to use Grotberg's model of resilience, described earlier in this chapter. Together with children and their parents, therapists can discover which of the fifteen factors in the categories I Have, I Can, and I Am the child already possesses and which ones could be (further) developed. Questions related to the *scale of psychological well-being* (see Figure 1, p. 18) may be helpful in the treatment of children; for example, children may be invited to draw different smileys at the points on the scale.

Furman and Aloha (2007) developed *Kids' Skills* in the 1990s in Finland. This is an SF method for helping children overcome emotional and behavioral problems, using a fifteen-step procedure, with the help of parents, friends, and other people close to the child. The main advantage of Kids' Skills is that inasmuch as children shy away from talking about problems, they enjoy improving their skills, which is something that can be done in a rewarding and enjoyable way. In addition, Kids' Skills fosters cooperation with parents by regarding them as partners who are willing and capable of supporting their children in developing these skills.

The first step in Kids' Skills is to convert problems into skills to be learned or to improve on. After the child expresses agreement regarding the skill he or she will be working on, a name is given to the skill, and the benefits of the skill are explored. The child may choose a *power creature* (animal, cartoon character) that can help him or her learn the skill. The child is then invited to recruit *supporters* (family, siblings, friends) and build confidence.

Exercise 101. SUPPORTERS

Invite clients—both children and adults—to answer the following questions:
- "Who are your main supporters?"
- "How do they support you?"
- "What positive things would they say about you if I asked them?"
- "How do you or did you support the people who support you?"

Exercise 102. BALLOON GAME

In this game, children get two minutes to write down (or draw) what they are good at. Then pairs are formed, and each pair blows up one balloon. The rules of the game are as follows:

1. Y ou play until one of you scores five points; he or she wins the game.
2. You can hit the balloon with your hands, but only after you say what you are good at (e.g., playing tennis or reading comic books).
3. The balloon must stay up in the air. You score points when your partner misses the balloon and the balloon hits the floor or when he or she can't say what he or she is good at
4. You can check your partner twice during the game. Stop the game and say "Check." Ask your partner to give you proof of what he or she has said.

This is a nice exercise for children, because usually they come up with far more things they are good at than they did when they made the list at the beginning of the game. This exercise is also useful for adults with low self-esteem.

A plan for celebration is then made with the child. The child demonstrates the skill (in a role play or in real-life situations) and later on practices by acting out the skill again and again. The child then celebrates his or her success and thanks the supporters. The child may also teach the skill to another child. If necessary, the child may start learning the next skill.

Homework Suggestions and Feedback

Berg and Steiner (2003) proposed a number of homework suggestions for children and families that can be divided into two categories: *do-more-of-what-works tasks*, which are done more frequently, and *do-something-different tasks*, which are suggested only under extreme circumstances, especially where adolescents are concerned.

They provide some guidelines and principles for suggesting homework. The experiment should be related to what clients want, as discussed during the first session. It should be doable and should usually involve a small step toward the clients' goal. The main purpose of the experiment is to elicit different reactions from those who play an important role in the child's life. The experiment or the homework alone rarely makes a difference; what matters are other people's responses to the child's execution of the experiment. If only the child is aware of the child's new behavior, it has a limited effect. It is important to generate a ripple effect that involves the observations and reactions of the people who are important to the child.

If therapists cannot think of an idea for an experiment, they should not force themselves to come up with one. Most experiments fall into the category of *doing more of what works*; the number of *do-something-different tasks* for children should be kept small. These experiments are useful for breaking chronic patterns that have everyone frustrated.

Behavior experiments that Berg and Steiner proposed include such things as flipping a coin. When the child wakes up, he flips a coin and when he throws tails, he engages in a secret new activity. If the child throws heads, it will be an ordinary day and the child does nothing different. The parents guess which way the coin landed each morning, and the child has to keep this information secret. At the next therapy session the parents compare notes with each other and with the child.

Another behavior experiment is the surprise task. Together with the child, the therapist finds out what the child can do that would really surprise his parents (making breakfast, cleaning his room), which then becomes a surprise the child can carry out himself. The child is asked to pay attention to the others' reactions. A surprise task is sometimes referred to as a technique of pattern disruption. Parents who claim that they 'have tried everything' often make progress when they carry out a surprise task.

Exercise 103. MARBLES IN A JAR

Invite the parents and the child to make a list of things that the child can do that are agreeable or impressive. Every time the child carries out a task assigned by the parents or the child engages in a desired behavior, the parents put a marble in a glass jar. In the evening, the parents and the child briefly discuss what each marble signifies and what went well that day. When the jar is full, the child receives a reward.

The predictable way in which parents react to their child's behavior may be disrupted if the parents do something different. For example, they can give a surprise kiss to the child or do something kind instead of becoming angry. The surprise can also come out of a wonder bag. The child and the parents each write down five wishes, which can be fulfilled, each on a separate piece of paper. The wishes are placed in separate bags and the bags are exchanged. Every week all family members pull a wish from the bag they received in the exchange, and each individual has a week to make the wish come true. Yet another behavior experiment is to pretend that the miracle has happened (or the goal is reached). After a clear description of what the miracle looks like (or the preferred future looks like), the child is asked to choose a day or part of a day for the miracle to occur. On that day the child pretends that the miracle has occurred. The child pays attention to who has noticed that he is acting as if the miracle has happened. Also a general observation task may be assigned to the child and parents. The therapist tells the child: Pay attention to the expression on your mom's face each time you start your homework without having to be told to. Or to the parents: Pay attention to the times when things are going well (or better, even just a little bit) at home, or: Observe the times when things are going well and do not need to change

Doing something fun with the child is a nice way to positively reinforce the desired behavior. Berg and Steiner describe three additional activities. For the first activity, called *magic five minutes*, parents spend five minutes with the child every day, regardless of how the child has behaved. The child gets to determine how the five minutes are spent. The second activity Berg and Steiner suggest is *horsing around* with the child every day, and for the third, the parents ask the child to take on a *big responsibility*, for example, preparing meals or running errands. This allows children to feel important and make a positive contribution to family life.

Berg and Steiner believe that parents and teachers have a *treasure box* full of tricks at their disposal, even if they are often unaware of this. It is often enough, therefore, to *do more of what works*.

They also suggested three techniques derived from hypnotherapy. The hand-on-your-hand technique is a form of cue conditioning, whereby the child carries a positive feeling from a previous situation into a situation where that positive emotion is needed. A connection is established between that positive feeling and a touch of the child's wrist. Parents demonstrate this to the child by touching the child's hand with their own. The goal is for the child to be able to conjure that positive emotion by himself in the future by briefly touching his or her own wrist. Children to pay attention in class for example can use concentration techniques; such as rubbing thumb and index finger together or placing one's hands on one's head. And imagining a safe place is a technique that offers children a feeling of security. It can be an existing or dreamed-up place that children can visit in their mind whenever they need to feel safe and relax.

More exercises that are suitable for children and adolescents include:

- You at Your Best (Exercise 32)
- Design Yourself a Beautiful Day (Exercise 83)
- What Went Well (Exercise 89)
- Three Blessings (Hunt the Good Stuff; Exercise 6)
- Older and Wiser Self (Exercise 17)
- Gratitude exercises (Exercises 67, 84, and 85)

As mentioned in Chapter 9, *building a culture of feedback* is essential in therapy. The Child Outcome Rating Scale (CORS) and Child Session Rating Scale (CSRS) were developed for working with children. The Young Child Outcome Rating Scale (YCORS) and Young Child Session Rating Scale (YCSRS) use emoticons (smileys) rather than words. The scales can be found at www.scottdmiller.com.

Many of the strategies used with children have also proved to be effective in working with clients with *intellectual disabilities* (Roeden & Bannink, 2007, 2009; Roeden, Maaskant, Bannink, & Curffs, 2011, 2012).

In the next chapter we will look at *social resilience*. Social resilience widens the perspective of researchers and therapists from a focus on individual capacities to the examination of ways to build more adaptive social environments for people, groups, organizations, and communities.

SUMMARY

- Not only adults, but also children may suffer from post traumatic stress disorder (PTSD); PTSD may look different in children of different ages.

- Most children recover, and some even grow after trauma; many children are resilient.
- Hope, optimism, and well-being are especially important for children.
- The role of parents and caregivers is to promote resilience and foster self-compassion in children, using positive reinforcement.
- A positive working assumption is that all parents and caregivers want what is best for their children—until proven otherwise. Child protection (ensuring the safety of children) is of utmost importance.
- Therapy with children and their families may be necessary. Instead of focusing on what is wrong with the child and family, the approach described in this book focuses on what is right with them and focuses on strengths and solutions. Homework suggestions for children and families are intended to direct clients' attention to those aspects of their experiences and situations that are most useful in reaching their goals.

PART THREE

SOCIAL RESILIENCE

CHAPTER 11

· · · · · · · · · · · · ·

Positive Relationships

Researchers studying people exposed to events such as accidents, war zone deployment, serious illness, or bereavement have found that social support and relationships with others in the time period following the event are key predictors of psychological recovery. These experiences may deepen people's bonds with family and friends, and they give the opportunity to see how deeply people care for one another. People may gain a new appreciation for the relationships they have and realize they can trust others to listen, care, and help. When family and friends are unsupportive or betray people's trust, the opposite effect can happen; they may feel alone and unworthy of love. But even in these cases, people may eventually form new, healthier relationships as a result of psychotherapy or groups such as Alcoholics Anonymous. They may learn that some people can be trusted, even if others cannot.

The primary protective factor against the development of PTSD is having relationships that provide care and support, create love and trust, and offer encouragement, both within and outside the family. King, King, Fairbank, Keane, and Adams (1998) found that social support was the major factor contributing to resilience in Vietnam war veterans.

Social resilience emphasizes the strengths and resources that encourage patterns of positive adaptation rather than sources of vulnerability that place people at risk (Masten & Wright, 2009). The term *social* widens the angle of researchers and therapists from a focus on individual capacities to the examination of ways to build more adaptive social environments for individuals, groups, organizations, and communities.

Social resilience is the capacity to foster, engage in, and sustain positive social relationships and to endure and recover from stressors and social isolation (Seligman, 2011). It is the glue that holds groups together, provides a purpose larger than the solitary self, and allows entire groups to rise to challenges.

Cacioppo and Patrick (2008) studied the concept of loneliness. They stated that humans are not particularly impressive physical animals. Humans do not have the benefit of natural weaponry, armor, strength, flight, stealth, or speed relative to many other species. It is their ability to reason, plan, and work together that sets them apart from other animals. Human survival depends on their collective abilities, their ability to join together with others in pursuing a goal, not on their individual might. The cohesiveness and social resilience of the group, therefore, matters.

Social resilience depends on the development of greater awareness of connections with others and capacities for social action that can lead to the attainment of both personal hopes and social purposes. Choices informed by social connection as well as personal values lead to resilient outcomes that are sustainable with respect to the social worlds in which people live as well as their personal motivations for success and long life.

In this chapter, the focus is on the impact of PTSD in relationships and how to build positive relationships—with or without therapy or coaching—with couples, groups, and teams. Therapists and whole teams of professionals working with trauma survivors are at risk for secondary traumatization but may also, just like their clients, survive and thrive.

STORY 35 *WHO MADE YOU SMILE AGAIN*

It doesn't matter who hurt you, or broke you down. What matters is who made you smile again.

—Author unknown

Exercise 104. SCALING RELATIONSHIPS

Reflect on your connections with other people each day. Each night, recall your three longest social interactions of the day and scale these from ten to zero according to how in tune and how close you felt to others. If you wish to, ask yourself what one point higher on the scale would look like and what you could do to get to a higher point on the scale.

Exercise 105. QUALITY TIME WITH FRIENDS

Positive relationships are very important. To help or encourage clients to spend quality time with friends, invite them to answer these questions:

- "When did you last really catch up with your friends?"
- "When was the last time you engaged in activities with your friends?"
- "When was the last time you did something for your friends?"
- "What may help you to set aside more time for paying attention to your friends?"
- "What could you do to find (more) friends?

RELATIONSHIPS AND PTSD

Trauma survivors with (symptoms of) PTSD may have trouble with their close family relationships or friendships. The symptoms of PTSD can cause problems with trust, closeness, communication, responsibility, assertiveness, and problem-solving. These problems may affect the way trauma survivors act with others. In turn, the way loved ones respond to them affects trauma survivors. A circular pattern can develop that may sometimes harm relationships.

In the first weeks and months following a trauma, survivors may feel angry, detached, tense, or worried. In time, most are resilient and able to resume their prior level of closeness in relationships. Yet the 5 to 10 percent of survivors who develop PTSD may have lasting relationship problems.

Survivors with PTSD may feel distant from others and feel numb.

They may have less interest in social or sexual activities. Because survivors feel irritable, on guard, jumpy, worried, or nervous, they may not be able to relax or be intimate. They may also feel an increased need to protect their loved ones. They may come across as tense or demanding.

Trauma survivors often have memories or flashbacks of the negative events. They might go to great lengths to avoid such memories. Survivors may avoid any activity that could trigger a memory. If survivors have trouble sleeping or have nightmares, both survivors and their partners may not be able to get enough rest. Survivors often struggle with intense anger and impulses. To suppress angry feelings and actions, they may avoid closeness. They may push away or find fault with loved ones and friends. Also, drinking and drug problems, used as a means to cope with PTSD, can destroy intimacy and friendships. Verbal or physical violence can occur. In other cases, survivors may depend too much on their partners, family members, and friends. This could also include people providing support, such as health care providers or therapists.

Dealing with these symptoms can take up a lot of the survivors' attention. They may not be able to focus on their partners or family. It may be hard to listen carefully and make decisions together with someone else. Partners may come to feel that talking together and working as a team are not possible.

Partners, friends, or family members may feel hurt, cut off, or down because survivors have not been able to get over the trauma. Loved ones may become angry or distant toward the survivors. They may feel pressured, tense, and controlled. The survivors' symptoms can make loved ones feel like they are living in a war zone or in constant threat of danger. Living with someone who has PTSD can sometimes lead the partner to have some of the same feelings of having been through trauma. Not surprisingly, social support may become more difficult if there is more than one person traumatized (in a family, in a group of refugees, in a group of soldiers).

In sum, people who are traumatized may have certain common reactions. These reactions affect the family, friends, and others around the survivor. They react to how the survivor is behaving, and this in turn comes back to affect the survivor.

Many trauma survivors do not develop PTSD. Also, many people with PTSD do not have relationship problems. Relationships with others can offset feelings of being alone and may help the survivors' self-esteem. This may help reduce depression and guilt. Relationships can also give survivors a way to help someone else. Helping others can reduce feelings of failure or feeling cut off from others. Last, relationships are a source of support when coping with stress.

POSITIVE RELATIONSHIPS

When asked to describe what positive psychology is about in two words or fewer, Peterson, cofounder of PP, replied, "Other people matter." Very little of what is positive in life is solitary. Is there someone in your life whom you would feel comfortable phoning at four in the morning to tell your troubles to? If your answer is yes, you will likely live longer than someone whose answer is no. In the Grant study (see Chapter 3),

---

Exercise 106. ACTS OF KINDNESS

Performing acts of kindness produces the single most reliable momentary increase in well-being of any PP exercise tested. Research has shown that this exercise will result in an increase in well-being, especially if people perform the five acts of kindness all in one day (Lyubomirsky, Sheldon, & Schkade, 2005).

Invite clients to care a bit less about what they need and care a bit more about what they can give. Invite them to set themselves the goal of performing five new acts of kindness in a single day (they should not do them every day, since this may become boring and less effective) sometime in the next six weeks. Ask them to aim for actions that really make a difference and come at some cost to them, such as donating blood, helping a neighbor with yard work, or figuring out a better way that their ailing father might manage his chronic pain. Ask them to be both creative and thoughtful and assess what those around them might need most. Ask them to make a point of carrying out all of the acts of kindness on a single day. At the end of the day, invite them to notice the good feelings that come with increasing their kindness. For lasting impact, ask them to make their kindness day a recurring ritual and to be creative each week. Ask them to find new ways to make a positive difference in the lives of others and to keep up this exercise for a few months to observe the difference it makes.

A variation is to invite clients to find one wholly unexpected kind thing to do tomorrow—"Just do it!"—and then notice what happens to their mood.

Isaacowitz, Vaillant, and Seligman (2003) discovered that the master strength in humans is the capacity to be loved. They found that the capacity to love and be loved was the single strength most clearly associated with subjective well-being at age eighty.

The American Psychological Association (APA; www.apa.org) described ten ways to build resilience (see Chapter 2). The first way is to make connections. Good relationships with close family members, friends, and others are important. Accepting help and support from those who care about you and will listen to you strengthens resilience. Some people find that being active in civic groups, faith-based organizations, or other local groups provides social support and can help with reclaiming hope. Assisting others in their time of need also can benefit the helper.

Of the virtues described in Chapter 6, the virtue *humanity* is a set of strengths focused on tending and befriending others. The three strengths associated with humanity are love, kindness, and social intelligence. Humanity differs from justice in that there is a level of altruism toward individuals included in humanity, more so than the fairness found in justice. That is, humanity, and acts of love, altruism, and social intelligence, are typically person-to-person strengths, while fairness is generally expanded to all.

STORY 36. *What You Give Is What You Get*

In the 1850s, immigrants to the United States received free grants of land if they were prepared to do the necessary work to make them livable. A family living on the East Coast undertook the long trip of several months, finally arriving in the middle of the continent. They stopped near a stream to feed their animals and children and met an old farmer who had been living in the area for many years. They asked him, "What is it like in this region? Is it a good place to plant our seeds, to build our farm, and to raise our children? How are the people here? Are they good? Are they cooperative?"

The farmer replied, "What were the people like in the East where you came from?" The head of the family replied, "Oh, they were awful and not at all cooperative!" The old farmer said, "I am sorry to inform you that it is exactly like that here. It would be better to continue your voyage and look elsewhere for your new home."

Then another family arrived, and they had also come from the East and traveled a long time. By chance they stopped at the same stream to feed their animals and children and met the same old farmer. Like the first family, they asked, "What is it like in this area? Is it a good place to plant our seeds, build our farm, and raise our children? How are the people here?" The farmer replied, "What were the people like in the East?" The family answered, "Oh, they were very kind, very helpful and cooperative." The old farmer said, "It is exactly like that here. My dear neighbors, welcome to your new land!"

—Peacock, 2001, pp. 135–136

APPROACH AND AVOIDANCE GOALS

Most people want to make connections and want to avoid loneliness. In this quest, approach and avoidance motives and goals are linked to different social outcomes (see Chapter 5). Social relationships entail both pleasure and pain. Potential social incentives include affiliation, affection, intimacy, friendship, and love. The benefits of having positive social relationships are numerous and well documented. Diener and Seligman (2002) identified the happiest people (i.e., the top 10 percent), and the one aspect of their lives they all had in common was that they had strong positive social relationships. On the other hand, there are also potential threats inherent in relationships, including conflict, rejection, humiliation, competition, and jealousy.

Approach social goals are strongly associated with outcomes defined by the presence of social rewards, such as affiliation and intimacy. For individuals who are largely approach oriented (they make connections) or find themselves in a reward-rich environment, pleasing interactions and relationships are defined as those that provide such rewards such as companionship and understanding; painful relationships are those that fail to provide these rewards. *Avoidance social goals* are strongly associated with outcomes defined by the presence of punishment, such as rejection and conflict. For individuals who are primarily avoidance oriented (they avoid loneliness) or find themselves in a threat-rich environment, pleasing interactions and relationships are defined as those that lack uncertainty, disagreements, and anxiety; painful relationships are those that possess these negative qualities. These social outcomes (e.g., intimacy, conflict) are predicted to combine and form global feelings about social bonds and relationship quality. Approach goals are generally associated with better results and more well-being than avoidance goals, although both approach and avoidance goals are necessary for successful adaptation. Whereas approach motivation facilitates growth and flourishing, avoidance motivation facilitates protection and survival.

Gable (2006) found that persons with strong approach motives were more likely to adopt short-term approach social goals (e.g., to make new friends, to be considerate), and those with strong avoidance motives were more likely to adopt short-term avoidance social goals (e.g., to not be lonely, to avoid conflict with a partner). Moreover, these motives and goals were associated with different social outcomes. Specifically, approach motives and goals were associated with positive social attitudes and more satisfaction with social bonds. Avoidance motives and goals were associated with more negative social attitudes and relationship insecurity.

COUPLES

Murray, Holmes, and Griffin (2003) studied what a *good marriage* looks like. They carefully measured what people think about their spouse: how good-looking, how kind, how funny, how devoted, and how smart he or she is. They posed the very same questions about the spouse to the closest friends of the other spouse, and they derived a discrepancy score: If someone thought more of his or her spouse than the friends did, the discrepancy was positive. If someone saw his or her spouse exactly as the friends did, the discrepancy was zero. If someone was more pessimistic about his or her spouse than the friends were, the discrepancy was negative. The strength of a marriage was considered to be directly a function of how positive the discrepancy was. Spouses with very strong benign illusions about their partners had much better marriages. The researchers believed this was likely to be because the spouse knew about these illusions and tried to live up to them. Their conclusion was that optimism helps love, and pessimism hurts.

The favorite song of US soldiers serving in Vietnam was a song by the Animals titled "We Gotta Get Out of This Place." The song was about the need to get out of the war because there was a better life for the soldiers and their partners elsewhere, providing a good example of approach motivation. Approach motivation generates greater positive affect and relationship satisfaction. Links between approach and avoidance motives and outcomes (see Chapter 5) have also been examined in romantic relationships (Impett, Gable, & Peplau, 2005). Romantic couples' motives for everyday relationship sacrifices (enacting a behavior that is not preferred, such as accompanying a partner to a dull work function, not spending time with friends, or having sex when not in the mood) were studied in a daily experience study that included a longitudinal component. The results showed that on days persons sacrificed for approach motives (e.g., to promote intimacy), they reported greater positive affect and relationship satisfaction. But, on days when they enacted the same behaviors for avoidance motives (e.g., to avoid conflict), the reported greater negative affect, lower relationship satisfaction, and more conflict. Sacrificing for avoidance motives was particularly harmful to the maintenance of relationships over time: the more individuals sacrificed for avoidance motives over the course of the study, the less satisfied they were with their relationships six weeks later and the more likely they were to have broken up. These results remained after controlling for initial levels of satisfaction.

Much research emphasizes the value of positive, approach-oriented emotions for broadening awareness and building social networks (Fredrickson, 1998).

According to Fredrickson, love can be defined as the resonance of positivity, a co-experiencing of positive emotions. Research with couples has indicated that in stable relationships, partners tend to express five times as many positive approach emotions toward each other as negative emotions, including both anger and avoidant emotions (Gottman, 1994). Gottman computed the *positivity ratio* of a marriage (see Chapter 7). He found that among flourishing marriages, positivity ratios were about 5:1. By sharp contrast, languishing and failed marriages had positivity ratios lower than 1:1.

Active and Constructive Responding

In line with the research mentioned above, Gable and colleagues (2004) demonstrated that how people celebrate is more predictive of strong relationships than how people fight. Partners may tell each other about a victory, a triumph, or good things that happen to them. How people respond can either build relationships or undermine them. There are four ways of responding:

1. *Active and constructive.* Verbal: "That's great, congratulations! I know how important this is to you." Nonverbal: Maintaining eye contact, displays of positive emotions such as smiling or laughing.

2. *Passive and constructive*. Verbal: "That's good news." Nonverbal: Little to no emotional expression..
3. *Active and destructive*. Verbal: "That sounds like a lot of responsibility to take on. Are you going to even spend fewer nights at home now?" Nonverbal: Displays of negative emotions such as frowning or crying.
4. *Passive and destructive*. Verbal: "What's for dinner?" Nonverbal: Little to no eye contact, turning away, leaving the room.

Only the first way helps in building positive relationships. Every time someone people care about tells them about something good that has happened to them, they should listen carefully and respond actively and constructively. The more time they spend reliving the event with the other person, the better. Seligman (2011) stated that once people start listening like this, other people like them better, spend more time with them, and share more of the intimate details of their lives with them. People who actively listen feel better about themselves, and all of this strengthens the skill of active, constructive responding.

In the same vein, *capitalization*, telling others about positive events in one's life, leading the other to respond in an active and positive way, generates additional affect over and above the positive affect associated with the event itself. Furthermore, the communicative act may involve rehearsal and elaboration, both of which prolong and enhance the experience by increasing its salience and accessibility in memory. In this way, capitalization builds personal and social resources.

However, perceived social support and received social support are not the same. They are differently associated with psychological benefits. Perceived social support is critical. Many survivors of disasters find benefit in the idea that other people are willing to help them. Received social support, on the other hand, may be a more mixed bless-

---

Exercise 107. ACTIVE-CONSTRUCTIVE RESPONDING

Invite clients to respond in a manner of genuine happiness, excitement, and active questioning to their partner when he or she shares an item of good news. This will allow their partner to reexperience the pleasure of the event and build a stronger, more positive relationship between them and their partner.

ing. Sometimes people receive social support when in fact they don't want social support. Therefore, the responsibility of other people is not only to offer support, but to offer it at a time and in a way that will be perceived as support. It may sometimes be wiser to withhold advice and simply validate feelings.

STORY 37. *It Is Not an Insane World*

A man had been serving in World War II. One day his wife said to him, "I want you to be able to talk to me about the war, because it may help us to understand each other. Did you really kill seventeen men?" Her husband nodded. The wife asked if he wanted to talk about it, but he said he didn't want to. He told her that he would rather think about the future—getting a new car, driving up to Vermont together and having some fun. They agreed that it wasn't an entirely insane world and concluded that at least their part of it didn't have to be.

—Wilson, 1955, p. 57

Therapy With Couples

Couples often come to therapy with a history of destructive and painful interactions, unable to work together to make much-needed changes. Usually they have little hope that their futures will be brighter than the past.

In therapy, it is important not to perpetuate this sense of failure, inadequacy, blame, and hopelessness by focusing on what the couple is doing wrong. Instead, a shift in the focus to what they are doing right, their future possibilities, their past successes, and their strengths and resources generates more hope and helps couples in building on what works and progressing (see Chapters 6 and 7).

According to Ziegler and Hiller (2001), the best predictor of success seemed to be whether, early on, both partners begin to identify their individual and relationship strengths and become motivated to work hard together to bring about mutually desired changes. These changes take place if the therapist is able to help the couple turn themselves into a *solution-building team* capable of tapping their own assets in a way that raises their hopes that things could be better. As partners feel themselves to be working as a solution-building team toward common goals, their hope, motivation, and effectiveness in making changes increases. And as they feel more hopeful about the future, they become more able to work collaboratively, both in therapy and in their everyday worlds.

From a traditional CBT point of view, couples who feel distressed need help with correcting their misinterpretations, untying the knots that twisted their communication, and tuning up their abilities to see and hear their partners' signals accurately (Beck, 1988). From a strengths-and-solutions point of view, distressed couples may need help in observing which interpretations are already right—those that don't have to change—and doing more of those. Instead of untying the knots that twist their communication, they may observe which parts of their communication are still sound and focus more on those. Finally, they may observe which capacities they already possess (and may indeed tune up) with regard to seeing and hearing their partners' positive signals instead of the negative ones.

For years, difficulties in relationships have been attributed to poor communication. In response, therapists have focused their efforts on improving communication between partners, especially about problems and the expression of emotions. While effective communication has been linked to marital satisfaction in the research literature, Gordon and colleagues (1999) suggested an alternative that is sometimes more effective: teaching *tolerance*. In particular, partners can be helped to become more tolerant (and probably more forgiving) when they adjust their expectations to the type of communication pattern they have. For example, avoidance of discussing problems and sharing emotions had less relation to marital satisfaction and happiness in couples that preferred more emotional and psychological space and less conjoint decision-making.

Bannink (2008b, 2009b, 2010b) offered many tips for couples with power struggles and conflicts:

- If there is a power struggle between two partners. suggest that they do something else, preferably something unexpected, and note the difference it makes.
- If there are arguments, ask clients what they do agree on.
- If there are arguments, ask clients if the situation could be worse. If so, how come it is not worse?
- If there is a conflict, ask both partners what the other partner could do to encourage them to adopt a different attitude.
- If there is a conflict, ask both partners what small signs they have detected that give them hope that the conflict can be resolved.

- If there are difficulties, invite both partners to notice what the other person is doing that is good for their relationship. (This is also useful as a homework suggestion.)

Therapy starts by building a positive *alliance* with both partners. It is important for therapists to start building this alliance with the person who is more likely to be there involuntarily. Sometimes a partner is brought in for therapy because the other partner wants him or her to change. The following questions about strengths and resources may be useful:

- "What is your partner good at?"
- "What do you appreciate in your partner?"
- "What do you like about him or her?"
- "What aspects of your partner are you proud of?"
- "What is positive about your relationship?"
- "How did you meet each other? What attracted you to him or her?"

This process of clients complimenting each other by describing each other's strengths is useful because it generates hopefulness and good-will, paving the way for the rest of the session to proceed more easily and in a more positive tone. *Honeymoon talk* (Elliot, 2012) is also useful, because it redirects the focus away from problems and toward previous successes in the relationship.

Needless to say, couples therapy is a balancing act for therapists: Each person should have equal time to tell his or her story and express his or her goals and solutions for a better future.

Both partners are invited to describe what they want different in their lives and in their relationship (their goal in coming to therapy). In this way, clients can move away from past problems and frustrations in their relationship to something more productive and satisfying. Working toward a common goal is important: "What would you like to see different in your relationship? What difference will it make if the other person changes in the direction you want him or her to change? What will be different between the two of you? What will you be doing differently then?"

In therapy with couples, partners sometimes want the other person to change, which puts them in a *complainant relationship* (see Chapter 4). Walter and Peller (2000) stated that clients often speak of what they do not want or what they want to eliminate from their lives. In interactional situations, clients often speak of what they want their partner *not* to do; their only course of action has been to try to get the other person to stop doing what they consider to be problematic behavior. The other partner is also in a strange position, in that his or her options are to either defend the present behavior or to stop what the other finds so problematic. He or she is still in the dark as to what the other does want to happen. Talking about what clients do want often opens up the conversation in a more positive direction.

Therapists may then ask about *exceptions*: "When is (was) there a moment or a time when things between the two of you are (were) better, even just a little bit?" If clients cannot find exceptions, invite them to observe these moments in the time leading up to the next session. Therapists may also use *scaling questions*:

- "Where on the scale from ten to zero would you like to end up (what will be a realistic goal), where ten means the best situation possible in your relationship and zero means the worst situation possible?"
- "At what point are you on the scale today (and why are you not lower)?"
- "How will you know you are one point higher on the scale? What will be different between the two of you? What will you be doing differently?"
- "At what point on the scale do you think therapy can be stopped?"

CASE 32. *Ask About Exceptions*

As therapists look for exceptions, they inquire about the couple's observations. One can distinguish between exceptions pertaining to the couple's desired outcomes (e.g., their preferred futures, their common goals) and exceptions pertaining to the problem. Here are examples of what a therapist might say to draw out exceptions pertaining to the goal:

- *Ask about exceptions.* "So when your goal has been reached (or the miracle has happened), one of the things that will be different is that you will talk to each other in a positive way about how your day has been. When do you already see glimpses of that? How is that different from what usually happens?"

- *Ask for details.* "When was the last time you and your husband talked in a positive way? What was it like? What did you talk about? What did you say? How did you react?"
- *Give positive reinforcement.* Nonverbal: Lean forward, raise your eyebrows, make notes (do what you naturally do when someone tells you something important). Verbal: Show interest. "Was this new for the two of you? Did it surprise you that this happened?" Pay compliments. "What do you think you did to make that happen? Where did you get the idea to do it that way? What great ideas you have! Are you someone who often comes up with the right ideas at the right time?"
- *Project exceptions into the future.* "On a scale of ten to zero, where ten means a very good chance and zero means no chance at all, how do you both rate the chances of something like that happening again in the coming week (or month)? What will help make that happen more often in the future? What is the most important thing you need to remember to make sure it has the best chance of happening again? If you were to do that, how will things be different in your relationship?"

CASE 33. *Relationship Questions*

A couple in therapy share a common goal: They wish to restore their relationship. Their relationship has been under much stress since they both returned from a tour of duty in Afghanistan a year ago.

After some *honeymoon talk*, the therapist decides to ask a number of relationship questions and invite other perspectives into the conversation (see Chapter 7). First, the therapist asks the husband, "How will your wife be able to tell that as a couple you are starting to get on the right track again? What will your wife say you are doing differently? What will your wife say about how she is reacting differently?"

Then the therapist asks the wife, "How will your husband be able to tell that as a couple you are on the right track again? What will your husband say you are doing differently? What will your husband say has been helpful in making that happen?"

The therapist also asks both husband and wife questions from an observer position: "How do you think your two children will be able to tell that things are going better between you? What will they see you doing differently together?"

The therapist then invites both partners to complete the VIA inventory of character strengths (see Chapter 6) and set a *strengths date* every week, using their top five character strengths during the date (see Exercise 108). Because husband and wife share curiosity as one of their top five strengths, they decide to visit some new museums together.

Homework and Feedback

Many of the homework suggestions described in Chapter 8 are also useful in therapy with couples. The suggestions are intended to direct the couple's attention to those aspects of their experiences and situations that are most useful in reaching their goals. In offering these suggestions, it is important for therapists to keep the following three questions in mind:

1. Does the couple have a well-defined common goal?
2. Do I have a visitor, a complainant, or a customer relationship with both clients? (see Chapter 4). Remember: As long as someone is not part of the solution, he or she is part of the problem.
3. Are there spontaneous or deliberate exceptions related to the couple's goal that happen already?

Building a culture of feedback is essential in psychotherapy, and no less so when working with couples. More information about the use of the Outcome Rating Scale (ORS) and the Session Rating Scale (SRS) can be found in Chapter 9. In couples therapy, both partners are in-

---

Exercise 108. STRENGTHS DATE

Planning a *strengths date* is a great way to enhance a relationship and to increase positive emotions for clients and their partners through understanding, recognizing, and celebrating each other's character strengths. To plan a strengths date, first invite clients and their partners to complete the VIA Survey of Character Strengths (see Chapter 6) to discover their top five strengths. Invite them to take as many of their top strengths as they see fit and sculpt an activity together that taps into the individual strengths of both of them.

vited to give feedback to their therapist by filling out the SRS (www. scottdmiller.com). When there is still time at the end of the session to briefly discuss the ratings, this can be done immediately. If not, therapists can come back to the couples' ratings at the beginning of the next session. No matter how high the ratings are, therapists should always ask the couple what they as therapists might do differently in order for the couple to score higher ratings next time.

The *Norway Feedback Project* investigated the effects of providing treatment progress and alliance information to both clients and therapists during couples therapy in Norway. Outpatients at a community family counseling clinic were randomly assigned to the treatment as usual (TAU) or feedback condition (using the ORS and SRS; see Chapter 9). Couples in the feedback condition demonstrated significantly greater improvement that those in the TAU condition at post-treatment, and achieved nearly four times the rate of clinically significant change. They also maintained a significant advantage on the primary measure at the six-month follow-up, while attaining a significantly lower rate of separation or divorce (Anker, Duncan, & Sparks, 2009).

A second study done by Anker, Owen, Duncan, and Sparks (2010) supported both the feasibility and the importance of the feedback intervention. The therapist–couple alliance significantly predicted outcome over and above early change, demonstrating that the alliance is not merely an artifact of client improvement, but rather a force for change in and of itself. The study also found that those couples whose alliance scores increased attained significantly better outcomes than those whose alliances scores did not improve. Together, these findings suggest that therapists should not leave the alliance to chance but rather routinely assess it and discuss it with clients in each session.

GROUPS

Furman and Aloha (2007) described an SF method called reteaming, consisting of twelve consecutive, logical steps intended to help individuals as well as groups and teams change for the better by facilitating the setting of goals, increasing motivation, and enhancing the cooperation needed to achieve these goals. Reteaming generates hope and optimism, builds motivation, and enhances creativity and cooperation between people. In reteaming, change is seen as a collective process, something done together with others. In most cases, people need help, support, and encouragement from others in order to change. Some of the steps are: to describe their dreams; identify and highlight the benefits of their goal; recruit supporters; envision progress; prepare for setback; and celebrate success.

For more information about the reteaming process, see www.reteaming. com.

Six elements may increase the success of groups:

1. Creating a climate of respect, tolerance, and trust. Everyone has a voice and is treated respectfully and equally.
2. Allowing communication to proceed in a flexible and spontaneous manner. Too much structure is counterproductive. Turn problem-focused conversations into solution-focused conversations. This generates mutual trust and appreciation, causing group members to feel encouraged to develop ideas and think of solutions.
3. Providing a context in which different points complement each other. New ways of looking at problems may thus emerge and new *problem-free* stories may be developed. This reassures group members about the situation.
4. Providing a context in which one can experiment with different viewpoints and uncertainty. This creates an opportunity for exploration.
5. Recognizing that consensus is unnecessary for and irrelevant to the creation or discovery of new possibilities. Because there is no emphasis on reaching consensus, one may discover that there are many ways of looking at a situation, one being no more correct than another.
6. Ensuring that there are no restrictive boundaries as to who does what. One often doesn't need to appoint people to execute

tasks or responsibilities. If group members notice that their knowledge and expertise are respected, they will be prepared to take more risks by undertaking additional action.

Group Therapy

In group therapy, the interpersonal process that develops in small groups is used to assist clients in achieving their individual goals. The term *group therapy* may refer to any form of psychotherapy delivered in a group format, but it is usually applied to psychodynamic group therapy and CBT. There are different types of groups: *support groups* like Alcoholic Anonymous, *skills-training groups* (e.g., anger management groups), and *psychoeducaton groups*. Apart from achieving individual goals, group therapy may be applied when group members (e.g., those living in a psychiatric setting or living in a home for intellectually disabled people) share a common goal, such as creating a positive atmosphere in the home where they live (Roeden & Bannink, 2007, 2009).

Group therapies are usually problem-focused, with the goal of enabling clients to confront their personal problems together. The goal in working with a group using a *strengths-and-solutions perspective*, how-

---

Exercise 110. SUCCESS, TALENT AND AMBITION

As a way of introduction, invite group members to talk in pairs for three minutes each about their success, talent, and ambition. Then invite each group member to give a short (one-minute) introduction of his or her partner to the rest of the group, making use of the success, talent, and ambition the member just shared. (This exercise is also useful in training listening skills.)

Exercise 111. ROUND OF COMPLIMENTS

Invite group members to write down their name on a sheet of paper and pass this sheet of paper around to each other. All members in turn write down which strengths, capacities, and resources they attribute to the person whose name is on the paper and then pass the paper to their neighbor. The paper, now filled with compliments, will finally end up with the first person. The paper can be folded concertina style to prevent anyone from reading the previous remarks.

---

ever, is different: to make the group strong and to help group members to help themselves find solutions to their problems and ignite "positive contagion" instead of negative contagion. The group is responsible for contributing their experiences. Members ask questions and are willing to share, give support, and make suggestions. Therapists are responsible for taking care of the climate, the interaction of group members, and the process of the group. Therapists' job is to stimulate the talk, involve everyone, and provide care for those who need it. A few suggestions for therapists working with groups are:

- Provide no individual counseling in the group.
- Keep eye contact with all group members, and give attention to everyone.
- Invite group members to talk, to answer, to react, and to help each other.
- Do not give answers yourself, but invite group members to do so instead.
- Do not work on individual relationships, but stimulate the relationship of the group.
- Do not engage in one-on-one discussion with group members, but keep discussion between group members.
- Refrain from giving personal opinions.
- Find strengths and resources of all group members (e.g., by offering the VIA strengths test; see Chapter 6) and look for resilience.

Homework and Feedback

Metcalf (1998) described a method of helping group members develop a homework task: When the goals of all clients in the group have been identified, the therapist encourages them to work toward their goals in between group sessions. For instance, he or she might say, "You all have good ideas about the moments when the problem is less of a burden to you. Now let's talk about what you can do until tomorrow meeting to keep the problem under control." When the goal is not yet clear, therapists can motivate clients to make good use of the time between sessions: They are invited to closely observe their daily activities until the next group session and to pay attention to when the problem does not bother them quite as much. The goal is for clients to keep track of exceptions to the problem so that they can describe these exceptions

Exercise 112. REFLECTED BEST SELF IN GROUP THERAPY

Have clients in group therapy follow these instructions:

- Ask the other group members to give you three written stories that describe when you made positive contributions in the group.
- Collect the stories and bring them together, looking for common themes, surprises, and insights.
- Synthesize these into a *best self-portrait* of you; summarize your findings or create a project based on the synthesis.
- Share the results with the other group members.

Exercise 113. POSITVE GOSSIP

Reduce negativity in a group or team and promote an upward spiral of positivity by ending negative gossip and replacing it with *positive gossip*. Positive gossip leads to the discussion of someone's attributes and successes. By painting a positive picture of other group or team members, people will, in an implicit way, exercise a positive influence on their relationships. People may think of their colleagues in a positive way: What in their qualities and capacities do they value? Which strengths do they attribute to them? How do they contribute to the group or team? Invite group or team members to speak about their colleagues in a positive way to others, with or without their colleague being present. Remember that when someone points their finger at another person (both in positive and negative gossip), there are three fingers pointing back at them!

You can invite them to do this exercise:

1. Form small groups of three people.
2. Have two of the members, A and B, gossip positively for two minutes about person C, as if he or she were not there and couldn't hear what is being said. Person C may turn his or her back to the other two persons while listening (C is not allowed to talk, but may say thank you at the end of the two minutes).
3. After two minutes, B and C gossip about person A, and, again after two minutes, A and C gossip about person B.

Although people may feel slightly uncomfortable during this exercise, they usually appreciate very much what is been said. Usually people do not get to hear so many positive things about themselves during the next session. At the end of the first group session, Metcalf suggested asking the following questions:

- "If a ten means that you have control over your life and a one means that the problem has control over you, where on that scale are you today?"
- "Where on the scale would you like to be when we meet again?"
- "What did you notice about yourself today that can help you reach that point on the scale?"
- "Does anyone have a suggestion for anyone else?"

As suggested homework, clients can then keep track of times when they have more control over their lives and problems (see Chapter 7 for the technique of externalizing the problem).

Other useful exercises are Compliment Box (Exercise 100) and Success Box (Exercise 114).

Building a culture of feedback is essential in psychotherapy, and this is true also when working with groups. More information about the use of the Outcome Rating Scale (ORS) and the Session Rating Scale (SRS) can be found in Chapter 9. The Group Session Rating Scale (GSRS) is a feedback instrument developed for working with a group. Group mem-

---

Exercise 114. SUCCESS BOX

Have group members make or buy a beautiful box together. All group members then anonymously submit three separate notes with solutions that have helped them successfully face or solve their problems. Examples of solutions include talking to a friend, taking long walks, or keeping a positive data log. When all notes have been placed in the box, they are removed and placed on the table. All group members can pick up one or two of the notes with solutions that are new to them (or that they want to try again) and try them out in a behavioral experiment.

---

bers give feedback at the end of every session on the same topics: (a) relationship with the leader and/or the group, (b) goals and topics, (c) approach or method, and (d) overall. For more information, see www.scottdmiller.com.

THE WORKPLACE

We spent about a third of our lives at work, and there is no better reason to ensure that the workplace is as healthy as possible. When referring to a healthy working environment, we think as much about physical as mental well-being. Job satisfaction, commitment, and employee perception of the organization are important factors. There is a clear connection between well-being at work and good health. Positive psychological development can be derived from a job where a high level of control and social support are possible to meet certain of the jobs inherent requirements.

Turner, Spencer, and Stone (2005) stated that the best way to improve the workplace is to create jobs whereby employees are encouraged to be active, both in their tasks and their environment. Autonomy, challenging work, and the possibility of social contact all contribute to the employee's feeling of competency.

Turner and colleagues also described the *job characteristics model*, in which three elements are important:

1, To experience work as useful
2. To feel responsible
3. To receive information about results

Individuals commonly report that what they like about work is the sense of meaning and purpose it gives them—that is, serving a goal larger than themselves. Finding ways to keep staff connected to a sense of purpose can motivate them and encourage more positive feelings. This can be done by having a strong vision or mission and talking about this more at meetings. Finding ways to tell inspiring stories about how the staff's work is affecting clients is another useful way to do this. It is important to find ways to optimize professional individual well-being and team well-being.

Individual Well-Being

Working in a team can create *individual well-being*: It provides a social network where one can find support and the idea of belonging. Within the team, high levels of clarity regarding expectations, goals, and the motivation needed to reach those goals will provide for increased well-being of the team. Team members with clear perceptions of the task to be performed report better psychological health than lone workers or team members lacking such clarity. The social context in the workplace is therefore important. Team members with high levels of team motivation are more motivated to contribute to the organization as a whole. There is also a positive connection between feeling good about the organization and an increased feeling of well-being (Turner et al., 2005).

There is a clear positive link between enjoying one's work and achievements and between a positive attitude and well-being. Well-being therefore yields better results. A positive attitude delivers more pleasant and better work, creating an upward spiral of positivity. The concepts of *therapist well-being* and *professional growth* are described in Chapter 12.

Secondary Post traumatic Success

Pope and Tabachnick (1994) found some alarming facts about the work psychologists do. Their research showed that 61 percent of about 500 psychologists reported at least one episode of depression during their career; 29 percent had experienced suicidal feelings, and 4 percent had actually attempted suicide. In 2006, the American Psychological Association's Board of Professional Affairs' Advisory Committee on Colleague Assistance (ACCA) issued a report on distress and impairment in psychologists. The report pointed out that depending on how depression is measured, its lifetime prevalence in psychologists ranges from 11–61 percent. In addition to depression, they found that mental health practitioners are exposed to high levels of stress, burnout, substance abuse, and vicarious traumatization. Seligman (2011, p. 1) stated, "While we do more than our bit to increase the well-being of our clients, psychology-as-usual typically does not do much for the well-being of its practitioners. If anything changes in the practitioner, it is a personality shift toward depression." *Secondary traumatic stress* (STS), also known as *compassion fatigue* or *vicarious traumatization*, is a condition characterized by a gradual lessening of compassion over time. STS is the combination of physical and emotional stress responses resulting from helping or wanting to help traumatized or suffering persons. It is common among professionals who work with trauma survivors, such as nurses, psychologists, first responders, and family members.

The symptoms of STS mimic those of PTSD. People may exhibit symptoms including hopelessness, a decrease in experiences of pleasure, constant stress and anxiety, sleeplessness or nightmares, and a pervasive negative attitude. This may have detrimental effects both professionally and personally, including a decrease in productivity, the inability to focus, and the development of feelings of incompetency and self-doubt.

For psychologists and other professionals to flourish even when working with trauma survivors, a number of important questions should be answered: How can therapy be more kind, not only for its clients, but also for its therapists? How can therapists prevent STS and be resilient, or recover from and even grow after STS? How can they survive and thrive, and ensure *secondary post traumatic success*?

The answer to these questions is that it is about time to take better care of ourselves as therapists by adopting a positive stance toward psychotherapy and paying attention to what we want to see expand in our clients and in ourselves. Many practitioners working in the fields of PP and SFBT have reported that they have a lighter workload, more energy to spare at the end of the day, and, ultimately, less stress.

From a PP point of view, Seligman (2011) stated that teaching PP, researching PP, using PP in practice as a coach or therapist, giving PP exercises to tenth-graders in a classroom, parenting little kids with PP, teaching drill sergeants how to teach about post traumatic growth, meeting with other positive psychologists, and just reading about PP all make people happier. From an SF point of view, Erickson (as cited in Rossi, 1980) stated that if people place the emphasis on what is positive—on the little movements that take place in a good direction—they are going to amplify these improvements, and this in turn will create more cooperation with other persons (partners, children, friends, and colleagues). The same mechanism applies in a client–therapist relationship.

STORY 38. *Water the Flowers, Not the Weeds*

In his book *Water the Flowers, Not the Weeds* (2001), Peacock tells how, after he gave a seminar to 250 managers, half of them bought a watering can. They put the cans, of all different sizes and styles, in plain sight in their offices to remind themselves that they were gardeners and that their job was to water what was working well in their organizations and in their personal lives.

Seligman (2011, p. 53) took watering the flowers even more literally:

I am a rose gardener. I spend a lot of time clearing away underbrush and then weeding. Weeds get in the way of roses; weeds are a disabling condition. But if you want to have roses, it is not nearly enough to clear and weed. You have to amend the soil with peat moss, plant a good rose, water it, and feed it nutrients. You have to supply the enabling conditions for flourishing.

Well-Being in a Team

Over the last few years, the interest in well-being and resilience has centered not only on individuals but also on teams. Initially, resilience is not reflected in team results nor in the quality of each individual employee. Resilient teams are teams wherein the team members react and cooperate with each other in a defined way. Characteristics of employees in resilient teams:

- Help each other to excel
- Openly share mutual evaluations
- Listen attentively to colleagues' advice
- Permit and accept critical comments
- Have fun and enjoy humor at work
- Support colleagues through difficulties
- Constantly seek solutions
- Are not disinclined to realign their opinions
- Do not avoid conflicts but constructively use them to attain deep dialogue

- Permit each other sufficient space to allow creativity and success
- Are modest enough to learn from each other

Team resilience is greater than the sum of the resilience of each individual member. It is concealed within the quality of the interactions between the members, which is illustrated in Story 39.

STORY 39. *Five Lessons From Geese*

A flock of geese, flying in a V-formation, has 71 percent greater flying range than a single bird flying alone. As each goose flaps its wings, it creates an uplift for the bird following. Lesson one is that people who share a common direction and sense of community can get where they are going quicker and easier because they are traveling on the thrust of one another.

Whenever a goose falls out of formation, it feels the resistance of trying to fly alone and quickly gets back into formation. Lesson two is that we would do well to stay in formation with those who are headed where we want to go and be willing to accept their help, as well as to give our help to others looking for support.

When the lead goose gets tired, another goose flies at the point position. It pays to take turns doing the hard tasks and to share the leadership. Like geese, we are dependent on each other's skills and capabilities; no person is right to lead in all circumstances and at all times. Lesson three is that leaders need to let go at times, and others must feel comfortable stepping forward.

When a goose becomes ill or wounded, two geese follow it down to help protect it. They stay with it until it is able to fly again or dies, and then they launch out with another formation or catch up with their flock. Lesson four is that we need to stand by each other in difficult times as well as when we are strong.

The geese honk from behind to encourage those up front to keep up their speed. Lesson five is to make sure our honking from behind is encouragement and not something else. Productivity is much greater in groups where there is encouragement.

—McNeish, 1972

Flourishing Teams

As stated earlier, Gottman (1994) indicated that in relationships that remain healthy, there are five positive remarks or signals for every negative or disapproving remark or signal. Research into the differences between *flourishing* teams and teams that fare less well or not at all well showed that in highly functioning teams, the *positivity ratio* is 5:1 or even 6:1 (Losada & Heaphy, 2004). As an example of these positive remarks or signals, helping co-workers with an upcoming project or presentation makes people happier. Altruists in the office are more likely to be committed to their work and are less likely to quit their jobs. Those who help others are happier at work than those who don't prioritize helping others.

A nice way of inviting team members to design their preferred future as a flourishing team and pathways toward it is to ask *future-oriented questions*, such as, "Suppose we were to meet at the airport and you were to tell me that you had won first prize in a contest for the best team. Your team is about to catch the plane to retrieve the prize. Of course there must be a speech. What are you going to tell the public about how you succeeded in becoming the best team? And whom are you going to thank for their help?"

Furman (1988) asks the *dream team question*: "How will your team function in the future when it works together like a dream team?" He proceeds to inquire about goal formulation and what the benefits of reaching the goal will be, in part to increase motivation. He encourages clients to view the path toward the goal as a step-by-step process and asks them what actions are needed tomorrow, next week, and next month. He also looks at the strengths and resources within and outside the organization and asks staff members to look for exceptions. Instead of using the term *exceptions*, he refers to *times when progress toward the stated goal took place during another project*. Questions include: "Who contributed to that? What about recent progress? Who or what made a difference? How did you do that?"

During a follow-up meeting, an assessment is done to find out what progress has been made and who deserves credit for it. *Appreciative inquiry* (AI), developed by Cooperrider and Whitney (2005), shares much common ground with PP and SF. AI is a method for realizing positive change in organizations by searching for the best in people, their organizations, and the relevant world around them. It involves systematic discovery of what gives life to a living system when it is most alive, most effective, and most constructively capable in economic, ecological, and human terms. It involves the art and practice of asking questions that strengthen a system's capacity to apprehend, anticipate, and heighten positive potential. Instead of negation, criticism, and spiraling diagnosis, there is discovery, dream, and design. AI assumes that every living system has many untapped and rich and inspiring accounts of the positive. Contrary to the problem-solving model, with its focus on problems, AI focuses on the already positive elements within the organization. There is another essential difference: Through AI, every employee is involved at the onset of the necessary change. Thereby, big changes can be realized in a very short space of time, since the fundamentals have been maximized. If, for example, an organization encounters dissatisfied clients, the question AI poses is not "What are we doing wrong to make our clients are dissatisfied?" but "At which point were our clients really satisfied with our organization?" A team is not asked, "Tell us why you have so much conflict?" but "Tell us about your team *at its best*."

In line with the story about geese (see Story 39), Stam and Bannink (2008) and Bannink (2010c) described the concept of *swarm intelligence*. They use the algorithm of a swarm of birds in their description of a positive team or organization. The human mind (and therefore also its intelligence) is a social phenomenon that arises through interaction in a social world. Human intelligence does, therefore, result from human communication. This happens through evaluating, imitating, and drawing comparisons with others' behavior and by learning from their experiences and successful solutions. It explains how, for example, a swarm of birds can demonstrate very intelligent and complex behavior despite their scant individual brain capacity. A swarm is therefore a system of social processes. Swarm behavior in humans can manifest itself by way of ideas, religious convictions, attitudes, behaviors, and everything else to do with the mind. And this is relevant to both teams and organizations. A computer model was developed to simulate swarm behavior, whereby it was discovered that only three rules were needed to make the program work:

- Retreat before you collide with the other.
- Try to fly as fast as the bird next to you in the swarm.
- Aim to fly at the center of the swarm from your own perspective.

Translated into practical applications for teams, *swarm intelligence* means:

- Know what is happening (be curious, nonjudgmental, inform others).
- Work with others to improve what is happening (find and apply solutions).
- Make it easy for the next person to do their work well (help the solutions work).

In considering these rules, it is clear that every rule links the lone bird with the other. The rules entwine individuals into a system (a team or organization). By implementing only these three simple rules, the spots on the screen behaved as a swarm, just like birds, fish, and bees. Migration can be explained by the birds' ability to combine a mutual goal (e.g., a meadow in the south of France) with an acute sensitivity to magnetic fields. A team's or organization's sensitivity is not attuned to magnetic fields but to communication, in which the following SF rules apply:

- If it works (better), do more of it.
- If it does not work, do something else.
- If it works, learn from each other and teach it to each other.

Everyone in a team or organization is responsible for the quality of his or her own personal interactions. Ghandi said, "Be the change you want to see in the world." With teams, this statement may be adapted to, "Be the change you want to see in your team."

Team Coaching

There exist many forms of *team coaching*, most of them still problem-focused. However, these models have in recent years increasingly become interested in PP and SFBT. In these approaches, strengths and solutions become the starting point, not the problem itself. Talking about problems creates problems; talking about solutions creates solutions. Positive coaching of teams is a goal- and competency-oriented form of coaching. It generates optimism and hope, increases self-efficacy, and contributes to more self-respect and a better-functioning team, even in the case of conflicts (Bannink, 2010b).

Exercise 116. HIGH-QUALITY RELATIONSHIPS

These four recommendations may help to build up high-quality relationships in the workplace. Cooperation in one or more of the following ways will create greater positivity. Ask team members to practice them throughout the day at every opportunity. Ask them to take note of how these recommendations differ from ignoring others or gossiping about them (in a negative way). Also ask them to pay attention to how others react and what differences this makes in their relationships. The four recommendations are:

1. Respect the other members; make sure you are there for them and pay attention to them.
2. Support the other members whenever you can.
3. Trust the other members and let them know that you trust them to help you.
4. Be playful together and have fun without a specific goal.

Exercise 117. APPRECATION WALL

This exercise takes about thirty minutes with a team. It helps people to get a clear view of what they and their colleagues do that works, creates energy, and strengthens relationships and trust. Hang a big sheet of paper on the wall with the names of all team members on it. Write on the top of the sheet: "WHAT WE APPRECIATE IN EACH OTHER." Then invite everyone to take a marker pen and write what he or she appreciates about what others do right under their names. When everyone is ready after about fifteen minutes, look with the team at what has been written. It may be interesting to talk about some of the appreciative statements. The team leader may ask questions, such as, "Who wrote this compliment? How did you notice this person has this capacity? What do you appreciate about it? What makes it valuable for you to have a colleague who does this?" Often the responses are enthusiastic. Complimenting people directly and accepting compliments can sometimes be awkward, but with this exercise it is usually easy and fun.

Glass (2009) compared *the broaden-and-build theory of positive emotions* (see Chapter 1) with SF and found many similarities. It appears to be the case that coaches generate positive emotions by asking questions in an open and positive way in combination with imagination, memory, and resources. This builds a wider thought-action repertoire. Thus, team members not only find more solutions for themselves but also generate more curiosity, openness, and acceptance of the thoughts of others. In this way, better team cooperation is achieved and the organization's results improve. Glass stated,

> Fredrickson's theory not only supports the power of Solution Focus in bringing the fruits of positive psychology to the workplace, but adds food for thought regarding the use and direction of SF in organizations and the aspects of SF we should focus on as practitioners in order to maximize what works (p. 39).

I also suggested the use of a combination of PP and SFBT in my book *Solution-Focused Leadership* (Bannink, 2010c).

Many of the applications and exercises in this book may also be useful in helping colleagues suffering from STS who want to recover and even grow and build resilience. Also, many exercises may be useful in building resilience with teams and organizations.

In the next chapter, we will look at the future of post traumatic success.

SUMMARY

- The primary protective factor against the development of PTSD is having relationships that provide care and support, create love and trust, and offer encouragement, both within and outside the family.
- Social resilience emphasizes strengths and resources that encourage patterns of positive adaptation.
- Approach and avoidance goals are linked to different social outcomes.
- In couples, active and constructive responding is the only way to build positive relationships.

- In couples therapy and in group therapy, clients are invited to formulate a (common) goal and find out what works and what might constitute progress.
- There is a clear connection between (individual and team) well-being at work and good health.
- Professionals working with trauma survivors are at risk for developing secondary traumatic stress (STS), but they may also survive and thrive. This is called *secondary post traumatic success*.
- Teams may flourish by asking questions that strengthen their capacity to apprehend, anticipate, and heighten positive potential. Instead of negation, criticism, and spiraling diagnosis, there is discovery, dream, and design.
- A goal- and competency-based form of coaching is described. It generates optimism and hope, increases self-efficacy, and contributes to more self-respect and a better-functioning team, even in the case of conflicts.

CHAPTER 12

••••••••••••

The Future of
Post Traumatic Success

Human beings are more often drawn by the future than they are driven by the past, and so a science that measures and builds expectations, planning, and conscious choice will be more potent than a science of habits, drives, and circumstances. That we are drawn by the future rather than just driven by the past is extremely important and directly contrary to the heritage of social science and the history of psychology. It is, nevertheless, a basic and implicit premise of PP and SFBT (Seligman, 2011). To further develop the science of human flourishing and to achieve the goal of complete mental health, whether in the realm of prevention or treatment, scientists must study the etiology of and treatments associated with mental health and develop a science of mental health. Theoretically, the largest challenge facing the field over the coming years is whether it will succeed in providing a useful alternative nonmedical paradigm for the study of post traumatic stress.

In this chapter, I will explore the possibility of changing the focus from post traumatic stress to *post traumatic success* in the fields of research and training. This may result in building the qualities that help individuals and communities not just to endure and survive, but also to flourish and thrive. Proust, a French novelist (1871–1922), wrote that the only real voyage of discovery consists not in seeking new landscapes but in having new eyes (1992).

RESEARCH

Prevention

Can *preventative resilience-building interventions* actually make people more resilient? Of course we want to promote resilience on a large scale. But, unfortunately, some preventative interventions have been surprisingly ineffective and even harmful. While the idea of preventing the development of trauma-related pathology in individuals exposed to high-stress situations such as abuse or combat has obvious merits, it is important to anticipate potential adverse consequences of these interventions (Bonanno, Westphal, & Mancini, 2011).

Critical incident stress debriefing (CISD), a single-session intervention that was widely expected to lower the incidence of psychopathology after traumatic events, highlights the importance of exercising caution when contemplating large-scale administrations of psychological interventions. However, Bonanno and colleagues (2011) found that multiple studies have shown that CISD is not only ineffective but actually may be psychologically harmful. Similarly, a review of a multiple-session intervention aimed at everyone exposed to a specific traumatic event concluded that there was insufficient evidence for the effectiveness of this intervention as well.

There have been a number of attempts to implement national programs aimed at the prevention of specific target problems, such as suicide. But large-scale public education programs have also been relatively ineffective in reducing suicide risk.

Two interrelated patterns of findings emerge from suicide prevention programs and from eating disorder programs. One is the relative ineffectiveness of universal curriculum-based programs that emphasize didactics. The other is the relatively greater effectiveness of intensive, interactive programs targeting at-risk groups.

Another unintended effect of resilience-building interventions is their potential to increase stigma attached to mental health problems experienced following exposure to potentially traumatic events. If people can be trained to be resilient, the absence of resilient outcomes may be attributed to a person's failure to benefit from training.

Perhaps the most crucial limitation of these programs is their almost exclusive focus on the individual. Resilience is not solely the province of personal strengths. Rather, there are multiple risk and resilience factors, only some of which have to do with personality and coping abilities. Environmental factors that increase or decrease risk for chronic post traumatic problems are still often neglected.

Unfortunately, the medical model did not move us much closer to the prevention of serious problems. Most prevention models were developed from an initial perspective of building competencies and not on correcting weaknesses. Research discovered that human strengths and virtues such as courage, optimism, interpersonal skills, hope, honesty, perseverance, and flow act as buffers against mental illness. Therefore, a science of human strengths is useful in helping us understand and learn how to foster these virtues in young people. Working on personal weakness and on damaged brains has rendered science poorly equipped to do effective prevention. Cofounders of PP Seligman and Csikszentmihalyi (2000) stated that practitioners should recognize that much of the best work they already do in the consulting room is to amplify strengths rather than repair the weaknesses of their clients.

Treatment

The strengths movement has two dimensions. One is that excellence is not the opposite of failure and that you will learn little about excellence from studying failure. The process of studying a phenomenon actually changes that phenomenon: We create new realities during the process of inquiry. Studying the bad, the worse, and the impossible produces its own ripple effects through the "mere measurement effect" (Morwitz & Fitzsimons, 2004). So does inquiry into the good, the better, and the possible.

My therapeutic model of *post traumatic success* is new. This is the first book about this promising approach, combining two recent approaches in psychotherapy that share a positive focus: positive psychology and solution-focused brief therapy. This implies that so far no research has been done. Of course, this model needs to be empirically tested and objectively evaluated. What criteria should be used to measure this model? How can we know whether this model leads to better therapy outcomes? Which mechanisms of change are operating? How is this model different from other approaches?

Research should be done on specific elements and how these may help certain populations or be used to address certain problems under specific conditions. The information obtained from research will also enable therapists to thrive in their profession instead of merely survive. Microanalysis of conversations (see Chapter 7) will be useful for this purpose. Pilot studies and larger studies with randomized control trials (RCTs) are needed, since this is the best way to determine the effectiveness of a given approach. These studies will help to develop the evidence base to support this model as an effective approach.

Further research will hopefully help to increase the number of clients who benefit from approaches to trauma. Cost-efficiency considerations along with social and technological changes can make this new model, which may well be as effective by telephone, Skype, or Internet as it is in the consulting room, the preferred approach for the future, particularly because it uses protocols that easily lend themselves to social media applications.

TRAINING

Until recently, the primary emphasis in the training of mental health workers was on human deficits and weaknesses. In this way, we became *victimologists and pathologizers*. Slowly but surely, however, there has been a shift toward a more positive focus (see Chapter 1). Seligman (2011) stated that over the last forty-five years he had taught almost every topic in psychology. However, he said, he had never so much fun teaching, nor were his teaching ratings ever so high, as when he was teaching PP. When he taught abnormal psychology, he could not assign his students meaningful, experiential homework; they couldn't become schizophrenic for a weekend. But in teaching positive psychology, he could assign a gratitude visit or the what-went-well exercise.

In future training, we have to find a new and more positive balance between a focus on pathology and a focus on the strengths and solutions of our clients and their environment. There should be a greater emphasis on using a positive lens, in addition to the negative lens used in traditional approaches. Ultimately, the aim is to create a large group of therapists who will use this positive approach to trauma and in turn can teach others. We need professionals to recognize that much of the best work they do is amplifying their clients' strengths and solutions rather than repairing their weaknesses and problems.

In training courses, there should also be a greater emphasis on *outcome measurement*. Conventional wisdom suggests that competence engenders, if not equals, effectiveness. As a result, there is a continuing education requirement designed to ensure that therapists stay abreast of developments that enhance the positive outcome of therapy. The vast majority of these trainings do not include any methods for evaluating the effectiveness of the approach. Instead, emphasis is placed on learning skills or techniques of a particular brand or style of therapy. But this emphasis on competence versus outcome decreases effectiveness and efficiency. Research has shown that there is no or little relationship between experience level and the effectiveness of therapists (Clement, 1994). Unlike product-oriented efforts the field has employed so far, outcome management results in significant improvements in effectiveness. Liberated from the traditional focus on models and techniques, therapists will be better able to achieve what they have always claimed to be in the business of doing: helping people change.

Focus on Clients' Well-Being

Our clients create meanings or definitions of reality through their use of words and talking to one another. Clients' capacity to change is connected to their ability to see things differently. De Jong and Berg (2002, p. 349) stated,

> These shifts in client perceptions and definitions of reality, which are a part of clients' solution building, occur most readily in conversations about alternative futures and useful exceptions. Solutions depend more on clients' capacity to develop and expand their definitions of what they want and how to make that happen than on scientific problem definition, technical assessment, and professional intervention.

By using their skills to sustain purposeful conversations, therapists allow clients to develop the expanded perceptions and definitions they need to live more satisfying and productive lives. Strictly speaking, therapists do not empower clients or construct alternative meanings for them; only clients can do that for themselves. However, therapists can assume and respect clients' competencies and have meaningful conversations with clients so they can create more of what they want in their lives.

Therefore, a focus on the art of psychotherapy may be added to the focus on techniques, and a focus on mental health may be added to the focus on mental illness. Reducing distress by making miserable people less miserable is just one side of our job, whereas building success by helping clients to survive and thrive is the other side (hence the subtitle of this book).

Gilbert (2010) stated that if science continues to show that one of the most important components of well-being is the ability to love and be loved, to care and to be caring, then our therapies, interventions, and training will become increasingly focused on that, be this in our clinics, schools, or workplaces.

Focus on Therapists' Well-Being

In Chapter 10, research was described showing that between 11 and 61 percent of psychologists have at least one depressive episode in their lives and that they are at risk for developing secondary traumatic stress. Anyone in the health or mental health community inherently knows about *compassion fatigue*, also known as *secondary traumatic stress* (see Chapter 11). It is a condition characterized by a gradual lessening of compassion over time, accompanied by symptoms such as hopelessness, a decrease in experiences of pleasure, an increase in stress and anxiety, and a pervasive negative attitude. In turn, this may lead to a decrease in productivity, an inability to focus, and the development of feelings of incompetence and self-doubt. In the medical professions this condition is often called *burnout*.

Research on microanalysis (see Chapter 7) has shown that positive talk leads to more positive talk, and negative talk leads to more negative talk. Thus, a therapist's use of positive content seems to contribute to the co-construction of an overall positive session, whereas negative content does the reverse.

Seligman described the impact PP has on its practitioners (2011). According to him, PP makes people happier. Teaching positive psychology, researching positive psychology, using positive psychology in practice as a coach or therapist, giving positive psychology exercises to tenth graders in a classroom, parenting little kids with positive psychology, teaching drill sergeants how to teach about post traumatic growth, meeting with other positive psychologists, and just reading about positive psychology all make people happier. Seligman reported that the people who work in positive psychology were the people with the highest well-being he had ever known.

De Jong and Berg (2002) described the impact of SFBT on its practitioners. They quoted practitioners working with domestic violence groups, groups for adolescent substance abuse offenders, and parents of adolescents on probation, as well as practitioners working with the entire range of clients in a community mental health clinic.

> When we used to do problem-focused work, it seemed we were tired all the time. We never seemed to know when a client was done with therapy, and often felt that we were doing all the work, and had to be the *expert* and figure out how to fix or cure the client . . . Solution-focused therapy was a breath of fresh air. All of a sudden, it was the client who determined when they were done with therapy. There were clear behav-

ioral indicators when the goal was reached. We . . . worked in collaboration with the client to figure out together what would be helpful. We no longer listened to months of problems, but were listening to strengths, and competencies, and abilities. We no longer saw clients as DSM labels but as incredible beings full of possibilities . . . We found we were definitively having more fun. (p. 322)

Many therapists grow weary and begin to wonder why they enlisted in this difficult job in the first place. So what keeps them from succumbing to burnout or getting a job that is more fun? Orlinsky and Ronnestad (2005) did a twenty-year, multinational study of 11,000 therapists and found that therapists stay in the profession not because of material rewards or the prospect of professional advancement, but because, above all, they value connecting deeply with clients and helping them to improve. On top of that, clinicians consistently report a strong desire to continue learning about their profession, regardless of how long they have been practicing. Orlinsky and Ronnestad found that *professional growth* is a strong incentive and a major buffer for burnout. What therapists seek in their professional careers and the satisfaction they receive from the work they do is called the *healing involvement*. This concept describes therapists at their best: It is about therapists' reported experiences of being personally engaged, communicating a high level of empathy, and feeling effective and able to deal constructively with difficulties. This healing involvement emerges from therapists' cumulative career development as they improve their clinical skills and increase their mastery, but an even more powerful factor promoting healing involvement is the therapists' sense of currently experienced growth—the feeling that they are learning from their day-to-day clinical work, deepening and enhancing their understanding in every session. This growth is fundamental to maintaining a positive work morale and clinical passion. A sense of having currently experienced growth reenergizes therapists, and it is their greatest ally against burnout.

Duncan (2010) stated that achieving a sense of healing involvement requires a continual evaluation of where you are compared to where you have been. Research literature offers strong evidence that not all therapists perform equally well and that most therapists are poor judges of client deterioration (see Chapter 9). They don't tend to be good judges of their own performance either. Sapyta, Riemer, and Bickman

(2005) asked clinicians of all types to rate their job performance from A to F. About 66 percent ranked themselves A or better. Not one therapist rated himself or herself as being below average! If you remember how the bell curve works, you know that this isn't logically possible. Therefore, some quantitative standard as a reference point is essential. Taking the time to measure outcomes—for example, by using the Outcome Rating Scale (ORS) and the Session Rating Scale (SRS) as described in Chapter 9—relates both to having an awareness of one's mastery over time and experiencing a sense of current professional growth. In this sense, it is clear that not only do clients benefit from the use of feedback forms, but therapists do as well. In the largest randomized clinical trial of couples therapy ever done, Anker and colleagues (2009) found that clients who gave their therapists feedback about the benefit and fit of services on the ORS and SRS reached clinically significant change nearly four times more than nonfeedback couples did. Tracking outcomes also improved the results of nine out of ten therapists. This finding implies that many therapists can become *supertherapists* if they are proactive about tracking their own and their clients' development.

In sum, many professionals working within the PP and SF model (psychotherapists, coaches, mediators, teachers) report the same experience but in the opposite direction: The positive focus in their work enhances their personal well-being and professional growth. Most professionals and trainers in SFBT also believe that adequate therapeutic skills can be achieved with less training time and experience than is the case for other psychological therapies.

Two more advantages of this model can be highlighted. One is the use of positive supervision and peer supervision models (Bannink, 2012b, 2014). With these models, far more cases can be reviewed using less time, with a focus on the strengths and solutions of colleagues instead of on their weaknesses and failures, leading to better results. The second advantage is that expertise in short-term, goal-focused and strengths-based therapies will, in these times of economic recession, render therapists highly marketable.

STORY 40. *Heaven or Hell*

A woman died and found herself standing in a beautiful banquet hall. A huge table running through the center of the hall was laden with the finest foods and wines. She thought, "This must be heaven!" She sat down at the table and then noticed something dreadful. Both her arms were in splints, so she could not bend her elbows. She could easily reach the delicacies but was unable to maneuver them to her mouth. The other people sitting around the table had the same difficulty: Their arms were also in splints and they could not eat or drink. They were angry, frustrated, hungry, and even crying, but nothing could save them from their fate.

"This can't be heaven," the woman thought; "this must be hell. I wonder what heaven is like." Her wish transported her to another banquet hall, but there she found that her and others' arms were in splints as well. But there was something different about this group of people, who all appeared happy and well fed. Then she saw what made the difference: Her fellow guests were not trying to bend their arms, but each person picked up a delicacy requested by the person opposite him or her. Others fed her, just as she fed them. "This is not just about food," she thought, for they also shared conversation. They exchanged stories, spread feelings of optimism, and joined in an experience of joyfulness, She decided, "This must be heaven."

—Author unknown

BUILDING BRIDGES

Until now, traditional approaches to trauma have been far apart from PP and SFBT. Maybe because I live in the Netherlands where we have to build bridges to survive (and thrive: we are one of the happiest nations in the world), but certainly, because it is my mission to make this world a better one (even if only in some small way), my aim is to build bridges between different fields within psychotherapy and beyond. In my profession as a mediator, I often use the saying "The wider the gap, the more beautiful the bridge."

With this model, I want to build bridges between research and training in the fields of traditional therapies, and research and training in PP and SFBT, so that they can benefit from each other and cooperate in making this world better instead bitter for our clients and ourselves. The landscape may remain the same, but with new eyes there is a real voyage of discovery waiting for us!

• • • • • • • • • • • • • •

CHAPTER 13

Frequently Asked Questions

It is said that the wise man is not the man who provides the right answers, but the one who asks the right questions. Below are my answers to twenty-three frequently asked questions. I welcome your inspiring answers and would like to invite you to email your suggestions to solutions@fredrikebannink.com.

Question 1: *What if my client has no goal?*
- Give your client compliments for showing up and talking to you.
- Ask your client who referred him to you and what he thinks the referrer wants to see different as a result of therapy.
- Discuss with your client the disadvantages or possible dangers of change.
- Invite the client to meet with you again in the future.
- Don't give any homework suggestions.
- See Chapter 4 (mandated clients) for further suggestions.

Question 2: *What if my client wants something that is not good for her?*
- Try to understand her perspective.
- Ask your client how this may be helpful to her.
- Ask your client what is happening in her life that tells her that

continuing this behavior (e.g., drinking alcohol or doing drugs) is good for her.
- Use the third-person perspective: "Supposing we asked your partner (children, colleagues) about how this might be helpful to you or to them, what do you think he (she, they) would say?
- It is only on the rarest occasions that taking away the self-determination of your client is necessary.

Question 3: *What if the goal of my client is unrealistic?*
- If there is no solution, there is no problem (but there is a fact of disability, see Chapter 5). A problem can be solved; a fact or disability cannot be solved, and has to be dealt with in the best possible way.
- If your client has an unrealistic goal (winning the lotto, wanting someone who died to be alive, wishing the accident had never happened), ask, "Supposing that was a reality, what difference would that make in your life?" Or ask your client what that would mean to him.
- Ask yourself whether you are dealing with not just a complaint or wish (to bring about a different feeling or a change in another person) but an actual goal, the attainment of which lies within the client's control (a soundly and positively formulated goal).

Question 4: *What if my client cannot visualize?*
- Find out with your client what the reason might be. Sometimes visualizing the preferred future or using imagery is difficult for clients (e.g., in the case of autism). Sometimes clients are reluctant to engage with imagery because of fears about what the image represents.
- Define what you mean by imagery.
- Start with positive and neutral images to find out whether your client has access to visual imagery.
- Ask your client to bring photos (e.g., of herself as a child, parents, or other relevant positive situations).
- Engage your client in relaxation procedures prior to imagery.
- Start with safe place imagery (see Exercise 81) and also end that way.
- Give your client imagery experiences in which she takes control (e.g., being the director on a stage).

- Use auditory, kinesthetic, olfactory, or gustatory stimuli instead of visual ones.

Question 5: *What if my client answers, "I don't know"?*
- Ask your client, "Supposing you did know, what would you say?" or "Supposing you did know, what difference would that make?"
- Ask your client, "Supposing I were to ask your partner (children, colleagues, best friend), what would they say? Would they be surprised? Which person you know would be least surprised?"
- Agree with your client: "Yes, I am asking you some tough questions; please take your time."
- Ask yourself, "Is it important to my client to know?"
- Ask your client, "How would your life be different if you did know? or "How would your life be better if you did know?" Or say, "Take a guess!"
- Say, "Of course you don't know yet, but what do you think?"
- Say to yourself that something important is probably going on at this point and allow your client more time.

Question 6: *What if my client does not want to talk about what happened to her, or what if there is a secret?*
- Put your client at ease and respect that she is not (yet) ready (and perhaps will never be ready) to tell you what is bothering her.
- Don't think it is necessary for your client to reveal her secret to you.
- Ask your client, "Supposing you did tell me what is bothering you, what difference would that make?"
- Ask your client, "Supposing there is a solution, what would your life look like then?"

Question 7: *What if my client cannot name any strength?*
- Help your client to explore areas of his life that are going relatively well, expressing curiosity for all of the client's life, not just problem areas;
- Ask your client what happens in his life that he would like to continue to happen, and link that to his strengths.
- Link these areas to therapy goals (see *competence transference* in Chapter 6);

- Ask coping questions and competence questions: "How do you manage? How do you cope with this situation? How is it that the situation is not worse?"
- Invite your client to fill out the VIA strengths survey on the Internet.
- Use the third-person perspective (see Chapter 7): "Supposing you had a twin brother or sister sitting right behind you, what would he or she say your strengths are?"

Question 8: *What if my client cannot find exceptions to the problem?*

Do you have a complainant relationship with your client? (see Chapter 4). If so, give only observational homework suggestions. Examples are:

- Ask your client to pay attention to what is going well and should stay the same, or pay attention to what happens in her life that she would like to continue to happen.
- Ask your client to observe the positive moments in her life so that she can talk about them next time you meet.
- Ask your client to pay attention to the times when things are going better so that she can talk about them next time.
- Ask scaling questions: "Observe when you are one point higher on the scale and what you and/or (significant) others are doing differently then."
- Ask your client to pay attention to what gives her hope that her problem can be solved.
- Use prediction homework: "Predict what tomorrow will be like, tomorrow evening find an explanation for why the day turned out the way it did, and then make a new prediction for the following day."
- Ask your client to pay attention to exactly what happens when an exception manifests itself so that she can tell you more about it: "What is different then, and what are (significant) others doing differently?"
- When a client in a complainant relationship thinks the other person is the problem and needs to change: "Pay attention to the times when the other person does more of what you want, to what is different then, and to what he or she sees you do then that is helpful to him or her."

- Ask your client to pay attention to what the other person does that is useful or pleasant and to the difference it makes so that you can talk about it next time.
- Have your client ask other people what exceptions they see.
- Ask your client, "Supposing you could find an exception, what difference would that make?"
- See Appendix B for finding exceptions pertaining to the goal and the problem.

Question 9: *What is the role of diagnosis in this model?*
- The role of diagnosis is important, but diagnosis should not only be about disorders (DSM-5) and what is wrong with your client, but should also be about strengths (VIA) and resources and what is right with him (see Chapter 6);
- Diagnosis should include an exploration of everything that works in your client's life.
- Diagnosis should be not only about the problem (problem analysis), but also about what the client wants to have instead of the problem (goal analysis).
- The problem-solving structure assumes a necessary connection between a problem and its solution, as in modern medicine. This assumption underlies the field's emphasis on assessing problems before making interventions. It is not (always) necessary to start treatment with assessing problems. Bakker and colleagues (2010) proposed the use of *stepped diagnosis* (see Chapter 4).
- Diagnosis is also about the alliance with your client: Is there a visitor, complainant, or customer relationship (see Chapter 4)?
- In CBT, *functional behavior analyses* can be made of problems and/or of exceptions to the problems (Bannink, 2012a).

Question 10: *What if my client is in a crisis situation or is suicidal?*
- Remember that clients in crisis quickly stabilize if they are invited to direct their attention to what they want to be different (goal formulation) and to make use of their past successes and their competencies.
- Ask *coping questions* and *competence questions:* "How do you manage to go on, given this difficult situation?"

- Install hope in your client: "What are your best hopes? What difference will that make?"
- Ask how you can be helpful: "How can I help you?"
- Ask if there is anyone else who knows of this situation with your client and how that is helpful.
- Be curious of what your client has already attempted since the start of the crisis and what has been helpful, even just a little bit.
- Remember that at least half of the sessions with a suicidal client should be spent on her reasons for living; the client is still alive.
- Ask your client what she would like to see different in her life or in her situation.
- Ask your client, "Supposing you felt calmer and everything became a bit more clear to you. What would be different then? What is the first thing you would do?"
- Ask your client, "How were you able to get up in the morning, come here, and ask for help?"
- Ask your client, "What are you doing to take care of yourself under these circumstances?"
- Ask your client, "Who (and what) do you think would help the most at this moment?"
- Ask how your client will get through the rest of the day.
- Ask your client, "What, in your opinion, is the most useful thing that I as a therapist can do?"
- Ask if things could be worse than they are now. If so, "How come things are not worse?"
- Ask your client, "What is the most important thing for you to remember in order for you to handle this situation?"
- Look for exceptions: "How often do you have these (suicidal) thoughts?"
- Ask scaling questions: "On a scale of ten to zero, where ten means that you're dealing optimally with the situation and zero means that you can't deal with it at all, how well are you dealing with all of this? How is it that you are already at that point on the scale? What would one point higher on the scale look like? How would you be able to tell that you were one point higher? How would you be able to go up one point? How motivated are you to go up one point? How much confidence

do you have that you will succeed in going up one point? What difference would it make for you if you went up one point?"

Question 11: *How many sessions are needed in this model?*
- In SFBT, the average number of sessions is three to four (with the same follow-up results as in problem-focused therapies).
- In this model, the number of sessions will be less than the average number of sessions in traditional psychotherapies, because if there is to be no assessment of the problem, the therapy will probably be briefer.
- Remember that the client defines the goal in therapy (and not the therapist) and indicates when to stop therapy. Usually this occurs at an earlier stage than the therapist might anticipate.
- Remember that, during the first session, the client is asked about when he would consider therapy to be successful and when it can end. This is indicative of the fact that therapy is limited and goal-oriented. This is different from traditional forms of psychotherapy, in which conversations about concluding therapy are only held when therapy is almost over.

Question 12: *Can I combine traditional therapy for trauma survivors with this model?*
- Yes, traditional therapies may be combined with this model.
- For example, the combination of EMDR and this model may be useful. First, the therapist invites the client to find exceptions to the problem. Then the therapist may suggest to the client that in order for her to move up the scale of well-being, a technique such as EMDR may be helpful.
- Keep your client in the expert position by, for example, asking her what she already knows about this technique or inviting her to find (more) information about EMDR on the Internet.
- Keep your client in the expert position by, for example, first explaining some traditional methods to your client (e.g., exposure, EMDR, compassion-focused therapy) and then inviting her to reflect on which method she may find most useful.

Question 13: *Can I ask my client to choose between traditional therapy models and this model?*
- As a therapist, you should have the skills to use both forms of therapy.

- Erickson, the famous psychiatrist-hypnotherapist, often gives his client the choice of two or more alternatives. The feelings of choice and freedom are maintained better than in a situation where the client is told exactly what to do. In fact, once your client chooses a particular alternative, he is probably more committed to that choice.

Question 14: *What if my client says: Tell me what to do; you are the expert!*
- Ask your client if in the past it has been useful when other people told her what to do.
- Ask you client if, before you offer some suggestions, she is willing to answer a few questions.
- Then ask her about exceptions to the problem and about her competencies and successes in the past.
- Keep your client in the role of co-expert. For example, explain that others have solved problems similar to the one the client has through X, Y, or Z. Invite your client to reflect on which solution she may find most useful.
- Invite your clients to do some behavioral experiments and to observe what difference they make. For example, ask your client to *pretend the miracle has happened* and observe the reactions of others.
- Take a cautious stance: "I think I do have an idea, but I am sure you have already tried it and it probably didn't help much . . . Did you ever try to . . . ?"

Question 15: *What if my client wants to find an explanation for what is wrong with him?*
- Remember we human beings are explanation-seekers.
- Also remember that you do not need to find an explanation in order to help your client reach his goal.
- Instead, ask your client, "Suppose you were to have an explanation, what difference would that make?"
- Ask, "How would an explanation be helpful to you?"
- Ask, "What part of the explanation do you already have?"
- Ask your client what he can do to come up with information that may be useful in finding the explanation he wants.
- Ask how you might be helpful in helping him to come up with an explanation.

- The focus on explanations may indicate that there is a complainant relationship with this client (see Chapter 4).

Question 16: *What if my client only wants to talk about her past?*
- Ask yourself whether you are you working with someone who is willing to change. Maybe you have a complainant relationship with your client (see Chapter 4) and should adjust your interventions accordingly.
- Ask yourself whether you are working on your client's goal. Make sure that the client wants to reach the goal more than you do.
- Ask your client, "How many sessions do you think you need to talk about your problematic past (and/or problematic present) before you are ready and able to talk about your preferred future?"
- Ask her how talking about the past will help her reach her goal.
- Ask her how she will know that she has talked enough about the past and can start looking at the future.
- The present and future determine how we look at our past: It is said that it is never too late to have a happy childhood. Ask your client three resilience questions about his or her past (see Chapter 7).

Question 17: *What if my client returns to problem-talk all the time?*
- Don't get discouraged, because this happens quite often.
- Gently interrupt your client and say, "OK, we'll come back to that." Once your client has moved on to a more clearly defined goal or can find exceptions to the problem, often there is no need or wish to return to the topic.
- Ask your client how long or how many sessions he thinks will be necessary before he can move on from talking about his problem to talking about what he wants and his preferred future.
- Consider whether you have a customer relationship with your client or maybe a complainant relationship (see Chapter 4). If you might have the latter, adjust your interventions accordingly.
- Ask your client, "How do you think that talking about your problem will help you reach your goal?"

- Say to your client that he must have a good reason for continuing to talk about his problem and invite him to tell you about this reason.
- Ask your client, "Supposing you said everything you wanted to say about your problem, what would change for you then?"

Question 18: *What if there is no progress or even deterioration?*
- If you have a positive alliance and your approach does not work, stop and do something else. Continuing with an approach that is not working and doing more of the same when there is no progress are two of the four pathways to impossibility, as described in Chapter 9.
- Remember what Einstein said: "Insanity is doing the same thing over and over again, expecting different results."
- Keep in mind that therapy should not be used for the purpose of just sustaining or maintaining clients.
- Remember that we therapists are very bad at identifying deteriorating clients and routinely overestimate our effectiveness (see Chapter 9).
- Don't assume that deterioration of your client's situation comes before the situation gets better. Instead, this is an indicator that portends a final negative outcome (see Chapter 9).
- Ask your client (or supervisor or colleagues) what you should do differently.
- If you have a negative alliance, refer your client to a colleague.
- More diagnosis may be needed (see Chapter 4 for the concept of *stepped diagnosis*).
- Invite others into the conversation (the client's partner, children, friends).
- Use the ORS and SRS (see Chapter 9).

Question 19: *What if I become irritated or discouraged or start to feel uncertain?*
- If you feel irritated, discouraged, or uncertain (*countertransference*), you need to focus more on the therapeutic alliance.
- Ask yourself what you can do differently to enhance the alliance (see Chapter 4) instead of thinking about what the client should do differently.
- Supposing you were one point higher on the scale of the alli-

ance than you are now, what would you do differently? How would your client react differently? This is a nice question to use in supervision or peer supervision.
- Give your client more compliments by focusing on his strengths, successes, and competencies;
- Use the past of your client to look for exceptions to his problem.
- Ask a supervisor or colleagues in peer supervision what you can do differently to enhance the alliance.
- Use the ORS and SRS (see Chapter 9).

Question 20: *What if my client becomes irritated or angry?*
- Validate her feelings. Tell your client than you are sure she must have a good reason for becoming irritated or angry and invite her to name the feeling.
- Tell your client to take all the time she needs to vent her emotions. Often this is helpful, because when the therapist has control, venting anger becomes less rewarding.
- Ask your client which strengths and resources she has to control her anger if she should want to do so.
- Take a time-out. Tell your client that you are leaving (e.g., to go to the bathroom) and will return after a while.
- End the session if you feel threatened and unsafe, and explain this to the client if possible.
- Ensure that during the next session a colleague is present who may help you if necessary.
- Always sit close to the door so that you are able to leave the room first.
- Use the ORS and SRS and ask the client what you as her therapist may do differently next time you meet.

Question 21: *What if my client has not done his homework?*
- Homework as seen in, for example, traditional CBT is no longer necessary. Homework is useful only if the client thinks it is useful.
- Ask yourself if homework suggestions will generate more information than you will receive if the client does not perform homework (see Chapter 8).
- Accept nonperformance as a message about your client's way of doing things rather than as a sign of resistance.

- Say to your client that you are sure he must have a good reason for not doing his homework and invite him to tell you more about this reason.
- Remember to keep a positive alliance with your client, even without him doing any homework.
- Only provide feedback for the client to reflect on, or assign an observational homework task. Your client may not yet or may no longer be in a customer relationship (see Chapter 4).
- Do you want too much too soon? Look for smaller changes, use scaling questions regarding the goal or the exceptions, or counsel the client not to move too fast.

Question 22: *What if my client has very complex problems?*
- Remember that complex problems do not need complex solutions, and that you as a therapist do not need to know as much as possible about your client's problems in order to effectively help her.
- *Occam's razor*, often expressed as the *law of parsimony*, is a principle that generally recommends, when one is faced with competing hypotheses that are equal in other respects, selecting the one that makes the fewest new assumptions.
- Use *skeleton keys*, as described in Chapter 8. You don't have to analyze each lock (e.g., each problem) before you can use these keys. This is an example of the use of Occam's razor.
- Follow Einstein's constraint: Everything should be kept as simple as possible, but no simpler.
- Read the story Brilliant Insights in Chapter 9 and see how complicated theoretical formulations often make things worse.

Question 23: *How do I cooperate with problem-focused colleagues?*
- Remember that it is very likely that at least some of your colleagues are still thinking and acting in a problem-focused way. Therefore, they place greater emphasis on problems (and are more prone to finding problems).
- Make sure you keep your client's goals in mind and that his goal is always your guide. It is easy to get distracted. Meetings with your colleagues may get bogged down in a lengthy discussion of problems or complaints about another person or other people. In a meeting, always ask what the goal of the meeting is so that you can work in a solution-focused way.

- Establish a positive framework. Making the (hidden) positive motivation of everyone involved explicit may put your colleagues at ease and allow them to work in a goal-oriented manner.
- Compliment your colleagues, and always explicitly express your appreciation of the progress being made and their collaboration.
- Regularly point out the successes and strengths of your colleagues and summarize them. Be generous.
- Use positive *guerrilla actions*. Now and then show your colleagues, without explaining too much, what it is exactly that you do when using PP and SFBT. For example, show them that you ask about exceptions to the problem and that you highlight areas of strengths and resources.
- Remember to be the change that you want to see in your team or organization.

APPENDIX A

■■■■■■■■■■■■■■

Protocols for the First Session

PROTOCOL FOR THE FIRST SESSION 1
(Submit all questions to each client present)

Building Rapport

Problem:
"What brings you here? How is that a problem for you? What have you already tried, and what has been useful?"

Goal Formulation:
"What would you like to be different as a result of these sessions?" Here the therapist may ask the *miracle question* (see Chapter 5) or other questions about goal formulation.

Exceptions:
"When have you caught a glimpse of this miracle? How did you make that happen?" Alternatively: "When is the problem absent or less noticeable? How do you manage that? Which personal strengths and resources do you use?"

Scaling:
- *Progress:* "Where are you now on a scale of progress of ten to zero? How do you manage to be at that point (and not lower)?"
- *Motivation:* "Where are you now on a scale of ten to zero, if ten means you're willing to give it your all and zero means you're not willing to put in any effort?"
- *Confidence:* Where are you now on a scale of ten to zero, if ten means that you are very confident and zero means you have no confidence at all that you can reach your goal?"

Concluding the session:

- If the client gives a concrete and detailed response to the miracle question or another question about goal formulation, suggest: "Pick a day in the coming week, pretend the miracle has happened, and observe what difference that makes."
- If the client does not give a concrete and detailed response to the miracle question or another question about goal formulation, suggest: "Pay attention to what happens in your life that gives you the sense that this problem can be solved." Alternatively: "Pay attention to what is happening in your life that you would like to keep happening because it's good (enough)."
- "Do you think that it would be useful for you to return?" If so: "When would you like to return?"

PROTOCOL FOR THE FIRST SESSION 2
(Submit all questions to each client present)

Build rapport and ask the four basis SF questions:

1. "What are your best hopes? What else?"
2. "What difference will that make? What else?"
3. "What is working? What else?"
4. "What will be the next signs of progress?" or "What will be your next step? What else?"

APPENDIX B

■■■■■■■■■■■■■

Protocol for Finding Exceptions

As you look for exceptions, you may inquire about the client's observations and, using the *interactional matrix* (see Chapter 7), about what important others might be able to perceive. You may distinguish between exceptions pertaining to the desired outcome (the goal) and exceptions pertaining to the problem. Submit all questions to each client present.

EXCEPTIONS PERTAINING TO THE GOAL

1. *Elicit.* "So, when your goal has been reached (or the miracle has happened), you will talk to each other about how your day has been. When do you already see glimpses of that? If your husband were here and I asked him the same question, what do you think he would say?"
2. *Amplify.* "When was the last time you and your husband talked to each other? Tell me more about that. What was it like? What did you talk about? What did you say? And what did he say? What did you do when he said that? What did he do then? What was that like for you? What else was different about that time? If he were here, what else would he say about it?"
3. *Reinforce.* Nonverbal: Lean forward, raise your eyebrows, make notes (do what you naturally do when someone tells you something important). Verbal: Show interest. "Was this new for you and him? Did it surprise you that this happened?" Pay compliments: "It seems that it was pretty difficult and that it required courage for you to do that, given everything that's happened in your relationship. Please tell me more."
4. *Explore.* "What do you think you did to make that happen? If your husband were here and I were to ask him that, what do you think he would say you did that helped him tell you more about his day? Where did you get the idea to do it that way? What great

ideas you have! Are you someone who often comes up with the right ideas at the right time?"

5. *Project exceptions into the future.* "On a scale of ten to zero, where ten means a very good chance and zero means no chance at all, how do you rate the chances of something like that happening again in the coming week (or month)? What would it take? What would help to have that happen more often in the future? Who needs to do what to make it happen again? What is the most important thing you need to keep remembering to make sure it has the best chance of happening again? What is the second most important thing to remember? What would your husband say about the chance of this happening again? What would he think you could do to increase that chance? If you decided to do that, what do you think he would do? If he were to do that, how would things be different for you (in your relationship)?"

EXCEPTIONS PERTAINING TO THE PROBLEM

1. *Ask about exceptions.* If the client cannot describe a goal (or miracle) and talks only in problem terms, say: "Please recall a time in the past week (or month, or year) when your problem was less severe, or when the problem was absent for a short period of time." Then continue with the five steps for exceptions pertaining to the goal (or miracle).

2. *Ask about progress.* All subsequent sessions commence with the exploration of positive differences. Ask: "What is better since the last time we met?" Remember to follow all five steps and to ask both individual and relational (interactional matrix) questions. After examining an exception, always ask: "What else is better?"

3. *Ask coping questions.* Sometimes the client is unable to find exceptions and the difficulties he or she faces are enormous. In that case, you may ask coping questions to find out what the client does to keep his or her head above water: "I'm surprised. Given everything that's happened, I don't know how you cope. How do you do that? Which of your personal strengths do you use? How do you keep your head above water?"

4. *Give acknowledgment.* If a client describes a prolonged unpleasant situation with ever-discouraging events, you might say: "I understand that you have many reasons to be down. There are so many things that turned out differently than you'd hoped. I won-

der how you've kept going and how you've been able to get up every morning and start a new day. Please tell me more."

5. *Use positive character interpretations*. If the client says he or she must go on, for example, for the children's sake, you might say: "Is that how you do it? You think of your children and how much they need you? You must be a really caring person. Please tell me more about what you do to take good care of them."

Protocol for Follow-Up Sessions

Submit all questions to each client present.

Use EARS (see Chapter 9):

- *Eliciting.* "What is better (since your previous visit)?"
- *Amplifying* (asking for details). "How does that work? How do you do that exactly? Is that new for you? What effect does that have on _____? What is different then between you and _____ ?"
- *Reinforcing.* Give the client compliments.
- *Start again.* "What else is better?"

(DeJong & Berg, 2002)

Do more of it. "What would help you to do that more often?" If nothing is better: "How do you cope? How do you get through that? How come things aren't worse? If you can continue to do that, would you have accomplished what you came here for?"

Scaling progress. "Where are you now? How did you make that happen? What does one point higher look like? What will be different then? How will you be able to get there? What will help you to do that? Who will be the first to notice? How would that person notice? How would she react? What difference will that make for you? At what point on the scale would you like to end up?"

Homework suggestions. If the client wants do homework, give behavioral tasks for a client in a customer relationship, observational tasks for a client in a complainant relationship, and no tasks for a client in a visitor relationship (see Chapter 4).

Future sessions. "Do you think it is useful for you to return? If so: "When would you like to return?"

■■■■■■■■■■■■■

Exceptions Journal

Invite clients to keep a journal recounting their thoughts, feelings, and actions when specific situations arise. Most therapies use a problem focus, which helps to make the client aware of his or her maladaptive thoughts and reveal their negative effect on his or her behavior. But journaling may also help the client find exceptions to the problem and show their positive effect on his or her thoughts and behavior.

However, you don't have to be ill to get better. All of us, including those of us who are therapists, can look at times when we are a bit closer to where we would like to be. Below are eighteen questions. You can answer just a few questions every day and vary them.

1. What is better today (even just a little bit)?
2. What else is better?
3. What did I do differently to make it better?
4. Who noticed this, and how?
5. If nobody noticed it, what could they have noticed about me, had they paid more attention?
6. What do I hope important others in my life will notice that I do differently?
7. What did I think or believe about myself that was helpful in making these exceptions happen?
8. What would others say about the way I made these exceptions happen? Which of my personal strengths, qualities, and abilities would they say were helpful?
9. What do I have to do to make these exceptions happen more often?
10. What will my life look like if these exceptions are happening more often?

11. How can important others help me to let these exceptions happen more often?
12. Whom can I invite to help me?
13. What will be the best way to ask them for help?
14. When I intend to repeat what is working, what should I do?
15. What should or could I think about myself or about others to be successful?
16. What will others say I should or could think to be successful?
17. What will others say I should or could keep on doing to be successful?
18. Which compliments can I pay myself today?

Externalizing the Problems

Name of the problem: _____

The problem controls me/us   I/we have control of the problem

   0   1   2   3   4   5   6   7   8   9   10

1. Circle your current state on the above scale.
   Where are you on the scale compared to the last time we met? If you went up on the scale, indicate how you managed that.

   _____

2. If you remain at the same level as last time, indicate how you managed to stay stable.

   _____

3. If you ended up lower on the scale, indicate what you have done before to get ahead again. What did you do in the past in a comparable situation that was helpful?

   _____

4. What have important people in your life noticed about you this past week? How has that influenced their behavior toward you?

   _____

Changing Perspectives

Differences in a question can make a difference. They invite clients to examine differences in perspectives. The first perspective is that of the self, the client's own point of view. The second perspective is that of the other, that is, the client is invited to respond as if he or she is speaking for someone else. In order to respond to such a question the client must set aside his or her own ideas for a while and imagine what the other person would say. The third perspective is one of distance, that is, the client can imagine what an observer would see. Each question and perspective encourages clients to think differently about the problem and solutions It is important to use the following sequence, starting with question 1 and then moving on to 2 and 3, especially when clients want someone else to change.

1. When this problem/issue is solved, what will you notice that is different about the other person? What will you see him/her doing differently? What else?
2. When this problem/issue is solved, what will this other person notice that is different about you? What will s/he see you doing differently? What else?
3. When this problem/issue is solved and an outside observer is watching you, what will this observer notice that is different about your relationship with the other person? What will this observer see both of you doing differently? What else?

Questionaire for the Referrer

1. In your opinion, what will be the best possible outcome of collaboration among you as referrer, the client, and me/our institution?

   _____

   _____

   _____

2. What are the client's strengths, and what aspects of his or her performance are satisfactory and should be maintained?

   _____

   _____

   _____

3. In your opinion, what resources does the client have?

   _____

   _____

   _____

4. What are the limitations we need to take into account?

   _____

   _____

   _____

5. What do you think will be the first sign that will indicate to the client that therapy is meaningful and useful? And what will be the first sign for you?

   _____

   _____

   _____

6. When does this already happen? Please give an example.

   _____

   _____

   _____

Thank you for your cooperation!

Session Rating Scale

Name _____

Age (Yrs):_____

ID # _____ Sex: M / F

Session # _____ Date: _____

Please rate today's session by placing a mark on the line
nearest to the description that best fits your experience.

| I did not feel heard, understood, and respected. | **Relationship** | I felt heard, understood, and respected. |

|—————————————————————————————|

| We did not work on or talk about what I wanted to work on and talk about. | **Goals and Topics** | We worked on and talked about what I wanted to work on and talk about. |

|—————————————————————————————|

| The therapist's approach is not a good fit for me. | **Approach or Method** | The therapist's approach is a good fit for me. |

|—————————————————————————————|

| There was something missing in the session today. | **Overall** | Overall, today's session was right for me. |

|—————————————————————————————|

SOURCE: www.scottdmiller.com. Reprinted with permission.

Certificate of Post Traumatic Success

Certificate of Post Traumatic Success

This certifies that

_____ (name)

has successfully

_____

_____ (goal)

This success was achieved by the following

_____

_____

_____

_____ (what worked)

Signed:_____

(name of therapist and date)

References

....

Affleck, G., Tennen, H., Croog, S., & Levine, S. (1987). Causal attribution, perceived benefits, and morbidity after a heart attack: An 8-year study. *Journal of Consulting and Clinical Psychology*, *55*(1), 29–35.

Ai, A. L., Cascio, T., S antangelo, L. K., & Evans-Campbell, T. (2005). Hope, meaning, and growth following the September 11, 2001, terrorist attacks. *Journal of Interpersonal Violence*, *20*, 523–548.

Ai, A. L., Tice, T. N., Whitsett, D. D., Ishisaka, T., & Chim, M. (2007). Posttraumatic symptoms and growth of Kosovar war refugees; The influence of hope and cognitive coping. *Journal of Positive Psychology*, *2*(1), 55–65.

Aldwin, C. M. (1994). *Stress, coping and development: An integrative perspective.* New York, NY: Guilford.

Allen, R. E., & Allen, S. D. (1997). *Winnie-the-Pooh on success.* New York, NY: Dutton.

American Psychiatric Association (1994). *Diagnostic and statistical manual of mental disorders* (4th ed.). Washington, DC.

American Psychiatric Association (2013). *Diagnostic and statistical manual of mental disorders* (5th ed.). Arlington, VA: American Psychiatric Publishing.

American Psychological Association. (n.d.). *10 ways to build resilience.* Retrieved from http://www.apa.org/helpcenter/road-resilience.aspx

American Psychological Association's Board of Professional Affairs' Advisory Committee on Colleague Assistance (ACCA). (2006, February). *Report on distress and impairment in psychologists.* Retrieved from www.apa.org/practice/.../assistance/monograph.pdf

Ankarberg, P., & Falkenstrom, F. (2008). Treatment with antidepressants is primarily a psychological treatment. *Psychotherapy Theory, Research, Practice, Training*, *45*(3), 329–339.

Anker, M. G., Duncan, B. L., & Sparks, J. A. (2009). Using client feedback to improve couples therapy outcomes; a randomized clinical trial in a naturalistic setting. *Journal of Consulting and Clinical Psychology*, *77*(4), 693–704.

Anker, M. G., Owen, J., Duncan, B. L., & Sparks, J. A. (2010). The alliance in couple therapy: Partner influence, early change, and alliance patterns in a naturalistic sample. Journal of Consulting and Clinical Psychology, 78, 635–645.

APA Presidential Task Force on Evidence-Based Practice. (2006). Evidence-based practice in psychology. *American Psychologist*, *61*(4), 271–285.

Aristotle. (1998). *Nicomachean ethics.* Mineola, NY: Dover.

Arntz, A., & Weertman, A. (1999). Treatment of childhood memories: Theory and practice. *Behaviour Research and Therapy*, *37*, 715–740.

Arts, W., Hoogduin, C. A. L., Keijsers, G. P. J., Severeijnen, R., & Schaap, C. (1994). A quasi-experimental study into the effect of enhancing the quality of the patient–therapist relationship in the outpatient treatment of obsessive-compulsive neurosis. In S. Brogo & L. Sibilia (Eds.), *The patient-therapist relationship: Its many dimensions* (p. 96–106). Rome, Italy: Consiglio Nazionale delle Ricerche.

Baker, W., & Ross, J. C. (2002). *George Eliot: A bibliographical history*. New Castle, DE: Oak Knoll Press.

Bakker, J. M., Bannink, F. P., & Macdonald, A. (2010). Solution-focused psychiatry. *The Psychiatrist*, *34*, 297–300.

Bannink, F. P. (2007). Solution-focused brief therapy. *Journal of Contemporary Psychotherapy*, 37(2), 87–94.

Bannink, F. P. (2008a). Posttraumatic success: Solution-focused brief therapy. *Brief Treatment and Crisis Intervention*, 7, 1–11.

Bannink, F. P. (2008b). Solution-focused mediation. *Conflict Resolution Quarterly*, 25(2), 163–183.

Bannink, F. P. (2009a). *Positieve psychologie in de praktijk* [Positive psychology in practice]. Amsterdam, Netherlands: Hogrefe.

Bannink, F. P. (2009b). *Praxis der losungs-fokussierte mediation [Solution-focused mediation in practice]*. Stuttgart, Germany: Concadora Verlag.

Bannink, F. P. (2010a). *1001 solution-focused questions: Handbook for solution-focused interviewing*. New York, NY: Norton.

Bannink, F. P. (2010b). *Handbook of solution-focused conflict management*. Cambridge, MA: Hogrefe.

Bannink, F. P. (2010c). *Oplossingsgericht leidinggeven [Solution-focused leadership]*. Amsterdam, Netherlands: Pearson.

Bannink, F. P. (2011). *Praxis der positiven psychologie [Positive psychology in practice]*. Göttingen, Germany: Hogrefe.

Bannink, F. P. (2012a). *Practicing positive CBT*. Oxford, UK: Wiley.

Bannink, F. P. (2012b). *Positieve supervisie en intervisie [Positive supervision and intervision]*. Amsterdam, Netherlands: Hogrefe.

Bannink, F. P. (2013). Positive CBT: From reducing distress to building success. *Journal of Contemporary Psychotherapy*. doi 10.1007/s10879-013-9239-7

Bannink, F. P., & Jackson, P. Z. (2011a). Positive psychology and solution focus: Looking at similarities and differences. *InterAction: The Journal of Solution Focus in Organisations*, 3(1), 8–20.

Bannink, F.P. (2013). Positive CBT. *Journal of Contemporary Psychotherapy*, 44, 1-8.

Bannink, F.P. (2014). *Positive Supervision*. Cambridge MA: Hogrefe Publishers.

Barakat, L. P., Alderfer, M. A., & Kazak, A. E. (2006). Posttraumatic growth in adolescent survivors of cancer and their mothers and fathers. *Journal of Pediatric Psychology*, *31*, 413–419.

Barrell, J. J., & Ryback, D. (2008). *Psychology of Champions*. Westport, CT: Praeger.

Baumeister, R. F., Bratlavsky, E., Finkenauer, C., & Vohs, K. D. (2001). Bad is stronger that good. *Review of General Psychology*, 5, 323–370.

Baumeister, R. F., Bratlavsky, E., Muraven, M., & Tice, D. M. (1998). Ego depletion: Is the active self a limited resource? *Journal of Personality and Social Psychology*, *74*, 1252–1265.

Baumeister, R. F., & Tierney, J. (2011). *Willpower*. London, UK: Penguin.

Bavelas, J. B., Coates, L. & Johnson, T. (2000). Listeners as co-narrators. *Journal of Personality and Social Psychology*, 79, 941–952.

Beck, A. T. (1967). *Depression: Clinical, experimental, and theoretical aspects*. New York, NY: Harper & Row.

Beck, A. T., Weissman, A., Lester, D., & Trexles, L. (1974). The measurement of pessimism: The hopelessness scale. *Journal of Consulting and Clinical Psychology*, 42, 861–865.

Beck, J. S. (2011). *Cognitive behaviour therapy: Basics and beyond* (2nd ed.). New York, NY: Guilford.

Beijebach, M., Rodriguez Sanches, M. S., Arribas de Miguel, J., Herrero de Vega, M., Hernandez, C., & Rodrigues-Morejon, A. (2000). Outcome of solution-focused therapy at a university family therapy center. *Journal of Systemic Therapies*, 19, 116–128.

Benard, B. (1991). Fostering resiliency in kids: *Protective factors in the family, school and community*. San Francisco, CA: Far West Laboratory for Educational Research and Development. (ED335781)

Benish, S. G., Imel, Z. E., & Wampold, B. E. (2008). The relative efficacy of bona fide psychotherapies for treating post-traumatic stress disorder: A meta-analysis of direct comparisons. *Clinical Psychology Review*, 28(5), 746–758.

Bennett-Levy, J., Butler, G., Fennell, M., Hackman, A., Mueller, M., & Westbrook, D. (2004). *Oxford guide to behavioural experiments in cognitive therapy*. New York, NY: Oxford University Press.

Berg, I. K., & Steiner, T. (2003). *Children's solution work*. New York, NY: Norton.

Beutler, L. E., Malik, M., Alimohamed, S., Harwood, T. M., Talebi, H., Noble, S., & Wong, E. (2004). Therapist effects. In M. J. Lambert (Ed.), *Bergin and Garfield's handbook of psychotherapy and behavior change* (5th ed., pp. 227–306). New York, NY: Wiley.

Bohlmeijer, E. & Bannink, F.P. Posttraumatische groei [Post traumatic growth]. In: E. Bohlmeijer, L. Bolier, G. Westerhof & J. Walburg (2013). *Handboek Positieve Psychologie*. Amsterdam: Boom.

Bonanno, G. A. (2004). Loss, trauma and human resilience. *American Psychologist*, 59, 1, 20–28.

Bonanno, G. A., Rennicke, C., & Dekel, S. (2005). Self-enhancement among high-exposure survivors of the September 11th terrorist attack: Resilience or social maladjustment? *Journal of Personality and Social Psychology*, 8(6), 984–998.

Bonanno, G. A., Westphal, M., & Mancini, A. D. (2011). Resilience to loss and potential trauma. *Annual Review of Clinical Psychology*, 7, 1.1–1.25.

Bower, J. E., Kemeny, M. E., Taylor, S. E., & Fahey, J. L. (1998). Cognitive processing, discovery of meaning, CD4 decline, and AIDS related mortality among bereaved HIV-seropositive men. *Journal of Consulting and Clinical Psychology*, 66(6), 979–986.

Branigan, C., Fredrickson, B. L., Mancuso, R. A., & Tugade, M. M. (2000). The undoing effect of positive emotions. *Motivation and Emotion*, 24, 237–258.

Brewin, C. R., Wheatley, J., Patel, T., Fearon, P., Hackmann, A., Wells, A., . . . Myers, S. (2009). Imagery rescripting as a brief stand-alone treatment for depressed patients with intrusive memories. *Behaviour Research and Therapy, 47*, 569–576.

British Psychological Society. (2011). *Response to the American Psychiatric Association: DSM-5 development*. Retrieved from http://apps.bps.org.uk/_publication-files/consultation-responses/DSM-5%202011%20-%20BPS%20response.pdf

Burns, K., Duncan, D., & Ward, G. C. (2001). *Mark Twain: An illustrated biography*. New York, NY: Knopf.

Bushman, B. J., Baumeister, R. F., & Stack, A. D. (1999). Catharsis, aggression, and persuasive influence: Self-fulfilling or self-defeating prophecies? *Journal of Personality and Social Psychology, 76*, 367–376.

Butler, L. D., Blasey, C. M., Garlan, R. W., McCaslin, S. E., Azarow, J., Chen, X., . . . Spiegel, D. (2005). Posttraumatic growth following the terrorist attacks of September 11, 2001: Cognitive, coping and trauma symptom predictors in an internet convenience sample. *Traumatology, 11*, 247–267.

Cacioppo, J. T., & Gardner, W. L. (1999). Emotion. *Annual Review of Psychology, 50*, 191–214.

Cacioppo, J. T., & Patrick, B. (2008). *Loneliness: Human nature and the need for social connection*. New York, NY: Norton.

Calhoun, L.G., & Tedeschi, R.G. (2000). Early posttraumatic intervention: facilitating possibilities for growth. In D. Patton & C. Dunning (Eds.), *Posttraumatic stress intervention: Challenges, issues, and perspectives* (pp. 135–152). Springfield, IL: Charles C Thomas.

Calhoun, L. G., & Tedeschi, R. G. (Eds.). (2006). *Handbook of post-traumatic growth: Research and practice*. Mahwah, NJ: Erlbaum.

Carroll, L. (1865). *Alice's adventures in wonderland*. New York, NY: Barnes & Noble.

Carver, C. S. (1998). Resilience and thriving: Issues, models, and linkages. Journal of Social Issues, 54, 245–266.

Carver, C. S., & Scheier, M. F. (1998). *On the self-regulation of behavior*. New York, NY: Cambridge University Press.

Charney, D. (2012, October 29). *Resilience lessons from our veterans*. Retrieved November 9, 2012, from http://www.youtube.com/watch?v=XoN1pv2JKpc

Chesterton. (1908). *Orthodoxy*. Nashville, TN: Sam Torode Book Arts.

Chin, D., Myers, H. F., Zhang, M., Loeb, T., Ullman, J. B., Wyatt, G. E., & Carmona, J. (2013). Who improved in a trauma intervention for HIV-positive women with child sexual abuse histories. *Theory, Research, Practice, and Policy, 8*.

Cialdini, R. B. (1984). *Persuasion: The psychology of influence*. New York, NY: Collins.

Clark, R.W. (1977). *Edison: The man who made the future*. London, UK: Macdonald.

Clement, P. W. (1994). Quantitative evaluation of 26 years of private practice. *Professional Psychology: Research and Practice, 25*(2), 173–176.

Cohen, L. H., Hetter, T. R., & Pane, N. (1998). Assessment of posttraumatic growth. In R. G. Tedeschi, C. L. Park, & L. G. Calhoun (Eds.), *Posttraumatic growth: Positive changes in the aftermath of crisis* (pp. 23–42). Mahwah, NJ: Erlbaum.

Constantino, M. J., Castonguay, L. G., & Schut, A. J. (2002). The working alliance: A flagship for the "scientist-practitioner" model in psychotherapy. In G. S. Tryon (Ed.), *Counseling based on process research: Applying what we know* (pp. 81–131). Boston, MA: Allyn & Bacon.

Cooperrider, D. L., & Whitney, D. (2005). *Appreciative inquiry: A positive revolution to change*. San Francisco, CA: Berett-Koehler.

Cooperrider, D. L. & Godwin, L. (2011) Positive Organization Development. In: K. Cameron & G. Spreitzer (Eds.). *The Oxford Handbook of Positive Organizational Scholarship*. Oxford: Oxford University Press.

Covey, S. R. (1989). *The seven habits of highly effective people*. New York, NY: Simon & Schuster.

Cryder, C. H., Kilmer, R. P., Tedeschi, R. G., & Calhoun, L. G. (2006). An exploratory study of posttraumatic growth in children following a natural disaster. *American Journal of Orthopsychiatry, 76*, 65–69.

Danner, D. D., Snowdon, D. A., & Friesen, W. V. (2001). Positive emotions in early life and longevity: Findings from the nun study. *Journal of Personality and Social Psychology, 80*(5), 804–813.

Davidson, R. J., Kabat-Zinn, J., Schumacher, J., Rosenkranz, M., Muller, D., Santorelli, S. F., . . . Sheridan, J. F. (2003). Alterations in brain and immune function produced by mindfulness meditation. *Psychosomatic Medicine, 65*, 564–570.

De Bono, E. (1985). *Conflicts: A better way to resolve them*. London, UK: Penguin.

De Castella, K., Goldin, P., Jazaieri, H., Ziv, M., Dweck, C. S., & Gross, J. J. (2013). Beliefs about emotion: Links to emotion regulation, well-being, and psychological distress. *Basic and Applied Social Psychology, 35*(6), 497–505. doi: 10.1080/01973533.2013.840632

De Jong, P., & Berg, I. K. (2002). *Interviewing for solutions*. Belmont, CA: Thomson.

De Shazer, S. (1984). The death of resistance. *Family Process, 23*, 79–93.

De Shazer, S. (1985). *Keys to solution in brief therapy*. New York, NY: Norton.

De Shazer, S. (1988). *Clues: Investigation solutions in brief therapy*. New York, NY: Norton.

De Shazer, S. (1991). *Putting difference to work*. New York, NY: Norton.

De Shazer, S. (1994). *Words were originally magic*. New York, NY: Norton.

Diener, E., & Seligman, M. E. P. (2002). Very happy people. *Psychological Science, 13*(1), 81–84.

Doctor, J. N., Zoellner, L. A., & Feeny, N. C. (2011). Predictors of health-related quality-of-life utilities among persons with posttraumatic stress disorder. *Psychiatric Services, 62*, 272–277.

Dolan, Y. M. (1991). *Resolving sexual abuse*. New York, NY: Norton.

Dolan, Y. M. (1998). *One small step*. Watsonville, CA: Papier-Mache.

Drucker, P. F. (2002). *Managing in the next society*. New York, NY: St. Martin's Press.

Druss, R. G., & Douglas, C. J. (1988). Adaptive responses to illness and disability: Healthy denial. *General Hospital Psychiatry, 10*(3), 163–168.

Duncan, B. L. (2005). *What's right with you: Debunking dysfunction and changing your life*. Deerfield Beach, FL: Health Communications.

Duncan, B. L. (2010). *On becoming a better therapist*. Washington, DC: American Psychological Association.

Duncan, B. L., Hubble, M. A., & Miller, S. D. (1997). Psychotherapy with "impossible" cases. New York, NY: Norton.

Duncan, B. L., Miller, S. D., & Sparks, A. (2004). The heroic client. San Francisco, CA: Jossey-Bass.

Duncan, B. L., Miller, S. D., Wampold, B. E., & Hubble, M. A. (2010). The heart and soul of change (2nd ed.). Washington, DC: *American Psychological Association*.

Dunigan, J. T., Carr, B. I., & Steel, J. L. (2007). Posttraumatic growth, immunity and survival in patients with hepatoma. *Digestive Diseases and Sciences, 52*, 2452–2459.

Dweck, C. S. (2006). *Mindset: The new psychology of success*. New York, NY: Random House.

Einstein, A. (1954). *Ideas and opinions*. New York, NY: Crown.

Elliot, A. J. (Ed.) (2008). *Handbook of approach and avoidance motivation*. New York, NY: Psychology Press.

Elliot, A. J., & Church, M. A. (1997). Approach-avoidance motivation in personality: Approach and avoidance temperaments and goals. *Journal of Personality and Social Psychology, 82*(5), 804–818.

Elliot, A. J., & Sheldon, K. M. (1998). Avoidance personal goals and the personality-illness relationship. *Journal of Personality and Social Psychology, 75*, 1282–1299.

Elliot, C. (2012). *Solution building in couples therapy*. New York, NY: Springer.

Emmons, R. A., & McCullough, M. E. (2003). Counting blessings versus burdens: An experimental investigation of gratitude and subjective well being in daily life. *Journal of Personality and Social Psychology, 84*, 377–389.

Epel, E. S., McEwen, B. S., & Ickovics, J. R. (1998). Embodying psychological thriving: Physical thriving in response to stress. *Journal of Social Issues, 54*, 301–322.

Erickson, M. H., & Rossi, E. L. (1989). *The February man: Evolving consciousness and identity in hypnotherapy*. New York, NY: Routledge.

Estrada, C. A., Isen, A. M., & Young, M. J. (1994). Positive affect improves creative problem solving and influences reported source of practice satisfaction in physicians. *Motivation and Emotion, 18*(4), 285–299.

Fagin-Jones, S., & Midlarsky, E. (2007). Courageous altruism: Personal and situational correlates of rescue during the Holocaust. *Journal of Positive Psychology, 2*(2), 136–147.

Flora, S. R. (2000). Praise's magic reinforcement ratio: Five to one gets the job done. *Behaviour Analyst Today, 1*, 64–69.

Folkman, S., & Moskowitz, J. T. (2000). Positive affect and the other side of coping. *American Psychologist, 55*(6), 647–654.

Fowler, J. H., & Christakis, N. A. (2008). Dynamic spread of happiness in a large social network: Longitudinal analysis over 20 years in the Framingham Heart Study. *British Medical Journal, 337*, a2338.

Frankl, V. E. (1963). *Man's search for meaning*. New York, NY: Vintage Books.

Franklin, C., Trepper, T. S., Gingerich, W. J., & McCollum, E. E. (2012). *Solution-focused brief therapy: A handbook of evidence based practice*. New York, NY: Oxford University Press.

Frazier, P., Steward, J., & Mortensen, H. (2004). Perceived control and adjustment to trauma: A comparison across events. *Journal of Social and Clinical Psychology, 23*, 303–324.

Fredrickson, B. L. (1998). What good are positive emotions? *Review of General Psychology, 2*, 300–319.

Fredrickson, B. L. (2000). Cultivating positive emotions to optimize health and well-being. *Prevention and Treatment, 3*, 0001a.

Fredrickson, B. L. (2009). *Positivity*. New York, NY: Crown.

Froh, J. J., Sefick, W. J., & Emmons, R. A. (2008). Counting blessings in early adolescents: An experimental study of gratitude and subjective well-being. *Journal of School Psychology, 46*, 213–233.

Furman, B. (1998). *It is never too late to have a happy childhood*. London, UK: BT Press.

Furman, B., & Ahola, T. (2007). *Change through cooperation: Handbook of reteaming*. Helsinki, Finland: Helsinki Brief Therapy Institute.

Furuya, K. (1996). *Kodo: Ancient ways: Lessons in the spiritual life of the warrior/martial arts*. Santa Clarita, CA: Black Belt Communications.

Gable, S. L. (2006). Approach and avoidance social motives and goals. *Journal of Personality, 71*, 175–222.

Gable, S. L., Reis, H. T., Impett, E. A., & Asher, E. R. (2004). What do you do when things go right? The intrapersonal and interpersonal benefits of sharing positive events. *Journal of Personality and Social Psychology, 87*(2), 228–245.

Galea, S., Vlahov, D., Resnick, H., Ahern, J., Susser, E., Gold, J., . . . Kilpatrick, D. (2003). Trends of probable post-traumatic stress disorder in New York City after the September 11 terrorist attacks. *American Journal of Epidemiology, 158*(6), 514–524.

Garmezy, N., & Streitman, S. (1974). Children at risk: The search for the antecedents of schizophrenia: Part 1. Conceptual models and research methods. *Schizophrenia Bulletin, 8*(8), 14–90.

Gassman, D., & Grawe, K. (2006). General change mechanisms: The relation between problem activation and resource activation in successful and unsuccessful therapeutic interactions. *Clinical Psychology and Psychotherapy, 13*, 1–11.

George, E. (2010). *What about the past? How does solution focus deal with that?* Retrieved from www.brief.org.uk/forum/viewtopic.php?f=18&t=76#p235

Gilbert, P. (2010). *Compassion focused therapy*. New York, NY: Routledge.

Gingerich, W. J., & Peterson, L. T. (2013). Effectiveness of solution-focused brief therapy: A systematic qualitative review of controlled outcome studies. *Research on Social Work Practice*. doi: 10.1177/1049731512470859

Gladwell, M. (2005). *Blink*. London, UK: Penguin.

Glass, C. (2009). Exploring what works: Is SF the best way of harnessing the impact of positive psychology in the workplace? InterAction: *The Journal of Solution Focus in Organisations, 1*(1), 26–41.

Gollwitzer, P. M. (1999). Implementation intentions: Strong effects of simple plans. *American Psychologist, 54*(7), 493–503.

Gordon, K. C., Baucom, D. H., Epstein, N., Burnett, C. K., & Rankin, L. A. (1999). The interaction between marital standards and communication patterns. *Journal of Marital and Family Therapy, 25*(2), 211–223.

Gottman, J. M. (1994). *What predicts divorce? The relationship between marital processes and marital outcomes.* New York, NY: Erlbaum.

Grant, A. M., & O'Connor, S. A. (2010). The differential effects of solution-focused and problem-focused coaching questions: A pilot study with implications for practice. *Industrial and Commercial Training, 42*(4), 102–111.

Gross, J. J., & Munoz, R. F. (1995). Emotion regulation and mental health. *Clinical Psychology: Science and Practice, 2*(2), 151–164.

Grotberg, E. H. (1995). *A guide to promoting resilience in children: Strengthening the human spirit.* The Hague, Netherlands: Bernard van Leer Foundation.

Isebaert, L. (2007). *Praktijkboek oplossingsgerichte cognitieve therapie.* Utrecht: De Tijdstroom.

Hackmann, A., Bennett-Levy, J., & Holmes, E. A. (2011). *Oxford guide to imagery in cognitive therapy.* New York, NY: Oxford University Press.

Haidt, J. (2006). *The happiness hypothesis: Putting ancient wisdom and philosophy to the test of modern science.* London, UK: Arrow Books.

Hannan, C., Lambert, M. J., Harmon, C., Lars Nielsen, S., Smart, D. W., Shimokawa, K., & Sutton, S. W. (2005). A lab test and algorithms for identifying clients at risk for treatment failure. *Journal of Clinical Psychology, 61*(2), 155–163.

Heath, C., & Heath, D. (2010). *Switch.* London, UK: Random House.

Hefferon, K., Grealy, M. N., & Mutrie, N. (2009). Post-traumatic growth and life threatening physical illness: A systematic review of the qualitative literature. *British Journal of Health Psychology, 14,* 343–378.

Henden, J. (2011). *Beating combat stress.* Oxford, UK: Wiley-Blackwell.

Henderson, N., & Milstein, M. M. (1996). *Resiliency in schools: Making it happen for students and educators.* Thousand Oaks, CA: Corwin Press.

Hershberger, P. J. (2005). Prescribing happiness: Positive psychology and family medicine. *Family Medicine, 37*(9), 630–634.

Hiatt, D., & Hargrave, G. E. (1995). The characteristics of highly effective therapists in managed behavioral providers networks. *Behavioral Healthcare Tomorrow, 4,* 19–22.

Howe, M. W., Tierney, P. L., Sandberg, S. G., Phillips, P. E. M., & Graybiel, A. M. (2013). Prolonged dopamine signaling in striatum signals proximity and value of distant rewards. *Nature.* doi:10.1038/nature12475

Ickovics, J. R., Meade, C. S., Kershaw, T. S., Milan, S., Lewis, J. B., & Ethier, K. A. (2006). Urban teens: Trauma, posttraumatic growth, and the emotional distress among female adolescents. *Journal of Consulting and Clinical Psychology, 74,* 841–851.

Impett, E., Gable, S. L., & Peplau, L. A. (2005). Giving up and giving in: The costs and benefits of daily sacrifice in intimate relationships. *Journal of Personality and Social Psychology, 89,* 327–344.

Isaacowitz, D. M., Vaillant, G. E., & Seligman, M. E. P. (2003). Strengths and satisfaction across the adult lifespan. *International Journal of Ageing and Human Development, 57*, 181–201.

Isebaert, L. (2007). *Praktijkboek oplossingsgerichte cognitieve therapie.* Utrecht: De Tijdstroom.

Isen, A. M. (2005). A role for neuropsychology in understanding the facilitating influence of positive affect on social behaviour and cognitive processes. In C. R. Snyder & S. J. Lopez (Eds.), *Handbook of positive psychology* (pp. 528–540). New York, NY: Oxford University Press.

Isen, A. M., & Reeve, J. (2005). The influence of positive affect on intrinsic and extrinsic motivation: Facilitating enjoyment of play, responsible work behaviour, and self-control. *Motivation and Emotion, 29*(4), 297–325.

Isen, A. M., Rosenzweig, A. S., & Young, M. J. (1991). The influence of positive affect on clinical problem solving. *Medical Decision Making, 11*, 221–227.

Joseph, S., & Linley, P. A. (2005). Positive adjustment to threatening events: An organismic valuing theory of growth through adversity. *Review of General Psychology, 9*, 262–280.

Jung, C. G. (1965). *Memories, dreams, reflections.* New York, NY: Random House.

Kabat-Zinn, J. (1994). *Wherever you go, there you are: Mindfulness meditation in everyday life.* New York, NY: Hyperion.

Kessler, R. C., Sonnega, A., Bromet, E., Higher, M., & Nelson, C.B. (1995). Post-traumatic stress disorder in the national comorbidity survey. *Archives of General Psychiatry, 52*, 1048–1060.

Keyes, C. L. M., & Lopez, S. J. (2005). Toward a science of mental health. In C. R. Snyder & S. J. Lopez (Eds.), *Handbook of positive psychology.* New York, NY: Oxford University Press.

King, L. A. (2001). The health benefits of writing about life goals. *Personality and Social Psychology Bulletin, 27*, 798–807.

King, L. A., King, D. W., Fairbank, J. A., Keane, T. M., & Adams, G. A. (1998). Resilience-recovery factors in post-traumatic stress disorder among female and male Vietnam veterans: Hardiness, postwar social support, and additional stressful life events. *Journal of Personality and Social Psychology, 74*, 420–434.

Klaver, M., & Bannink, F. P. (2010). Oplossingsgerichte therapie bij patienten met niet-aangeboren hersenletsel [Solution-focused brief therapy with patients with brain injury]. *Tijdschrift voor Neuropsychologie, 5*(2), 11–19.

Kleiman, E. M., Adams, L. M., Kashdan, T. B., & Riskind, J. H. (2013). Gratitude and grit indirectly reduce risk of suicidal ideations by enhancing meaning in life: Evidence for a mediated moderation model. *Journal of Research in Personality.* doi: http://dx.doi.org/10.1016/j.jrp.2013.04.007

Kuiper, E. C., & Bannink, F. P. (2012).Veerkracht, een pleidooi voor het bevorderen van veerkracht in de jeugdhulpverlening [Resilience, a plea for enhancing resilience in youth care]. *Kind and Adolescent Praktijk, 3*, 134–139.

Kuyken, W., Padesky, C. A., & Dudley, R. (2009). *Collaborative case conceptualization.* New York, NY: Guilford.

Lally, P., Jaarsveld, C. van, Potts, H., & Wardle, J. (2010). How are habits formed: Modelling habit formation in the real world. *European Journal of Social Psychology, 40,* 998–1009.

Lamarre, J., & Gregoire, A. (1999). Competence transfer in solution-focused therapy: Harnessing a natural resource. *Journal of Systemic Therapies, 18*(1), 43–57.

Lambert, M. J., & Ogles, B. M. (2004). The efficacy and effectiveness of psychotherapy. In M. L. Lambert (Ed.), *Bergin and Garfield's handbook of psychotherapy and behaviour change* (5th ed., pp. 139–193). New York, NY: Wiley.

Lambert, M. J., Whipple, J. L., Vermeersch, D. A., Smart, D. W., Hawkins, E. J., Nielsen, S. L., & Goates, M. (2002). Enhancing psychotherapy outcomes via providing feedback on patient progress: A replication. *Clinical Psychology and Psychotherapy, 9,* 91–103.

Leckman, J. F., & Mayes, L. C. (2007). Nurturing resilient children. *Journal of Child Psychology and Psychiatry, 48*(3–4), 221–223.

Lepore, S. J., & Revenson, T. A. (2006). Resilience & posttraumatic growth. In L. G. Calhoun & R. G. Tedeschi (Eds.), *Handbook of posttraumatic growth: Research and practices* (pp. 24–46). Mahwah, NJ: Erlbaum.

Libby, L. K., Eibach, R. P., & Gilovich, R. (2005). Here's looking at me: The effect of memory perspective on assessments of personal change. *Journal of Personality and Social Psychology, 88*(1), 50–62.

Lieberman, M. D., Eisenberger, N. I., Crockett, M. J., Tom, S. M., Pfeifer, J. H., & Way, B. M. (2007). Putting feelings into words. *Psychological Science, 18*(5), 421–428.

Linley, P. A., & Joseph, S. (2004). Positive change following trauma and adversity: A review. *Journal of Traumatic Stress, 17*(1), 11–21.

Linley, P. A., Joseph, S., & Goodfellow, B. (2008). Positive changes in outlook following trauma and their relationship to subsequent posttraumatic stress, depression, and anxiety. *Journal of Social and Clinical Psychology, 27,* 877–891.

Litt, A. (2010). Lusting while loathing: Parallel counterdriving of wanting and liking. *Psychological Science, 21*(1), 118–125.

Losada, M. F., & Heaphy, E. (2004). The role of positivity and connectivity in the performance of business teams: A nonlinear dynamics model. *American Behavioral Scientist, 47*(6), 740–765.

Luthar, S. S., Cicchetti, D., & Becker, B. (2000). The construct of resilience: A critical evaluation and guidelines for future work. *Child Development, 71*(3), 543–562.

Lyubomirsky, S. (2008). *The how of happiness.* New York, NY: Penguin.

Lyubomirsky, S., Sheldon, K. M., & Schkade, D. (2005). Pursuing happiness: The architecture of sustainable change. *Review of General Psychology, 9,* 111–131.

Macdonald, A. J. (2011). *Solution-focused therapy: Theory, research & practice* (2nd ed.). London, UK: Sage.

Mangelsdorf, J. (2013). Comprehensive growth ability: Thriving after traumatic and ecstatic life events. Presentation at the third World Conference of the International Positive Psychology Association.

Marx, G. (2002). Groucho and me: *The autobiography.* London: Virgin.

Masten, A. S. (1989). Resilience in development: Implications of the study of successful adaptation for developmental psychopathology. In D. Cicchetti (Ed.), *The emergence of a discipline: Rochester symposium on developmental psychopathology* (pp. 261–294). Hillsdale, NJ: Erlbaum.

Masten, A.S. (2001). Ordinary magic: Resilience processes in development. *American Psychologist, 56,* 227–238.

Masten, A., & Wright, M. O. (2009). Resilience over the lifespan: Developmental perspectives on resistance, recovery and transformation. In J. W. Reich, A. J. Zautra, & J. S. Hall (Eds.), *Handbook of adult resilience* (pp. 213–237). New York, NY: Guilford.

McCraty, R., Barrios-Choplin, B., Rozman, D., Atkinson, M., & Watkins, A. D. (1998). The impact of a new emotional self-management program on stress, emotions, heart rate variability, DHEA and cortisol. *Integrative Physiological and Behavioral Science, 32*(2), 151–170.

McElwee, N. (2007). A focus on the personal and structural: Resilience explored. *Child and Youth Services, 29*(1), 57–69.

McFarlane, A. C., & Yehuda, R. (1996). Resilience, vulnerability, and the course of posttraumatic reactions. In B. van der Kolk, A. C. McFarlane, & L. Weisaeth (Eds.), *Traumatic stress: The effects of overwhelming experience on mind, body, and society.* New York, NY: Guilford.

McKay, K. M., Imel, Z. E., & Wampold, B. E. (2006). Psychiatrist effect in the psychopharmacological treatment of depression. *Journal of Affective Disorders, 92*(2–3), 287–290.

McMillen, J. C., Smith, E. M., & Fisher, R. H. (1997). Perceived benefit and mental health after three types of disaster. *Journal of Consulting and Clinical Psychology, 65*(5), 733–739.

Menninger, K. (1959). The academic lecture: Hope. *American Journal of Psychiatry, 12,* 481–491.

Metcalf, L. (1998). *Solution focused group therapy.* New York, NY: Free Press.

Milam, J. E., Ritt-Olson, A., Tan, S., Unger, J. B., & Nezami, E. (2005). The September 11th 2001 terrorist attacks and reports of posttraumatic growth among a multi-ethnic sample of adolescents. *Traumatology, 11,* 233–246.

Milam, J. E., Ritt-Olson, A., & Unger, J. B. (2004). Posttraumatic growth among adolescents. *Journal of Adolescent Research, 19,* 192–204.

Miller, S. D., Hubble, M. A., & Duncan, B. L. (Eds.). (1996). *The handbook of solution-focused brief therapy: Foundations, applications and research.* San Francisco, CA: Jossey-Bass.

Miller, S. D., Duncan, B., & Hubble, M. A. (1997). *Escape from Babel: Toward a unifying language for psychotherapy practice.* New York, NY: Norton.

Miller, S. D., Hubble, M. A., & Duncan, B. L. (2007). Supershrinks: Learning from the field's most effective practitioners. *Psychotherapy Networker, 31*(6), 26–35.

Miller, W. R., & Rollnick, S. (2002). *Motivational interviewing: Preparing people to change* (2nd ed.). New York, NY: Guilford.

Mischel, W., & Ayduk, O. (2004). Willpower in a cognitive-affective processing system: The dynamics of delay of gratification. In R. F. Baumeister & K. D. Vohs

(Eds.), *Handbook of self-regulation: Research, theory, and applications* (pp. 99–129). New York, NY: Guilford.

Mischel, W., Shoda, Y., & Rodriguez, M. L. (1989). Delay of gratification in children. *Science, 244*, 933–938.

Monson, C. M., Schnurr, P. P., Resick, P. A., Friedman, M. J., Young-Xu, Y., & Stevens, S. P. (2006). Cognitive processing therapy for veterans with military-related posttraumatic stress disorder. *Journal of Consulting and Clinical Psychology, 64*(5), 898–907.

Morwitz, V. G., & Fitzsimons, G. J. (2004). The mere-measurement effect: Why does measuring intentions change actual behavior? *Journal of Consumer Psychology, 14*(1–2), 64–74.

Moskowitz, G. B., & Grant, H. (Eds.). (2009). *The psychology of goals*. New York, NY: Guilford.

Murray, S. L., Holmes, J. G., & Griffin, D. W. (2003). Reflections on the self-fulfilling effects of positive illusions. *Psychological Inquiry, 14*, 289–295.

Myers, D. G. (2000). The funds, friends and faith of happy people. *American Psychologist, 55*, 56–67.

Neff, K. D. (2011). Self-compassion, self-esteem and well-being. *Social and Personality Psychology Compass, 5*(1), 1–12.

Neff, K. D., & Vonk, R. (2009). Self-compassion versus global self-esteem: Two different ways to relating to oneself. *Journal of Personality, 77*(1), 23–50.

Nolen-Hoeksema, S. (2000). Growth and resilience among bereaved people. In J. E. Gillham (Ed), *The science of optimism & hope: Research essays in honor of Martin E. P. Seligman* (pp. 107–127). Philadelphia, PA: Templeton Foundation Press.

Nolen-Hoeksema, S., & Davis, C. G. (2005). Positive responses to loss. In C. R. Snyder & S. J. Lopez (Eds.), *Handbook of positive psychology* (pp. 598–607). New York, NY: Oxford University Press.

Norcross, J. C. (2002). Empirically supported therapy relationships. In J. C. Norcross (Ed.), *Psychotherapy relationships that work: Therapist contributions and responsiveness to patients*. New York, NY: Oxford University Press.

Oettingen, G. (1999). Free fantasies about the future and the emergence of developmental goals. In J. Brandtstadter & R. M. Lerner (Eds.), *Action & self-development: Theory and research through the life span* (pp. 315–342). Thousand Oaks, CA: Sage.

Oettingen, G., Hönig, G., & Gollwitzer, P. M. (2000). Effective self-regulation of goal attainment. *International Journal of Educational Research, 33*, 705–732.

Oettingen, G., Pak, H., & Schnetter, K. (2001). Self-regulation of goal setting: Turning free fantasies about the future into binding goals. *Journal of Personality and Social Psychology, 80*(5), 736–753.

Oettingen, G., & Stephens, E. J. (2009). Fantasies and motivationally intelligent goal setting. In G. B. Moskowitz & H. Grant (Eds.), *The psychology of goals* (pp. 153–178). New York, NY: Guilford.

O'Hanlon, B. (1999). *Evolving possibilities*. Philadelphia, PA: Brunner/Mazel.

O'Hanlon, B. (2000). *Do one thing different*. New York, NY: Harper Collins.

O'Hanlon, B., & Bertolino, B. (1998). *Even from a broken web*. New York, NY: Wiley.

O'Hanlon, B., & Rowan, R. (2003). *Solution oriented therapy for chronic and severe mental illness.* New York, NY: Norton.

O'Leary, V. E., & Ickovics, J. R. (1995). Resilience and thriving in response to challenge: An opportunity for a paradigm shift in women's health. *Women's Health: Research on Gender, Behavior and Policy, 1,* 121–142.

Ong, A. D., Bergeman, C. S., Bisconti, T. L., & Wallace, K. A. (2006). Psychological resilience, positive emotions, and successful adaptation to stress in later life. *Journal of Personality and Social Psychology, 91,* 730–749.

Orlinsky, D., & Ronnestad, M. H. (2005). *How psychotherapists develop: A study of therapeutic work and professional growth.* Washington, DC: American Psychological Association.

Panksepp, J. (1998). *Affective neuroscience.* New York, NY: Oxford University Press.

Papp, P. (1983). *The process of change.* New York, NY: Guilford.

Park, C. L., Cohen, L. H., & Murch, R. L. (1996). Assessment and prediction of stress-related growth. *Journal of Personality, 64*(1), 71–105.

Park, C. L., & Helgeson, V. S. (2006). Introduction to the special section: Growth following highly stressful life events: Current status and future directions. *Journal of Consulting and Clinical Psychology, 74*(5), 791–796.

Park, S. S. (2006). *Exposure to community violence and aggressive beliefs in adolescents: Role of posttraumatic growth and developmental resources.* PhD dissertation, Fuller Theological Seminary, School of Psychology, United States. Retrieved December 23, 2009, from Dissertations & Theses: A&I (Publication No. AAT 3209664).

Peacock, F. (2001). *Water the flowers, not the weeds.* Montreal, Quebec: Open Heart.

Peterson, C. (2006). The values in action (VIA) classification of strengths. In M. Csikszentmihalyi & I. Csikszentmihalyi (Eds.), *A life worth living: Contributions to positive psychology* (pp. 29–48). New York, NY: Oxford University Press.

Pinker, S. (2012). *The better angels of our nature.* London, UK: Penguin.

Piper, W. E., Ogrodniczuk, J. S., Joyce, A. S., McCallum, M., Rosie, J. S., O'Kelly, J. G., & Steinberg, P. I. (1999). Prediction of dropping out in time-limited, interpretive individual psychotherapy. *Psychotherapy: Theory, Research, Practice, Training, 36*(2), 114–122.

Plaud, J. J. (2001). Positive reinforcement. *Living and Learning, 1,* 3.

Pope, K. S., & Tabachnick, B. G. (1994). Therapists as patients: A national survey of psychologists' experiences, problems, and beliefs. *Professional Psychology: Research and Practice, 25,* 247–258.

Prochaska, J. O., Norcross, J. C., & DiClemente, C. C. (1994). *Changing for good.* New York, NY: Morrow.

Proust, M. (1992). *In search of lost time.* New York, NY: Modern Library.

Rakel, D.P.,Hoeft, T.J., Barrett, B.P., Chewning, B.A., Craig, B.M. & Niu, M. (2009). Practitioner empathy and the duration fo the common cold. *Family Medicine 41,* 7, 494-501.

Reed, M. B., & Aspinwall, L. G. (1998). Self-affirmation reduces biased processing of health-risk information. *Motivation and Emotion, 22,* 99–132.

Roberts, M. C., Brown, K. J., Johnson, R. J., & Reinke, J. (2005). Positive psychology for children. In C. R. Snyder & S. J. Lopez (Eds.), *Handbook of positive psychology*. New York, NY: Oxford University Press.

Rock, D. (2009). *Your brain at work*. New York, NY: HarperCollins.

Roeden, J. M., & Bannink, F. P. (2007). *Handboek oplossingsgericht werken met licht verstandelijk beperkte clienten* [Handbook for solution-focused interviewing with clients with mild intellectual disabilities]. Amsterdam, Netherlands: Pearson.

Roeden, J. M., & Bannink, F. P. (2009). Solution focused brief therapy with persons with intellectual disabilities. *Journal of Policy and Practice in Intellectual Disabilities*, 6(4), 253–259.

Roeden, J. M., Maaskant, M. A., Bannink, F. P., & Curffs, L. M. G. (2011). Solution-focused brief therapy with people with mild intellectual disabilities: A case series. *Journal of Policy and Practice in Intellectual Disabilities*, 8(4), 247–255.

Roeden, J. M., Maaskant, M. A., Bannink, F. P., & Curffs, L. M. G. (2012). Solution-focused coaching of staff of people with severe and moderate intellectual disabilities: A case series. *Journal of Policy and Practice in Intellectual Disabilities*, 9(3), 185–194.

Rosenhan, J. (1973). On being sane in insane places. *Science*, 179, 250–258.

Ross, M., & Wilson, A. E. (2002). It feels like yesterday: Self-esteem, valence of personal past experiences, and judgments of subjective distance. *Journal of Personality and Social Psychology*, 82, 792–803.

Rossi, E. L. (Ed.). (1980). *The nature of hypnosis and suggestion by Milton Erickson* (collected papers). New York, NY: Irvington.

Rothman, A. J. (2000). Toward a theory-based analysis of behavioural maintenance. Health Psychology, 19, 64–69.

Rowe, G., Hirsh, J. B., & Anderson, A. K. (2007). Positive affect increases the breadth of attentional selection. *Proceedings of the National Academy of Sciences of the United States of America*, 104, 383–388.

Rubin, L. (1996). *The transcendent child*. New York, NY: Basic Books.

Rutter, M. (1985). Resilience in the face of adversity. *British Journal of Psychiatry*, 147, 598–611.

Sagi-Schwartz, A., Bakermans-Kranenburg, M. J., Linn, S., & van IJzendoorn, M. H. (2013). Against all odds: Genocidal trauma is associated with longer life-expectancy of the survivors. *PLoS ONE 8*(7): e69179. doi:10.1371/journal.pone.0069179

Saleebey, D. (Ed.) (2007). *The strengths perspective in social work practice*. Boston, MA: Allyn & Bacon.

Salter, E., & Stallard, P. (2004). Posttraumatic growth in child survivors of a road traffic accident. *Journal of Traumatic Stress*, 17, 335–340.

Sapyta, J., Riemer, M., & Bickman, L. (2005). Feedback to clinicians: Theory, research and practice. *Journal of Clinical Psychology*, 61(2), 145–153.

Schroevers, M. J., Helgeson, V. S., Sanderman, R., & Ranchor, A. V. (2010). Type of social support matters for prediction of posttraumatic growth among cancer survivors. *Psychooncology*, 19(1), 46–53.

Seery, M. D., Holman, E. A., & Silver, R. C. (2010). Whatever does not kill us: Cumulative lifeline adversity, vulnerability and resilience. *Journal of Personality and Social Psychology, 99*(6), 1025–1041.

Selekman, M. D. (1993). *Pathways to change: Brief therapy solutions with difficult adolescents.* New York, NY: Guilford.

Selekman, M. D. (2010). *Collaborative brief therapy with children.* New York, NY: Guilford.

Seligman, M. E. P. (2002). *Authentic happiness.* London, UK: Brealey.

Seligman, M. E. P. (2011). *Flourish.* New York, NY: Free Press.

Seligman, M. E. P., & Csikszentmihalyi, M. (2000). Positive psychology: An introduction. *American Psychologist, 55*, 5–14.

Seligman, M. E. P., Reivich, K., Jaycox, L., & Gilham, J. (1995). *The optimistic child.* Boston, MA: Houghton Mifflin.

Seligman, M. E. P., Steen, T. A., Park, N., & Peterson, C. (2005). Positive psychology progress. Empirical validation of interventions. American Psychologist, *60*(5), 410–421.

Sharot, T. (2011). *The optimism bias.* New York, NY: Random House.

Siegel, D. J. (1999). *The developing mind.* New York, NY: Guilford.

Siegel, D. J. (2001). Toward an interpersonal neurobiology of the developing mind: Attachment relationships, "mindsight" and neural integration. *Infant Mental Health Journal, 22*, 67–94.

Siegel, D. J. (2010). *Mindsight.* New York, NY: Bantam.

Smock, S., Froerer, A., & Bavelas, J. B. (in press). Microanalysis of positive and negative content in solution focused brief therapy and cognitive behavioral therapy expert sessions.

Snyder, C. R. (2002). Hope theory: Rainbows in the mind. *Psychological Inquiry, 13*, 249–275.

Snyder, C. R., & Lopez, S. J. (2005). *Handbook of positive psychology.* New York, NY: Oxford University Press.

Snyder, C. R., Michael, S. T., & Cheavens, J. (1998). Hope as a psychotherapeutic foundation of common factors, placebos and expectancies. In M. A. Hubble, B. Duncan, & S. Miller (Eds.), *Heart and soul of change* (pp. 179–200). Washington, DC: American Psychological Association.

Solzhenitsyn, A. I. (1973). *The Gulag Archipelago, 1918–1956.* New York, NY: Harper & Row.

Stam, P., & Bannink, F. P. (2008). De oplossingsgerichte organisatie [The solution-focused organisation]. *Tijdschrift VKJP, 35*(2), 62–72.

Stams, G. J., Dekovic, M., Buist, K., & Vries, L. de (2006). Effectiviteit van oplossingsgerichte korte therapie: Een meta-analyse [The efficacy of solution-focused brief therapy: A meta-analysis]. *Gedragstherapie, 39*(2), 81–94.

Tamir, M., & Diener, E. (2008). Approach-avoidance goals and well-being. In A. J. Elliot (Ed.), *Handbook of approach and avoidance motivation* (pp. 415–430). Mahwah, NJ: Erlbaum.

Tamir, M., Mitchell, C., & Gross, J. J. (2008). Hedonic and instrumental motives in anger regulation. *Psychological Science, 19*, 324–328.

Tedeschi, R. G., & Calhoun, L. (2004). Posttraumatic growth: A new perspective on psychotraumatology. Psychiatric Times, 21, 4.

Tedeschi, R. G., & Calhoun, L. G. (2006). The posttraumatic growth inventory: Measuring the positive legacy of trauma. *Journal of Traumatic Stress*, 9(3), 455–471.

Tedeschi, R. G., & McNally, R. J. (2011). Can we facilitate posttraumatic growth in combat veterans? *American Psychologist, 66*, 19–24.

Turnell, A., & Edwards, S. (1999). *Signs of safety. A solution oriented approach to child protection casework.* New York, NY: Norton.

Turner, C., Spencer, M. B., & Stone, B. M. (2005). Effect of working patterns of UK train drivers on fatigue: A diary study. *Shiftwork International Newsletter, 22*, 150.

Ungar, M. (2008). *A brief overview of resilience: How does the concept help us understand children's positive development under stress.* Retrieved from http://www.tlpresources.ca/policyresearch_conference_NDRY_2008/Michael_Ungar_English.pdf

U.S. Department of Veterans Affairs. (n.d.). *PTSD in children and teens.* Retrieved from www.ptsd.va.gov/public/pages/ptsd-children-adolescents.asp

Vaillant, G. E. (1995). *Adaptation to life.* Cambridge MA: Harvard University Press.

Vasquez, N., & Buehler, R. (2007). Seeing future success: Does imagery perspective influence achievement motivation? *Personality and Social Psychology Bulletin, 33*, 1392–1405.

Walter, J. L., & Peller, J. E. (1992). *Becoming solution-focused in brief therapy.* New York, NY: Brunner/Mazel.

Walter, J. L., & Peller, J. E. (2000). Recreating brief therapy: Preferences and possibilities. New York, NY: Norton.

Wampold, B. E. (2001). *The great psychotherapy debate: Models, methods and findings.* Hillsdale, NJ: Erlbaum.

Wampold, B. E., & Bhati, K. S. (2004). Attending to the omissions: A historical examination of evidence-based practice movements. *Professional Psychology: Research and Practice, 35*(6), 563–570.

Watzlawick, P. (1976). *How real is real?* New York, NY: Random House.

Watzlawick, P., Weakland, J. H., & Fisch, R. (1974). *Change: Principles of problem formation and problem resolution.* New York, NY: Norton.

Werner, E. E. (2004). What can we learn about resilience from large scale longitudinal studies? In S. Goldstein & R. B. Brooks (Eds.), *Handbook of resilience in children.* New York, NY: Kluwer.

White, M., & Epston, D. (1990). *Narrative means to therapeutic ends.* New York, NY: Norton.

Williams, T. (2012, June 8). Suicide outpacing war deaths for troops. *New York Times.* Retrieved from http://veteransforcommonsense.org/2012/06/11/suicides-outpacing-war-deaths-for-troops/

Wilson, S. (1955). *The man in the gray flannel suit.* New York, NY: Four Walls Eight Windows.

Wilson, T. D. (2011). *Redirect: The surprising new science of psychological change.* New York, NY: Little, Brown.

Wilson, T. D., Centerbar, D. B., Kerme, D. A., & Gilbert, D. T. (2005). The pleasures of uncertainty: Prolonging positive moods in ways people do not anticipate. *Journal of Personality and Social Psychology*, 88(1), 5–21.

Wittgenstein, L. (1968). *Philosophical investigations* (G. E. M. Anscombe, Trans., 3rd ed.). New York, NY: Macmillan. (Original work published 1953)

Wolin, S. J., & Wolin, S. (1993). *Bound and determined: Growing up resilient in a troubled family.* New York, NY: Villard Press.

Woodward, C., & Joseph, S. (2003). Positive change processes and post-traumatic growth in people who have experienced childhood abuse: Understanding vehicles of change. *Psychology and Psychotherapy: Theory, Research and Practice*, 76(3), 267–283.

Yalom, I. D. (2008). *The gift of therapy.* New York, NY: HarperCollins.

Young, S. (2010). *Solution-focused schools.* London, UK: BT Press.

Youssef, C. M., & Luthans, F. (2007). Positive organizational behaviour in the workplace: The impact of hope, optimism, and resiliency. *Journal of Management*, 33, 774–800.

Ziegler, P., & Hiller, T. (2001). *Recreating partnership.* New York, NY: Norton.

Zimmerman, M., McGlinchey, J. B., Posternak, M. A, Friedman, M., Attiullah, N., & Boerescu, D. (2006). How should remission from depression be defined? *American Journal of Psychiatry*, 163, 148–150.

Websites

■■■■■■■■■■■■■■

www.asfct.org
Association for the Quality Development of Solution-Focused
Consulting and Training (SFCT)

www.authentichappiness.org
Seligman with positive psychology questionnaires

www.brief.org.uk
BRIEF, an SF training institute in London

www.billohanlon.com
O'Hanlon, author

www.brieftherapysydney.com.au
Brief Therapy Institute of Sydney, Australia

www.brief-therapy.org
Brief Family Therapy Center, Milwaukee, Wisconsin

www.centerforclinicalexcellence.com
ICCE, a worldwide community dedicated to promoting
excellence in behavioral healthcare services (Miller)

www.ebta.nu
European Brief Therapy Association (EBTA)

www.edwdebono.com
De Bono, author

www.enpp.eu
European Network for Positive Psychology (ENPP)

www.fredrickson.socialpsychology.org
Fredrickson, researcher of the broaden-and-build theory of positive emotions

www.fredrikebannink.com
Author of this book

www.gingerich.net
Gingerich with SFBT research

www.heartandsoulofchange.com
Duncan, author

www.ippanetwork.org
International Positive Psychology Association (IPPA)

www.korzybski.com
Korzybski Institute, an SF training institute in Belgium

www.positivemeetings-app.com
Bannink positive meetings app

www.positivepsychology.org
Pennsylvania University (Seligman)

www.posttraumatic-success.com
Bannink on posttraumatic success

www.pos-cbt.com
Bannink on positive CBT

www.ppc.sas.upenn.edu/ppquestionnaires.htm
Penn University with positive psychology questionnaires

www.reteaming.com
Furman, SF team coaching and Kids' Skills

www.scottdmiller.com
Miller with the ORS and SRS

www.sfbta.org
Solution-Focused Brief Therapy Association (SFBTA)

www.sfwork.com
Centre of Solution Focus at work

www.solutionsdoc.co.uk
Macdonald with SF research

www.solutionfocused.net
Institute for Solution-Focused Therapy (Dolan)

www.solworld.org
Solutions in Organisations Link (SOL)

Index

......

medical model, 39, 40
medical setting
  positive affect in, 183–86
meditation
  loving-kindness, 126, 206
  mindfulness, 174
memory(ies)
  sparkling, 121
Menninger, K., 79, 227
mental contrasting, 102–3
  exercise, 103
  in goal setting, 232
  reverse, 232
mental health
  advances in, xii
Mental Health Team of Doctors Without Borders, 381
mental imagery, 153
mental road map, 227
metaphor of shattered vase, 28–29
Metcalf, L., 303
Michael, S.T., 80
microanalysis
  of dialogue, 144–46
migration, 313
Milam, J.E., 24, 263
Miller, S.D., 84, 131, 224, 245, 247, 249, 250
Miller, W.R., 72–73
Mindful Attention Awareness Scale (MAAS), 14
mindfulness, 126–27
mindfulness-based cognitive therapy (MBCT), 126–27
mindfulness-based stress reduction (MBSR), 126
mindfulness-based therapy
  in trauma therapy, 18
mindfulness exercise, 206
mindfulness meditation, 174
mindset
  growth, 226–28
"miracle question," 177
Mischel, W., 170
Mitchell, C., 11–12
MLQ. see Meaning in Life Questionnaire (MLQ)
moment(s)
  defining, 115

Monson, C.M., 41
Mortensen, H., 23–24
Moskowitz, J.T., 7
motivation
  approach, 103
  assessing, 127–31
  avoidance, 103
  to change, 130–31
  intrinsic, 178
motivational interviewing
  principles of, 72
multiple options
  exercise, 205
Muraven, M., 171
Murray, S.L., 291
Mutrie, N., 25
"my kids keep me going"
  case example, 19–20

narrative(s), 147–52
  digressive, 147
  progressive, 147
  stability, 147
  types of, 147–52
National Comorbidity Survey (NCS)
  on PTSD, 16
NCS. see National Comorbidity Survey (NCS)
Neff, K.D., 120, 267
negative affect, 2, 6
  balancing with positive affect, 11–12
negative emotions
  positive emotions vs., 174
  reducing, 174–76
negative feedback
  therapist's asking for, 250
negative stories
  types of, 147
negativity bias, 34
neurogenesis, 33
neurolinguistic programming (NLP), 101
neurosis(es)
  war. see post traumatic stress disorder (PTSD)
neutral language
  in therapeutic alliance, 75
Nietzsche, 14, 157

usefulness
    through simplicity, xvii

Vaillant, G.E., 46, 289
validation
    in context for change, 75–78
value(s)
    in line with your, 172
"value positivity" story, 10–11
value time
    exercise, 128
valued-added state, 15
Values in Action (VIA) Survey of
    Character Strengths test, 48,
    113, 114
Vasquez, N., 153, 161–62
"venting anger feeds the flame" story,
    175
VGCt. see Dutch Association for
    Behaviour and Cognitive thera-
    pies (VGCt)
VIA Survey of Character Strengths,
    299
vicarious traumatization, 307
victim(s)
    seeing oneself as, 150–52
victim or survivor
    exercise, 151
victory box
    exercise, 263
violence
    decline of, 13
visitor relationship, 189
    in therapeutic alliance, 68–69
visualization
    lack of, 327–28
    positive, 99

Waite, T., 15–16
wall
    appreciation, 314
Walter, J.L., 105, 128, 132, 159,
    192–93, 234–35, 296–97
Wampold, B.E., 18, 41, 183, 233, 249,
    250
wanting
    liking vs., 100

war neurosis. see post traumatic stress
    disorder (PTSD)
Water the Flowers, Not the Weeds, 308
Watzlawick, P., 50, 233, 243
"We Gotta Get Out of This Place," 291
Weakland, J.H., 50
websites, 113, 369–71
Weertman A., 154
Weissman, A., 79
well-being
    in children, 265–66
    clients, 321
    elements of, 47
    promoting, 136
    psychological, 17, 17f, 277
    scaling, 130
    subjective, 8
    in team, 309–10
    in workplace, 306–7
well-being theory, 47–48
Werner, E.E., 257–58
"what are your best hopes?", 54–55
"what difference will that make?",
    55–57
    case example, 57
    exercise, 143
"what do you want to continue to
    happen?"
    case example, 193
"what have you done today that is
    good for you"
    exercise, 136
"what helped you survive?"
    case example, 150
"what is better?"
    exercise, 217
"what was good about this experi
    ence?"
    case example, 118–19
"what will be the next signs of prog-
    ress?", 59–61
"what will be your next step?", 59–61
"what works?", 57–58
    focus on, 111–39
"what would you like to keep the way
    it is?"
    exercise, 112
"what you give is what you get" story,
    289–90

About the Author

....

Fredrike Bannink is a clinical psychologist and a child psychologist. She has a therapy, training, coaching, and mediation practice in Amsterdam, the Netherlands. She is a trainer/supervisor for the Dutch Association for Behaviour and Cognitive therapies (VGCt) and cofounder and chair of the Association's Solution-Focused Cognitive Behavioural Therapy Section. She is a lecturer at various postgraduate institutes.

She teaches CBT, solution-focused brief therapy, and positive psychology to psychologists and psychiatrists, and solution-focused interviewing to medical professionals. She is a trainer for the Mental Health Team of Doctors Without Borders. In addition, she provides in-company training courses in solution-focused brief therapy and positive psychology at mental health care institutions; for companies, she organizes coaching and leadership trajectories.

Fredrike Bannink is also a Master of Dispute Resolution, an International Full Certified ADR Mediator, and a mediator for the Court of Amsterdam. She is the author of many international publications in the fields of solution-focused brief therapy, solution-focused coaching, solution-focused mediation/conflict management, solution-focused leadership, positive psychology, and positive CBT. Since 2004, she has been writing and presenting worldwide on the topic of bridging traditional approaches with solution-focused and positive psychology approaches.

Not surprisingly, her top strength (according to the VIA strengths test) is *curiosity and interest in the world*.